M000307899

READING
THE RED BOOK

READING THE RED BOOK

An Interpretive Guide to C.G. Jung's *Liber Novus*

SANFORD L. DROB

Foreword by Stanton Marlan

Spring Journal Books
New Orleans, Louisiana

© 2012 by Spring Journal, Inc.
All rights reserved.

Spring Journal™, Spring: A Journal of Archetype and Culture™, Spring Books™,
Spring Journal Books,™ Spring Journal and Books™, and Spring Journal Publications™
are all trademarks of Spring Journal Incorporated. All Rights Reserved.

Published by
Spring Journal, Inc.;
627 Ursulines Street #7
New Orleans, Louisiana 70116
Website: www.springjournalandbooks.com

Cover Image and Excerpts from:
The Red Book by C.G. Jung.
Edited by Sonu Shamdasani.
Translated by Mark Kyburz, John Peck, and Sonu Shamdasani.
Copyright © 2009 by the Foundation of the Works of C.G. Jung. Translation
copyright © 2009 by Mark Kyburz, John Peck, and Sonu Shamdasani.
Used by permission of W.W. Norton & Company, Inc.

Cover design and typography by:
Northern Graphic Design & Publishing
info@ncarto.com

Text printed on acid-free paper

Library of Congress Cataloging-in-Publication Data Pending

TABLE OF CONTENTS

ACKNOWLEDGMENTS

I would like to thank W.W. Norton & Company for their generous permission to quote extensively from *The Red Book* by C.G. Jung, edited by Sonu Shamdasani, translated by Mark Kyburz, John Peck, and Sonu Shamdasani. Copyright © 2009 by the Foundation of the Works of C.G. Jung. Translation copyright © 2009 by Mark Kyburz, John Peck, and Sonu Shamdasani. I would also like to thank W.W. Norton for their permission to use as the cover image for this book Jung's painting, which appears on page 119 of *The Red Book*. I am greatly appreciative of Sonu Shamdasani's marvelous work as the editor of *The Red Book*. His meticulous and comprehensive editing and annotations are of immense assistance to all readers of this difficult but highly rewarding work. In addition, the painstaking efforts of *The Red Book's* translators, Mark Kyburz, John Peck, and Sonu Shamdasani, have not only been critical for my own work, but should be applauded for making Jung's opus accessible to a broad reading public.

I am also indebted to Princeton University Press for permission to make extensive quotations from C.G. Jung's Psychological Types, Volume 6 of *The Collected Works of C.G. Jung*. © 1971, 1999 Princeton University Press. Reprinted by permission of Princeton University Press.

My heartfelt gratitude goes to Stanton Marlan, who carefully reviewed the entire manuscript, and through a series of long and enlightening conversations, helped me to greatly improve and clarify the ideas expressed in this work.

Murray Stein's illuminating lectures on *The Red Book*, which he delivered on-line and video-recorded for the Asheville Jung Center in January and May, 2010 have proven an important stimulus to my own thinking.

I would like to thank Pat Berry, Paul Bishop, John Hill, and Robert Romanyshyn for their valuable comments and suggestions on earlier drafts of this book. I also want to thank Northern Graphic Design and Publishing for designing the cover, typesetting, and preparing the manuscript for publication.

I am also thankful to Amarilla Sanders for reviewing the entire manuscript and in assisting with the verification of quotations from Jung's works.

I am deeply indebted to my publisher, Nancy Cater, for her faith in my resolve to embark upon and complete this project, and for her assistance during each phase of its production. I also want to thank Aryeh Maidenbaum, for his encouraging me to present my thematic approach to *The Red Book* at the Jung on the Hudson series, and the students and faculty at Fielding Graduate University's program in Clinical Psychology who have found Jung and his *Red Book* to be of sufficient interest to developing clinicians to attend and become engaged in my various seminars and lectures on this work. Indeed, this work evolves out of my series of seminars on *The Red Book* that I presented to students at Fielding Graduate University in 2010-11 and at the Jung on the Hudson series of the New York Center for Jungian Studies in July 2010.

The Red Book is an immense, complex work, one that requires multiple readings and much reflection to even begin to grasp its intellectual, spiritual, aesthetic, and personal content. One who ventures to do so and to present a full commentary on its substance within two and one half years of its publication runs the risk of making premature judgments and errors of interpretation that would be eliminated by repeated review and the reconsideration of one's thinking over a longer period of time. In this context the usual authorial disclaimer, "I am solely responsible for the errors, etc.," takes on more than the usual significance.

Sanford L. Drob
March 28, 2012

FOREWORD

BY STANTON MARLAN

Sanford Drob's *Reading The Red Book: An Interpretive Guide to C.G. Jung's Liber Novus* is a welcome and important addition to the rapidly growing body of literature that has emerged since the publication of Jung's now-famous but once secret and mysterious *Red Book*. I believe that Dr. Drob's book is the first full-length study of *The Red Book* to be published in English, and it arrives in the midst of considerable excitement and controversy. *The Red Book* has been compared to many of the major classics of Western literature, including Nietzsche's *Zarathustra*, St. Augustine's *Confessions*, Dante's *Divine Comedy*, Goethe's *Faust*, and to Blake's illuminated manuscripts as well as those of the high Middle Ages. Indeed, there are those who hale the publication of *The Red Book* as the most important document in the Jungian corpus—a book that will revolutionize our understanding of Jung and his work. On the other hand, there are others who believe it should never have been published at all and who lament its appearance, viewing it as a private journal that adds little to what is already known about Jung's ideas. Heated arguments have ensued. Still others have sought a middle road. Murray Stein, for example, has commented, "One can err on both sides [of the controversy] and here you have the extremes .... It's not easy to get the proportion right or to find a way to talk about this strange work in a way that holds it but doesn't over or underestimate its value."[1]

Sanford Drob's reflections steer clear of both extremes. While he deeply appreciates *The Red Book*, he is able at the same time to reflect on it critically, and thus he achieves this elusive "holding" and balance of perspectives. By analyzing *The Red Book* in terms of its underlying questions and problems, *Reading The Red Book* provides both a guide to *The Red Book's* major themes and facilitates the reader's own interpretation and, moreover, his personal encounter with this important work.

---

[1] Personal communication from Murray Stein, December 2011.

Perhaps it is not surprising that extreme differences of opinion cluster around *The Red Book,* a book replete with dramatic contrasts and oppositions. It has been called an "impossible book," a "book that is not a book," because of its highly personal nature and its internal contradictions.[2] On the other hand, James Hillman has positively imagined these "contradictions" as "contraries necessary to each other" and the book as a poetic text that "opens the soul to living" in our age of scientific rationalism, an important example of "what is to come."[3]

A difficulty for readers of *The Red Book* is its challenge to our modern intellect and imagination. What the nascently alchemical Jung called the "melting together of sense and non-sense"[4] is nearly impossible to understand from within our taken-for-granted categories. Even Jung's own continuing attempt to describe his experience of the seemingly contradictory aspects of the psyche, using phrases such as *complexio oppositorum* and *mysterium coniunctionis,* can become too easily assimilated and intellectualized, thus becoming benign clichés for the darkness, complexity, and profundity of the numinous unknown that Jung called the unconscious. What seems important in reading *The Red Book* is an appreciation of its radical vision, a vision that points beyond any conventional sense of meaning. In *The Red Book,* Jung tries to convey this radicality by using the neologism *Übersinn,* which was translated as "supreme meaning." The difficulty of understanding Jung's intent is noted by Wolfgang Giegerich who points out that *Übersinn* implies a meaning that is "over," "beyond," in "excess of meaning," even "counter-meaning."[5] He states that what Jung has in mind in *The Red Book* is "outrageous."[6] For Hillman, Jung's vision jars even the most knowledgeable readers. It shocks and "pushes us to the very limits of mind and language," and we are "lived by powers we pretend to understand."[7]

---

[2] Wolfgang Giegerich, "*Liber Novus,* That is, The New Bible: A First Analysis of C.G. Jung's *Red Book,*" *Spring: A Journal of Archetype and Culture* 83 (Spring 2010): 361-411, p. 362.

[3] James Hillman, C.G. Jung *Red Book* Symposium, Library of Congress, 6-19-10.

[4] Giegerich, p. 384.

[5] *Ibid.,* pp. 383-384.

[6] *Ibid.,* p. 383.

[7] Hillman, *Red Book* Symposium.

In a review of *The Red Book* entitled "Fantastic Voyage," John Tarrant compares Jung's book to the "late Buddhist sutras, in which we are confronted with thousand-armed deities and paradoxes and impossible statements that nonetheless make you feel changed after connecting with them."[8] It is not an uncommon experience to feel somehow changed after reading *The Red Book*. Might we imagine such a change as the result of an encounter with the numinous, a quality of fear and awe in the face of a *tremendum* hard to define or understand? In such a case, understanding is not only standing above, "overmeaning," but also a standing "under" which requires a descent and a decentering, a "going under" that results in a defeat for and relativization of the ego.

Such an encounter and experience with the unconscious brought Jung to the edge of his sanity, but his psychic strength and character allowed him to use his experience to forward a new vision of psychology and theology. During Jung's time, he was not the only one to react to the perception that something had been left out of our vision of the soul: the seething irrationalism below the surface of European culture.[9] Many creative artists, writers, poets, and painters were, like Jung, experimenting with ways to access this unacknowledged depth. Tarrant noted, "Jung in common with other prominent figures (like Kandinsky) had terrible dreams of destruction overwhelming the land. We know now that Europe was heading toward a century of war."[10] In response, creative thinkers were turning away from traditional ways of understanding and seeking a deeper meaning of life:

> Rilke was writing sonnets—which he received more or less as dictation—to Orpheus, Yeats was studying automatic writing, and Eliot was trying to educate his unconscious creative processes by immersing himself in great literature. Picasso was experimenting with Cubism. The Dada movement was for a while closely linked to the Jungians. The idea that something had to come from the depths was important.[11]

---

[8] John Tarrant, "Fantastic Voyage: *The Red Book* by C. G. Jung," excerpted from the *Shambhala Sun*, May 2010, http://www.shambhalasun.com/index.php?option =com_content&task=view&id=3525&Itemid=0.

[9] *Ibid.*

[10] *Ibid.*

[11] *Ibid.*

The Red Book was ultimately Jung's reaction to the creative urgings of his imagination in response to personal and collective crises. He noted in *The Red Book*:

> I have learned that in addition to the spirit of this time there is still another spirit at work, namely that which rules the depths of everything contemporary. The spirit of this time would like to hear of use and value. I also thought this way, and my humanity still thinks this way. But that other spirit forces me to speak beyond justification, use, and meaning. .... The spirit of the depths took my understanding and all my knowledge and placed them in the service of the inexplicable and the paradoxical.[12]

The "inexplicable and paradoxical" that Jung speaks of here remained with him throughout his life and in his works, from *The Red Book* to the *Mysterium Coniunctionis*. From its nascent beginnings to its mature form, Jung's work forges a vision of the unity of opposites, of wholeness, and the self that is almost unbearable for the ego to tolerate.

British Jungian analyst Neil Micklem has noted that there is still a tendency in reading Jung to pass over the shock and radicality of his vision.[13] Micklem emphasizes the importance of paradox rather than unity and notes that paradox usually gets glossed over as our attention moves toward the more attractive idea of the vision of the unity of the opposites. Micklem points to the image of the hermaphrodite in the last print of the *Rosarium Philosophorum* in Jung's essay "The Psychology of Transference" and notes that most people see it as a symbol representing an integrated wholeness without letting themselves experience its grotesque and monstrous character. Edinger gives another example of the monstrous in the image of the "Extraction of Mercurius and the coronation of the Virgin" from Reusner's *Pandora* (1582) and humorously speaks of it in the context of the Christian *Weltanschauung* as analogous to "a cuckoo's egg that's been laid in somebody else's nest" and from which "something unexpected is going to hatch."[14] French philosopher Jacques Derrida has likewise linked the monstrous with

---

[12] C.G. Jung, *The Red Book*, as quoted by Tarrant.

[13] Niel Micklem, "I Am Not Myself: A Paradox," in Jung's Concept of the Self: Its Relevance Today, papers from the public conference organized in May 1990, by the Jungian Postgraduate Committee of the British Association of Psychotherapists.

[14] Edward F. Edinger, *The Mysterium Lectures: A Journey through C.G. Jung's* Mysterium Coniunctionis (Toronto: Inner City Books, 1995), p. 135.

the future. Drob quotes Derrida's notion that "the future is necessarily monstrous: the figure of the future, that is, that which can only be surprising, that for which we are not prepared, you see, is heralded by a species of monsters. A future that would not be monstrous would not be a future."[15] I would claim that *The Red Book* is just such a "monstrosity" and like Edinger's cuckoo's egg, it has now been laid in the spirit of our times and is bringing many surprises in its wake.

Jung's discoveries pushed him to imagine a psychology beyond Freud's vision. He struggled to speak about the spirit of the depths in a way that also went beyond translating the living psyche into what he felt was the Procrustean bed of a "scientific" *Weltanschauung*. In *The Red Book*, Jung's experiments were leading him into the future of a psychology that was revising and transforming our understanding of "the unconscious," and his experiences presented in *The Red Book* are at the foundation of his understanding, and continue to transform our understanding, of the soul. Of all Jung's works, *The Red Book* is perhaps the most enigmatic and difficult. It is most prone to misunderstanding and perhaps this is one of the reasons why those who lament its publication fear that it could damage Jung's reputation. While I suspect there will be those who use this text to defame Jung, I know there are others who are inspired by it, and *The Red Book* is, to my mind, clearly a document important to Jungian scholarship. I am one for whom the publication and translation of *The Red Book* is a gift, and I am grateful for the untiring hard work, sacrifice, and scholarship of Sonu Shamdasani and his erudite colleagues Mark Kyburz, John Peck, and others who helped bring this work into the public domain— with great care and beauty.

Yet, for those of us who care that Jung's vision receives a fair reading, good Jungian scholarship now requires that we engage with Jung's text with the utmost integrity, neither blindly idealizing nor reacting out of uninformed prejudice. Shamdasani notes, "In a critical sense *Liber Novus* does not require supplemental interpretation, for it contains its own interpretation."[16] In a certain sense, it is true that Jung in his "hermeneutic experiment"[17] supplies us with his own interpretations

---

[15] Note 19, in Notes to Chapter 7, this volume, p. 289-90.
[16] Sonu Shamdasani, Introduction to *The Red Book, Liber Novus* by C.G. Jung, ed. Sonu Shamdasani, trans. Mark Kyburz, John Peck, and Sonu Shamdasani (New York: W.W. Norton, 2009), p. 203.
[17] *Ibid.*, p. 203.

in an ongoing way throughout the text. I believe Jung's own reflections need to be honored and given due respect. However, it is also the case that there are important limitations on anyone's personal judgment about the meaning of their own work. Perhaps this is implied when Shamdasani says, in the last sentence of his Introduction, "Thus this introduction does not end with a conclusion, but with the promise of a new beginning."[18] However, it should be emphasized that Jung's personal reflections are now in the public domain, and interpretations will be and need to be made. I would venture to say that a book as complex and multidimensional as *The Red Book* needs ongoing and multiple interpretations, and it certainly will receive many over the coming years. One can only hope that these interpretations will have integrity and will emulate the care that has already been given to the text in the framing it has received by those involved in its publication.

Sanford Drob's guide to reading *The Red Book* is such a text. He is a formally trained psychologist and philosopher and a respected interpreter of the Kabbalah. He knows Jung's work well and has published an earlier, highly regarded book, *Kabbalistic Visions: C.G. Jung and Jewish Mysticism*, and many scholarly articles about Jung and archetypal ideas. Drob examines Jung's *Red Book* in a narrative, thematic, and conceptual framework. He is appreciative and critical in his examination of Jung's text from a multi-leveled perspective. Along with his earlier work, the publication of *Reading The Red Book: An Interpretive Guide to C.G. Jung's Liber Novus* establishes Drob as an important and unique voice in Jungian scholarship.

Drob takes *The Red Book* metaphorically as an archetypal dream, a vision of something beyond its meaning for a single individual, and as a dream for the future psychology. As a dream, Drob asks what *The Red Book* compensates for in contemporary psychology and points to the way psychology has fallen prey to a scientized and medicalized vision of psychotherapeutic work. For Drob, *The Red Book* helps awaken us to the depth of the soul and shows that psychology can (and, from my perspective, must) also involve a search for "meaning and wisdom rather than just knowledge per se."[19] For Giegerich, *The Red Book* is of little value to a current psychology. He writes, "It is a

---

[18] *Ibid.,* p. 221.
[19] Drob, this volume, p. 263.

new publication, but it should not be a *Liber Novus* for us. Its value is two fold; it provides us with a rich source for gaining insight into the formation of and deeper motivation behind Jung's thought and, beyond Jung, into one episode of intellectual history, and it is a mine of interesting symbolism and theosophic speculation."[20] While for Drob, on the one hand, *The Red Book* is also an important, even necessary, contribution to understanding Jung, intellectual history, and symbolism, it is also of great value to the continuing development of current psychology and analysis. It is truly a *Liber Novus*, a new book!

For this and other reasons, I am highly appreciative of Sanford Drob's study of *The Red Book*—for his engagement with the enormity of the task and for his passion, scholarship, and refusal to simplify. He notes, "We cannot hope to understand *The Red Book* at all unless we suspend our demand for simple univocal ideas and answers."[21] Drob follows his own dictates with intelligence and integrity, with the heart of a spiritual seeker and the mind and eye of a scholar. From the moment I began reading Drob's text, I was deeply engaged in his presentation and interpretation of Jung's vision. I learned a great deal and have been grateful to have Drob as a companion in my own attempt to deepen my understanding of Jung and of his epochal *Red Book*. I am certain that others will have a similar experience.

Stanton Marlan
Pittsburgh, PA
December 10, 2011

---

[20] Giegerich, "*Liber Novus*, That is, The New Bible", *Spring*, p. 409. These differences of perspective confirm for me that there can be multiple strong and scholarly readings of Jung's text.

[21] Drob, this volume, p. 4.

INTRODUCTION

Jung held that dreams are challenges to the assumptions and complacency of the ego, compensations for one-sided conscious attitudes, or messages from the unconscious that prompt us to question the value and direction of our current modes of thinking, feeling, and living. By this definition, Jung's *The Red Book* or *Liber Novus* (*New Book*) is akin to a "dream," not the dream of any individual, but a dream of the discipline and practice of psychology. Like many dreams, the "dream" that is *The Red Book* is at once magnificent and grotesque, and our first response, if we do not simply forget or ignore it, is to contemplate its strangeness, and as James Hillman would say, "seethe in its juices," allowing ourselves to be immersed in its narrative and painted images. Coming to us from psychology's now distant past, this "time capsuled" volume is the suppressed masterwork of one of psychology's giants. Its emergence in our own era after more than 80 years of frozen secrecy, at a time when psychology as a discipline believes itself to have moved beyond its literary, philosophical, and theological roots, comes as an even greater shock to us today than had *The Red Book* been presented to the public in Jung's own time. In all likelihood, psychology as a discipline will ignore this "dream" from its own past, just as most dreams are forgotten or ignored. It may be, however, that psychology ignores *The Red Book* "dream" at its own peril, and misses an important opportunity to regain an audience with its own soul.

The current work, which examines *The Red Book* from a thematic and conceptual perspective, will ultimately ask the question of the meaning of *The Red Book* for contemporary psychology. What questions does *The Red Book* ask, and what psychological attitudes does it challenge or compensate for? However, before we can inquire into *The Red Book's* contemporary meaning, the work must be read, its fundamental themes and concepts grappled with, and its meaning placed within the context of its own era and Jung's full body of work. We must come to grips with *The Red Book's* understanding of God, prophecy, science, reason, evil, love, the hero, death, and the soul, to name just a handful of its salient themes. A great deal of contemplative, associative, and amplificatory work must be completed, and other, perhaps less ambitious goals, achieved, before we can address the question of *The Red Book's* meaning for contemporary thought. Still, the commentary in the pages to follow is written with this latter goal in mind. In the final chapter, I will return to the metaphor of *The Red Book* as psychology's "dream."

Jung warned against the illusion that one could provide a definitive interpretation of a dream, or produce an ultimate psychological theory. He held that the various psychological theories extant in his day were a function of the "psychological types" of their creators, and for this reason could only yield a partial or relativized truth. In writing this work I have become acutely aware of how my own "personal equation" has dictated its contents. Although I have endeavored to be balanced and as comprehensive as possible, I found that my main focus has been on *The Red Book's* theoretical rather than its narrative and symbolic content. I have become convinced that while *The Red Book* narrative centers around Jung's soul-finding journey, its greatest value may be in its ideas on such themes as God, humanity, madness, chaos, death, science, reason, knowledge, language, logic, and evil. I am of the view that *The Red Book* has a strong intellectual core, one that makes it an important document in the history of psychology and, moreover, in the history of ideas, and it is this conviction that has guided my approach to the work. As such, my first task has been to articulate and comment upon the book's main ideas. A second goal of the present work is to describe the dialectic of Jung's inner exploration and spiritual journey, and to examine this dialectic's significance for the process of "individuation" in the life-journeys of contemporary readers. Jung himself held that his life work was in many ways an elaboration of themes first presented in *The Red Book*, and as such a third goal of this book is to trace the development of *The Red Book's* themes and ideas in Jung's earlier and later writings. Finally, I have endeavored to place *The Red Book* in the context of several spiritual traditions (including Gnosticism, Christianity, and the Kabbalah), some of Jung's antecedents (e.g. Nietzsche), his contemporaries (e.g. Heidegger, Sartre, Wittgenstein, Buber), and subsequent thinkers (e.g. Derrida), who seem to echo or serve as a valuable counterpoint to Jung's ideas.

However, as will become evident, following up on *The Red Book's* threads in Jung's other writings and the traditions and works of other thinkers must be a highly selective enterprise in a work of this length.

As this book proceeds, I hope to make clear that *The Red Book* raises and provides valuable and at times highly original insights into a wide variety of philosophical, theological, and psychological questions that have helped define the spiritual and intellectual life of the last century. I also hope to show how *The Red Book* is vitally relevant to our own time. While Jung *raises* many questions in *Liber Novus*, he answers few, as he tends to circle around the problems that concern him and try out various possibilities. In *Scrutinies,* Jung's soul tells him, "The uncertain way is the good way: Upon it lie possibilities" (*The Red Book*, p. 335). Indeed, Jung rarely reaches a final perspective or conclusion on any of the conceptual or life problems that he considers, and many of the "views" that one finds in *The Red Book* are reversed or balanced by their opposites in other parts of the book (as well as in Jung's later writings). It is almost as if Jung held that a better description of the world, and especially the psyche, arises from encounters with significant questions, conflicts, and dilemmas rather than through the provision of purported, and inevitably fallible answers. It is in this spirit of heightened respect for inquiry that the present work has been written.

I am not a Jungian analyst, nor do I identify myself as a Jungian, but rather as a psychologist who is deeply appreciative of Jung's thought, while at the same time cognizant of its historical context and potential limitations. While I believe that my treatment of *The Red Book* is a sympathetic one and I have been moved by its words, paintings, and beautiful illuminated presentation, I do not hesitate to raise questions about Jung's approach to various issues, including his *Red Book* views on science, reason, love, and the willing of evil, and his suggestion that spiritual wisdom and enlightenment must involve an inner, solitary journey. In many instances, without providing anything resembling an "answer," I raise questions that the reader will want to consider for him or herself.

As this work evolved I became increasingly convinced that only a dual approach could do adequate justice to *The Red Book's* contents. One approach involves following the work serially, and commenting upon it chapter by chapter. While this approach is in many ways the most rich and comprehensive, it runs the risk of losing the forest for the trees, particularly in the case of a work like *The Red Book*, which documents a spiritual and intellectual journey that evolves dialectically over the course of its lengthy narrative, but is in no way organized thematically, and abruptly ends without a clear conclusion. A second approach involves a re-organization of the material along thematic lines. While this approach has the advantage of increased clarity, it runs the risk of losing touch with the work's narrative structure, and thus with its very life. The current work is thus a combination of these two approaches. I have followed *The Red Book* serially, chapter by chapter, but have divided my commentary into thematic sections, some of which introduce considerable material from other parts of *The Red Book*, in order to attain comprehensiveness and clarity. Further, throughout the text I have considered ideas from Jung's other published works, as well as the works of other thinkers, that shed light on *The Red Book* material.

The reader will note that while I have commented at some length on many of *The Red Book's* paintings, I have devoted by far the major portion of this commentary to Jung's text.[1] Many of the paintings in *The Red Book* strike me as efforts to produce psychic and spiritual experiences, particularly experiences of wholeness, and, beginning with *Liber Secundus*, they do not in the main serve as illustrations to the narrative or ideas of the text within which they are embedded. Indeed, some of the paintings create a second imaginal narrative or structure in *The Red Book* that is interspersed or superimposed upon the linguistic one. They illustrate the point that theology and even psychology can be articulated in media other than words. My reaction to them is itself mainly imaginal, and thus in some instances my reaction is not adequately expressible in words. In many instances, the paintings' contents, when they are specifiable, relate more to the mythological than to the conceptual aspects of *The Red Book*, and while I have in some instances endeavored to articulate these mythic aspects, insofar as they shed light on the work's thematic content, I will leave it to others to explore these connections in greater detail.

In the course of writing this book it has become clear to me that thousands of pages can (and will) be written about *The Red Book*, from a wide variety of perspectives, and it is clear that no one author can hope to grasp more than a portion of its potential depth and meaning.[2] I am also well aware that for some readers the very process of interpreting the images and even the narrative content of *The Red Book* will be seen as an effort at rational and conceptual control that will rob the work of its transformative power.[3] However, while I believe that there is great value in allowing oneself to become enveloped, enthralled, shocked, and disturbed by the images and words of *The Red Book*, there is also great value in subjecting this work to interpretive and conceptual analysis. Indeed, Jung himself undertook such analysis in what the book's translators have spoken of as the "conceptual" layer of *The Red Book* text (p. 222), and there is thus reason to believe that Jung held such analysis to be critical to the soul-finding, individuating journey that he had embarked upon.

In presenting his book in the manner of a medieval religious manuscript (carefully copied and edited from less elaborate non-illuminated versions), Jung clearly signaled his conviction that *The Red Book* is an extremely important work, and, moreover, one that is religious or spiritual in form and content. However, as one leafs through its pages, *The Red Book* may prompt an unusual reaction. One is captivated by the paintings and the calligraphy but is not initially inclined to *read* the work, any more than one would read the *Book of Kells* or any other illuminated manuscript of old. The immense size and weight of the facsimile edition, along with the haunting beauty and mystery of its illustrations lead one to approach this book with a certain caution—it is hardly the sort of work that one curls up with in bed or reads on the morning train. And yet it is a work that, above all else, must be read; read, and then studied and reflected upon, as it not only provides a valuable key to the development of Jung's thought, but raises a series of profound questions on a range of topics that continue to be of relevance to our own lives and time. In the present work, I propose to *read The Red Book*, and, in the course of this reading, wrestle with the questions it asks, in the hope of experiencing something new, seeing life from a new perspective, and perhaps being personally transformed in the process.

NOTE ON REFERENCES

References in this interpretive guide are to the English language edition of C.G. Jung's *The Red Book, Liber Novus,* ed. Sonu Shamdasani, trans. Mark Kyburz, John Peck, and Sonu Shamdasani (New York: W.W. Norton & Company, 2009).

References to *The Red Book* are placed in parentheses within the text of this guide. *The Red Book* is abbreviated to "RB", followed by the page number, and when appropriate, the modifier "a" or "b", e.g. "(RB, p. 303a)". The modifier "a" or "b" is used as many of the pages in *The Red Book* are printed with two columns of text on each page. The modifier "a" refers to text in the left column of the page, while "b" refers to text in the right column of the page.

References to Sonu Shamdasani's Introduction to *The Red Book* are abbreviated to "RB Intro," followed by the page number and the modifier "a" or "b", e.g. "(RB Intro, p. 303a)".

References to the editorial footnotes in *The Red Book* are to page number only, without the "a-b" modifier, for example, "(RB, p. 290, n. 149)".

All references in this guide to Jung's Images, or Paintings, are placed in bold in parenthetical references, and refer to the page numbers in *Liber Primus* and *Liber Secundus*, the calligraphic text at the beginning of *The Red Book*.

Jung numbered the pages in *Liber Primus* only on the front of each page, not on the back, in this way: Fol. i, Fol. ii, Fol. iii, Fol. iv, Fol. v, Fol. vi, and Fol. vii. Thus both the front and back of the first page are numbered "Fol. i". In my references to the Images in *Liber Primus*, I reference *The Red Book* Fol. page number and then follow it with either "a" or b", with "a" indicating the front side of the folio page and "b" representing the back side of the page, e.g. "**(RB Image, Fol., p. iv b)**".

Jung numbered *Liber Secundus* beginning with page number "1" and, unlike the page numbering in *Liber Primus*, he numbered both the front and back of each page. Thus, my parenthetical references to the Images in *Liber Secundus* utilize page numbers only, e.g. "(**RB Image, p. 29**)".

References to the *Collected Works of C.G. Jung* (Princeton, NJ: Princeton University Press, 1954-1973) are abbreviated to "CW", followed by the volume number and the paragraph number, e.g. "(CW 6, § 105)" or by a page number range "(CW 8, pp. 67-91)".

References to Supplementary Volume A of Jung's *Collected Works*, *The Zofinga Lectures*, trans. Jan van Heurck (Princeton: Princeton University Press, 1983) are abbreviated to "CW A" followed by the paragraph number, e.g. "(CW A, § 25)".

References to Supplementary Volume B of Jung's *Collected Works*, *Psychology of the Unconscious: A Study of the Transformations and Symbolisms of the Libido. A Contribution to the History of the Evolution of Thought*, trans. Beatrice M. Hinkle (Princeton: Princeton University Press, 1991) are abbreviated to "CW B" and followed by either a paragraph number or page number, e.g. "(CW B, § 3)" or "(CW B, pp. 1-5)". This work was originally published as *Wandlungen und Symbole der Libido* in 1912, and I have adopted the convention, used by Shamdasani in his Introduction and Notes to *The Red Book*, of referring to it in my text with the English translation of its original title, *Transformations and Symbols of the Libido*.

Transformations and Symbols of the Libido was considerably revised by Jung in 1952, and appears as Vol. 5 of his *Collected Works*, with the title, *Symbols of Transformation*. Wherever possible I have cross-referenced pages in the later revision that contain text *parallel* to the original 1912 work, e.g. "(CW B, § 441; cf. CW 5, § 432)".

References within the main text to C.G. Jung, *Memories, Dreams, Reflections*, recorded and edited by Aniela Jaffe (New York: Vintage Books, 1989) are abbreviated to "MDR" followed by the page number, e.g. "(MDR, p. 294)".

Biblical and other scriptural references are cited by book, chapter, and verse, e.g. "(Isaiah 53:1-4)".

All other references are indicated with endnotes and are not in parenthetical references.

Since Jung referred to his work both as the "*Red Book*" and as "*Liber Novus,*" these appellations will be used interchangeably in this guide.

The "S" in the term "Self" is capitalized in those instances where it refers to Jung's archetype of the Self or is used in a manner commensurate with Jung's concept, except in those instances where it appears in a quotation and is not there capitalized. Following the convention of Jung's translators both the term "God" and "Gods" are capitalized throughout this work.

Chapter 1

Jung's Prologue: Inspiration and Knowledge from the "Depths"

The Red Book: Liber Primus

"Prologue: The Way of What Is to Come," pp. 229-31**

The Red Book opens with the first of Jung's paintings, the letter "D", from the title, *Der Weg des Komenden* ("The Way of Things to Come"), superimposed upon a small lakeside town that is dominated by a church and its steeple. Mountains and fair weather clouds can be seen in the background, and an ancient or medieval sailing vessel drifts close to shore. The masted vessel, which seems suitable for a lone adventurer, signals the beginning of a journey, one that will take Jung into the primitive depths and the astral heights. This scene, which is peaceful, indeed idyllic, in the center, has much that is troubling around its edges—a harbinger of things to come. Astrological objects and symbols range across the sky, and below there are strange, perhaps primitive, plants and corals in a dark lake. The staff of the letter "D" contains a flaming cauldron, and a serpent wearing a golden crown rises high above it. We will later see that the serpent is one of the faces of Jung's own soul, and that Jung himself will eventually be granted a golden crown from the heavens.

** **Note:** Jung's chapter headings, which appear in quotes and bold headings throughout the text are quoted from C.G. Jung, *The Red Book, Liber Novus*, ed. Sonu Shamdasani, trans. Mark Kyburz, John Peck, and Sonu Shamdasani (New York: W.W. Norton & Company, 2009).

The text of *Liber Primus* begins with four biblical quotations: the first two and the fourth are from Isaiah, and the third is from the Gospel of John. V. Walter Odajnyk[1] suggests that the four quotations express four progressive themes that occupy Jung in *The Red Book*. The first (from Isaiah 53:1-4) begins, "Who hath believed our report?" and announces Jung's concern with prophecy and the nature of his own *prophetic* calling, a calling that, as we will see, he alternately embraces and rejects during his *Red Book* period. The second quotation (Isaiah 9:6) begins, "For unto us a child is born," and heralds Jung's interest not only in the nature and meaning of Christ, but also in a series of "new Gods" that are effectively "born" in *The Red Book's* pages. The third quotation (John 1:14) which begins, "And the Word was made flesh and dwelt among us," announces Jung's notion that a newly born God has been incarnated in man, an idea that in *Liber Novus* evolves into the notion that God is manifest and known through a deep understanding of what Jung will later come to term the "Self." Finally, the fourth quotation, from Isaiah 35:1-8, says, "The wilderness and the solitary place shall be glad for them; and the desert shall rejoice, and blossom as the rose," and effectively declares the grace and redemption that will result from Jung's new revelation, the birth of the new God and his incarnation in humanity.

We should also note that the three quotations from Isaiah describe the *paradoxical* traits and effects of the redeemer: "He is despised and rejected by men," he is a "tender plant" (Isaiah 53:1-4) and a child (Isaiah 9:6), and in his wake the desert shall blossom, the blind shall see, the lame shall leap, the dumb shall sing, and "the parched ground shall become a pool" (Isaiah 35:1-8). We will see that concern with paradox and the coincidence of opposites is a theme that will dominate *Liber Novus* and thereby set the tone for much of Jung's later thought. We will return to each of Jung's prologue themes many times in this book.

Jung's use of the phrase "The Way of What is to Come" (*Der Weg des Kommenden*) has resonances with both eastern and western spiritual traditions, bringing to mind both the Chinese "Tao" (way, route, or path) and the future coming of Christ.[2] Jewish law is also described with the term "the way" (*halakha*—literally, "the path that one walks"). Murray Stein has suggested as an alternate translation of this opening phrase "The way of the one who is coming,"[3] thus drawing a connection to Jung's *Red Book* interest not only in Christ, but in a post-Christian God, religion, and humanity.

A CONTEMPORARY PROPHET?

The question of Jung's prophetic aspirations looms large throughout *The Red Book*, and it is important that we consider this issue at the outset, even if the question can only be fully addressed after a complete reading of *Liber Novus* in the context of Jung's later work. There are passages in *The Red Book* that *seem* to confirm the extreme, and to some, outrageous claims of Richard Noll that Jung viewed himself as a Christ figure and the leader of a religious cult.[4] At various points in *Liber Novus*, we find Jung healing a sick and dying God (RB, p. 282a ff), speaking of giving birth to his God (RB, p. 289a), and being told that he is indeed a prophet and even Christ himself (RB, p. 252b). However, we also find, in keeping with *The Red Book's* many paradoxes, that Jung turns out to be the sort of prophet or redeemer who announces to the world that there is, in effect, *no prophet or redeemer at all*, and that each individual must find his or her own spiritual way. While Jung may have nonetheless seen himself as a sort of prophet (or "anti-prophet") during his *Red Book* period, he could not, on the basis of his own "prophecy," have viewed himself as the leader of a religion or cult, or even the head of a school. He sums up his mission with the words, "I give you news of the way of this man. My path is not your path, therefore I cannot teach you" (RB, p. 231b). As we will see, Jung's goal in *The Red Book* was to encourage others to discover their own "soul" and assume responsibility for their own lives, and while in *The Red Book* he provided a broad road map for this "individuation" process, he clearly rejected the view that it could be achieved through an attachment to Christ or any other prophet or redeemer. Interestingly, years later, in his "Foreword to Suzuki's 'Introduction to Zen Buddhism'" (1939), Jung approvingly quotes D. T. Suzuki that "satori" is a highly individual experience: "A Master says to his pupil: 'I have really nothing to impart to you, and if I tried to do so you might have occasion to make me an object of ridicule. Besides, whatever I can tell you is my own and can never be yours'" (CW 11, § 895, n. 31).

In the *Black Books*, where Jung recorded the experiences that were later described in *Liber Novus*, Jung's soul specifically tells him that his calling is "The new religion and its proclamation" (RB Intro, p. 211, citing *Black Book* 7, p. 92c). However, as Shamdasani points out, rather than prophesying a new faith, Jung's interest moved in the direction of understanding the psychology of religion (RB Intro, p. 212). Shamdasani cites Cary Baynes' notes of her discussions with Jung during the early 1920s, at a time when Jung was still working on *The Red Book*. Baynes wrote that Jung had informed her that his discourses with Elijah, Philemon, etc. derived from the same source that inspired Buddha, Mani, Christ, and Mohammed, but that Jung had refused to identify with these experiences and steadfastly remained a psychologist endeavoring to understand the nature of religious experience (RB Intro, p. 213).

In *The Red Book*, Jung is in the process of formulating his theory of *individuation*, and, as we will see, this theory is naturally expressed in Jung's own, highly *individualized* terms. As such, in *Liber Novus* and throughout his career, Jung struggled with his personal mission and his role as a guide for others. On the one hand, Jung harbored the idea that his work had the potential to provide what was lacking in western civilization,[5] while on the other hand, he rejected the notion that he was the founder of a school or that anyone should or even could be a "Jungian."[6] The question of Jung's understanding of his role in relation to the individuation and spiritual fulfillment of others is highly complex and, as with so many other of Jung's attitudes and ideas, we will find that a simple "yes" or "no" answer does not do justice to Jung's position. We cannot hope to understand *The Red Book* at all unless we suspend our demand for simple, unequivocal ideas and answers. Jung himself declares that his major "innovation" in *Liber Novus* is the proclamation of the "coincidence of opposites" (RB, p. 319a), and his approach to many of the issues and problems raised in The *Red Book* involves conflict, paradox, and even contradiction.

THE TWO SPIRITS

Jung begins the main text of *Liber Primus* with a distinction between the "spirit of this time" (*Der Geiste dieser Zeit*) and the "spirit of the depths" (*Der Geist der Tiefe*) (RB, p. 229b). Jung is moved by the latter spirit, which promises to grant him a form of insight and wisdom that is not conditioned by the empty practicalities that he believed to characterize his own time. He writes that while the spirit of this time promotes "use and value," the spirit of the depths is "beyond justification, use and meaning" (RB, p. 229b). Jung relates that his pride originally blinded him and he was caught up in the experimental, scientific, skeptical world-view that characterizes the "spirit of this time." However, the greater power of the "spirit of the depths" took from him his "belief in science," brought him back to the simplest of things, and brought his knowledge and understanding to serve the "inexplicable and paradoxical" (RB, p. 229b). Throughout his career, Jung will be torn between the present and the eternal, and between science and mystery, as his claims to have achieved an empirical psychology will be counterbalanced by an absorption in the forgotten disciplines of Gnosticism and alchemy and a fascination with the numinosity of the collective unconscious. The distinction between the "spirit of this time" and the "spirit of the depths" nicely captures the conflict that will color and prove so fruitful for Jung's life's work.

Jung's discussion of the spirit of the depths raises the question of whether there is indeed a form of *gnosis* that is not conditioned by time and place. He identifies the "spirit of this time" with science and the "spirit of the depths" with spiritual "understanding" (RB, p. 230b), suggesting that while science is conditioned by history, a form of understanding is trans-temporal. Indeed, it is the quest for such a trans-temporal, transcultural, "Platonic" understanding that fueled Jung's early interests in mythology and which conditioned his inquiries into the archetypes of the collective unconscious. Years after writing *The Red Book*, in an essay entitled "What India Can Teach Us" (1939), Jung echoed his early distinction between the two spirits:

> The true genius…speaks to a temporal world out of a world eternal. Thus he says the wrong things at the right time. Eternal truths are never true at any given moment in history (CW 10, § 1004).

SENSE, NONSENSE, AND THE GOD YET TO COME

Jung introduces another important theme in the opening paragraphs of *Liber Novus*, the distinction between *sense* and *nonsense*, and their relationship to what he calls the "supreme meaning" (*Übersinn*) and "*the God yet to come*" (*der kommende Gott*) (RB, p. 229b). "God" (in a wide range of conceptions and guises) is a major theme in *The Red Book*, and throughout its pages, Jung struggles to resignify and recreate the Gods who have lost their authority, significance, and very existence in the wake of the science and relativism of Jung's time. Jung's reference to the "supreme meaning" or "over-meaning" and its connection with "God" may give the impression that he is positing a fundamental philosophical or theological principle. However, Jung himself suggests that his "supreme meaning" is not so much the underlying principle or "God" of our present world, but is rather "the path, the way and the bridge to what is to come" (RB, p. 229b).

For Jung, the supreme meaning, which gives rise to an image of "the God yet to come," is "the melting together of meaning and absurdity, sense and nonsense" (RB, p. 229b). Indeed, Jung states that God has a shadow (*Schatten*), and this shadow is "nonsense" (*Unsinn*) (RB, p. 230a). Jung's focus on meaning and absurdity introduces what might be termed an existential and even postmodern element into his worldview. Jung was acutely aware of the loss of meaning that resulted from the Enlightenment and the mechanized world picture that followed in its wake. He considered this loss of meaning when years after the composition of *The Red Book*, he stated in his seminar on Nietzsche's *Zarathustra*:

> …we don't know what the purpose of life is, don't even know whether it *has* a purpose…we are quite safe in believing that this life is mere meaningless chaos because that is what we see…We belittle chance and don't admit that chance is the master…the main thing is chaos and chance—that is a pretty fair picture of the world.[7]

In the opening pages of *Liber Primus*, Jung chooses to embrace the absurd and the nonsensical as a moment in his conception of the divine, a moment that is set against and integrated with its opposite—fullness of meaning. While the integration of evil into the self and the image of God is a familiar theme in Jung's later writings, here in *The Red Book* Jung seeks to integrate *meaninglessness* into his conception of God and the world. He explains that "The highest truth is one and the same with the absurd" (RB, p. 242a), and just as "day requires night and night requires day, so meaning requires absurdity and absurdity requires meaning" (RB, p. 242a).

While Jung might have at times preferred to remain in a purely *meaningful*, Platonic world of symbols, ideas, and archetypes, he came to believe that no contemporary view of the psyche or formulation of the God-idea could fail to include the nonsensical, the meaningless, and the absurd. In *Scrutinies*, when Jung's spiritual guide and alter ego Philemon comes to describe the highest God, Abraxas, he portrays him as the "cruel contradictoriness of nature" (RB, p. 350b), a nature that has no meaning inherent in itself. We will see that Jung has more than one strategy for preserving or re-creating God in the face of relativism and science. However, here at the beginning of *The Red Book*, he recognizes that if God is to survive his "death" at the hands of Nietzsche and science, the deity must embody the very relativism and meaninglessness that was thought to have killed him.

Jung holds that we can experience the world and ourselves as both infinitely meaningful and infinitely contingent. In *Psychological Types*, which Jung authored during a hiatus in his work on *The Red Book*, he writes:

> The fact that there are two distinct and mutually contradictory views eagerly advocated on either side concerning the meaning and meaninglessness of things shows that processes obviously exist which express no particular meaning, being in fact mere consequences or symptoms; and that there are other processes which bear within them a hidden meaning, processes which are not merely derived from something but which seek to become something, and are therefore symbols. (CW 6, § 822)

Jung's comments here are set in the context of a discussion of the neurotic's view of his symptoms, but they apply equally to his general conception of the human psyche and the world as a whole. Indeed, Jung's view in *The Red Book* is that any conception of man or God that does not encompass both of these poles is woefully incomplete.

From a purely logical perspective it can be argued that an "Absolute" must be *infinite*, and for such an Absolute to exclude something from itself (e.g. absurdity and meaningless) would be tantamount to surrendering its infinitude. Jung himself suggests that the supreme meaning is infinite when he writes: "The supreme meaning is great and small, it is as wide as the space of the starry Heaven, and narrow as the cell of the living body" (RB, p. 230a). Its all-encompassing nature demands that it includes not only the meaningful but also the absurd.

SPEAKING NONSENSE IN THE NAME OF SENSE

There is another perspective that we can take upon Jung's conception of *Ubersinn*, and this involves the notion that the *supreme meaning* is achieved only through a process in which one transgresses the boundaries of *conventional meaning* and speaks or writes in a manner that initially appears to be nonsense.[8] As the philosopher Richard Rorty and others have suggested,[9] this process is evident in poetry, where an initially "nonsensical" metaphor that is articulated in the "jungle" beyond the "clearing" of normative meaning stretches our notion of significance and expands the horizon of what can be cognized and understood. Jung himself makes use of a very similar metaphor when he suggests that he only gained his freedom and became a "prophet" when he permitted his mind to wander in the chaotic forest of wild animals (RB, p. 250b, p. 251a). Indeed, much of the difficulty (and promise) of *The Red Book* derives from the fact that in it Jung is wandering in the (as yet nonsensical) forest, and it was only after the work's completion that he became fully engaged in the task of expanding the clearing of meaning to include what he had experienced during his *Red Book* period.

Explanation and Understanding

Jung discusses his spiritual experiences and ideas from the perspectives of both the spirit of the depths and the spirit of this time, and in the process articulates a set of ideas that, without Jung making it explicit, mark his dissension and break from Freud. Jung relates that the *spirit of the depths* moved him to regard the "small, narrow, and banal" as one of "the essences of the Godhead," the very aspect of divinity that heals "the immortal" (RB, p. 230a) within him. Perhaps more significantly, the spirit of the depths informed Jung that he himself is "an image of the unending world [and] all the last mysteries of becoming and passing away live in [him]" (RB, p. 230a). Finally, Jung learned that "the spirit of the depths in [him] was at the same time the ruler of the depths of world affairs" (RB, p. 230b, p. 231a). Later in *The Red Book*, Jung will generalize these ideas into the "certainty" that one reaches God through a communion with the Self (RB, p. 338b).

However, for the *spirit of this time* these ideas are nonsense, and Jung says that at least for a while he found such notions "ridiculous and revolting" (RB, p. 230a). From the perspective of "this time," the image of God that Jung was forming was a function of his individual psychology, and Jung indicates that he struggled to formulate an explanation along these lines. For a time he came close to inventing such an account—one, we might imagine, that would have been along Freudian lines.

It will be instructive to inquire into the *sort* of individual explanation that Jung might have devised for his spiritual experiences (without suggesting that this particular or even type of explanation actually applies to Jung). To do this we need only to recall Freud's analysis of Daniel Paul Schreber's 1903 book, *Memoirs of My Nervous Illness*. Freud's interpretation, which was published in 1911 as "Psychoanalytic Notes on an Autobiographical Account of a Case of Paranoia,"[10] explained Schreber's psychotic symptoms, which included his being effeminized and penetrated by the "rays of God," as a manifestation of repressed homosexual wishes. Jung, who claimed that he originally brought the Schreber case to Freud's attention (CW 5, § 458, n. 65), was initially deeply impressed by Freud's interpretation. However, by the time Jung published *Transformations and Symbols of the Libido* in 1912, he had begun to see similarities between psychosis and mythology that could not be explained in Freudian terms, and to seriously question the sexual theory of the libido and its role in psychosis that Freud had put forth in connection with the Schreber case (CW B, § 219 ff.; cf. CW 5, § 190 ff.). While Jung himself never published an interpretation of Schreber's "delusions,"[11] other Jungians, notably Hillman[12] and Adams,[13] have argued that Freud failed to take Schreber's experience on its own terms, as a genuine religious experience. Given that Jung started to record his own religious experiences shortly after he began questioning Freud's interpretation of Schreber's delusions, it is hard to imagine that he did not have this interpretation in mind when he (Jung) thought to give his experiences an "individual" explanation.[14]

Nevertheless, Jung clearly rejected such causal, individual explanations for his spiritual experiences. He says that while the spirit of this time prompted him to speak in terms of "reasons and explanations" (*Gründe und Erklärungen*) (RB, p. 230b), he was in the process of rejecting this whole mode of comprehension, and sought to establish for himself another form of *understanding*. Indeed, Jung avers that while *understanding* is "a bridge and possibility of returning to the path," *explanation* is "arbitrary and sometimes even murder"

(RB, p. 230b). Jung is here developing the phenomenological approach to psychic experience that he was to retain throughout his career. It is a position similar not only to the phenomenology of Edmund Husserl (1859-1938)[15] but also to the views of Wilhelm Dilthey (1833-1911),[16] who had contrasted what he termed "*verstehen,*" i.e., interpretive or participatory understanding, with causal explanation.

Jung's aversion to causal explanations in psychology took critical form in his 1914 paper, "On Psychological Understanding" (CW 3, pp. 179-193), where he wrote that objective/causal explanations are totally appropriate "in all sciences that are not psychology" (CW 3, § 395). However anyone who tries to understand a work of art like Goethe's *Faust,* for example, or any other meaningful human product from a causal standpoint, is like

> a man who tries to understand a Gothic cathedral under its historical, technical, and finally its mineralogical aspect. But where is the meaning of the marvelous edifice? Where is the answer to that all-important question: what goal of redemption did the Gothic man seek in his work, and how have we to understand his work subjectively, in and through ourselves? (CW 3, § 396)

For Jung, *Faust* and any other work of art or meaningful human product "is understood only when it is apprehended as something that becomes alive and creative again and again in our own experience" (CW 3, § 398).

THE INDIVIDUAL AND THE UNIVERSAL

In a letter written during his *Red Book* period to Hans Schmid, Jung describes a certain form of understanding as "a fearfully binding power, at times a veritable murder of the soul" that "flattens out vitally important differences." Jung continues that understanding that conforms "with general points of view, has the diabolical element and kills." It has the tendency to "wrench…life out of its own course, forcing it into a strange one in which it cannot live."[17] It is clear that Jung was highly suspicious not only of causal explanations in psychology but of any mode of explanation or understanding that attempts to comprehend the individual's experience in general terms. As *The Red Book* progresses we will see the development of Jung's veneration for the individual and for "difference." At the same time, Jung will develop a concept of the individual in relation to the collective and the universal man. This tension (and balance) between the individual and the collective will become a major theme in Jung's psychology.

The tension between the individual and the universal has a bearing on our overall understanding of *The Red Book*. Is *Liber Novus* simply a record of Jung's unique experiences, idiosyncratic ideas, and personal journey, or does it move beyond Jung himself into a description of the journey of the universal man and woman? While Jung adamantly denied that *The Red Book* was art, claiming that it was instead a natural psychical expression (MDR, pp. 185-6)[18], I believe that his comments years later on the nature of art and literature have an important bearing on *The Red Book's* generalizability. In "Psychology and Literature" (1930, rev. 1950), Jung writes:

> The essence of a work of art is not to be found in the personal idiosyncrasies that creep into it—indeed, the more there are of them, the less it is a work of art—but in its rising above the personal and speaking from the mind and heart of... mankind. (CW 15, § 156)

In his early review of *The Red Book*, Wolfgang Giegerich took Jung to task for regarding his fantasy productions as nature, happenings, events, and processes rather than artistic creations.[19] According to Giegerich, Jung *failed* to lift his purely subjective experience into the realm of thought and intersubjectivity,[20] and thus failed to turn his experiences into a work of either art or science that could (like Dante's *Divine Comedy* or Nietzsche's *Zarathustra*) be accessible to a general reader. For this reason, says Giegerich, *The Red Book* remains *absolutely* esoteric.[21] My own view is that in writing *The Red Book*, Jung was at all times struggling with the very question of how his (indeed, how anyone's) unique experience can be generalized to others, and that this genuine, *generalizable*, struggle is a source both of the work's difficulty and one of its great strengths. Giegerich's claim that *The Red Book* is an "impossible" book, because its tone is prophetic yet it refuses to speak in general terms, both hits and completely misses the mark, for the writing of *The Red Book* was itself an effort to engage the problem and paradox of comprehending the universal in the particular.[22] As we proceed we will see how much of the experience and thought recorded in *The Red Book* is generalizable beyond Jung's own private world. Perhaps, *Liber Novus* will provide an illustration of Aristotle's dictum that the universal is "implicit in the clearly known particular."[23]

AN INTOXICATING MADNESS

Jung records that the spirit of the times accused him of "madness," and Jung says that he must agree, adding, however, that his madness is great and intoxicating as well as ugly. The depths affirm that all that Jung has spoken of, the great, the intoxicating, the ugly, as well as the sick, the mundane, and the ridiculous *exist*, and, further, that they are all "the one essence of God" (RB, p. 230b). The supreme meaning can be recognized both in laughter and in worship, and what's more, the supreme meaning is "a bloody laughter and a bloody worship" (RB, p. 230b).[24] One cannot arbitrarily judge that one aspect of the world is more spiritual, godly, or valid than any other. All is part of the "sum of life" (RB, p. 230b). We will see that as *The Red Book* progresses, Jung's soul will implore him to *accept everything*, and Jung will struggle to comply with this demand, a demand that he will at times find overwhelming. Here, for example, his "humanity" tells him that his talk about the supreme meaning is cold and desolate (RB, p. 230b), and that the spirit of the depths demands too much blood, destruction, and sacrifice. The depths, however, inform Jung that his path is one that will indeed involve sacrifice and isolation, as only the "desert within (him)" can free him from the "world of this time" (RB, p. 230b). Jung relates that hearing this caused his "humanity" to fall silent as his spirit experienced the "belief, hope and…daring" to proceed on the path prepared for him by the spirit of the depths. Jung says that language fails him on this path and that he must "speak in images" (RB, p. 231b). By "images" we might understand both the painted images of *The Red Book* and the imagistic language of its narratives.

SIGNS, DREAMS, AND VISIONS

Jung writes that he needed a "visible sign" to demonstrate that it is the "spirit of the depths" that rules world affairs. The sign came to him in a series of visions, dreams, and coincidences (what Jung will later call "synchronicities") that accompanied the outbreak of the First World War. His visions, which occurred from October, 1913 to July,

1914, involved floods that devastated and killed "countless thousands" across Europe, "a sea of blood over the northern hills" (RB, p. 231a), a terrible cold that froze seas, rivers, and every green thing, and a summer frost that turned the leaves of a fruitless tree "into sweet grapes full of healing juice," which Jung then distributed to the "waiting throng" (RB, p. 231a). Jung relates that at the time war broke out he was in Scotland and needed to embark on a fast and direct ship for home. On this journey, he tells us, he encountered "colossal cold… the flood, (and) the sea of blood" (RB, p. 231a). He reports that he also encountered a "barren tree whose leaves the frost had transformed into a remedy." Jung says that he "plucked the fruit and gave it to you" (RB, p. 231a), presumably referring to the wisdom he is giving to the reader. It was this synchronous experience that brought Jung to the realization, as he later told Eliade, that he was not experiencing schizophrenia but rather the "subsoil of the collective unconscious."[25]

It is here, however, that Jung cautions, *It is no teaching and no instruction that I give you*" (Jung's italics). As we have already suggested, the fruit that Jung is distributing to the "great waiting throng" represents the wisdom that each must find his own way, and that each must live his own life: "The way is within us, but not in Gods, nor in teachings, nor in laws" (RB, p. 231b). One must not be eager to "gobble up the fruits of foreign fields," as one is oneself "the fertile acre." "There is only one way and that is your way" (RB, p. 231b). While Jung regards himself as transmitting something of great significance to humanity, he insists that he is "no savior, no lawgiver, no master teacher" (RB, p. 231b). Human beings are past the point where they can regard themselves and be treated as children. Providing them with laws and making things easier for them can now only lead to "wrong and evil" (RB, p. 231b). If anything, Jung is a *prophet of individuation*. Only by standing apart, and by each finding his own path and dignity can individuals achieve true fellowship, love, and community. The path is difficult, as both God and the world are "crossed by chaos" (RB, p. 231b), and "one must be "patient with the crippledness of the world…" (RB, p. 231b).

THE METAPHYSICAL GOD

Jung's talk of the "supreme meaning" and "the God yet to come" raises for us the question of whether Jung is speaking in metaphysical or psychological terms. In his later work Jung will make a distinction between the metaphysical God, about which he claimed to know nothing (CW 14, § 7), and the "archetype" or God "image" (CW 9ii, § 73), which he held to be a proper subject of psychological inquiry. However, here in *The Red Book*, where Jung has jettisoned any claim to be functioning as an empirical scientist, this distinction is not at all clear. Indeed, Jung states that the supreme meaning is "image and force in one" (RB, p. 230a), suggesting that it is both a "phenomenon" for human consciousness and an active power in the external world. Further, while other Gods have died in the course of time, the supreme meaning is eternal (RB, p. 230a). Already in the opening chapter of *The Red Book*, we find what appears to be a metaphysical understanding of the "absolute" or God, an understanding that will only become more varied and complex as we proceed through *The Red Book*, and which will culminate in the highly metaphysical "Seven Sermons to the Dead." In spite of his later distinction between metaphysics and psychology, there can be little doubt that in *The Red Book* Jung is struggling with ideas that can be regarded as metaphysical and theological.

Chapter 2

The Search for the Soul

The Red Book: Liber Primus

"Chapter I: Refinding the Soul," pp. 231-2

T he letter "D" that opens the title of this chapter, *Die Wiederfindung der Seele* ("Refinding the Soul"), fully encloses a white dove, which as we will later learn, is another manifestation of Jung's soul, the soul that Jung now seeks to rediscover. The search for the soul links Jung to a literary tradition that runs from Virgil to Dante to Goethe. It is a goal that distinguishes Jung from Freud, and signals Jung's distance in *The Red Book* from both psychoanalysis and psychiatry. Whereas Freud's self-analysis remained largely focused upon the meaning of dreams and psychological symptoms, Jung understood his own inner journey as a search for the depths and meaning of life itself, a search that, by his own account, brought him to the brink of madness.

Jung relates that his visions of October 1913 occurred at a point in his life when he had achieved "honor, power, wealth, knowledge, and every human happiness" (RB, p. 231b). In this he was much like Faust prior to embarking on the "soul-making" journey described by Goethe, and indeed it is clear from *The Red Book* and elsewhere in his writings that Jung saw himself as a Faustian figure.[1] At this point in his life, which coincided temporally with his break from Freud, Jung lost desire for the superficial trappings of life (RB, p. 232a), was gripped by the spirit of the depths, and overcome with horror.

"THIS LIFE"

It was at this point, "after long years of wandering" (RB, p. 232a), that Jung returned to his soul. Surprisingly, given the fact that Jung has just spoken of losing his desire for the trappings of worldly success, he states that "this life" is the path to the divine. He even goes so far as to say that the way of this life is the *only* way and that any other path to the divine is false (RB, p. 232a). We might ask whether Jung has not contradicted his earlier claim that each must find his own path and that "there is only one way and that is your way" (RB, p. 231b). Moreover, while the celebration of "this life" does at times occur in Jung's later writings, it is the withdrawal from this life, and in particular, a withdrawal from his interaction with his fellow men that is prominent throughout *The Red Book*. Even in this chapter Jung writes that in wandering with his soul he will "ascend to [his] solitude" (RB, p. 232a). This is but one of the many dialectical tensions that pervades *The Red Book*.

Interestingly, the affirmation of "this life" distinguishes Jung from the Gnostics, whose notions permeate much of Jung's thought during this period and figure prominently in *The Red Book*, and especially in the "Seven Sermons to the Dead." The Gnostics held that this world was worthless and irredeemable, and spoke of an inner realization that propels one beyond this cosmos. Indeed, in the "Seven Sermons" Jung (through his alter ego, Philemon) will make such typically Gnostic proclamations as "Weakness and nothingness here, eternally creative power there. Here nothing but darkness and clammy cold there total sun" (RB, p. 354 a, b). But in *Liber Primus* Jung takes precisely the opposite point of view: "the one thing I have learned is that one must live this life...This life is the way, the long sought-after way to the unfathomable, which we call divine...all other ways are false paths" (RB, p. 232a). This perspective, which Jung maintained as he matured, is much more Kabbalistic than Gnostic, as the Kabbalists held that humanity's task was not to escape one's life but rather to live in and repair this world. Indeed, we will (in Chapter 12) see that Jung later wrote about being in accord with the Lurianic notion that humanity partners with God to restore a broken world.[2] In fact,

Jung's interest in *this world* in *The Red Book* and elsewhere helps to counter the accusations made by Buber and others that Jung substitutes a thoroughly introversive, Gnostic vision of life and God for a dialogical, world-engaging one.

SCIENCE AND THE SOUL

Jung describes his struggle with the scientific status of psychology and his efforts to turn the soul "into a scientific object" (RB, p. 232a). He states, "I had to accept that what I had previously called my soul was not at all my soul but a dead system," and he writes that he had come to the realization that his soul cannot be an object of study, judgment, and knowledge. We will see that this is but an intimation of the radical critique of science that Jung puts forth as his thinking develops in *Liber Secundus*.

DESIRE AND IMAGE

Jung writes that one must turn one's desire "away from outer things" if one wants to reach the soul. While one "becomes a fool through endless desire," one who possesses his desire rather than being possessed by it is able to grasp his soul. Jung here adopts a view that is reminiscent of Hegel and anticipatory of the French psychoanalyst Lacan, that the soul finds itself in its desire. On the other hand, Jung's claims that "desire is the image and expression of the soul"[3] (RB, p. 232b), that "the image of the world is half the world" (RB, p. 232b), and "the wealth of the soul exists in images" (RB, p. 232b) sets the tone for a long tradition in analytic and archetypal psychology which holds that life is lived not in the world of matter or ideas, but in the world of images and the imagination. As we proceed through *The Red Book*, we will see how seriously Jung takes the image as a "reality" in its own right.

"Chapter II: Soul and God," pp. 233-4

ON DREAMS

The drop-case "S" that begins this chapter is superimposed upon a picture of a white dove and a serpent, which as we have seen, are symbols of Jung's soul. Jung's journey to discover his soul continues, and he writes that for many years he wandered, having forgotten that he even possessed a soul (RB, p. 233a). However, his soul announced herself in dreams, which he affirms are the soul's "guiding words" (RB, p. 233b). Here, by suggesting that dreams have spiritual significance, Jung links himself to earlier (e.g. biblical) traditions of dream interpretation, and clearly departs from Freud's understanding of dreams as disguised wish-fulfillments rooted in the personal unconscious. In addition, Jung adopts a view of the *prospective function* of dreams that he will maintain for the rest of his career: "Dreams pave the way for life, and they determine you without your understanding their language" (RB, p. 233b).

Is the Soul a God?

Jung describes his soul as both a child and a maiden and wonders if his soul is a god. He affirms that his soul "lies behind everything" (RB, p. 233b), and says that if he crosses the world this is ultimately in the service of finding his soul, an idea that echoes the Hasidic notion that one who is moved to travel to a distant place does so in order to "raise divine sparks" that are unique to his mission in life, an act which is at the same time a discovery of the roots of one's soul.

Jung writes that "God" and one's soul or Self is always in the "other," unexpected place: "If you are boys, your God is a woman…The God is where you are not" (RB, p. 234a). We are seeing the beginnings of Jung's thinking about the shadow and the anima, and his view that the individual is only completed through that which is opposed to, rejected by, and greater than one's conscious ego.

Knowledge of the Heart

Jung speaks of the paradox involved in finding one's soul, stating that his directed efforts were never rewarded, and that his discoveries were always in places that he could not have foreseen (RB, p. 233a, b). He writes that scholarliness, which "belongs to the spirit of this time," is by itself insufficient to grasp the soul, as "the soul is everywhere that scholarly knowledge is not" (RB, p. 233b). The soul can only be approached through a "knowledge of the heart" (*Wissen des Herzens*), a phrase Jung may have borrowed from Pascal (RB, p. 233, n. 54). Jung writes that the heart is both "good and evil" (RB, p. 234a) and that knowledge of the heart can only be attained "by living your life to the full" (RB, p. 233a).

There are places in *The Red Book* where Jung suggests that intuitive knowledge is superior to argument and reason. For example, regarding his assertion that one reaches God by uniting with oneself (RB, p.

338b), Jung protests that this idea was neither wished for nor expected, and that indeed he consciously hoped that he could disown it as a deception. However, the idea "seized [him] beyond all measure," and he was certain of its truth (RB, p. 338b). Jung remarks, "No insight or objection …could surpass the strength of this experience," and while Jung claims that he himself could explain the experience away in terms that would "join it to the already known," this "would be unable to remove even the smallest part of the knowledge…" (RB, p. 338b).

We will see that Jung's inner guide, Philemon, is also certain of his intuitions, but couches this certainty in a way that has it passing through the sieve of doubt. When asked about the veracity of his "Seven Sermons," Philemon avers that while he is uncertain that what he knows is the best knowledge, his knowledge nevertheless involves a direct apprehension of things as they are in themselves (RB, p. 348b). In the examples just cited, neither Jung nor Philemon considers the possibility that their intuitions might simply be mistaken; this despite the fact that in other places in *The Red Book*, Jung holds that one who becomes enslaved to thinking vs. feeling or vice versa, ends up in error (RB, p. 247b), that our concepts, unlike existing things, can yield and be in error (RB, p. 303a), that the universe is governed by chance (RB, p. 350b), and that "yes and no are both true and untrue" (RB, p. 303a).

Reflections on Jung's Theory of Knowledge

Renos Papadoupolos has suggested that Jung wavered between two conceptions of knowledge, a Platonic/Gnostic conception, in which one can achieve certainty or gnosis through an intuition of essences (e.g. the archetypes), and a dialectical or constructivist one, in which all so-called truths must be complemented by their opposites and in which so-called "knowledge" is always colored by the "personal equation" (or psychology) of the knower.[4] This tension, already evident in *The Red Book*, was, I believe, never fully resolved or even adequately recognized by Jung. Conceivably there is a *coincidentia oppositorum* between Jungian certainty and Jungian open-mindedness, but it is not one that is readily apparent from a reading of Jung himself. We will return to this issue in Chapter 11 when we reexamine Philemon's claim that "things are as I know them" (RB, p. 348b) in the First Sermon to the Dead.

While Jung does not offer a formal or systematic theory of knowledge in *The Red Book*, there is much in *The Red Book* that supports an open-ended epistemological point of view. Throughout *The Red Book* Jung challenges the assumptions of traditional and modernist epistemology implicit in such oppositions as real vs. imaginary, sanity vs. madness, science vs. magic, and rational vs. irrational. While Jung often appears to place his weight on the side of the "debased" pole of each of these dichotomies, e.g. by extolling magic and intuition and critiquing science and reason, we will see that he does not ultimately reject the poles that he has critiqued, but rather holds that each pole must be balanced by, and is indeed intertwined with and dependent upon its presumed contrary. Jung's view anticipates the perspective that Jacques Derrida would develop 60 years later— which not only redresses the imbalance resulting from the tradition's "privileging" of certain critical ideas over their opposites, but works to unsettle the very system of oppositions upon which much of traditional epistemology is based. For Jung in *The Red Book*, as it will be for Derrida, the impact of this gesture is to create a tolerance for ambiguity (RB, p. 244b) and difference (RB, p. 348a), and thereby open new modes of thought and experience that would be closed to us if we remained fast within the orbit of the traditional oppositions.

On Being Guided by One's Soul

Jung makes a number of existential pronouncements in this chapter. One particularly existential formulation Jung provides is that "The spirit of the depths demands: 'The life that you could still live, you should live'" (RB, p. 234a). However, Jung's "existentialism" is quite equivocal, and at any rate, certainly not one that is rooted in the individual's consciously directed will. He writes that he has learned that he is simply a "symbol" or "serf" of his soul, one who is "completely subjugated, utterly obedient" (RB, p. 234a). He castigates himself for his ambition and his desire to be a "prophet" (RB, p. 233a), writing that learning that he is "in fact the servant of a child" (i.e. his soul), provided him with the "extreme humility" that he needed, presumably as a compensation for his earlier grandiosity. However, becoming his soul's servant is a prescription for Jung, but not for everyone. In his next chapter, entitled, "On the Service of the Soul," Jung will write that only those who believe they are their soul's masters need become her servant, while those who have served her should become her master (RB, p. 235b). Philemon will later warn Jung not to subjugate himself to his soul (RB, p. 343a), and Jung will eventually disobey his soul's dictates (RB, p. 358a). However, at this point in *The Red Book*, Jung surrenders his will and his reason to the service of what he will later describe as the "anima" archetype. Later Philemon will tell Jung: "Whoever lives invents his life for himself" (RB, p. 357a); and the question of whether the individual should be guided by his own will as opposed to a guiding voice from the unconscious will become a major issue for Jungian psychology. There are dangers associated with being a servant of the soul or the unconscious; indeed, Jung will later describe Hitler as such a servant, as a man who "listens intently to a stream of suggestions from a whispered source and then *acts upon them*."[5]

THE INNER CHRIST

Chapter II of *Liber Primus* concludes with some comments on the nature of Christ and Christianity. One should not be a Christian, but should rather seek Christ within oneself, and actually *become Christ*, otherwise one "will be of no use to the coming God" (RB, p. 234b). Jung's meaning here is as yet unclear, but as *The Red Book* develops Christ will become an existential symbol, both of the sacrifice that one must make in order to find one's soul, and as an example of one who has taken his life into his own hands and has been true to his essence and his love (RB, p. 356a). In Jung's later work, Christ becomes an important symbol of the Self (CW 9ii, pp. 36-71), and the call to find Christ within oneself becomes a call to individuation (CW 9ii, §§ 123-125).

"Chapter III: On the Service of the Soul," pp. 234-5

Jung speaks about his hesitance to follow his soul, stating that he is terrified to enter her darkness. He says that his joy at rediscovering his soul "was not genuine," but he nonetheless commits himself to trusting and even loving her. Jung's anxiety derives from his view that an approach to one's own soul initially sinks one into meaninglessness and disorder, a disorder that is the origin of both the soul's power and terror.

ORDER AND CHAOS

Jung asserts that meaninglessness and chaos is the "other half of the world" (RB, p. 235a), and no one can be complete or have a full understanding of the world without embracing its chaotic and meaningless elements. Order and meaning are lacking in that they are in a state of having already become, while chaos and meaninglessness are in a process of becoming (RB, p. 235a). Jung thus suggests that the experience of chaos is the price we pay for our freedom and creativity. According to Jung, the wedding between order and chaos produces the divine child and the supreme meaning, a meaning "beyond meaning and meaninglessness" (RB, p. 235a) and for this reason, while one must realize that one's fear of the soul is reasonable and one's doubt is justified, one must overcome the temptation to be guided by these misgivings. When one becomes open to one's soul, the flood of chaos merges with order and meaning.

Jung is here introducing ideas that will become a dominant theme in *The Red Book* and enter into the core of his psychology: the coincidence of opposites and the need to embrace what is alien, dark, and chaotic in the world and Self. Later in his career Jung will discover that "chaos" is an important stage in the alchemical work (CW 12, § § 334, 356; CW 13, §157; CW 14, §§ 183, 253, 552), a work he will declare to be analogous to, if not identical with certain psychological processes leading to individuation (CW 12, §§ 185, 306, 342; CW 14, § 679).

Jung asserts that one must submit to what one fears and love what one is horrified by (RB, p. 235b). One must even be willing to eschew virtue if one becomes enslaved to it. As we have seen, a person must be willing to *reverse his position vis a vis* the soul: if he believes he is master, he must become its servant; if he believes that he is its servant, he must become its master. Jung's notions of compensation and the shadow are already implicit in these reflections. We might say that there is no single prescription for psychological growth; those who live on the side of order and meaning must embrace their shadow side of chaos, and vice versa. And, while Jung sees the dangers in embracing what brings fear and horror to one's ego, Jung's journey in *Liber Novus* suggests that this is precisely the path to individuation.

"Chaos," in the sense of a disorganized and disorganizing confrontation with the depths of the soul and the world, plays an important role in *The Red Book*. Jung made a study of Nietzsche's

Zarathustra in 1914 (RB Intro, p. 202), and he was likely inspired by Zarathustra's aphorism that "one must have chaos if one is to give birth to a dancing star."[6] "There in the world of chaos," Jung writes, "dwells eternal wonder…Man belongs not only to an ordered world, he also belongs to the wonder-world of his soul. Consequently you must make your ordered world horrible…" (RB, p. 264a). As *The Red Book* progresses, Jung speaks of his own descent into chaos:

> Everything inside me is in utter disarray. Matters are becoming serious, and chaos is approaching. Is this the ultimate bottom? Is chaos also a foundation? If only there weren't these terrible waves. Everything breaks asunder like black billows. (RB, p. 298a)

The descent into chaos is perilous, but it also yields great rewards: "If one opens up chaos, magic also arises" (RB, p. 314b). Psychic chaos is beyond logic, reason, expectation, and control:

> If one has done one's best to steer the chariot, and then notices that a greater other is actually steering it, then magical operation takes place. One cannot say what the effect of magic will be, since no one can know in advance because the magical is lawless, which occurs without rules and by chance so to speak. (RB, p. 314b)

The "greater other" Jung speaks of might be regarded as equivalent to the gods, the archetypes, the collective unconscious, and especially the "Self" that Jung will later contrast with the conscious, rational ego.

Jung's guide, Philemon, teaches that "the chaos…is without measure and utterly boundless, to which justice and injustice, leniency and severity, patience and anger, love and hate, are nothing" (RB, p. 350b). Chaos, to use Nietzsche's phrase, is "beyond good and evil," yet in spite, or even because of this, it enters into the essence of the divine: "*The one eye of the Godhead is blind, the one ear of the Godhead is deaf, the order of its being is crossed by chaos*" (RB, p. 231b, Jung's italics).

With his encounter with eastern alchemy in 1928 (RB, p. 360),[7] and then European alchemy in the 1930s, Jung discovered a tradition that provided support for his view that an encounter with chaos is instrumental to the development and individuation of the psyche. Jung viewed the alchemist's efforts to create gold as a symbol of their quest to transform the adept's soul, and he saw the alchemist's equivalence of *prima materia* with "chaos" as a verification of his view that chaos is the fundamental ingredient of psychological transformation. The European alchemists spoke of the "chaotic waters," which served as the raw material for creation (CW 14, § 252) prior to the separation of the opposites symbolized by the "firmament." Jung understood the alchemists to hold that all material transformation and psychic healing arises through chaos, quoting the alchemist Dorn on the disintegrating, yet reintegrative effects of disorder:

> Man is placed by God in the furnace of tribulation, and like the hermetic compound he is troubled at length with all kinds of straits, divers calamities, anxieties, until he dies to the old Adam and the flesh and rise again as in truth a new man. (CW 14, p. 353, n. 370)

For Jung, the psychological meaning of such "transformation by chaos" is a confrontation with one's personal, and moreover, the collective unconscious. While an encounter with the collective unconscious can have a disintegrating effect upon the ego, there exists in the midst of the chaos of the unconscious a source of unity, symbolized in alchemy by a globe (CW 14, p. 364, n. 393), which provides the seeds for a higher integration of the Self (CW 12, § 96).

The notion that chaos plays a critical role in all forms of creativity and change is a prominent theme in the Kabbalah, which was a major spiritual source and foundation for western alchemy. For example, the Kabbalist Joseph Ben Shalom of Barcelona (c.1300) held that there is no creation, alteration, or change in which the abyss of nothingness does not, at least for "a fleeting moment," become visible.[8] Late in his life Jung celebrated his discovery that in the 16th century the Kabbalist Isaac Luria had introduced the symbols of *Shevirat ha-Kelim*, the Breaking of the Vessels, and *Tikkun ha-Olam*, the Restoration of the World.[9] These symbols express the notion that the structures of God, world, and self must each be broken and a portion of the "original chaos" reintroduced in order for there to be a creative restoration and emendation of the world and the individual's soul.

The idea of an "irrational chaos" as a precondition for transformation, rebirth, and creativity is also not without its dangers, and was likely a factor in Jung's initial optimism regarding the Nazi state. In an interview conducted on December 26, 1969, and which Richard Noll quotes from the Jung Biographical Archives, Jolande Jacobi relates:

> His idea [about the Nazi movement] was that chaos gives birth to good or something valuable. So in the German movement he saw a chaotic (we could say) pre-condition for the birth of a new world.[10]

"Chapter IV: The Desert," pp. 235-6

Jung discusses the poles of retreating from and engaging with his fellow men as pathways to the soul. He says that by turning himself away from men and things he became wholly identified with his thoughts, and then found that he needed to further detach himself from them. In the process his soul became a virtual desert, and by turning his creative energy towards this desert, he found that his soul would green and bear "wonderful fruit" (RB, p. 236a). Presumably this is a reference to the process of "active imagination" that Jung developed during the period of *The Red Book*, a process that begins with a passive observation of images, scenes, and figures as they emerge into awareness from the unconscious, and is completed through the active engagement with them that, as we will see, is Jung's *modus operandi* in *Liber Secundus*.

Jung, of course, was not the first to retreat to a real or imagined desert as a means of spiritual transformation. In Nietzsche's *Zarathustra*, we read:

> In the loneliest desert…the second metamorphosis occurs: here the spirit becomes a lion who would conquer his freedom and be master in his own desert. Here he seeks out his last master: he wants to fight him and his last god; for the ultimate victory he wants to fight with the great dragon.[11]

According to Jung, one will be tempted to, but must refrain from, making an early return to the world of things, men, and thoughts. Only after one has discovered one's soul can one live in harmony with men, thoughts, and things, and avoid being their slave or fool. The ancients who retreated into solitude found a world of symbols, an "abundance of visions" (RB, p. 236a, b). While it was easier for the ancients to "live their symbols" as the world "had not yet become real for them" (RB, p. 236a), Jung will soon embark on a modern form of the retreat into visionary solitude.

ON THE CREATIVE POWER OF LANGUAGE

At the close of this chapter, Jung comments on the role of language in the discovery of the soul, and the constructive or creative power of words: "When you say that the place of the soul is not then it is not. But if you say that it is then it is" (RB, p. 236b). He notes that the ancients considered the word a creative act. The contemporary reader will note that this is not only an ancient idea, but a postmodern one as well. Jung will consider the constructive theory of language later in *The Red Book*, but he will be more equivocal in his assessment of it.

Jung then tells us that the "oldest and truest" words are those "that oscillate between nonsense and supreme meaning" (RB, p. 236b). One might add that such oscillation is also true for the *newest* words (for example, those of the poet that press up against the boundaries of sense), and indeed Jung holds that the words and images of the ancients "show the way of what is to come" (RB, p. 236b). We might say that the margins of "sense" move as time goes on, so each generation must produce literature, metaphors, and theories that straddle the margins between sense and nonsense in the search for soul and meaning. In the process language is brought up against the boundary of what Jung here calls the "true" and what the psychoanalyst Jacques Lacan referred to as the "real." In order to reach the spirit of the depths one must escape from the "ruling discourse" of one's time. While this can perhaps be achieved outside of language,[12] for example, in experiences of the numinous and in trauma and suffering, it can also be *pointed* to within language, through words that border on the nonsensical, and thus escape from the shackles of accepted meaning. We might say that in *The Red Book*, Jung is struggling to do just this— to speak nonsense that leads us to a new sense, one that is both ancient (pointing backwards to the Gnostics) and contemporary (pointing forwards towards a new man and God).

"Experiences in the Desert," pp. 236-7

ON INTENTIONS

Jung continues to approach and struggle with his soul, arriving at "an undergrowth of doubt, confusion, and scorn" (RB, p. 236b). He experiences himself as poor, empty, thirsty, and weak, as if he is in a desert, and he wishes to be near his soul so that he can "feel the breath of [her] animating presence" (RB, p. 236b). Jung's soul reprimands him for his lack of patience, and moreover for his desires and intentions. His soul asks, "Do you still not know that the way to truth stands open only to those without intentions?" (RB, p. 236b). One is here reminded of the Buddhist paradox that enlightenment only comes when one is not seeking it, and Nietzsche's dictum that "He who seeks, easily gets lost."[13] Jung responds that a true commitment to life would be to "grow like a tree that...does not know its law" (RB, p. 236b), adding that intentions are actually inimical to life. When we have an intention, we presume that we can somehow know in advance the direction of light, truth, and soul, but in so doing we completely miss the mark. Jung is here laying the groundwork for his critique of the conscious ego and his theory of the Self. As he will later claim, the individuated or self-realized individual is one who thinks, feels, and acts from a center in his psyche that is guided by, but does not originate with the conscious ego. If we become too caught up in our plans and intentions, we will be blind to the experiences and opportunities that come from the "other," i.e. from the outer world, and, especially, from the unconscious.

UNITY IN DIFFERENCE: ON JUNG'S INNER FIGURES

Jung's soul warns him that he is not writing to feed his vanity but rather to enter into a genuine dialog with her. Jung tells us that now, in his "twenty-fifth night in the desert" (RB, p. 237a), his soul has awakened and is no longer a shadowy entity, but rather one who can approach him as a separate free-standing being. Yet Jung had earlier stated that everything said by his soul is also his own thought (RB, p. 236b). A question arises as to how Jung can regard his soul, and each of the other figures he will encounter in *The Red Book*, as separate entities who can challenge, instruct, and advise him. Are they not simply aspects of his own psyche? Is the self singular and unified, or is it a chorus of distinct voices and personalities? To what extent is this an issue that is unique to Jung? Is Jung describing experiences of "dissociation," here and in *Memories, Dreams, Reflections,* when he speaks specifically of having two personalities as a child (MDR, p. 45), and if so, are such dissociative experiences necessarily pathological?[14] Further, are we all not "multiple personalities," and is it even possible to achieve a unified Self? We will not resolve these questions here, but we should note that Jung himself held that a major task of individuation is precisely to unify the disparate voices of our psyche, in *complexio oppositorum.*

The question of "unity in difference" is not only a problem for psychology, but is also a fundamental philosophical issue that manifests in humanity's conception of the divine. For the Christian Church, it is the basic mystery of theology—the unity of Father, Son, and the Holy Spirit. For Hindus, it is the struggle to reconcile the polytheism of their mythology and folk-religion with the singular unity of Brahman; for the Kabbalists, it is task of uniting the disparate *Sefirot* (aspects of God) and *Partzufim* (faces of God) with a radically monotheistic faith. Each of these theological quandaries might be said to both complement and reflect the divided-yet-unitary nature of the human personality.

On Simplemindedness

Chapter IV concludes with an ode to simplemindedness and a rejection of the "cleverness" that characterizes the "spirit of this time." Wisdom, Jung tells us, is itself simple-minded. This is because "cleverness couples itself with intention" (RB, p. 237a) and as we have seen, truth, life, and wisdom are quite foreign to intention and the ego. Yet Jung does not want to abandon cleverness for simple-minded foolishness, as he holds that only by combining the two, by becoming "clever fools" (RB, p. 237a), is it possible to approach the "supreme meaning." Here we have another of *The Red Book's* paradoxes and *coincidentia oppositorum.* Much can be said about the integration of cleverness with foolishness. Clinically, it is imperative that we both be clever and simple-minded with our patients. In listening to their material we must be astute and analytical, but we must also allow ourselves to be open and simple-minded and even to be fooled on occasion—for if we always guard against being fooled, and insist on

never *being the fool*, we may fail to open ourselves to others in a manner
that will allow them to share their inner worlds.

"Chapter V: Descent into Hell in the Future," pp. 237-240

DIVINE ASTONISHMENT

Jung descends deeper into his own darkness, his spirit remains
tormented, and he experiences himself as a victim of his own thinking.
"When can I order my thinking to be quiet, so that my thoughts, those
unruly hounds, will crawl to my feet?" (RB, p. 238a) He bemoans
the fact that his howling thoughts prevent him from clearly
apprehending his soul's face and hearing her voice. Jung senses that
he is choking on his own knowledge, and he begs for protection against
the "serpent of judgment" (RB, p. 238a). Here we are witness to one
of the first of Jung's many *Red Book* diatribes against science: "Keep it
far from me, science that clever knower, that bad prison master who
binds the soul and imprisons it in a lightless cell" (RB, p. 238a). It is
clear that Jung is of the view that all of his thinking and judgment, all
of his psychiatric knowledge, will be of no avail to him in his "dark
night of the soul." Rather, he wishes to "persist in divine astonishment"
(*göttlicher Fassungslosigkeit*) (RB, p. 238a), and it is only in that mood,
from that perspective, that he will be able to behold his soul's wonders
and light. In Rudolph Otto's[15] terms, Jung seeks a numinous
experience, an experience of the *mysterium*, that fearful yet fascinating
and awe-inspiring rapture that lifts one from the despair of the everyday
and allows one to experience self and world as bathed in the darkness
of terror and/or the light of wonder, awe, and spiritual affirmation.

DIVINE MADNESS

Jung resumes his reflections on madness and the quest for the soul.
He tells his prospective readers: "It is unquestionable: if you enter into
the world of the soul, you are like a madman, and a doctor would consider
you to be sick" (RB, p. 238a). Jung links himself to a tradition that regards
certain forms of madness as a divine visitation, stating that there is a "divine
madness [*göttlichen Wahnsinn*] which is nothing other than the
overpowering of the spirit of this time through the spirit of the depths"
(RB, p. 238b). The notion of "divine madness" has a venerable history,
having been described in Plato's *Phaedrus* and the *Aeneid* of Virgil.

Nietzsche held that "there is always some reason in madness,"[16] and he has Zarathustra ask, "... do you want to go the way of your affliction, which is the way to yourself?"[17]

Jung's idea here is that it is only by challenging what one's time regards as reasonable, comprehensible, and true that one gains access to one's soul and an intuition of God. As we have seen, if we are to reach the divine, the "reality" of the "ruling discourse" must be set aside in favor of an experience that initially appears to be fantastic, mad, and nonsensical. Jung associates this divine reality with chaos, the irrational, life, and the imagination. Jung himself finds these ideas difficult, and at one point in *The Red Book,* he states, "I don't want to be divine but reasonable" (RB, p. 291b). However, Jung is of the view that the "divine astonishment" (RB, p. 238a) he seeks to make his desert bloom will also result in madness. A religion, i.e. contemporary Christianity, that is lacking in madness, lacks divine life, but one who enters into such life, who enters into the realm of the soul, would be considered mad, not only by a physician but also by himself.

The problem of madness pervades *The Red Book*, and prompts the reader to ask a number of questions. Was Jung truly psychotic or verging on psychosis as he later claimed? Or is Jung's "psychosis," simply a literary device, or perhaps even a conceit, an inflated effort to provide himself with the imprimatur of "divine madness," the stamp of prophesy, or the credentials of a spiritual savant? Is Jung's method of "active imagination" in *The Red Book*, in which various spiritual and mythical figures appear and dialog with Jung, a genuine means of self-discovery, or as Wolgang Giegerich has suggested, a "*simulation* of an 'authentic representation of an unconscious process,'"[18] and if so, does this in some way apply to active imagination in general and call into question the use of this technique? One problem with understanding Jung's visions as an authentic product of the collective unconscious is that many of the figures and themes contained within them appear to reflect Jung's readings during the period of *The Red Book's* composition. As Giegerich ungraciously puts it, "Over long stretches the book appears to be much like a subjective recapitulation of what one might find in textbooks of religious and mythological phenomenology."[19] I will return to this problem later, where I will argue that the issue of "learnedness" vs. an "authentic representation of the unconscious" does not result in an either/or proposition.

Jung himself says that he overcame his "madness" when after having been caught up in the "spirit of this time," he was overcome by the "spirit of the depths" (RB, p. 238b). Presumably, it was not simply an immersion in the unconscious but rather Jung's capacity to both experience, contain, transform, and be transformed by the influx of the spirit of the depths that enabled him to overcome his madness and experience his own creative renewal. Nietzsche had, in his early writings, spoken of the need for the Apollonian (rational) spirit to contain the influx of Dionysian impulses in the production of a higher, creative man. For Jung this process must move beyond containment into a dialectic that yields a symbolic transformation. This dialectic is evident in the alteration and interaction between visionary experience and rational reflection that occurs throughout *Liber Novus*, what *The Red Book's* translators refer to as the descriptive and conceptual layers of the text (RB, p. 222). It is this very dialectic that was ultimately productive of Jung's own theoretical corpus.

Years after terminating his work on *The Red Book*, Jung, in *Mysterium Coniunctionis* (1955-6), commented on the difference between an "anticipated" and "real" psychosis. His comments bear quoting at length as they are fully pertinent to his *Red Book* experiences:

> ...there is an enormous difference between an anticipated psychosis and a real one, but the difference is not always clearly perceived and this gives rise to uncertainty or even a fit of panic. Unlike a real psychosis, which comes on you and inundates you with uncontrollable fantasies irrupting from the unconscious, the judging attitude implies a voluntary involvement in those fantasy-processes... The avowed purpose of this involvement is to integrate the statements of the unconscious, to assimilate their compensatory content, and thereby produce a whole meaning which alone makes life worth living and, for not a few people, possible at all. The reason why the involvement looks very like a psychosis is that the patient is integrating the same fantasy-material to which the insane person falls victim because he cannot integrate it but is swallowed up by it. (CW 14, § 756)[20]

Part of the difficulty with divine madness is that it contrasts markedly with the profound tranquility that is often associated with an experience of God. Indeed Jung himself states:

> Every man has a quiet place in his soul, where everything is self-evident and easily explainable, a place where he likes to retire from the confusing possibilities of life, because there everything is simple and clear, with a manifest and limited purpose. (RB, p. 295b)

One might suppose that it is this "quiet place" that is the goal of spiritual practice in certain forms of both eastern and western meditation. Yet as we have seen, such tranquility may preclude the very "chaos" that Jung understands to be the origin of creative fantasy and the vehicle to the soul's depths. Jung tells us that if the walls of a man's quiet place are broken "the overwhelming stream of chaos will flood in (RB, p. 295b, p. 296a) and magic will arise (RB, p. 314a). For Jung, the divine madness produces an "irrational truth" that proceeds out of chaos and breaks the bonds of conventional thought and discourse (RB, p. 295a). His views on madness are premonitory of the postmodern rejection of "reality" as it is defined by "common practice and consent."

In *The Red Book*, Jung's soul tells him, "You wanted to accept everything. So accept madness too. Let the light of your madness shine and it will suddenly dawn on you. Madness is not to be despised and not to be feared, but instead you should give it life" (RB, p. 298a). For Jung:

> Madness is a special form of the spirit and clings to all teachings and philosophies, but even more to daily life, since life itself is full of craziness and at bottom utterly illogical. Man strives toward reason only so that he can make rules for himself. Life itself has no rules. That is its mystery and its unknown law. What you call knowledge is an attempt to impose something comprehensible on life. (RB, p. 298a)

Yet Jung does not rest with a "madness" that remains disorganized and chaotic. At the close of *The Red Book* he writes that he was indeed struggling with madness during the period of its composition: "To the superficial observer, it will appear like madness. It would also have developed into one, had I not been able to absorb the overpowering force of the original experiences. With the help of alchemy, I could finally arrange them into a whole" (RB, p. 360).

Thus for Jung, at least after his encounter with alchemy, madness and chaos became one pole of a dialectic that is complemented by wholeness and comprehension. In alchemical terms *solve* is complemented by *coagulum*, and in the language of the Kabbalah, the *Shevirah*, the "breaking of the vessels" (in which the order of self and God is broken apart and the original chaos of creation makes a reappearance) is followed by *Tikkun*, the restorative process in which self and world are reorganized into a (divine) whole.

THE ORIGIN OF MEANING

Jung writes that a new life develops out of a mixture of "depths and surface" (RB, p. 239a). However, this life does not come from events in the external world, but is rather a change that occurs within the individual. Indeed, it is a change that is only perceptible from within, for it involves a resignification of events by the human subject: *"Events signify nothing, they signify only in us. We create the meaning of events. The meaning is and always was artificial. We make it."* (RB, p. 239a) Further,

> The meanings that follow one another do not lie in things, but lie in you, who are subject to many changes, insofar as you take part in life. Things also change, but you do not notice this if you do not change. But if you change the countenance of the world alters. (RB, p. 273b)

In the "Seven Sermons to the Dead," we read, "you must not forget that the Pleroma has no qualities. We create these through thinking" (RB, p. 348a).

These rather clear constructivist pronouncements do not, however, comport very well with Jung's later ideas on the collective unconscious. This is because Jungian "archetypes" yield trans-individual and even transcultural meanings that are brought to the world by a collective, objective psyche, as opposed to an individual or existential one. Jung expressed this view in his 1934 monograph, "Archetypes of the Collective Unconscious," where he wrote that while we assume that the meaning of things is assigned by ourselves, these meanings are ultimately "founded on primordial archetypal forms" (CW 9i, § 69). Further,

> The forms we use for assigning meaning are historical categories that reach back into the mists of time—a fact we do not take sufficiently into account. Interpretations make use of certain linguistic matrices that are themselves derived from primordial

images…everywhere we find ourselves confronted with the
history of language, with images and motifs that lead straight
back to the primitive wonder-world. (CW 9i, § 67)

In *The Red Book* Jung gives voice to a more balanced view of the
origins of significance when he says the "*meaning of events is the supreme
meaning*" and this meaning resides neither in events nor in the soul
but is rather "the God standing between events and the soul" (RB, p.
239a), a God that is a mediator and a bridge, presumably between
the meaningful and the absurd (RB, p. 239a), and between the
subjective and the objective. Jung is here of the view that God is the
act of signification that makes an arbitrary and inherently meaningless
cosmos meaningful. While at times in *The Red Book* Jung holds that
the world itself is meaningless and it is the psyche that provides it
with meaning, he ultimately adopts a dialectical view in which meaning
arises out of an interaction between the psyche and the world.

With the benefit of *The Red Book* we might incline to the view
that Jungian archetypal meanings are *iridescent* concepts that lie on
the cusp between the subjective and the objective. The questions
of subjective vs. objective might best be answered with a response
of *both and neither*. Perhaps embracing this ambiguity is a path to
wisdom and to the discovery of one's soul. Again, the coincidence of
opposing attitudes and ideas becomes a major theme, if not the major
theme, in *The Red Book*.

THE MEANINGFUL AND THE ABSURD

A similar dialectic is evident in Jung's discussion of meaning and
the absurd. While in *The Red Book* the descent into the "depths" is
mainly identified with chaos, madness, "frightfulness and cruelty" (RB,
p. 238b), in Jung's later work the collective unconscious is also seen
as a source of abundant meaning. In the latter view, the individual is
not simply thrown into a meaningless world from which he must create
significance, but is rather the heir to a vast tradition of collective
meanings or archetypes that reside within the depths of his or her own
psyche. In Jung's later formulation, as the Self develops in the second
half of life, one's ego is compensated through the assimilation of
archetypes that lend meaning to one's life and make one whole. While
in *The Red Book* Jung had not as yet arrived at a clear formulation of

this problem, we have seen that by holding that the *supreme meaning* is a coincidence of absurdity and meaning, *The Red Book* provides a vehicle for integrating these two points of view. Wisdom lies in understanding that both life and the world are each deeply absurd *and* infinitely meaningful.

Indeed, meaning is dependent upon meaninglessness and vice versa, as it can be argued that the greatest potential meaning arises, not in a world that is filled with meaning and significance from the start, but rather in one that is, at least on its face, almost completely chaotic, nonsensical, and absurd. For it is in such a (near) meaningless world that the struggle to find or forge meaning has the greatest significance, and therefore bears the most fruit. Just as courage and compassion find their maximum expression under threatening, dire circumstances,[21] meaning reaches its greatest significance in the context of a world that appears to be devoid of all sense. Jung writes that absurdity is the background contrast against which meaning can be perceived, and that meaning is best observed when a meaningful light is suddenly revealed against a curtain of meaningless darkness (RB, p. 242a). We might add that the reverse is equally true as well—as the world seems most chaotic and absurd when something very meaningful, such as a loved one, is suddenly taken from us. Here we should note that the book of *Genesis* speaks not of an eternally meaningful world, but one that God forged out of the empty chaos, the *tohu v' bohu*, that preceded the introduction of light (Genesis 1:2). As we have seen, for Jung, the "supreme meaning" is dependent upon an original chaos, and is a blending together of meaning and absurdity.

On the Death of the Hero

Jung introduces a theme that he will return to several times in *The Red Book*, and on which he will elaborate in the next chapter, "The Murder of the Hero." He speaks of his own participation in this murder, the guilt that is on his hands, and yet the necessity that this murder should take place. It is imperative that the hero die if the individual is to find his own way, his own meaning; for as long as one is possessed by a hero, meaning is external to oneself. As Zarathustra declared: "Companions, the creator seeks, not corpses, not herds and believers. Fellow creators, the creator seeks—those who write new values on new tablets."[22] One might think that for Jung the hero must be murdered so that one can become a hero to oneself. But Jung takes this idea a step further and declares that instead of murdering their noble, brave, and courageous brother, men should *sacrifice the hero in themselves*, destroying all pretense of a heroic source of absolute meaning and value. What must be sacrificed is the view that certain things *are good*, certain acts *are necessary*, and that certain goals *must be attained* (RB, p. 240a). In our time, Jung says, the heroic source of value is a princely ruler who has gained entry within us and as the "spirit of this time," a spirit of reason and science, has brought both immeasurable good and "fascinated men with unbelievable pleasure" (RB, p. 240a). However, this ruler is associated with a cult of consciousness and the elevation of the ego, each of which must be radically questioned if not "murdered" within oneself.

Jung's view of the hero in *The Red Book* is at odds with his understanding of the hero in his earlier (and even in some of his later works), and, to a certain extent it is, as we will see, even at odds with the apparent theme of certain paintings that adorn *Liber Secundus*. In *Transformations and Symbols of the Libido* Jung understood the hero as symbolic of the individual's identification with, and efforts to overcome, the regressive forces of the unconscious that strive to retain the merger of the ego with the mother (CW B, § 585; cf. CW 5, § 575). Indeed, in *Transformations*, the hero's separation and liberation from the mother is the key to understanding both mythology and the process of human development,[23] and in that work Jung thereby adopts a sort of "heroic ideal." *The Red Book*, however, is, as John Beebe has put it, "a post-heroic work," where the hero ideal is criticized and abandoned.[24] Jung often identified the hero with the ego, and while in his later work, he would not have countenanced the ego's complete demise, he was (as he is here in *The Red Book*) certainly suspicious of the ego's domination of the psyche. When we come to examine Jung's *Red Book* paintings of Atmavictu and the dragon (**RB Images, p. 117, p. 119, p. 123**), we will see that subsequent to the hero's murder, he reemerges in a more temperate form that surrenders a portion of his control to the powers of the underworld.

"Chapter VI: Splitting of the Spirit," p. 240-1

THE RAPACIOUS BEAST WITHIN

Jung's search for his soul continues with a descent into the underworld. He reports that "To journey through hell means to become Hell oneself" (RB, p. 240a), and he relates that he has exchanged his humanity for a "monstrous animal form" and can no longer recognize himself. In anticipation of the merciless self-criticism he will levy against himself in *Scrutinies,* Jung writes, "perhaps I ensnare myself in self-deceit and monkey business, and I am a rascal grinning at myself in the mirror, a fool in my own madness" (RB, p. 241a). Again, Jung engages the "spirit of the depths", who asks him to remain calm, to which Jung objects that a spirit who "overthrew the mighty Gods who mean the most to us" (RB, p. 240a) cannot make such a demand.

Jung finds himself being transformed into a "rapacious beast" (RB, p. 241b), one that carries murder and war within itself. Jung is in conflict with himself, as he is both "the murderer and the murdered" (RB, p. 241b). He entertains committing murder and fears death. Jung's transformation in hell into a murderer, a madman, and a beast brings to mind Goethe's statement that he had never encountered a crime that he could not imagine himself committing. By plunging ourselves, at least on the level of fantasy, into the most repugnant side of the human spirit, we not only prepare ourselves to recover our own shadow, but perhaps also extend our capacity to empathize with those unfortunate souls (both victims and perpetrators) for whom murder, rape, and other appalling crimes are a reality, and not only a fantasy. As we will see, Jung is of the view that such "criminals" are the overt expression of what is covertly present in himself (and everyone).

ANOTHER WORLD

Jung rages against his soul as he debates with her the question of whether his soul's light is of this or another world. Jung says indignantly that he knows of no other world but this one, to which his soul replies: "Should it not exist because you know nothing of it?" (RB, p. 240b). The argument, as it turns out, is a "civil war" (RB, p. 241a) within Jung himself, as Jung's soul informs him that it is she who gives Jung his words. Jung remains indignant, telling his soul that she had "donned the mask of a God," but now wears "the mask of a devil" (RB, p. 241a).

Jung's debate with his soul about the possibility of "another world" is reflected later in his theory of the archetypes, which he held were akin to the Platonic forms, but which are known only through their effects in worldly human experience. Jung will, throughout his career, exhibit an ambivalence about "metaphysical" statements regarding "another world." While he generally held that as an empirical scientist he had no warrant for making such statements, he nonetheless at times suggests the possibility of an order that transcends the causal framework of science (CW 8, pp. 404-415, 417-519).

TEXTUAL CONTRADICTIONS

We cannot analyze this material (and much of the material in *The Red Book*) without becoming embroiled in a series of textual contradictions and other difficulties. For example, Jung says that it is the "spirit of the depths" that overthrew the Gods (RB, p. 240b) and that "The God becomes sick if he oversteps the height of the zenith" (RB, p. 241b); whereas later in *The Red Book* he squarely places the blame for God's sickness on "science," which Jung associates with the "spirit of this time." Throughout *The Red Book*, Jung is struggling with conflicting feelings, intuitions, and ideas; in a work of this sort we can hardly expect him to present a consistent point of view. Indeed, he will later tell us that his "innovation" in *The Red Book* is the bringing together of the opposites (RB, p. 319a), and he will provide his readers with examples of truths that can only be expressed in contradictory terms (RB, p. 304b, p. 314a). One is here reminded of Walt Whitman's "Song of Myself", where the poet writes, "Do *I contradict myself*? Very well then *I contradict myself*, (I am large, I contain multitudes)."[25]

"Chapter VII: Murder of the Hero," pp. 241-2

In Chapter VII Jung returns to the already familiar themes of the death of the hero and the relationship between meaning and the absurd. He has a vision in which he joins a youth on a "high mountain" and together they murder Siegfried, the legendary hero of the German and Norse epics. The murder is illustrated, somewhat crudely, in a small painting in **RB Image, Fol., p. iv b** of *Liber Primus*, the calligraphic parchment text. Jung is tormented by this act and feels certain that he must kill himself if he cannot "solve the riddle of the murder of the hero" (RB, p. 242a). He hints that Siegfried embodies the spirit and hope of the German people, and it is for this reason Jung feels that he must commit suicide in order to spare the hero's life (RB, p. 242b). Yet Jung's "murder of the hero" has enormous implications for Jung's own life and thought. We can surmise at least several meanings for Siegfried's demise:

(1) Jung identifies with Siegfried, speaking of him as "my power, my boldness, my pride" (RB, p. 242b), and the murder is thus a killing off of Jung's ambition and his narcissistic investment in his dominant thinking function, an aspect of himself that he regards as "beautiful," but which is perhaps inimical to Jung's journey. In his 1925 seminar on analytical psychology Jung spoke of having killed his inner hero, his intellect.[26] The murder of Siegfried represents an opportunity for spiritual renewal, since "our Gods want to be overcome" precisely so that they can be renewed within ourselves (RB, p. 242a). "Men kill their princes," Jung tells us, because "they cannot kill their Gods," Gods that are actually contained within themselves (RB, p. 242a).

(3) The murder of the hero symbolizes Jung's (and our) existential quest to construct his (and our) own projects, meanings, and identity. Later in *The Red Book*, Jung will tell us: "The image of the hero was set up…through the appetite for imitation. Therefore the hero was murdered, since we all have been aping him" (RB, p. 249b). "It belongs to this mystery that man is not redeemed through the hero, but becomes a Christ himself" (RB, p. 253b).

(4) In a conversation with the English psychiatrist E.A. Bennet in 1956, and later published by Bennet's wife,[27] Jung recounted a dream he had in 1913 in which a "primitive man" implored Jung to shoot Siegfried, and from which Jung awoke with great remorse and the thought that he must take his revolver and shoot himself. This dream is a near perfect parallel to Jung's account of Siegfried's murder in *The Red Book*. Jung explained to Bennet that the primitive man

represented the collective unconscious, over against the "accepted achievements" of the current age. In this way the "murder of the hero" becomes an assassination of the "spirit of this time" by "the spirit of the depths."

(5) The "murder of the hero" can also be understood in connection with Jung's departure from (and symbolic murder of) Freud. Siegfried is known as "Sigurd" in the ancient legends, and is the posthumous son of "Sigmund!" Here, it is worth noting that while Freud had selected Jung as his successor precisely because of his Aryan qualities (to prevent psychoanalysis from being seen as a "Jewish national affair"[28]), Jung murders Siegfried, who is an important symbol of Aryan consciousness. However, as Stein, points out, Jung chose not to fight Freud and his faction for the presidency of the International Psychoanalytic Association in 1914, where he may well have prevailed, and instead resigned his presidency on April 20, 1914, the day after beginning work on his nearly abusive self-criticism in *Scrutinies*.[29] The murder of Siegfried may thus be seen as both an aggression against Freud and a displacement of that aggression onto one that is Freud's antithesis.

Jung returns to the question of the hero, imitation, and discipleship in the next chapter ("The Conception of God"), where he writes: "The Gods do not want imitators: The new God laughs at imitation and discipleship. He needs no imitators and no pupils" (RB, p. 245a). Indeed, the hero must fall because he "demands imitation," and the new God must move "into the self," become "his own follower in man" (RB, p. 245a), and imitate no one but himself. These ideas are very similar to those of Nietzsche, and they shed light on Jung's 1912 letter to Freud, in which Jung offers a direct quotation from *Zarathustra*:

> One repays a teacher badly if one remains only a pupil
> And why, then, should you not pluck at my laurels?
> You respect me; but how if one day your respect should tumble?
> Take care that a falling statue does not strike you dead!
> You had not yet sought yourselves when you found me.
> Thus all believers—.
> Now I bid you lose me and find yourselves;
> And only when you have all denied me will I return to you.[30]

The murder of the hero raises the question of Jung's own status as a hero; the tendency to worship Jung as a spiritual hero in some circles and to demonize him in others.[31] In *The Red Book*, the "murder of the hero" is a station on Jung's journey to discover his soul. We will see, however, that the hero will be revived and reconstructed as the dialectic of the journey moves on to later stages.

THE "TRANSITION FROM ABSURDITY TO ABSURDITY"

The murder of the hero provides Jung a new context in which to discuss meaning and absurdity. Jung, in his vision, is on the verge of suicide for having killed Siegfried when the "spirit of the depths" saves him from this fate with the words, "The highest truth is one and the same with the absurd" (RB, p. 242a). For this reason Jung must accept the "absurdity" of having killed Siegfried. Jung explains that meaning requires absurdity just as day requires night, and that "meaning is a moment of transition from absurdity to absurdity" (RB, p. 242a). Years later Jung will expand on this idea when in his *Seminar on Zarathustra*, he says, "...we are quite safe in believing that this life is mere meaningless chaos because that is what we see...".[32] However, "if you see nothing but chaos that amounts to an unconscious condition...The world is an order only when somebody experiences that order...it is a chaos if nobody experiences it as a cosmos."[33]

Chapter 3

Of Gods, Heroes, and Prophets

The Red Book: Liber Primus, cont.

"Chapter VIII: The Conception of God," pp. 242-5

THE GOD THAT IS TO COME

Jung's soul reminds him of the parable of the mustard seed (Matthew 13:31-32), in which the smallest of all seeds grows into a powerful tree. We soon learn that the death of the hero has planted a seed that will grow into a new God. Jung is now intoxicated with a "powerful voice" that speaks to him of a "you who are to come" (RB, p. 243a). In contrast to Nietzsche's Overman, this "you" is not (simply) a new man but is a "veritable God," a "new spark of eternal fire," who will be manifest to men in "what they hate, fear, and abhor" (RB, p. 243a). Jung avers that this is a God who men pray to in "terror, fear, and doubt," a God whose very life originates in those who have overcome themselves and who have then, paradoxically, "disowned [this] overcoming" (RB, p. 243a). He says that with the death of the hero, a God emerges from "the terrible ambiguity, the hateful-beautiful, the evil-good, the laughable-serious, the sick-healthy, the inhuman-human, the ungodly-godly" (RB, p. 243b). Here Jung is anticipating his later concept of both the Self and God as a *"coincidentia oppositorum."*

Jung, avows that the new God is born out of the tension of the opposites and indeed that he is "born as a child from my own human soul," which comes into being with the death of the hero, the death of perfection (RB, p. 244b). As Shamdasani points out, for Jung the "divine child" is a symbol that emerges as a herald of the development of the Self (RB, p. 234, n. 58), and in a 1919 letter to Joan Corrie, Jung spoke of the divine child as a reborn God and transcendental or universal Self (RB, p. 354, n. 123). We know from Jung's later writings that the Self archetype is empirically indistinguishable from the archetype of God, and in this section of *The Red Book*, we see a hint of the ambiguity between God and Self that is so characteristic of several of Jung's later writings.

GOD, SELF, AND AMBIGUITY

Both Nietzsche and Jung understood the development of the Self, of the "new man," in terms of a coincidence of opposites which re-incorporates the rejected pole of a number of value pairs, the most general of which is the pairing of good and evil. Jung here speaks of a new "relative" God, who in contrast to the old "absolute" deity, encompasses "the fullness of life" and embodies the polarities and contradictions of the human spirit (RB, p. 243b). He asks, "How can man live in the womb of God if the Godhead himself attends to one-half of him?" (RB, p. 243b).

The idea of an "evil side of God" appears in various religious traditions, for example, the demonic deities of Buddhism[1] and the *sitra achra* ("Other Side") of the Kabbalist's *Ein-sof* (Infinite).[2] Jung affirms that before Christ could ascend to heaven, he first had to journey through hell and become the Antichrist (RB, p. 243b). In a passage that Giegerich[3] cites as an example of *The Red Book*'s hubris, Jung writes: "No one knows what happened during the three days Christ was in Hell. I have experienced it" (RB, p. 243b). In the Corrected Draft of *The Red Book*, Jung states more modestly, "but this can be guessed;" however, it is clear that Jung was here making the claim that it was his "journey to Hell" and his becoming Hell himself (RB, p. 240b, p. 244a) that enabled him to reach this new, presumably fuller, conception of the divine. It was as a result of this journey that Jung realized that the divine is a coincidence of opposites and that "Unequivocalness is simplicity and leads to death," while "ambiguity is the way of life" (RB, p. 244b). Certainly, *The Red Book* is ambiguous in many of its notions and ideas, and as Shamdasani points out, years after he stopped working on *Liber Novus,* Jung wrote to the Kabbalah scholar Zwi Werblowsky that his own ambiguity "corresponds to the nature of being" (RB, p. 244, n. 142).

Jung implores us to be careful in our own journey to hell, to proceed as a coward rather than as a hero ("since nothing is more dangerous than to play the hero" RB, p. 244a). He provides us with descriptions of hell, most of which are variations on the theme that in Hell "everything good is also bad" (RB, p. 244b). However, one of hell's features is that "you must think and feel and do everything that you do not want" (RB, p. 244a), which incidentally (with regard to thinking and feeling) is the experience of many individuals who enter Jungian-oriented analysis.

ON THE COINCIDENCE OF OPPOSITES

Jung's ideas on equivocalness and ambiguity merge with his understanding of *coincidentia oppositorum,* the co-existence, blending, and interdependence of opposites. The doctrine of the coincidence of opposites has historically been associated with *mystical* thought, but has also made its appearance in both eastern and western philosophical traditions. Philosophers, ranging from Nagarjuna to Nicholas of Cusa, Meister Eckhardt, and G.W.F. Hegel, have held that the poles of at least certain philosophical and theological contraries do not exclude one another but are actually necessary conditions for the truth of their opposites. For example, Hegel argued that

> every actual thing involves a coexistence of opposed elements. Consequently to know, or, in other words, to comprehend an object is equivalent to being conscious of it as a concrete unity of opposed determinations.[4]

The notion of a "coincidence of opposites" takes center stage in late Jewish mysticism. Rabbi Dov Baer (1773-1827), a leading Hasidic thinker, wrote "within everything is its opposite and also it is truly revealed as its opposite,"[5] and maintained that the union of opposites on earth brings about the completeness (*shelemut*) of God on high.[6] The 20th century physicist Neils Bohr stated that while the opposites of what he called "superficial truths are false," the opposites of "deep truths" are true as well.[7] In recent years, philosophers, following the lead of Jacques Derrida, have deconstructed traditional oppositions, and marshaled the gesture involved in *coincidentia oppositorum* in an effort to overcome the privileging of certain ideas and establish the contingency of the entire dichotomous system. Amongst the oppositions to have received such deconstructive attention are word and thing, knowledge and error, sense and nonsense, presence and absence, permanence and change, identity and difference, public and private, freedom and necessity, God and humanity, good and evil, spirit and nature, and mind and matter.

As we have seen, the notion of *coincidentia oppositorum* plays a central role in Jung's search for his own soul in *The Red Book*, and it also becomes a fundamental tenet of his later thought. Throughout his career, Jung held that a "non-rational," imaginative, and symbolic union of opposites enables the individual to transcend conflict and achieve individuation. Indeed, Jung held that there is a non-rational instinctive human function, which he termed the "transcendent function," that spontaneously mediates and combines opposites through the production of fantasies and symbols and which enables the individual to gain a new perspective and a more encompassing and rewarding attitude toward what he formerly regarded to be an insoluble dilemma or personal struggle (CW 8, pp. 67-91). Unlike Hegel, whose dialectic of opposing principles and ideas was presumably rational and conscious in its origin and application, Jung held that the transcendent function is non-rational and involves a combination of conscious and unconscious processes. In his later work, Jung regarded the coincidence of opposites to be constitutive of both the God archetype and the Self.

The Red Book is replete with Jung's not as yet fully formed ideas on the coincidence of opposites, and we see him struggling to make sense of the personal experiences that led him to become captivated by this notion and regard it as his personal "innovation" (RB, p. 319a). In *Liber Novus* he considers a variety of oppositions: meaning and nonsense, fullness and emptiness, love and hate (RB, p. 343b), action and thought (RB, p. 293b), madness and reason (RB, p. 317b), pleasure and thinking (RB, p. 247a), above and below (RB, p. 315a), etc. Jung is of the view that the poles of an opposition are either identical or interdependent. He tells us, for example, "immense fullness and immense emptiness are one and the same" (RB, p. 273b), thinking and feeling "are each other's poison and healing"

(RB, p. 248a), and "If no outer adventure happens to you, then no inner adventure happens either" (RB, p. 263a).

Jung says that one only achieves a "presentiment of the whole" (RB, p. 248a) and can only "achieve balance" by nurturing one's "opposite." However, doing so is very difficult, as nurturing the opposite of one's own thoughts, feelings, and attitudes "is hateful to you in your innermost core, because it is not heroic" (RB, p. 263a). Jung's polemic against the heroic in *The Red Book* is in part grounded in the idea that the image of the hero is insulated from the negative poles of the features that make him/her heroic, and thus the effort to imitate the hero is inimical to one's full desire (RB, p. 249b).

Jung relates that the "new God" he speaks of in *The Red Book*, the one that has been reborn subsequent to his demise at the hands of Nietzsche and science, is a union of opposing principles that occurs within Jung's own psyche (RB, p. 254b). Presumably, Jung holds that the new God also develops through the reconciliation of opposites in the mind and souls of individuals other than himself. Jung is here again hinting at the identity of the God and the Self archetypes, an idea that figures so prominently in his later psychology.

If God is associated with the union of opposites within the human psyche, it is the "serpent" that keeps the opposites apart: "It is always the serpent that causes man to become enslaved now to one, now to the other principle, so that it becomes error" (RB, p. 247b). However, Jung is not completely of one mind regarding the unity of opposites. While it is absolutely necessary to unite the opposites in one's quest for one's soul, their *complete* unity is not desirable, since the *conflict* between the opposites (as opposed to their union) produces interest and activity. Jung is concerned that with the union of the opposites everything will come to a standstill (RB, p. 319b). As we will see, the devil, in one of his dialogs with Jung, suggests that "the conflict of opposites belong(s) to the inescapable conditions of life" (RB, p. 318b), and Jung's soul asks him if he could even live "without divisiveness and disunity" (RB, p. 319b). This is because one needs to "get worked up about something, represent a party, overcome opposites, if you want to live" (RB, p. 319b). Life itself is the overcoming of opposites; when they have been *completely overcome* one has no further reason to live in this world. This is made clear in *Psychological Types*, where in the course of a discussion of the

Hindu conception of the opposites, Jung writes: "He who has...gradually given up all attachments and is freed from all pairs of opposites reposes in Brahman alone" (CW 6, § 328).

Indeed, we can gain considerable insight into the theme of the coincidence of opposites as it appears in *The Red Book* by examining this same theme as it is treated, more systematically, in Jung's major "scientific" work of the period, *Psychological Types*, which was apparently written between July 1919 and February 1920 (RB, p. 305, n. 230) during a hiatus in Jung's work on *Black Book 7*, one of the notebooks that was eventually incorporated into *The Red Book*. *Psychological Types* is an extremely wide-ranging work that is loosely structured around Jung's examination of the "type problem" in philosophy, literature, biography, and psychology. By "type" Jung refers specifically to personality types that are characterized by the functions of thinking, feeling, sensation, and intuition, and the dichotomy introversion/extraversion (CW 6, § 835). Jung holds that a complete understanding of the psyche can neither be achieved through thinking (science) nor feeling, but only via a higher third principle that unites them, *creative fantasy* (CW 6, § 86). Indeed, for Jung, psychology cannot be fully grounded in either thought or feeling. If grounded in the former, it loses its connection with life; if grounded in the latter, it loses its claim to validity.

Jung extends this notion of complementarity to his critique of Freudian and Adlerian psychology, each of which neglects the principles that are considered fundamental for the other (instinct for Freud and the aims of the ego for Adler). Both Freud's and Adler's psychologies are complete on their own terms, but are found to be incomplete when examined in light of the principle that grounds the opposing theory. Interpretations can always be made that accord both with Freud's "infantile wishes" and Adler's aims of "security and differentiation of the ego" (CW 6, § 89), but such interpretations offer only partial truths that cannot claim total validity. While these two perspectives potentially complement one another, they are each incomplete because they reject the reconciling principle of the imagination (CW 6, § 93). Later in *Psychological Types*, Jung tells us that it is only through the imagination and its production of symbols, in particular religious and spiritual symbols (CW 6, §§

824-5), that we are able to transcend and reconcile the demands of instinct (Freud) with the aims of the ego (Adler).

Neither reason nor feeling can produce symbols (CW 6, § 179), which must arise unconsciously and spontaneously through the vehicle of the imagination, which "alone has the power to supply the will with a content of such a nature that it can unite the opposites" (CW 6, § 185). Jung allows that the opposites can in certain respects be reconciled through art, but he is critical of Nietzsche and others who place too much stock in aesthetic experience and fail to recognize the overarching importance of spiritual and religious symbols. Jung is certainly skeptical of any effort to achieve an intellectual reconciliation of the opposites. While he initially suggests that "It remains an open question whether the opposition between the two standpoints can ever be satisfactorily resolved in intellectual terms" (CW 6, § 93), he is later quite emphatic: "opposites are not to be united rationally...[that is] precisely why they are called opposites" (CW 6, § 169). For Jung, "opposites can be united only in the form of a compromise, or irrationally...only...through living" (CW 6, § 169). The idea here is familiar to psychotherapists: a patient who finds himself on the horns of a conflict between his homosexuality and the demands of the Catholic church, for example, may not be able to resolve this conflict in intellectual terms, but can come to lead a life in which the conflict is accepted and thereby transcended.

While Jung says that he rejects the idea of a rational reconciliation of the opposites, several of his remarks, including those on Freud and Adler, suggest the need for a *theoretical* synthesis. With regard to the opposition between fantasy and reality, Jung proposes that we "have a right on purely empirical grounds to treat the contents of the unconscious as just as real as the things of the outside world" (CW 6, § 279), a proposal that bears comparison, yet stands in contrast to Husserl's phenomenology, where the contents of experience are, as it were, equalized through a bracketing of the question of their "reality." Jung's remark that "theosophy and spiritualism are just as violent in their encroachments on other spheres as materialism" (CW 6, § 279) seems to invite a theoretical perspective that might be inclusive of each. Jung makes parenthetical reference to Hegel's efforts to theoretically reconcile the opposites, but criticizes Hegel on the grounds that although "intuitive ideas" underlie Hegel's system, they remained subordinated to intellect (CW 6, § 340). In his discussion of William James, Jung considers the conflict between intellectual and intuitive truths and accepts James' pragmatic eclecticism as a necessary part of the solution to the problem of conflicting foundations in philosophy and psychology. However, Jung ultimately concludes that both conceptualism and pragmatism are inadequate to the task of integrating "logically irreconcilable" views, as they inevitably lead to a loss of creativity. Only a "positive act of creation" can "assimilate...the opposites as necessary elements of co-ordination" (CW 6, § 541). In commenting on the coincidence of opposites, Jung suggests that when one travels far down the path of a given perspective, its opposite emerges; however, only a few "reach the rim of the world, where its mirror-image begins" (CW 6, § 281). We might presume that these are the few who discover their souls.

Jung holds that past religions and philosophies have utilized different principles in uniting the opposites. For Christians, it is the worship of God; for Buddhists, the realization and development of the Self; and for Goethe, it is "the worship of the soul, symbolized by the worship of women" (CW 6, § 375). Jung takes a special interest in the Christian mystic and philosopher, Meister Eckhardt, who wrote of a coincidence of opposites between God and man, and who sought to unite the opposites by discovering God within his own soul (CW 6, §§ 416-21), a task that also occupies Jung throughout much of *The Red Book*.

The doctrine of *coincidentia oppositorum* is a powerful idea, but like all ideas, it has its limitations and potential dark side. First, the suspicion arises that at times a simple, perhaps too simple, route to profundity and depth is to hold that it is to be found where one least expects it: in chaos as opposed to order, meaninglessness as opposed to meaning, darkness as opposed to light, and relativism, or even evil, as opposed to virtue. Further, we might ask if Jung's readiness to embrace certain opposites, e.g. the chaotic as a source of creative energy, might not have its dangers. Wasn't it just such an analysis that caused him to, at first, be ambivalent, if not optimistic, about the Nazi state?[8] In November 1932, just a few months prior to Hitler's swearing in as Germany's chancellor, Jung lectured:

> There are times in the world's history—and our own time may
> be one of them—when good must stand aside, so that anything
> destined to be better first appears in evil form. (CW 17, § 321)

As we will see, Jung will later hold that even the coincidence of
opposites must be tempered by its own opposite, "absolute opposition"
(CW 13, § 256). At the time Jung published this idea (1943), the
opposition between good and evil had never been clearer.

GOD, SELF, AND EVIL

Jung considers the Christian notion that "God is love" and protests,
"but what is more ambiguous than love" (RB, p. 244b), and surely
from any post-Freudian viewpoint he is correct. Still, we might ask
whether we should not be entitled to an ideal in our God, even if we
must acknowledge the shadowy evil in ourselves and the absurdity in
our world. While the argument that both God and Self, in order to
be complete and encompass the fullness of life must embody disvalues
as well as values (e.g. love as well as hate), may enable us to accept the
fullness of our being, it may also work as an excuse or rationalization
for our own malevolent actions. Jung may well be correct in the
assertion that one who fails to acknowledge his own dark side runs
the risk of being dominated by it, but it does not follow from this
that we should abandon all of our ideals and our attempts to live up
to them. Nietzsche, Freud, and Jung, by holding up a mirror to
humanity's shadow side, served as a valuable compensation for the
unreflective "faculty psychology" and "character virtue ethic" that
preceded them, but this does not mean that virtues and ideals must
be abandoned altogether.

It will be instructive here to examine the notion of the evil side of
God, as it appears in the Jewish mystical tradition, especially as Jung,
much later in his career, will turn to this tradition to explicate his own
understanding of the shadow side of God and man.[9] The Kabbalistic
view of evil, while acknowledging evil's metaphysical and psychological
reality, is more friendly to "virtue" than Jung appears to be in *The Red
Book*. In the early Kabbalistic work, *Sefer ha Bahir*, we read "The Holy
One praise be He has a trait (*middah*) which is called Evil."[10] Further,
the *Zohar*, the *locus classicus* of the Kabbalah, recites: "the angel of
death...should not be banished from this world. The world needs

him...It is all necessary, good and evil.[11] However, the *Zohar* explains that evil is necessary as the means for the realization of the good:

> there can be no true worship except it issue forth from darkness, and no true good except it proceed from evil. And when a man enters upon an evil way and then forsakes it, the Holy One is exalted in glory...[12]

Further, the rabbis affirmed that the "Evil Impulse" was an essential motivating factor in human life, holding that "were it not for the *Yetzer ha-Ra* (the "Evil Impulse"), no one would build a house, take a wife, give birth, or engage in commerce" (Genesis Rabbah 9:7).

The later Kabbalistic symbol of *Tikkun ha-Olam* (repair/restoration of the world) has its foundation in these ideas. *Tikkun* embodies the notion that it is precisely a world of evil, strife, disorder, chaos, and opacity that brings forth the activities in humankind that concretely realize the values that an Infinite God could only create in the abstract. The deity must create evil, for without evil, there could be no good. It is only in a world of ignorance that knowledge can be gained, and only in an evil and tragic world that kindness and compassion can be realized. "We live in the worst of all possible worlds in which there is still hope," says the contemporary rabbinic sage, Adin Steinsaltz, "and that is the best of all possible worlds."[13] It is the best world, because only an enormously challenging world, on the brink of disaster, but in which there is yet hope, concretely realizes the limits of human potential and establishes man as a partner with God in its repair and restoration. This is a notion that Jung welcomed years later when he wrote to his disciple, James Kirsch:

> The Jew has the advantage of already having anticipated the development of human consciousness in his spiritual history. By that I mean the Lurianic level of the Kabbalah, the breaking of the vessel, and human help in its reconstitution. Here for the first time the idea emerges that man must help God to repair the damage which creation has caused. Here for the first time the cosmic responsibility of man is acknowledged.[14]

DESIRE

We have seen that Jung suggests that the quest for God and soul is at least in part a quest for the actualization of one's own desire. He now proceeds to develop this idea further. Jung writes. "You arrive at [God] in yourself and only through yourself seizing you. It seizes you in the advancement of your life" (RB, p. 245a). Further, "You find yourself in your desire, so do not say that you desire in vain" (RB, p. 245b). The "desire" Jung has in mind is not the desire for worldly pleasures, and it is certainly not the desires one believes one has because of one's identifications with others; rather, it is a desire for a truer Self: "If you desire yourself, you produce the divine son in your embrace with yourself" (RB, p. 245b).

Jung returns to the question of desire several pages later when he writes:

> It is no small matter to acknowledge one's yearning. For this many need to make a particular effort at honesty. All too many do not want to know where their yearning is, because it would seem to them impossible or too distressing. And yet yearning is the way of life. If you do not acknowledge your yearning, then you do not follow yourself, but go on foreign ways that others have indicated to you. (RB, p. 249b)

Jung is here formulating an existential notion of desire that can be profitably contrasted with the Freudian notions of drive and object love. Jung's ideas here are in the philosophical tradition of Hegel, Nietzsche, and more recently, Jacques Lacan, who held that the aim of analysis is for the subject to recognize the truth of his/her desire through a process of stripping away the desire that originates in the other.

"Chapter IX: Mysterium Encounter," pp. 245-8

ELIJAH AND SALOME: THE UNION OF THE SACRED AND PROFANE

Jung begins this chapter with a description of his encounter with Elijah the prophet and Salome,[15] the step-daughter of King Herod, who the New Testament describes as requesting and causing the death of John the Baptist (Mark 6:21-29, Matthew 14:6-11). A simple painting illustrates these biblical figures (**RB Image, Fol., p. v b**). Jung describes being led into a high hall by Elijah, where on a glittering wall he sees the reflected images of "Eve, the tree, and the serpent" (RB, p. 245b), and also catches sight of Odysseus on the high seas. The mixture of Jewish, Christian, and Greek themes is one that recurs in Jung. For example, years later in *Memories, Dreams, Reflections* (MDR, p. 294), he describes his 1944 vision of the Kabbalistic union between *Tifereth* and *Malchuth*, immediately followed by "the Marriage of the Lamb" in Jerusalem and Zeus consummating the mystic marriage, as it is described in the *Iliad.* Indeed, the effort to bring together Athens and Jerusalem is an old theological stratagem, hardly unique to Jung, but one that characterizes much of his thought.

Jung is initially shocked to hear Elijah call Salome his daughter, and horrified by Salome's insistence that he, Jung, must love her. Jung is further disturbed by Elijah's claims that he and Salome have from eternity been "one" and that Salome actually loved John the Baptist, the man whose head she had severed and brought to Herod on a platter. Jung calls the relationship between Elijah, the holy man, and Salome, "a bloodthirsty horror" "and a "symbol of the most extreme contradiction" (RB, p. 246b), to which Elijah responds, "We are real and not symbols" (RB, p. 246b), suggesting to Jung that he cannot evade their significance by turning them into symbolic representations. Nonetheless, the union of Elijah and Salome represents a *coincidentia oppositorum* between the sacred and profane, and also, as Jung himself was to make explicit in his own commentary on this chapter (RB, p. 365a), between the archetypes of the wise old man and the *anima*, the erotic, feminine aspect of the human psyche. That Jung must "love" Salome suggests that he must learn to love the shadow and anima aspects of himself.

THE MYSTICAL FALL INTO CHAOS

Jung describes a "mystery play" that takes place in a "deep place like the crater of a volcano" (RB, p. 247a). Jung enters the crater, where he "gives birth to the children of chaos", and he himself is "smelted anew" (RB, p. 247a). The mystery play involves several paradoxical themes, including the embrace of the worthless along with the worthy, the origin of chaos in form, and the connection between the godly and the satanic (RB, p. 246a). Jung relates that he has descended into the "source of chaos" (RB, p. 247a), and that this descent brought him into contact not only with his own origins but (since he is part of the world's matter and formation) with "the primordial beginning of the world" (RB, p. 247a). Here Jung anticipates Heidegger's notion that one achieves insight into the being of the world through an existential confrontation with being as it is manifest in oneself. Jung's fall into chaos provides him with the opportunity to forge a new beginning. He notes that previously his participation in life has been only through a consciousness that is "formed and determined," but that this is incomplete because "the unformed and undetermined aspects of the world are also given to me" (RB, p. 247a). As we have seen, Nietzsche understood chaos as the source of creativity, and Jung later identified creative chaos with the unconscious.

Jung, in *The Red Book* and elsewhere, has a somewhat ambivalent view of chaos, which he seems to both invite and *struggle against*, the latter through a plethora of images, symbols, myths, and archetypes, each of which contains chaos with form. One criticism that can be levied against Jungian psychology as it is generally presented in his *Collected Works* is that it over-proliferates and objectifies subjective meaning in an effort to *avoid* meaninglessness, chaos, and death. However, in *Liber Novus*, the balance is tipped in the opposite direction, as "chaos" often takes center stage. We will return to this problem later in this book.

THE UNION OF THINKING AND FEELING

Jung considers the opposition between "forethinking" and "feeling." This is another opposition critical to Jung's realization of his soul. Jung states that the "forethinker is a seer" and "pleasure is blind" (RB, p. 247a). However, the latter's *power* is necessary if forethinking is to arrive at actual thinking and form. The two are equiprimordial and "in nature intimately one." It is only in man that "the separate existence of both principles becomes apparent" (RB, p. 247b). The notion that thinking and feeling complement one another, seen here in nascent form in *The Red Book*, becomes an important theme in *Psychological Types*. There, Jung argues that an exclusive reliance upon science and intellect "shut[s] us out from other, equally real provinces of life" (CW 6, § 85). On the other hand, Jung asserts that when Faust exclaims "feeling is all," he merely goes to the other extreme and fails to achieve the totality of life and wholeness of psyche in which feeling and thinking are united in a third and higher principle (CW 6, § 85).

In *Psychological Types* Jung holds that the bridge that unites feeling and intellect is "given us in creative fantasy" (CW 6, § 85). He then comments, "If psychology remains for us only a science, we do not penetrate into life…" (CW 6, § 86). We will see that as *The Red Book* proceeds Jung becomes increasingly critical of what he will describe as the "poison" of science. In *Psychological Types* Jung is of the view that not only the human psyche, but also the discipline of psychology is incomplete without the union of the "functions" of feeling and thinking. That such union is only achieved through "creative fantasy" provides something of a justification for Jung's entire *Red Book* project, which is in large measure an exercise of Jung's own creative fantasy and imagination. Freud reflected that his own case studies read like literature;[16] Jung, in spite of protestations to the contrary, went on to produce a literary work in *The Red Book*, in the tradition of Dante's *Inferno* and Nietzsche's *Zarathustra*.

As we have seen, Jung witnessed a reflection of "Eve, the tree and the serpent" (RB, p. 245b) as he was led by Elijah into a large hall. Now, focusing on the serpent, Jung tells us that it is the source of man's failure to acknowledge the balance between thinking and feeling (RB, p. 247b), and that this inevitably leads to error. Yet while the serpent is a symbol of enmity between *logos* and *eros*, it is also a symbol of serpentine movement and *longing*, and thus becomes a bridge that connects the opposing principles. We have already seen how, for Jung, desire, yearning, and longing is the way to an actualized life. We now see that it is through such longing that one energizes one's thinking and gives direction to one's feeling, thereby forming the imaginative bridge between the two functions.

Jung reflects that because he was a "thinker," pleasure appeared to him as the contemptible Salome; had he been a "feeling" type, thought would have appeared to him as the serpent. "The thinker's passions are bad," and "the thoughts of one who feels are bad" (RB, p. 248a). It is for this reason, and in order to correct Jung's psychic imbalance, that Salome insists that he must love her. "The thinker feels the disgust of feeling," and "the one who feels thinks the disgust of thinking." But thinking and feeling are thus "each other's poison and healing" (RB, p. 248a), and one only gains a vision of the whole by embracing one's opposing principle. Jung concludes with a prayer: "May the thinking person accept his pleasure, and the feeling person accept his own thought" (RB, p. 248b).

We here see Jung's theory of compensation of functions and attitudes in its nascent form. In *Psychological Types* Jung places the "realization of unconscious contents" at the core of analytic therapy because it is only through such realization "that compensation may be re-established" (CW 6, § 695). Jung observes (in agreement with Aldolphe Maeder) that one's contrary functions and attitudes are excluded from consciousness and their energy builds up in the unconscious until "the repressed unconscious contents break through in the form of dreams and spontaneous *images*" (CW 6, § 694). We might understand Jung's images and dreams in *The Red Book* in precisely these terms. That Jung should have these experiences soon after his break from Freud, and that *The Red Book* is at least on its face a world apart from Freudian analysis, suggests that *Liber Novus* was itself an irruption of ideas and attitudes that Jung had repressed during his psychoanalytic period.

LOGOS AND EROS: JUNG'S COMMENTARY ON THE MYSTERIUM ENCOUNTER

We are fortunate to have Jung's own extended commentary on Chapter IX and X of *Liber Primus*, the "Mysterium Encounter" and "Instruction" chapters, which has been published as "Appendix B" of the English language edition of *The Red Book*. Jung writes that while the (narrative) "images" that appear in these chapters came to him as "visions," these images "personify principles accessible to thinking and intellectual understanding" (RB, p. 365a). In particular, the figures of Elijah and Salome, "the old sage and the young maiden," respectively signify the spiritual principle of Logos and the un-spiritual principle of Eros. While the former principle represents order and stability, the latter "is dissolution and movement" (RB, p. 365b), and the two are complementary and interdependent. These "primordial images" belong to "general human history," and for this reason they are common parlance in philosophy and poetry. Such "primordial images" can seize and "take hold of a man" (RB, p. 365b), causing him to be "entranced, possessed, and confused," a notion that is symbolized by the serpent in Jung's fantasy.

Jung says that the fact that he envisioned Salome as Elijah's daughter indicates that at least here Eros is subordinated to Logos.

The appearance of Eve at the beginning of the fantasy, together with the tree and the serpent, is another manifestation of Eros, this time in the form of "temptation," which gives way to the image of the wanderer, Odysseus, as a symbol of the "adventurous possibilities" that Eros arouses and inspires (RB, p. 366a). Jung states that while in his own case "Logos undoubtedly has the upper hand," and that this may account for the fact that Eros is represented by the blind and "not-so-pleasing figure of Salome" (RB, p. 366a), this subordination of Eros results in an imbalance in the personality, moral suffering, or psychological sickness. Jung affirms,

> Only one way remains open to whoever wants to free himself from this suffering: he must accept the repressed part of his soul, he must love his inferiority, even his vices, so that what is degenerate can resume development. (RB, p. 366a)

Jung comments on the appearance of Eve and Mary in his fantasy. Each represents an aspect of Eros: Eve the carnal side and Mary the spiritual side of this principle (RB, p. 367a). To the extent that Jung remained with Eve and Salome as representations of Eros, the principle remained blind, but "the vision of the mother of God" (RB, p. 367a) moves him from a carnal to a spiritual form of love (RB, p. 367a).

The appearance of Christ and Buddha (RB, p. 248b) in the next chapter, "Instruction," is interpreted in the context of the relationship between spirituality and the corporeal world (RB, p. 367a). Whereas Christ overcame the world by burdening himself with suffering…Buddha overcame both the pleasure and suffering of the world by disposing of each (RB, p. 367a). Jung writes that as a result of his transcendence of both suffering and desire, Buddha "entered into nonbeing, a condition from which there is no return," and thus represents a "higher spiritual power" than Christ. Because Buddha is "unaffected and untouchable" (RB, p. 367a, b), he is surrounded by a "blazing fire" (RB, p. 367b; cf. RB, p. 248b: "circle of fire").

The Buddha's solution is not, however, adequate for "the living I" and its passions,[17] which requires a unity between Eros and Logos, not their dissolution. While Eros, unguided by Logos, can be devastating in its effects (a "bloodthirsty Kali[18] who devours the life of man from within"— RB, p. 367b), when Eros is reunited with Logos (when feeling is united with "forethinking"), the "conflict between spirit and flesh" is potentially resolved. Interestingly, Jung here suggests that the union of Logos and Eros is dominated by Logos. The fact that Elijah "leans against a marble lion" (RB, p. 367b; cf. RB, p. 248b) expresses his power, and as Logos, "Elijah assumes control over developing awareness" (RB, p. 367b).

"Chapter X: Instruction," pp. 248-51

THOUGHTS "OUTSIDE" THE SELF

Jung again finds himself in the presence of Salome and Elijah and he tells the latter that the previous night he had experienced a "longing" in their presence, and that while he does not like being in their house he feels "more real" there (RB, p. 248b). As he follows Elijah and Salome into the house, Jung has a vision of Mary, Jesus, St. Peter, and Salome as the Buddha in the form of a "many-armed bloody goddess," which in the *Black Book* he describes as a girl with black hair—his own soul (RB, p. 248, n. 187). Jung enters into a dialog with Elijah about his resistance to Salome's love and his ignorance of why he is drawn to the prophet's house. Jung confesses that he had a "doubtful and uncertain thought," a "far-fetched" and "dangerous" idea. Elijah admonishes him for identifying himself too closely with his thoughts, explaining, "your thoughts are just as much outside yourself as trees and animals are outside your body" (RB, p. 249a). This way of thinking, which is reminiscent of the early Wittgenstein's suggestion (following the 18th century German thinker, Georg Christoph Lichtenberg[19]) that thought could be expressed with the phrase "it thinks" in the manner of "it rains,"[20] allows Jung to distance himself from and express the "unbelievable" thought that Salome must love him because he resembles either John the Baptist or Elijah himself. Jung adds that he rejected this thought, because he is really quite the opposite of Elijah, and that Salome must actually love him because "she loves her badness in [Jung's] badness" (RB, p. 249a). We then hear from Salome that she and Jung are brother and sister, having both been born of Mary, "the mother of our savior" (RB, p. 249b). Jung again protests that this assertion must be the result of a "devilish spell" (RB, p. 249b), and he tries to distance himself from this idea by again claiming that Elijah and Salome (as well as Mary) are "symbols," to which Elijah again responds that on the contrary they are most certainly real.

THE RISK OF SOLIPSISM

The question of thoughts existing outside oneself, like natural objects, is suggestive of Jung's later notion of the "objective psyche." Certainly, given Jung's views about the collective unconscious, archetypal thoughts, dreams, and visions have an "objective" source and are not generated by the individual subject. From the phenomenological perspective which generally informs his thinking, Jung suspends the distinction between real and illusory experiences, a distinction that later in *The Red Book* he will specifically reject (RB, p. 282b, p. 283a). Indeed, as we will see, a major theme of *The Red Book* is that there is a sense in which the thoughts and images of one's imagination are as every bit as, if not more real, than the "external" objects of science and everyday life. Further, the view that the individual subject is not the source of his "own" language is hardly unique to Jung, and is present in such thinkers as Heidegger, Lacan, and Hillman, each of whom in their own way see the subject or ego as constructed by, as opposed to constructing, his/her words.

We should note, however, if only in passing, some potentially troubling implications of Jung's acceptance that his thoughts (and specifically the thought that he and Salome are born of Mary) are not generated by his personal psyche, but derive from an outside source. In spite of Jung's efforts to diffuse the issue of his prophethood, the thought that Jung is the son of Mary and that he himself is Christ (RB, p. 252b), if interpreted literally, is an enormous inflation that might on its face lend support to those, like Richard Noll, who would argue that Jung saw himself as a religious redeemer.[21] This charge appears to be strengthened by the fact that the declaration that Jung is Christ comes from an "outside source." On the other hand, we know that for Jung, Christ becomes a symbol of the Self, and even here, in *The Red Book*, Christ represents the capacity of the individual to assume responsibility for his/her own existence. In this sense, not only Jung, but each individual is potentially Christ, and as we will see, Jung holds that it is in its identification with Christ, and assuming personal responsibility, that the "I" actually assumes an "inferior position" (RB, p. 368b).

Nevertheless, the very notion that one's thoughts are external objects, like animals and trees,[22] can lead to either the complete disappearance of the subject or to solipsism, the idea that "I" am the only consciousness or self. To a solipsist, all things are equally presentations to one's own mind; there is no difference in kind between one's own thoughts and nature's animals and trees, because the only thing that properly exists is the self. If all things, including one's thoughts are "external objects" (as Elijah suggests to Jung), then the distinction between external and internal is vitiated and the self either disappears in a welter of disenfranchised experiences or becomes all that there is. (Indeed, as we will see, later in *The Red Book*, Jung declares that one cannot know anything beyond oneself [RB, p. 306b]). It is the latter that appears to be the main danger in *The Red Book*, as it is not only Elijah's proclamation but Jung's general *self-absorption* in this work that treads dangerously close to a solipsistic point of view. Whatever *The Red Book's* other merits, the potential madness that Jung himself recognized within it appears to be closely tied to his over-absorption with the self.

JUNG'S EXISTENTIAL PROJECT

It is here that Jung makes the comments on yearning and desire that I quoted earlier in connection with *Liber Novus*, Chapter VIII. Jung, as we have seen, informs us that the way to discover our own yearning is by overcoming our resistance to it. One who does not follow his or her desire exchanges his or her life for "an alien one" (RB, p. 249b), deceives him/herself and others, leads a life of apish imitation, and infects others with this apish attitude. Jung adopts an almost *Sartrian* existential posture when he proclaims: "To live oneself means: to be one's own task," and "...you must be your own creator" (RB, p. 249b). However, in order to do this one does "not begin with the best and the highest, but with the worst and the deepest" (RB, p. 249b, p. 250a). This helps explain why Jung must accept Salome's (his "evil" soul's) love, and perhaps even why (apart from any ego-inflation) Jung is to be identified with Christ, who for Jung is the model of a fully actualized and individuated Self. We have seen that for Jung the "New God" emerges from "the terrible ambiguity" of what is hateful and beautiful, evil and good, etc. and refuses to be *followed* as a hero. If Jung had not made it previously clear, we now understand that the Self emerges from the same ambiguity and refuses to *follow* a hero-god. By loving Salome, Jung in effect accepts his shadow and anima, forges a new self, is identified with Christ, and ushers in the new God.

THE DEMONIC DIVINE

Jung's vision of Salome as the Buddha and a "many-armed bloody goddess" further underscores the ambiguity of both God and the Self. Upon its publication, the original manuscript of *The Red Book* was on display at the Rubin Museum in New York, which is especially notable for its collection of Himalayan paintings expressive of the demonic divine,[23] some of which depict the Buddha as a multi-armed wrathful figure. These paintings are generally understood as a paradoxical vehicle for the expression of the power of compassion. The paradox is in part explained via the notion that the divinity's powerful wrath serves as a means for destroying the obstacles to compassion, wisdom, and enlightenment.[24] For Jung, it would also express the coincidence of good and evil in the archetypes of God and the Self.

"I AM NOT THE SON OF GOD" (BUT HIS MOTHER)

Jung again comments on Salome's identification of him with Christ. He explains, "I do not myself become the supreme meaning" (RB, p. 250a). A variant of a portion of this chapter in the *Corrected Draft* substitutes "the Son of God" for "the supreme meaning" (RB, p. 250, n. 192), suggesting that for Jung, during the writing of *Liber Primus*, Christ and the supreme meaning are closely related. Later in his career, in *Aion*, Jung will make an explicit connection between Christ and the Self (CW 9ii). Taken together, these ideas suggest a relationship between God, the Self, and the supreme meaning. Further, the Self, as a *coincidentia oppositorum,* unites the sense and nonsense that earlier in *Liber Novus* "melted together" in the supreme meaning.

Jung tells us, "Although I am not the son of God myself, I represent him nevertheless as one who was a mother to the God..." (RB, p. 250a). Jung will later explain how he heals the sick God Izdubar (RB, p. 278ff) and in effect gives (re)birth to him, but here the claim is made that God's being develops within Jung as a result of his own self-transformation. Jung's thinking is difficult to pin down, but he suggests that such transformation occurs as he incorporates his feeling-function (represented by Salome, his soul) and permits the chaos of his thoughts to develop like a "forest of wild animals" within his psyche.

A note to the English text indicates that in the *Draft* version of *Liber Novus*, Jung describes his "transformation" as occurring when he "went over to pleasure, as [he] was a thinker" (RB, p. 250, n. 197). In the main text, Jung writes that he "believed in the order of the world and hated everything disorganized," but that he only became a "prophet" when he "found pleasure in the primordial beginning (i.e. chaos), in the forest, and in the wild animals" (RB, p. 251a).

How can we understand these ideas? If, as Jung seems to suggest, the divine is identified with the "supreme meaning," which as Jung explains is itself a "melting together" of sense and nonsense, order and chaos, etc., we can understand the claim that such "coincidentia" as they occur within the individual (and collective) psyche are productive of the "supreme meaning," and therefore "give birth" to (or minimally, reveal) God. As the individual embraces his anima and shadow, as he incorporates functions that initially seem alien to the psyche, a transformation takes place that unites the very opposites that are productive of the divine. Jung later termed the foundation of this process "the transcendent function" (CW 8, pp. 67-90; CW 6, § 828) because it is an aspect of the psyche that *transcends* and unifies opposing tendencies and attitudes. While Jung specifically denied that the transcendent function has any metaphysical implications (CW 6, § 828), we have good reason to surmise that this function is also "transcendent" in the sense of reaching towards the beyond. In commenting on the "procreative" union between "forethinking" and "pleasure" that occurs within his own psyche, Jung says, "It would be madness to claim that they are in this world" (RB, p. 251a).

A THEOLOGY OF TRANSFORMATION

Jung is aware of the inflationary danger of his views of himself as a "prophet," the son of Mary, and the representative of God: "I am in danger of believing that I myself am significant since I see the significant" (RB, p. 251a), and we may here either fault (or excuse) Jung for failing to frame these insights into himself as insights into "psyche" in general, in which all men and women share. Putting aside the question of Jung's personal inflation, we can attend to the question of the nature and value of the "theology of transformation" set forth in these passages.

Jung's theology of transformation is actually a theology of *transformation* and *expansion*, as his approach to God and the "supreme meaning" is one in which the psyche is transformed in order to expand its horizons to include aspects of conscious (and unconscious) experience that have hitherto been unknown, rejected, suppressed, or ignored. As it was for Freud, the entire thrust of Jung's psychology is a reaching towards and expansion into the *unknown*.

If we take a very broad view, one that places Jung within the context of the history of western thought, we see that he is part of a trend beginning with the Enlightenment and continuing to this day which seeks to open up the possibilities of human thought, action, and experience. This trend began with the Enlightenment's rejection of dogma and authority and the institution of rational reflection and empirical observation. It continued with Kant's recognition of the contributions of the human subject to perception and understanding, and was further expanded via Hegel's insistence that all particular perspectives in philosophy are incomplete and must be critiqued and transcended in favor of more comprehensive points of view that are themselves subject to the same dialectical criticism. Western consciousness was further expanded by the historicists (e.g. Vico, Hegel, and Marx), who wrote of the contributions of history and culture to knowledge. The phenomenology of Edmund Husserl and Wilhelm Dilthey's *verstehen* approach to interpretive understanding expanded western conceptions of "knowledge" to include modes of apprehension that were not conceptualized in purely naturalistic and positivistic terms. By unsettling traditional oppositions and elevating the importance of the formerly debased poles of opposing ideas, Nietzsche, and later Derrida, not only produced a transvaluation of values, but also expanded the horizon of knowledge and understanding to include ambiguity, difference, playfulness, and irony. Wittgenstein added complexity to our conception of ourselves and the world by bringing attention to the role of language in constructing (and misleading) thought and experience. Freud and other psychoanalysts expanded the horizons of experience through their attention to unconscious affects, attitudes, and ideas; and Jung expanded the horizon of the self through his insistence that experience must be informed by multiple functions (sensation, feeling, reason, and intuition) and by such collective archetypes as the *anima* (*animus*) and the Shadow. We ourselves might expand upon Jung's nascent *Red Book* theology to include a theological perspective on each these trends. If, as mystics and negative theologians have proclaimed, God is the unknowable, ineffable ground of cosmos and consciousness, our approach to God must not involve a dogmatic claim to knowledge, but rather a continuing expansion of psyche and culture into hitherto unknown, uncharted, and chaotic realms. God, in this view, is associated with an open economy of thought, action, and experience, and one becomes open to God when one begins to realize such an economy within oneself. Perhaps this is the personal "transformation" that, in Jung's view, gives birth to the divine.[25]

"Chapter XI: Resolution," pp. 251-55

The final chapter of *Liber Primus* contains some of its most interesting and provocative passages. Jung begins with a vision of a battle between a white serpent and its apparently stronger, black counterpart. Yet the white serpent prevails; and, the "black serpent pulls itself back" (RB, p. 251b), the forward section of its body turning white. Jung discourses with Elijah about this battle and speculates about its significance: "Should it mean that the power of the good light will become so great that even the darkness that resists it will be illuminated by it?" (RB, p. 251b). We will see that Jung holds that the very conflict between good and evil in the individual is itself "productive of self-sacrifice" and the good; and, as Jung, quoting Heraclitus, puts it in *Psychological Types*, "war is the father of all" (CW 6, § 87). We soon learn that the white and black serpents are associated with the divine: "I see the divine child, with the white serpent in his right hand, and the black serpent in his left hand" (RB, p. 252a). Then, Jung has a vision of Christ on the cross "in his last hour and torment" (RB, p. 252a). The black serpent, now at the base of the cross, winds itself around Jung's own feet, as Jung spreads his arms wide and assumes the countenance of a lion. As Jung finds himself incomprehensibly forced to imitate the final torment of Jesus, Salome informs him, "You are Christ" (*Du bist Christus*) (RB, p. 252b). The blind Salome then wraps her hair around Jung's feet, and then suddenly, she exclaims that she sees light and is cured of her blindness. The serpent, which had entwined itself around Jung's body causing Jung's blood to spill down the mountainside, now falls weakly to the ground. Elijah the prophet, who according to ancient tradition will "herald the coming of the messiah," instructs Jung to "write exactly what you see" (RB, p. 252b).

"GOD DEVELOPS THROUGH THE UNION OF THE PRINCIPLES IN ME"

Jung has here described an experience in which he is in effect deified and attains Christ's powers of spiritual healing. Looked at metaphorically, we might say that Jung needed to experience a union between the spiritual principle represented by Christ and the earthly, instinctual principle, represented by the black serpent, in order to achieve mastery as a psychotherapeutic healer of the soul. As we have seen and will explore later in detail, Jung held that each must find the Christ within himself (RB, p. 234b), and this discovery equates with the assumption of responsibility for one's own existence (RB, p. 356b). This can occur only with the merging of spirit and matter, and of good and evil, within one's psyche.

Jung has the insight that the two serpents represent a fight within himself between forethinking[26] and love, and that this battle is necessary in order for Jung to ascend to love, which is the essence of Christ. Jung associates thinking with darkness, night, and the right, and love with light, day, and the left, a reversal of his earlier vision of the divine child, who held the white serpent in his right hand and the black serpent in his left; perhaps this suggests the fluidity between good and evil and their propensity to exchange places with one another. More significantly, the conflict between thinking and feeling is a struggle that is within each man's nature (RB, p. 253a). This struggle leads to a coincidence of opposites between thinking and feeling; thinking is associated with "aloneness" and love or feeling with "togetherness," the two "need one another, yet they kill one another" (RB, p. 253a). Jung explains further that "Love is empty without thinking, thinking hollow without love" (RB, p. 253b).

Jung's efforts to unify thinking and feeling, and a host of other oppositions, is his *modus operandi* in *The Red Book*. Here Jung makes the startling claim that the union of thinking and feeling is the very condition for the birth of the divine: "The God develops through the union of the principles in me. He is their union" (RB, p. 254b; cf. RB, p. 254, n. 38). As we have seen, it is in this chapter of *Liber Primus* that Salome tells Jung that he is Christ (RB, p. 252b). This attribution becomes understandable (if no less shocking to our contemporary ears) in the context of Jung's later view that the union of opposing principles is the path to the Self, which is itself symbolized in the image/archetype of God and Christ.

FURTHER THOUGHTS ON PROPHECY

In his commentary on *Liber Novus*, Chapter 11 (Resolution), which is published in Appendix B of *The Red Book*, Jung comments on the identification of his "I" with Christ. He says "the I" (his I) is jubilant over its spiritual power, and in its excitement is "tempted to arrogate prophethood" (RB, p. 367b). Indeed, this is evident in Jung's own claim that he *represents* the Son of God (RB, p. 250a), as well as in Salome's assertion that he is Christ (RB, p. 252b). However, Jung says that it is absurd to hold that by identifying itself with Christ the "I" presumes "excessive importance" (RB, p. 368b). On the contrary, by being identified with Christ, the "I" assumes "a decidedly inferior position," because it no longer has "the advantage of being part of the crowd rallying behind a powerful figure" (RB, p. 368b), and must, in effect, be responsible for its own life and redemption. As we will see, this is consistent with Jung's "existential" view of Christ in *The Red Book*, especially in *Scrutinies*, where Jung's guide, Philemon, says that Christ represents the idea that one must *not* follow Christ but lead one's own life in a manner that is true to one's essence and love (RB, p. 356a). Here in this commentary Jung writes that while the traditional Christian solution of redemption *through* Christ appeals to the child in each of us, it is ultimately unsatisfactory, because "every child wishes to grow" (RB, p. 368a), and with this growth the assumption of personal responsibility and redemption is inevitable. Thus, in *The Red Book* Jung is already well on the way to developing his conception of Christ as a symbol of the individuated Self.

THE RED BOOK AND THE BIRTH OF GOD

We have seen that Jung holds that God develops through the union of the principles of forethinking and feeling within the Self. We might now go a step further and surmise that *the very act of writing The Red Book*, an act of "creative fantasy" which unites thinking and feeling, gives birth to God! The notion that one becomes or gives birth to a God through intellectual or creative work, however jarring to our contemporary sensibilities, is hardly original to Jung and goes back at least as far as ancient Greece, where it was thought that through the life of reason one could partake of divinity and effectively become divine. Aristotle implied that through intellectual contemplation man identifies with God,[27] and Plotinus wrote of "enacting the noblest life [and] acquiring identity with the divine."[28] The notion of divinization through reason reappears in Hegel, who held that the Absolute achieved its fullest expression and actuality in the self-conscious development of reason in humanity, and that his own philosophy was that expression and development, thereby suggesting that his *own writings were generative of the Absolute or God*. We should also note that the idea of man becoming God appears in the New Testament, where men are spoken of as participating in the divine nature (2 Peter 1:4), a theme that was amplified by the early church fathers who held that God had become human in order that we may become divinized ourselves.[29] Finally, in the Kabbalah we find the notion that one should write a *Sefer Torah*, for in doing so one is credited with having created God.[30]

The notion that *Liber Novus* both illustrates and effects a divinization process provides insight into why Jung treated *The Red Book* with such reverence, and why he produced it as a calligraphic illuminated manuscript, in the style of the Bibles of medieval Europe. However, we must not forget that it is not just Jung who becomes Christ, but each man, and mankind as a whole (RB, p. 253b). According to Jung, each individual stands in for humanity as a whole: "As a man you are part of mankind, and therefore you have a share in the whole of mankind, as if you were the whole of mankind" (RB, p. 253a).

On Willing Evil

Jung returns to the theme that what we find abhorrent is actually a part of our very being, and moves from the *coincidentia oppositorum* between thinking and feeling to the unification of the good and evil will. Jung tells us: If you kill your enemy, you also "kill that person in yourself" (RB, p. 253a). A person must recognize that he wants the very evil that he fights against; what's more, one must come to *will* that very evil, otherwise one will never get beyond projecting one's own evil onto others (RB, p. 254a). In speaking about the atrocities of the First World War, Jung says that instead of blaming these atrocities on forces outside oneself, one must actually will this great evil with one's own heart (RB, p. 254a); only in this way can one draw close to Christ's mystery, take the destructiveness of humanity back into oneself, and be ready, like Christ, to sacrifice oneself. Jung writes, "Drink your fill of the bloody atrocities of the war, feast upon the killing and destruction, then your eyes will open, you will see that you yourselves are the bearers of such fruit" (RB, p. 254a). Jung will later argue that the dark or barbaric side of the German psyche had been repressed by Christianity, and that the lesson of the first World War was that this "blonde beast" must be acknowledged and affirmed if it is to be brought to a creative rather than destructive resolution (CW 10, §§ 16-17).

Jung is reported to have provided at least one of his analysands similar advice years later when, according to Irene Champernowne, who had been in analysis with Jung in the 1930s, Jung made anti-Semitic remarks and encouraged his patients to do the same as a means of staying in touch with one's "shadow."[31] The idea here is that by willing evil, rather than projecting it outward onto the other, one is forced to recognize its true source within oneself, and only then will one cease fighting against one's projections. In this manner, "the frightfulness become[s] so great that it can turn men's eyes inward, so that their will no longer seeks the self in others but in themselves" (RB, p. 254b). Jung seems certain about this: "I saw it. I know that this is the way. I saw the death of Christ and I saw his lament" (RB, p. 254b). Indeed, Jung appears to identify this process of willing "this greatest evil with your whole heart" (RB, p. 254a) with Christ's taking on the sins of humanity unto himself.

In spite of its apparent radical honesty, there are problems with this line of reasoning not the least of which is that those who will evil and "drink [their] fill of...bloody atrocities" (RB, p. 254a) rarely arrive at the sort of non-projective clarity about evil and attain the personal transformation that Jung describes; rather, more often they continue with even stronger projections as a means of justifying themselves. One can agree that we must come to recognize that on some level we will the very things we find abhorrent in ourselves and others, but this is not achieved by an *identification* with that will. Jung, at various points in his career, recognized this (e.g. in his 1945 essay, "After the Catastrophe," CW 10, pp. 194-217). However, here in *The Red Book* we may be witness to another line of thinking that would later lead Jung to be so terribly mistaken, and to even join in the optimism, about Nazi Germany.

Chapter 4

Soul-Making Encounters

The Red Book: Liber Secundus

Several markers distinguish *Liber Secundus* from *Liber Primus*. In *Liber Secundus* Jung greatly expands his catalog of internal figures and multiplies the archetypal encounters that enrich his experience and understanding of God, religion, and the soul. Graphically, as Jung moves from parchment to paper (RB Intro, p. 202), the calligraphy becomes larger, and the paintings, which were mainly small adornments in *Liber Primus*, become grander, more detailed, colorful, and aesthetically rich—expanding to the point where at times they become visually (and even thematically) dominant over the written narrative. As *Liber Secundus* proceeds, the paintings achieve independence from the text and create their own psychological and theological narrative that is, in effect, superimposed upon the written one.

Liber Secundus begins with a brief section entitled "The Images of Erring" (RB, p. 259a), which serves the same function as Jung's "Prologue" to *Liber Primus*. The entire section consists of two quotes from Jeremiah (23:16, 23:25-28) in which the prophet distinguishes between false prophets who "speak a vision of their own heart" or who prophesize with lies by saying, "I have dreamed, I have dreamed," and true prophets who speak "out of the mouth of the Lord." As an introduction to *Liber Secundus*, this quotation invites the reader to judge for himself which kind of prophet he has encountered, and is about to encounter in Jung. Stein has aptly pointed out that the quotation from Jeremiah is ironic,[1] for Jung is clearly one who "prophesizes" from his imagination, if not from his dreams.

Visually, *Liber Secundus* begins with a large drop case "D," the first letter of "*Die Bilder des Irrenden*" ("The Images of Erring"). Contained within this "D" is a single eye, with a bright red iris. The eye is surrounded by what is apparently a cross section of the earth's crust, with its earth-toned layers and tectonic shifts, cracked and fissured nearly throughout. The impression given by **RB Image, p. 1** is that of the mind's eye penetrating layers of a psychic past that is riddled with displacements and fractures.

Jung is about to engage in a series of encounters with archetypal figures, encounters that provide us with a model of the individuation process.

"Chapter I: The Red One," pp. 259-61

Jung envisions himself as a guard standing atop a castle's highest tower, and the small image that opens this section (**RB Image, p. 2**) depicts a figure with a horn strapped across his back looking out into the distance over a tower wall. Jung writes that a small dot in the distance slowly comes into focus as a horseman in a red coat. Jung calls this horseman "The Red One," but will soon identify him as the devil. Jung enters into a dialog with the Red One and suggests that there is something worldly or pagan about him. Jung asks the Red One if he has "ever broken [his] heart over the mysteries of our Christian religion" (RB, p. 259b), to which the devil responds that Jung is good at divining riddles but is "unbelievably ponderous and serious" (RB, p. 259b). The Red One further accuses Jung of judging him too harshly, and of taking the scriptures too literally, and he asks Jung if he is "something of a saint" or a sophist (RB, p. 260a). Jung responds that "no one is allowed to avoid the mysteries of the Christian religion unpunished," as Christianity is the task and destiny of Western man.

The Devil and the Jews

The Red One immediately raises the question of the Jews, arguing that there are Jews who have achieved goodness without "need for your solemn gospels" (RB, p. 260a). Jung's response is interesting, especially in light of the accusations of anti-Semitism levied against him by Freud, and which followed Jung throughout his life. Jung asks the Red One if he has "ever noticed that the Jew lacks something—one in his head, another in his heart, and he himself feels that he lacks something?" (RB, p. 260a). The Red One now accuses Jung of being a "Jew hater," to which Jung responds that because the Jews "lack" something (i.e. the mysteries of Christ) and do not want to admit it, they are particularly sensitive to criticism. Years later, in a letter to James Kirsch, Jung would observe: "The Jew directly solicits anti-Semitism with his readiness to scent out anti-Semitism everywhere,"[2] but here he suggests that the Jews' sensitivity is directly related to their refusal to accept Christ. The Red One, who is a thinly disguised substitute for Nietzsche, tells Jung that "Only Christianity, with its mournful escape from the world" could have made Jung "so ponderous and sullen" (RB, p. 260b). Nietzsche in *Zarathustra* said:

> As long as there have been men, man has felt too little joy: that alone, my brothers, is our original sin. And learning better to feel joy, we learn best not to hurt others or to plan hurts for them.[3]

The Red One tells Jung that he is spoiling the fun; since life does not require seriousness, it is better if Jung would "dance through life" (RB, p. 260b).

Jung, anticipating his later misgivings about Nietzsche's Dionysian prescription[4] (he will shortly reveal his own attraction to it), responds that dancing is no option, as dancers are either ridiculous or attempt to "dance for their gods" (RB, p. 260b) by reenacting antiquity. The devil responds that perhaps "dancing" is just a symbol for some "third thing." (We can speculate that for Jung, this "third thing" is "creative fantasy," which in *Psychological Types* is said to reconcile thought and feeling.) At this moment, the Red One turns a tender flesh color; his garments, now green, "burst into leaf" and he reveals himself as "Joy." Jung responds that perhaps there is "a joy before God" that he is yet to discover, and he calls the Red One his "beloved" and asks to take his hand.

This is clearly a transformational moment for Jung, and thus we cannot take to heart his defense of Christianity and its traditional vilification of the Jews. Indeed, in the name of the devil Jung ridicules the very anti-Semitism he was accused of harboring. Jung suggests that this "devil" was a devil that was specific to him, a devil that brought joy like "a warm southerly wind with swelling fragrant blossoms" (RB, p. 260b), and caused him to sweetly forget himself and his seriousness. Jung describes this devil as his own "other standpoint" and advises his would-be readers that if ever they have the opportunity to discourse with their own devil they should do so in all seriousness (RB, p. 261a).

Joy

Jung makes several interesting comments on the equation of the devil with "joy." He says that he and the devil can agree that joy is "neither lust nor madness," but "the most supreme flowering and greening of life" (RB, p. 261a). Yet joy is always ephemeral, and for this reason one can neither make a pact with nor capture the devil. Further, the pursuit of joy is not only vain but also evil, as it leads to pleasure, which itself leads one to Hell. Jung's formula of joy→pleasure→hell is somewhat surprising given his earlier discussion of the importance of feeling. In light of the fact that the issue of "joy" arises in the context of Jung's discussion of anti-Semitism, we should note that the Hasidim, who inherited the Jewish mystical tradition from the Kabbalah, held that joy, especially as it arises in song and dance, is a form of divine worship and a precondition for spiritual elevation.[5]

Jung's Psychological Standpoint

In the end, Jung says that he came to terms with his devil by accepting some of the devil's joy just as the devil accepted some of Jung's seriousness. Jung tells us that he treated his devil as a "real person" and that it is important "to take seriously" all of the inhabitants of the inner world, adding that "they are real because they are effectual" (RB, p. 260b). He suggests that while the devil is "an independent personality" (RB, p. 261a), the conversation with him took place within his (Jung's) own psyche. Further, "[t]aking the devil seriously" means to "accept your own other standpoint" (RB, p. 261a). Here we can gain some insight into the Jung's attitude toward his visions in *The Red Book*: his perspective is not that of a psychotic, who would take his visions to be real manifestations of an *external* reality, but rather that of a psychologist, who understands that the visions arise from an inner, psychological world, and that the figures he encounters represent compensations for the one-sided attitudes of his own ego. Jung later tells us that the "appearance of living figures should not be taken personally" (RB, p. 368a) as they are primordial, general images.

The question arises as to whether we today can follow Jung by encountering and dialoging with our own inner figures as Jung did in *The Red Book*. Certainly, such techniques as active imagination permit one to enter into an imagined dialog with figures encountered in one's fantasies and dreams and to "learn from them" in a manner similar to the way Jung learned from his. Such "dreaming the dream onward" is a technique that has its place in psychotherapeutic practice. Nevertheless, while Jung himself advised at least one of his followers to create her own *Red Book*,[6] we ourselves run the risk of falling into an "imitation of the hero" if we consciously endeavor to have our own transformative visions through an encounter and dialog with mythical figures of the distant past.

"Chapter II: The Castle in the Forest," pp. 261-65

This chapter begins with an image (**RB Image, p. 5**) of a castle amidst a lake, woods, and mountains. Jung describes how he loses his way and takes up lodging in a small castle where he meets an old scholar who appears to have dedicated himself to research and science (RB, p. 261b), but who has been made modest and fearful before the vastness of knowledge. Jung writes that this is "an ideal though solitary existence" (RB, p. 262a), and it is in some ways not unlike the life he will periodically retreat to years later in his tower at Bollingen, on the shore of Lake Zürich.

In his quarters, Jung becomes obsessed with what he describes as the irritating and hackneyed thought that the old man has a young beautiful daughter kept as a prisoner in the castle, and who awaits her savior. Suddenly, "a slim girl, pale as death" (RB, p. 262a), appears at Jung's door, and Jung, overcome by the triteness of this vision, says,

"I am truly in Hell—the worst awakening after death, to be resurrected in a lending library" (RB, p. 262a). Jung here struggles with his own elitism, and asks if he must atone in hell for an insult to the "lower half of average human taste" (RB, p. 262a). Jung comes to have pity and compassion for the young girl, and she feels vindicated when he finally recognizes that in spite of being banal, she is real. Jung comes to regard the girl as beautiful, feels love for her, and engages with her in a dialog about the nature of "ultimate truths."

BANALITY, COMPENSATION, AND ONE'S PERSONAL "HELL"

Jung listens carefully when the young maiden speaks of the universal validity of the fairy tale, and when she tells him that only what he calls "banal and hackneyed contains the wisdom" that he seeks (RB, p. 262b). The girl dissolves into darkness but not before giving Jung "greetings from Salome" (RB, p. 263a). We soon learn that Jung regards the old man and his daughter to be the equivalents of Elijah and Salome, who he had encountered in *Liber Primus*. Further, the young maiden is the soul of the old man, as well as *Jung's soul*, which, as we will learn momentarily is, for Jung, always the opposite of one's biological gender.

The notion that wisdom is to be found in banality serves as an important compensation to Jung's "heaviness" and "profundity" in *The Red Book*, just as the Red One's "joy" served as a compensation for Jung's "seriousness." Soon, in his 1918 essay, "The Role of the Unconscious," Jung will write:

> Whenever life proceeds one-sidedly in any given direction, the self-regulation of the organism produces in the unconscious an accumulation of all those factors which play too small a part in the individual's conscious existence. For this reason I have put forward the compensation theory of the unconscious as a complement to the repression theory. (CW 10, § 20)

We have seen how Jung described his involvement in the trite story of the scholar's daughter as a descent into hell. He now provides a general observation stemming from his particular case: "Your Hell is made up of all the things that you always ejected from your sanctuary" (RB, p. 264b). It is only by paying attention to one's hell, by "quietly look(ing) into everything that excites your contempt or rage" (RB, p. 265a), that one can "give soul to the souless" and "redeem your other unto life" (RB, p. 265a). It is for this reason that the rediscovery of one's soul and the process of individuation involve suffering and sacrifice.

INNER AND OUTER ADVENTURE

Jung continues with further reflections on the coincidence and balance of the opposites. The first balance he considers is between "outer" and "inner" adventure. If one has no adventures (presumably in the "everyday world"), one becomes hemmed in by the limits of one's own imagination and the expectations of others (RB, p. 263a). It is only through testing one's upper and lower limits, and by following the "devil" into adventure, that one comes to know one's real limitations. "Man lives in two worlds," an inner world and an outer one; only a fool lives in one or the other (RB, p. 264a). A second balance must be achieved between the uncommon and the ordinary. Jung confesses that he preoccupied himself to such a degree with the rare, the hidden, and the undiscovered that the *ordinary* within him suffered and "began to hanker after life" (RB, p. 263a). It was because of his own repression of the ordinary that he had his trite adventure with the scholar's daughter where he learned the significance and power of ordinary life, embodied in fairy tales and the common stories of mankind. Jung is in the process of formulating his notion that fairy tales and myths express the archetypes of the collective unconscious. The young maiden of his vision, like Salome and the devil before her, teaches Jung to crave what he "formerly derided" and consider as "feeble and wasted" what he formerly loved (RB, p. 263b).

Jung does not comment on the fact that few, if any, "outer" adventures are recorded in *The Red Book*. Indeed, the entire work could be said to remain within the bounds of the imagination. We know from *Memories, Dreams, Reflections* that in retrospect Jung felt that the only reason he kept his sanity during the period of *The Red Book* was that he had a family and career that anchored him to the external world (MDR, p. 189), but we glean little or nothing of this from *The Red Book* itself. Occasionally Jung's "real life" enters briefly into the narrative, as when he tells the scholar's daughter "By God, I love you—but— unfortunately I am already married" (RB, p. 263a), but otherwise the work remains almost exclusively within an imagined, visionary realm. We should not necessarily fault Jung for this; indeed, *The Red Book's* originality and power derives from its intense imaginative focus. However, we will see (in Chapter 9) that when Jung gave up work on *The Red Book* in 1930, this inaugurated a period of greater collegial involvement and participation in public and professional life (MDR, p. 197), suggesting that Jung may have needed to abandon his intense inner focus in order to achieve a balance of the "inner" and the "outer."

MASCULINE AND FEMININE

Jung next engages in a very interesting discussion of the masculine and the feminine, which yields yet another compensation or balance of opposites. A man "should not seek the feminine in women" (RB, p. 263b) but rather in himself, as he possesses the feminine as a key element in his psyche. Indeed, even "the most masculine man has a feminine soul, and the most feminine woman has a masculine soul" (RB, p. 263b). A man who recognizes his feminine soul is first able to treat a woman as a person, i.e., as an individual with whom he can truly identify. Further, by recognizing the opposing gender within oneself one is freed from the possibility of becoming enslaved by members of the opposite sex. Jung's advice to men: "It is good for you once to put on women's clothes…through becoming a woman you attain freedom from women" (RB, p. 263 b, p. 264a). Jung asserts that a man only becomes complete when he accepts his femininity and a woman is only complete when she accepts her masculinity. One's opposite gender is "bound up with evil," and for this reason "people hate to accept their own other" (p. 264a). However, accepting (what Jung will later call) one's *anima* (for a man) or one's *animus* (for a woman) completes one as a person. Jung raises the intriguing possibility of a post-gendered consciousness when he speaks of going "beyond the gendered and yet remain(ing) within the human" (RB, p. 264b).

This discourse, and related discussions elsewhere in *The Red Book*, make clear that the experiences recorded in *Liber Novus* were foundational for Jung's conception of the *anima* archetype and its relationship to the soul. We have already seen that Jung experienced an autonomous feminine presence within his psyche, which he related to as his "soul." Years later, reflecting on the experiences that he had set down in *The Red Book*, Jung said,

> I was greatly intrigued by the fact that a woman should interfere
> with me from within. My conclusion was that she must be the
> 'soul', in the primitive sense, and I began to speculate on the
> reasons why the name 'anima' was given to the soul...Later I
> came to see that this inner feminine figure plays a typical, or
> archetypal, role in the unconscious of a man.... (MDR, p. 186)

"Situation" Ethics

Jung warns that one cannot discover one's soul by simply following the "rule" of going beyond one's gender, for following such a rule makes one "dry, hard, and inhuman" (RB, p. 264b). One must transcend one's gender for what Jung calls "human reasons," reasons that are different for each individual and each situation. Jung does not specify in detail what he means by "human reasons," but he provides an example in the compassion he showed for the scholar's daughter. Jung writes: "If you act from your humanity, you act from that particular situation without general principle, with only what corresponds to the situation" (RB, p. 264b). While the general rule "also has meaning" and "comprises much venerable work of the human spirit," one is only "human...all too human" (an apparent reference to Nietzsche's 1878 work, "Human All Too Human") when one does justice to the *situation* (RB, p. 264b). Here Jung rejects Kantian ethics, which is based on generalizable rules, and propounds the sort of existential "situation ethics" that Sartre would advocate in the 1930s and 40s. While such situationalism may, at least on the surface, also appear to be "un-Jungian" in light of his understanding of the archetypes as transcultural and universal, it is a position he continued to maintain throughout his career. In an extemporaneous talk entitled "Good and Evil in Analytical Psychology," which he published in 1959, Jung defended the notion that those who are forced to make unique ethical decisions "condemned by current morality" are often true to their "innermost nature and vocation." Jung states:

> Without wishing it, we human beings are placed in situations
> in which the great "principles" entangle us in something and
> God leaves it to us to find a way out. (CW 10, § 869)

Recent discussions of ethics in Jungian psychotherapy, for example in the work of Luigi Zoja, underline the significance of the "grey zone" situational choices that must be made in the course of the psychotherapeutic process, and which often cannot be settled by appeals to rules or ethical maxims.[7]

Jung returns to a familiar theme when he asserts that one must make one's "ordered world horrible" in order to enter the "whirl of chaos" and the "wonder world of the soul" (RB, p. 264a). Jung's thinking here echoes Nietzsche's declaration that chaos gives "birth to a dancing star."[8] Years later, in his *Seminar on Zarathustra*, Jung commented on this same passage from Nietzsche:

> a certain lack of orientation, a vagueness, a feeling of…drifting, finding no direction and meaning in life. In certain stages of analysis, particularly in the beginning, people realize very clearly that they have chaos in themselves and they feel lost in it…Now Nietzsche's idea is that out of that lack of order a dancing star should be born.[9]

Jung remained of the view that it is only by allowing oneself to become lost in the chaotic and horrifying forces of the unconscious that one becomes truly creative, achieves completion as a human being, and liberation of one's soul. In *Psychology and Alchemy*, Jung writes:

> In alchemy the egg stands for the chaos…Out of the egg…will rise the eagle or phoenix, the liberated soul, which is ultimately identical with the Anthropos who was imprisoned in the embrace of Physis. (CW 12, § 306)

Still, the embrace of disorder is not without its dangers, as one

> must not underestimate the devastating effect of getting lost in the chaos, even if we know that it is the sine qua non of any regeneration of the spirit and the personality. (CW 12, § 96)

As *Liber Secundus* develops, Jung's attitude towards chaos becomes ambivalent, but as we will see below, his immersion in chaos and disorder is critical to his soul-finding journey and marks *The Red Book* as the "deconstructive" phase of his life's work.

"Chapter III: One of the Lowly," pp. 265-67

A new chapter begins with a brilliant painting (**RB Image, p. 11**), a mosaic of colored elements that diminish in size, creating the illusion of depth and distance as one's eyes move towards its center. One surmises that Jung is constructing a whole self out of various fragments. The sense of depth and perspective, virtually unique in *The Red Book*, gives the image the quality of introspection.

Jung describes an encounter with a lowly individual, an unshaven "tramp" or "rogue." Jung is concerned that anyone should see him speaking with this "former convict," who talks on about the murder of a tyrant, the simple pleasures of the cinema, and his desire to marry a woman who had carried another man's "bastard" child. The rogue had lost an eye in a brawl with the woman's former lover and subsequently went to prison. He acknowledges that his woman had lost interest in him but says, rather naively, "Once I find a proper job we can get married right off" (RB, p. 266a). The tramp says that there is something wrong with his lungs, but expresses optimism that they will soon improve. Jung thinks otherwise and puts the man up in a room next to his own quarters in a humble lodge. After a time Jung awakens to the sound of "an uncanny moan and gurgle mixed with a half-stifled cough" (RB, p. 266a). Jung arises from bed and goes to the tramp's aid, who by now is expectorating enough blood to form a puddle on the floor. Jung sees that the "hand of death lies on him" (RB, p. 266a), and the man dies in Jung's arms, his blood literally on Jung's hands.

ON "HEIGHTS" AND "DEPTHS"

Jung uses this tragic and not unrealistic vision as an occasion for considering the experience of one's "depths." Reflecting on what the rogue has told him, Jung thinks that there is a certain beauty in the feeling that one has hit bottom with nowhere to go but up (RB, p. 265b). Jung seems to empathize with the "lowly" man, and he writes, "We [all] stand on the spikey stones of misery and death" (RB, p. 266a). Just as the scholar's daughter represented an aspect of Jung that called for admission into his psyche, the destitute, now dead tramp "wants admittance" (RB, p. 266a) into Jung's soul as well, and Jung must find a way to grant him entrance. Jung realizes that he himself must experience "the bottommost" if he is to have hope for personal renewal. He suggests that in contrast to experiencing the "heights," which are unique to each individual, hitting bottom puts one in contact with one's fellow man in a way that success and achievement can never do. Further, one must be conscious of one's depths: if one has never hit bottom, it is dangerous to imagine that one cannot do so. The capacity to fall is present in all of us, and we restrict our "human potential" when we attribute "lowliness" to others that we believe can never be realized in ourselves.

It is interesting that Jung here maintains that we only enter into a "collective" form of consciousness, "the general life as a being", when we plumb our "depths" (RB, p. 266b). Jung writes, "your heights are your own mountain, which belong to you alone" (RB, p. 266b). He holds this to be the case, even though he believes that when we are in the "heights," i.e., at our best, "imagination is at its strongest" (RB, p. 266b). Thus, while in *Psychological Types* Jung pointed to "creative fantasy" as the "third" that draws upon collective symbols and thereby unites the divergent tendencies of the psyche (CW 6, § 84ff), in *The Red Book* he appears ambivalent regarding the proposition that the *imagination* is the key to the *collective*. His view, at least in the present chapter, appears to be that we reach our collective humanity only through our participation in the "least common denominator," while creative imagination expresses our individuality. Yet, Jung sows the seeds for a collective notion of creative fantasy on the very page where he appears to have foreclosed this idea; for he says that even when we believe that we are exercising will and making decisions, we are actually being directed by the "great wind of the world" (RB, p. 267a). This wind sinks us into "black depths" but also grants us a glimpse of our "golden light" (RB, p. 267a). Indeed, it is the very process of being cast into the depths that allows us to grasp our "heights" and experience the "bath of rebirth" (RB, p. 266b), leading to "singleness" of intent and what Jung would later call "individuation." It seems, then, that we do not create our own "heights," but rather experience them only after being cast into our depths by the world. We see here yet another blending of opposites in Jung's thought, between the abyss of despair and the heights of creativity.

In both this and the previous chapter Jung struggles with a conflict between his scholarly elitism and his desire to enter into community with the common man. In "The Castle in the Forest" the scholar's daughter represents what Jung regards to be the "lower half of average human taste" (RB, p. 262a), which Jung holds in contempt but which he thinks is nonetheless the key to a common "fairy-tale" wisdom that must be integrated into his psyche. Here, in "One of the Lowly," the destitute rogue, with whom Jung is embarrassed to be seen, leads him to a consideration of his depths, without which he cannot participate in common humanity and enter the "bath of rebirth" (RB, p. 266b).

LIVING TOWARDS DEATH

The death of the tramp prompts Jung to make some fascinating observations about the relationship between death and personal realization. Jung writes:

> The knowledge of death came to me that night, from the dying that engulfs the world. I saw how we live towards death, how the swaying golden wheat sinks together under the scythe of the reaper like a smooth wave on a sea beach. He who abides in common life becomes aware of death with fear. Thus the fear of death drives him toward singleness. He does not live there, but he becomes aware of life and is happy since in singleness he is one who becomes, and has overcome death. (RB, p. 267a)

According to Jung, it is only by "becoming" that one moves beyond mere existence and "grows aware of life" (RB, p. 267a). Later in *Liber Secundus,* Jung observes that, "Joy at the smallest things comes to you only when you have accepted death" (RB, p. 275a). Further, death clarifies our vision of things (RB, p. 274b), "teaches [one] how to live" (RB, p. 275a), and provides life with its meaning (RB, p. 275a). At one point, Jung exclaims, "How much our life needs death!" (RB, p. 274b). In an entry to *Black Book* 5, Jung writes "To attain individuality, we need a large share of death" (RB, p. 370b, Appendix C).

These statements clearly anticipate the notion of "Being-towards-death" that Martin Heidegger would put forth in *Being and Time*[10] in the 1920s. Indeed, there is much in *The Red Book* that comports not only with Heidegger's existential understanding of death but with Sartre's existential view of freedom and authenticity as well. As we have seen, Jung is adamant that the individual should not follow a personal or spiritual model but should instead assume personal responsibility for his or her own life:

> If you live according to an example, you thus live the life of that example, but who should live your own life if not yourself? So live yourselves. (RB, p. 231b)

While Christianity understood that redemption was only through Christ, Jung said, "The time has come when each must do his own work of redemption" (RB, p. 356b). For Jung, the divine is instantiated in man precisely through a rejection of imitation and the assumption of individual responsibility (RB, p. 245a). The latter involves a descent into the shadow depths of one's soul. Jung alludes to Kierkegaard when he writes that while one must become the author of one's own existence (RB, p. 249b), one must do this "with fear and trembling" (*mit Furcht und mit Zittern*) (RB, p. 244a).

Yet Jung is ambivalent with regard to these existential postulates, and especially regarding the notion of radical freedom that later came to be associated with existential philosophy. In *Liber Secundus,* Jung writes, "You had the thought that your movements came from you and that it needed your decision and efforts...But with every conceivable effort you would have never achieved that movement and reached those areas to which the sea and the great wind of the world brought you" (RB, p. 266b, p. 267a).

Neither do Jung's *Red Book* views on death always comport with an existential outlook. Toward the end of *Liber Secundus,* Jung suggests that by taking death into himself the individual surrenders his "personal striving...For everything that previously lurked hungrily in him no longer lives with him in his day. His life is beautiful and rich, since he is himself" (RB, p. 323a). This notion, that the consciousness of death leads one to surrender personal striving and desire, is more Buddhist than existentialist in character, and suggests that for Jung, individuation is not a matter of fulfilling personal desires. As is the case with so many of the topics and questions Jung considers, his views on death range wide, moving readily between poles that more "consistent" thinkers might regard as contradictions. Jung will have more to say about death when he encounters "Death" in person, in *Liber Secundus,* Chapter VI.

"Chapter IV: The Anchorite," pp. 267-70

Jung next describes a vision (December 30, 1913) in which he follows footprints under a desert sun to the abode of an anchorite. Jung had ended the previous chapter with a resolve to seek "the place of the inner life" (RB, p. 267b), and he now encounters a man who for the past ten or more years had withdrawn from society into the Libyan desert in order to lead a contemplative life focused on a deep reading of the gospels and communion with Christ.

ON LANGUAGE AND INTERPRETATION

Jung queries how it is that the anchorite can have occupied himself all of these years with only a copy of the gospels, and the anchorite replies that a book can be read many times and new thoughts occur with each reading. The anchorite adds that Jung must be a pagan if he truly sees one and the same meaning each time he reads a holy book. According to the anchorite, while men endeavor to assign a singular meaning to scripture "in order to have an unambiguous language" (RB, p. 268b), no "succession of words" has an unambiguous single significance. Further, "only to the all-knowing is it given to know all the meanings" (RB, p. 268b).

Jung asks whether the anchorite, like "a few Jewish scholars" (RB, p. 268b), believes that scripture has both an exoteric and esoteric meaning. The anchorite describes this as a "bad superstition," and he appears to maintain, instead, like many postmodernists, that textual meaning changes, and that such changes are revealed with the changing circumstances and perspective of the reader (RB, p. 268a). We should here recall that Nietzsche, in his *Notebooks* of 1886-8, had repeatedly stated that there are no facts only interpretations.[11] Jung seems to be struggling with this issue, and we will shortly see that he endorses fixed meanings as a sort of bulwark against the flux, an idea that seems to contradict, or at least set limits upon his view of the importance of chaos.

The conversation moves into other issues pertaining to the philosophy and theology of language, as the anchorite discourses on the question of whether language (i.e., the "word" or "Logos" in the Gospel of John) is itself a reality (as opposed to reality's representation). The anchorite relates that prior to becoming a Christian, he had been a pagan philosopher who had taught both Greek philosophy and the "new" system of Philo the Jew to his many students. The anchorite's discourse here is not completely transparent, but his view seems to be that for Philo, "words and names" attained divine power but were divorced from the life of mankind. The anchorite warns against such an elevation of language, saying that "words should not become Gods" (RB, p. 268b). According to the anchorite, while the Gospel of John echoes Philo's notion that "God was the word," it does so in the context of the passion of Christ, in which the word became incarnated in man, and thus infused with life (RB, p. 269a).

Years later, Jung will argue that "the danger that faces us today is that the whole of reality will be replaced by words" (CW 10, § 882). This is because men and women, especially those who dwell in cities, "lack all contact with the life and breath of nature" and know natural objects like rabbits and cows only by their words or pictorial representations.

We thus find Jung, in *The Red Book*, struggling with questions pertaining to the nature of language and the possibility of an objective representation of the world. Jung is especially concerned with the question of whether words point to specifiable ideas, kinds, and things, or are rather always subject to an indefinite series of reinterpretations. This was a question that was paramount in the minds of many intellectuals during the period that Jung was writing *The Red Book*. It was, for example, around this time that a young Ludwig Wittgenstein was writing in his *Notebooks* the ideas about language that were to eventuate in the "picture theory of meaning" in his *Tractatus Logico Philosophicus*.[12] In that work we find the idea, which Wittgenstein himself was later to repudiate, that the fundamental units ("Names") and statements ("Elementary Propositions") in language pictured unique states of affairs in the world, i.e. "atomic facts", thereby saving language, thought, and reality from an indefinite regress of interpretations. Wittgenstein was later to abandon the picture theory of meaning for the notion of "meaning as use," which opened up nearly infinite possibilities of linguistic interpretation and understanding.[13] Jung, in *The Red Book*, seems to be torn between these two views: on the one hand, he considers the idea that language and the world are fluid and open to indefinite interpretations; on the other hand, he is attracted to the notion that there are specifiable meanings, archetypes, that can be grasped and circumscribed by words.

While in his dialog with the anchorite Jung suggests that the reinterpretability thesis is a Jewish doctrine, he also attributes it to the Gnostics, stating that the idea that "the sequence of words have many meanings...does not sound properly Christian" (RB, p. 271a). Jung accuses the Gnostics of being "the worst of all the idolators of words..." (RB, p. 271a). Indeed, Jung bemoans the fact that in our scientific age, words have replaced the Gods. Later in *Liber Secundus* the sick god Izdubar asks Jung "Have you no Gods anymore?" To which Jung responds, "No, words are all we have...Science has taken from us the capacity of belief" (RB, p. 279a).

A RAMPART AGAINST THE FLUX

While in his *Draft* to an earlier section of *The Red Book* (*Liber Primus*, Ch. VIII), Jung noted that "You read as much into a book as out of it" (RB, p. 244, n. 145), Jung here suggests that while "things" are subject to limitless interpretations, "words" can set limits to meaning (RB, p. 270a). (This is apparent in the writing of biography or history, where ambiguous events are described in a narrative that provides them with a circumscribed, if not completely definite significance.) Jung writes that we must accept both the limitless and the limited, "since life flows not only down an infinite path but a finite one" (RB, p. 270a). However, since the infinite and unbounded give rise to anxiety (RB, p. 270a), we seek a constraint on meaning: "You cry out for the word which has one meaning and no other, so that you escape boundless ambiguity" (RB, p. 270a). Jung goes so far as to say that "the word becomes your God, since it protects you from countless possibilities of interpretation" (RB, p. 270a). He suggests that "the word is a protective magic against the daimons of the unending" (RB, p. 270a), and at this point in *The Red Book*, he seems to ignore or reject the views that such protection is either futile, or that the effort to stem the tide of meaning and interpretation can quickly lead to dogmatism. Jung recognizes that when one "breaks the wall of words [one] overthrows Gods and defiles temples," but he holds that "no one should shatter the old words, unless he finds the new word that is a firm rampart against the limitless and grasps more life in it than the old word" (RB, p. 270a).

While at many points in *The Red Book* Jung adopts a relativist and constructivist view of meaning and knowledge, at this point in *Liber Secundus* he holds that a circumscribed and life-affirming system of thought and language is superior, or at least complementary, to an infinite and boundless one, even if it appears the latter has a stronger claim to truth. This is a view that Jung became increasingly attracted to in the years subsequent to his work on *Liber Novus*. While Jung, like Nietzsche, insisted that one must be open to chaos, Jung was not quite willing to hurl himself into that chaos without recourse to a belief system. Having seen the demise of the "system of the Gods," Jung ultimately replaced it with a "system of archetypes" that served both as a new rampart against the flux, and a new source of collective meaning.

As we have seen, in *The Red Book* there is a tension between and blending together of existential and mythological views of life and the world, a tension that reflects the distinction between an open-ended and determinate view of the nature of linguistic meaning. According to the former world-view, one discovers the depths of one's soul through a courageous encounter with chaos, madness, and the infinite possibilities of sense and nonsense. According to the latter, one develops one's soul through the assimilation of a personal/collective myth, which occurs through an encounter with the enduring meanings of the archetypes of the collective unconscious. This tension between the existential and the mythological is reflected in the double view of language in *The Red Book*.

Narrative "Truth"

Questions surrounding the ambiguity of reality and text have direct implications for the practice of analytic and other forms of dynamic psychotherapy. If things, images, and words are inherently ambiguous and subject to indefinite reinterpretation, we lose the possibility of attaining a definitive interpretation of a symptom or dream, or arriving at a narrative "truth" about the self. Jung, of course, was too committed a Platonist to surrender all "truth," and while he acknowledged the role of "chaos" as a phase in the individuation of the Self, he ultimately, even in *The Red Book*, his most radical and skeptical work, questioned the wisdom of deconstructing the ramparts against it. Jung had already focused upon collective meanings in his 1912 work, *Transformations and Symbols of the Libido*, and this focus is, in various places, carried over into *The Red Book*, and *The Red Book's* tension between Platonism and relativism, which is paralleled by Jung's description of the supreme meaning as a fusion of sense and absurdity (RB, p. 229b).

A DECONSTRUCTIVE MOMENT

On balance, however, *The Red Book* represents the "chaotic," deconstructive moment or phase in the development of Jung's analytic psychology, while his later emphasis upon the collective meanings constitutes its reconstructive moment. We might ask what Jungian psychology would look like had Jung remained fully in the throes of the chaos, ambiguity, and relativism that he advocated at many points in *Liber Novus*? *The Red Book* may be quite shocking to many Jungians, and one reason for this is that it is far more deconstructive (of science, reason, meaning, etc.) than any of Jung's other works.

Why, we might ask, is *The Red Book* more "deconstructive" and relativistic than Jung's later writings? An answer might be forthcoming if we consider Jung's own psychology during the period of the work's development and composition. As Stein has pointed out, *The Red Book* represents Jung's "mid-life" crisis, a "destructuring" and entering into "liminality," which was followed by a restructuring phase,[14] one that took hold with Jung's work on alchemy. Schwartz-Salant makes a similar point, when he argues that Jung's confrontation with chaos and disorder in *The Red Book* facilitated his confrontation with his own narcissism and resulted in his personal transformation. It is for this reason, according to Schwartz-Salant, that disorder plays a much more significant role in *The Red Book* than in Jung's later work.[15] Later, when Jung came to make a deep study of what he understood to be the psychological implications of European alchemy, he concluded that a chaotic phase in the alchemical process (the *nigredo*) is followed by an integrative phase (*albedo, citrinitas,* and *rubedo* (CW 14, § 307) in which the archetypes of the shadow, *anima/animus,* and the *senex* (wise old man), are integrated in the realization of a whole self.

UNLEARNING

Two other themes make their appearance in Chapter IV of *Liber Secundus*: the values of "unlearning" (*Umlernen*—retraining, new learning, or changing of one's ideas) and "solitude." The anchorite who, as we recall, had been a pagan philosopher before taking up the gospels, tells Jung that he "spent many years alone with the process of unlearning" (RB, p. 269a) in order to effect his conversion. The anchorite reflects that for a "successful teacher" such as himself, it is "difficult or even impossible" to unlearn what one has been teaching. I am here reminded of Thomas Kuhn's observation that in order for an old scientific paradigm to be replaced by a new one, scientists of the generation that supported and taught the original paradigm must either retire or die[16]—such is the hold of ideas on man's psyche!

Later in his career, Jung will speak of the benefits of "unlearning" in a more practical, psychotherapeutic context, when he will exhort psychotherapists to "Learn the best, know the best—and then forget everything when you face the patient." (CW 10, § 882). In this view one must forget or at least "suspend" one's learning and theories in order to listen to and experience the patient in his or her uniqueness.

The Value of Solitude

Jung reflects upon the value of solitude: "In the desert the solitary is relieved of care and therefore turns his whole life to the sprouting garden of his soul, which can flourish only under a hot sun (RB, p. 269b). As we have seen, in *Liber Primus* Jung described his own imaginative solitary experiences in the desert, and the entire *Red Book* can be understood as a witness to the soul-making opportunities afforded by solitude. While Jung often couches his search for his soul in terms of interactions and dialogs with various "others," it is clear that each of these others, each of these figures, are products of his imagination, and while they each reflect archetypal attitudes or principles, they are all, in an important sense, aspects of Jung himself. Martin Buber will later criticize Jung for making the encounter with God a solitary, interior affair, as opposed to an "I-thou" encounter with fellow human beings and the world,[17] and indeed, as we will soon see, Jung himself expresses some doubts about the anchorite's solitary quest and suggests the possibility that religious meaning is best obtained by one who is "nearer to men" (RB, p. 272b). A similar question arises with respect to the role of isolation versus interaction in the discovery of one's soul. Jung's appeal to *so many imaginary others* raises doubts about his claim that the solitary can discover his soul in his own garden.

"Chapter V: Dies II (Day II)," pp. 270-73

Chapter V opens with an image of the philosophical tree (**RB Image, p. 22**). While the philosophical tree was often spoken of as an "inverted tree," having its roots in heaven and its branches in the earth (CW 13, § 410), the tree depicted here appears to be rooted and blooming equally in both heaven and earth, suggesting that the psyche has its roots both in "heavenly" and "netherworldly" forces. Indeed, much of *The Red Book* is predicated on this very notion—that the individual must accept, even nourish, those personal characteristics and aspects of the self that one would otherwise find repugnant, dark, and evil. Here, in this chapter of *The Red Book*, Jung will declare that one must descend into darkness in order to ascend to the sun god, Helios, and experience the light within oneself (RB, p. 272b). In his 1945 essay on "The Philosophical Tree," Jung wrote: "A person whose roots are above as well as below is thus like a tree growing simultaneously downwards and upwards. The goal is neither height nor depth, but the center" (CW 13, § 333).

"No More Prayers"

Jung has a vision of "four white horses, each with golden wings" (RB, p. 270b) that pull the carriage with which the god Helios moves the sun across the sky. Jung recalls that the anchorite, who he now refers to as Ammonius, had reminded him to say his morning prayers with the rising of the sun (RB, p. 270b). Jung finds himself becoming critical of the anchorite, reflecting that the anchorite's declarations that texts have multiple meanings and that "John brought the Logos to man" sound more Gnostic than Christian (RB, p. 271a). Further, Jung cannot comply with the anchorite's reminder to pray, for the anchorite does not know that Jung as a modern man has "no more prayers" (RB, p. 270a). Jung can, however, pray *to the sun* (rather than praying to God *with the sunrise*) for "one can never escape the age-old dreams of mankind" (RB, p. 271a). Jung questions how Ammonius could have endured his life as an anchorite for even a year, and then suddenly, to his own surprise, Jung finds himself praying to a scarab and worshipping a stone.

While it is clear that Jung prays (RB, p. 248b, p. 303a) and recites incantations (RB, pp. 284-86, p. 353b) at several places in the course of *The Red Book*, in *Scrutinies* he suggests that there is no value in prayer or worship of the Gods (RB, p. 351b), and that one's prayers are best directed at one's own "inner infinity" (RB, p. 354a). In line with this view, Jung will in 1934 compare prayer to paying attention to the dreams that one has when confronted with a problem that cannot be resolved through one's own resources (CW 9i, § 44), and towards the end of his life in 1958 he will suggest that prayer involves a compensation for "the superstitious belief in man's will and ability" (CW 10, § 679).

Jung now has a second encounter with the anchorite, one that does not end well. Jung explains to Ammonius that he could not pray to the Christian God but that in a dream he had prayed to the sun, and in his "absentmindedness," had also prayed to a scarab and to the earth. Surprisingly, the anchorite is not initially disturbed; he tells Jung that the prayer to the sun will suffice and that Jung shouldn't regret or condemn himself for these actions. Ammonius proceeds to tell Jung how he was drawn to Christianity, which he had first understood in terms of Egyptian teachings about the dismembered and resurrected God Osiris, and which even black slaves from the region of the Nile understand in a simpler form. Jung and the anchorite then reflect upon the nature of religion, Ammonius suggesting that all religions are the same in their "innermost essence" and that "every subsequent form of religion is the meaning of the antecedent" (RB, p. 272b). These quasi-Hegelian ideas are considered only in passing.

JUNG AS PAGAN AND SATAN

Jung begins to irritate the anchorite by questioning whether Ammonius might better succeed in learning the meaning of a religion that "is yet to come" if he ended his isolation and were "nearer men" (RB, p. 272b). Ammonius defends his life in the desert, but makes a crucial verbal slip when he says, "Here you can see the countenance of the sun every day, you are alone, you can see glorious Helios…"(RB, p. 272b).[18] Catching himself, the anchorite exclaims, "Helios—no, that is pagan," and now blaming Jung for having re-inserted the pagan god into his mind, Ammonius declares that Jung is Satan, and tries to lunge at Jung, who is, however, untouchable because he is "far away in the twentieth-century" (RB, p. 272b).[19]

Welcoming the anchorite's charge that he is the devil, Jung comments, "*He who comprehends the darkness in himself, to him the light is near*" (RB, p. 272b). Jung adds that one who "*climbs down into his darkness*" ascends to the "*fire-maned Helios*" (RB, p. 272b). It is clear that Jung is here rejecting the anchorite's version of Christianity in favor of a more polytheistic paganism that incorporates elements of the dark side of divinity and the Self. In *Psychological Types* Jung considered St. Anthony's warning to his disciples that the devil comes in many disguises. In what can readily be interpreted as a comment on the anchorite in *The Red Book*, Jung remarked that the devil is "the voice of the anchorite's [St. Anthony's] own unconscious, in revolt against the forcible suppression of his nature" (CW 6, § 82). In *The Red Book* we learn that because Jung "accepted [his] own darkness," he "had to appear to [the anchorite] as the devil," and unlike the anchorite who "was sucked empty by the desert" (RB, p. 273a), Jung "ate the earth…(and) drank the sun, and…became a greening tree that stands alone and grows" (RB, p. 273b).

Meaning, Psyche, and World

We have already seen how Jung, in *Liber Primus* and throughout *The Red Book,* suggests that events only have meaning within the human psyche (RB, p. 239a). He now makes some interesting comments on the "secret life" or soul that exists in all things, and how the spirit of the world, the *anima mundi,* is inextricably *bound with the soul of man.* All things, Jung says in an idealist and vitalist moment, live off one's life-force, and "Nothing happens in which you are not entangled in a secret manner; for everything has ordered itself around you and plays your innermost" (RB, p. 273a). Jung's *metaphysical* meaning here is not completely transparent, but his *psychological* point is clear: the anchorite erred in attempting to find himself through contemplating the meaning of scripture. He would have been better served had he engaged in an encounter with himself. Jung says, the anchorite "wanted to find meaning in the outer. But you find meaning only in yourself…"(RB, p. 273b) This is because "the meanings that follow one another do not lie in things" but rather lie in one who participates in life (RB, p. 273b). It is senseless to look for meaning in things (or in scripture) for if "you change, the countenance of the world alters" (RB, p. 273b). In this, Jung is expressing a stoic, inspired attitude that is essential to most, if not all psychotherapies, from psychoanalytic to cognitive and narrative forms of treatment. The psyche is comprised of meanings, and it is the alteration of these meanings, as opposed to the objects to which they purportedly refer, that is the goal (almost by definition) of all psychotherapeutic treatment. Jung, in this section of *The Red Book*, takes this idea a step further, as he appears to be of the view that the world itself is directly affected by psychical events. This is an idea that Jung will pick up on years later when his interest turns to the phenomena involved in synchronicity and parapsychology (CW 8, pp. 404-415 and pp. 417-519).

"Chapter VI: Death," pp. 273-75

The text of Chapter VI explores Jung's encounter with death, and it is prefaced with a painting (**RB Image, p. 29**) of a fearsome multi-armed beast, rising out of a cool sun in a dark indigo night. One could certainly take such a foreboding image for "death," but in the text Jung describes "death" as "wearing a black, wrinkled coat" (RB, p. 273b). We will later suggest, in connection with a similar beast in **RB Image, p. 61**, that the monster in **RB Image, p. 29** may be Jung himself!

In the text, Jung now follows his "brother," the sea, to a "broad dead lake" and then to a "remote horizon, where the sky and the sea are fused into infinity" (RB, p. 273b). There Jung meets Death, "gaunt and with a deeply serious look in his eyes" (RB, p. 273b), and this encounter prompts a series of new reflections on the significance of death for life. Flowing past him in an "enormous stream," Jung sees animals, insects, a forest, faded flowers, a "dead summer," and "densely pressed multitudes of men, old men, women and children..." all heading for their dissolution in a "a sea of blood" (RB, p. 274b) from which there arises a "new sun," one that emanates from darkness and shines "bloody and burning like a great downfall" (RB, p. 274b).

Jung writes that one must taste "the coldness of death" if one is to have clarity of vision (RB, p. 274b). Jung now speaks of a death drive: "Life wants to live and to die, to begin and to end" (RB, p. 274b). A balance must be struck between life and death, but modern man has dangerously tipped the balance in favor of life. However, death is the condition for the full life: "If I accept death, my tree greens" (RB, p. 274b). Jung again anticipates Heidegger when he writes: "Without death, life would be meaningless...limitation enables you to fulfill your being" (RB, p. 275a).

Shamdasani (RB, p. 274, n. 74) notes that Jung had accepted the death instinct in *Transformations and Symbols of the Libido*. There, Jung had described how "the active fructifying (upward striving) form of the libido is changed into the negative force striving downwards towards death" (CW B, § 606; cf. CW 5, § 596, "an unconscious longing for death"). It is important, however, to distinguish between these intimations of a "death instinct," and the view, expressed by Jung in *The Red Book*, that death is a condition for the meaning of life. These two ideas (one quasi-biological, the other existential) are quite distinct, though Jung in *Transformations and Symbols of the Libido* hints at a possible relationship between the biological and the existential when he writes that the "the highest summit of life is expressed through the symbolism of death...for creation beyond oneself means personal death" (CW B, § 441; cf. CW 5, § 432). Jung is here speaking quite literally and biologically, i.e., that the "coming generation is the end of the preceding one" (CW B, § 441), but we might also understand him as making the claim that a death (or at least transcendence) of the personal ego is implicit in the creative and generative acts that give meaning to self and others.

Evil and Virtue

Jung writes that his confrontation with and comprehension of his own darkness plunged him "into the depths of the millennia," resulting in his rebirth as his "phoenix ascended" (RB, p. 274b). Jung again engages in the play of opposites, commenting that in his own time the virtues had been transformed into their contraries, and that now evil stands behind one's virtues and is actually the substance of those virtues themselves. Jung's meaning here is not transparent, but we might consider at least three possibilities (a *fourth* will be considered shortly): (1) *psychologically*, without an acknowledgment of evil, one's virtues become subject to destructive unconscious impulses and archetypes—thus *recognition* of one's evil is the *sine qua non* of actual good; (2) *metaphysically*, only in a world of manifest evil, one on the brink of moral disaster, can virtues reach their highest expression— thus the existence of evil is a condition for the actualization of the good; (3) *historically*, Satan, who had been "locked in the abyss for a millennium" and considered nothing but a "children's fairy tale" (RB, p. 274b), must be reinstated, if both God and the human soul are to be redeemed and fulfilled. Behind this last possibility is Jung's view that Christianity had been prematurely grafted onto a barbaric German psyche, and that it is only through the re-emergence of this barbarism that there can be a creative revitalization of the European spirit and a new experience of the divine (CW 10, § 16-17). In any case, one who wishes an encounter with his soul must taste of both the devil and hell.

It is one thing to philosophize about the significance of death and the evil that "stands behind one's virtues," and quite another thing to actually experience the death and evil within oneself. Jung now describes a "satanic apparition" in which he exalts "blood and murder" and sees the "beauty of bloody acts of violence" (RB, p. 275a). Recognizing the repulsive arising within himself, Jung "curses the hours of [his] birth seven times" (RB, p. 275a), and apparently wavers between suicide and awaiting his "second birth." After three nights of immersion in death, life begins to stir within him again.

Jung, of course, is not the first to recognize a certain beauty and even value in violence and evil—Dante's *Inferno* is a poetic vision of sadism and torture, and it lies at the very heart of western culture. We have already seen how in the East, the "demonic divine" harnesses wrath and other evil traits in the service of compassion. I am also reminded of the Talmudic saying: "The greater the *yetzer hara* (evil impulse), the greater the *tzaddik* (saint)" (Talmud Tractate *Succah* 52a), which can been interpreted to suggest that the *tzaddik* harnesses intense drives for sex, power, and aggression into his or her compassionate and other positive works. We thus have a fourth interpretation of Jung's "claim that evil stands behind one's virtues": It does so by supplying the energy that drives them.

"Chapter VII: The Remains of Earlier Temples," pp. 275-77

This chapter is prefaced with a painting of a generally blue-toned circle within which are two egg-shaped images that surround tiny human figures wearing large pointed hats (**RB Image, p. 32**). Shamdasani (RB, p. 275, n. 81) points out that this painting resembles the mosaics found in Ravenna, which Jung had visited in 1913 and 1914. Many of the images in *The Red Book* leave one with the impression of a whole composed of fragmented or mosaic elements (e.g. **RB Images, p. 36, p. 72, p. 79, p. 115, p. 133, p. 135**), perhaps suggesting the process whereby fragmented psychical states are integrated and articulated into a united Self.

THE CRITIQUE OF "IDEALS"

In a rather odd adventure (indeed, they are all odd), Jung encounters two of his former interlocutors, the "Red One" and Ammonius (the anchorite), walking together in a meadow carpeted with flowers. Recall that the "Red One" appeared to Jung as his "devil," and that Jung himself had been the devil for Ammonius. Neither of these figures is happy to see Jung. They each claim that Jung had influenced them profoundly, but in each case the influence was for ill. Ammonius says that Jung's remark that closeness with others was required to reach "the higher mysteries" stunned him "like infernal poison" (RB, p. 275b), first prompting him to form a "monastery with the brothers" (RB, p. 275b), and later leading him to visit Alexandria out of an "insatiable greed to see the world" (RB, p. 276a). There Ammonius became involved with drinking and women before coming to his senses and returning to the monastery. The Red One, for his part, was so influenced by Jung's seriousness that he entered a monastery himself, did penance, and was converted to Christianity, hardly a fit outcome for the devil. Eventually, the two found one another and became inseparable, if quarrelsome, companions. Jung humorously describes how Ammonius finds the devil necessary to help him command others' respect, and how the devil must make an "arrangement with the clergy", if he doesn't want to lose his clientele (RB, p. 276a).

However, Jung faults each of them for becoming mired in the "burial ground of all outlived ideals" (RB, p. 276b). Indeed, Jung had titled a previous draft of this section, "Degenerate Ideals" (RB, p. 275, n. 80). Jung, too, was a slave to ideals prior to his first encounter with the Red One, but had since experienced the transvaluation of his earlier values, in part due to the Red One's influence. Jung, in a Nietzschean mood, now provides a general critique of ideals which he sees as the perishable products of human meaning-making. One who believes that he is living his ideals suffers from "delusions of grandeur" and behaves like a lunatic hero, at which point his ideals "crack open" and "play carnival" with him (RB, p. 276b).

THE "NATURAL BEING"

However, now that his "ideals have come down," Jung experiences a "greening" as a "natural being" (RB, p. 276b). The ideals, symbolized by the anchorite and the Red One, stand as "remains of earlier temples" (RB, p. 276b), but Jung has "greened and bloomed from within," and, at least for the time being, is able to live happily without attachment to either the world or spirit, allowing "the suffering and joy of men [to] pass over [him] with equanimity" (RB, p. 277a). Jung suggests that this "natural state" is one in which he is not conscious of himself— for the moment one becomes self-conscious, one falls "from one grave into another" (RB, p. 277a) in the endless cycle of rebirths that caused the Buddha to eventually give up on rebirth altogether (RB, p. 277a). Jung suggests that by giving up on ideals (and presumably by surrendering the desires that ideals entail) one is at least metaphorically freed from the cycle of reincarnation. He writes, "Neither good nor evil shall be my masters," and as such Jung can now exist "from [his] own force" (RB, p. 277b), take responsibility for himself, "talk to the trees and the forest wild life", and live in nature. In this condition, Jung says, he is ready to wander to the east (RB, p. 277b).

What are we to make of this "nature" state that Jung describes? Certainly, he is not positing it as some kind of goal or ideal—after all, it resulted precisely from the demise of all ideals. Jung suggests that this state came about once he abandoned his struggle with God (RB, p. 277a); but as we will see in the next section, it is this very struggle that is now renewed with great force in a surprising way.

THE PATH TO INDIVIDUATION

As Stein has pointed out, each of Jung's imagined encounters in the opening chapters of *Liber Secundus* involves a confrontation with a life attitude or collective archetype that must be assimilated and differentiated from on the path to Jung's individuation.[20] In his confrontation with the Red One, Jung assimilated the attitude of pleasure and joy; with the maiden in the forest, he came to accept the wisdom in ordinariness and "banality;" with the rogue, he acknowledged the significance of one's "depths" and despair; in his confrontation with Death, he came to recognize the great significance of death for the fulfilled life; and, as we have just seen, in his interactions with the anchorite, he learned the necessity of abandoning outmoded and outlived ideals. While Jung argues with several of these figures, and ultimately moves on from each of them, these "soul-making encounters" constitute the early stages of Jung's path to individuation and the re-discovery of his soul. While one may not necessarily follow Jung in assimilating and differentiating from the precise psychic contents symbolized by the inner figures in *The Red Book*, the way to individuation is clear. One find one's soul, and becomes a fully individuated self, through an imaginative and/or life process in which one confronts, embraces, differentiates from, and ultimately alters one's personal "devil," i.e. the rejected, "other" aspects of one's psyche. As we have seen, Jung's message is that we must take our own devil seriously (RB, p. 261a). However,

> Taking the devil seriously does not mean going over to his side, or else one becomes the devil. Rather it means coming to an understanding. Therefore you accept your other standpoint. (RB, p. 261a)

As Stein notes, it is not only Jung who changes as a result of his encounters with his inner figures, but these figures change as well.[21] It is clear, for example, that Ammonius and the Red One have themselves been altered, and as will become evident, Philemon, who is perhaps the most significant inner figure in *The Red Book*, is himself transformed over time, as he moves from being a cryptic and reticent figure to an active guide and teacher. We might say that individuation, which is nothing if not a creative process, has the potential to impact the world as well as the Self, and to actually alter the manner in which the archetypes of the collective unconscious manifest themselves both in the individual and the collective.

Chapter 5

The Healing of Izdubar

The Red Book: Liber Secundus

"Chapter VIII: First Day," pp. 277-81

In one of *The Red Book's* most dramatic and memorable episodes, one that provides an important key to understanding his entire oeuvre, Jung tells of his encounters with the sick God, Izdubar. This God, who Jung pictures with a full page painting in **RB Image, p. 36,** is described as possessing a ruffled black beard "decked with exquisite stones" (RB, p. 278a), two bull horns rising from his head, with a "rattling suit of armour" over his chest, and carrying a "sparkling double axe in his hand" (RB, p. 278). Yet Izdubar's face reveals a "consuming inner fear and his hands and knees tremble" (RB, p. 278a), a fear that intensifies when Jung explains to him the spherical nature of the earth and other proven truths of science.

Izdubar is another erroneous[1] name for the god Gilgamesh, who is thought to have been a historical Sumerian king who was later deified. Jung had written about "Gilgamesh" in *Transformations and Symbols of the Libido*, where he described Gilgamesh as a powerful hero (CW B, § 310; cf. CW 5, § 293). In *The Red Book* Izdubar is the ailing God who Jung must heal and in effect re-create.

In Jung's painting, a tiny figure worshipping at Izdubar's feet highlights the God's enormous size. Izdubar is surrounded by snakes and reptiles. Shamdasani notes that the image very much resembles an illustration in a book by Wilhelm Roscher (1884), a copy of which Jung owned (RB, p. 277, n. 96).

A second illustration (**RB Image, p. 37**) introduces the chapter. A primitive man holds a serpent over his head that bursts into a star. This is adjacent to a scene in which a star in space is surrounded by a serpentine form, possibly symbolizing the "evil" aspect of one's inner star (RB, p. 354a). Later in the chapter there is another pleasing image (**RB Image, p. 40**) in which the drop-case "I" that serves as an illustration for the word "Ich" (I) traverses a serpentine form. Behind it is a dark purple space occupied by snakes and four strange insect-like creatures in each corner.

THE POISON OF SCIENCE

Jung writes that Izdubar has been lamed by science, a science that humanity has grown accustomed to, but which, Jung acknowledges, has somewhat lamed man as well. Science, Jung informs Izdubar, has also taken from man his capacity to believe in the gods. Jung acknowledges that while science is "poison", it also contains "truth," a juxtaposition that Izdubar finds unfathomable. The God asks Jung whether "our astrologers and priests also speak the truth" (RB, p. 278b), to which Jung responds that there are two sources of truth: one, from science, which is derived from a knowledge of "outer things," and another, from the priests, which is derived from "inner things." Yet Jung acknowledges that he, as a man of his time, no longer has Gods, but only "words" (RB, p. 279a). Izdubar asks if these words are "powerful," and marvels that Jung's science has not succeeded in producing human immortality.

JUNG'S CRITIQUE OF SCIENCE

In *The Red Book*, Jung is highly critical of science, a posture that contrasts with his general attitude in his *Collected Works*, where he frequently describes himself as a physician who has great respect for empirical scientific methods. Reading the *Collected Works* may lead one to conclude that Jung's method is more phenomenological or hermeneutic than natural-scientific, and there are indeed places where he casts science, reason, and technology in a negative light (for example, in *Aion* where he writes about the "Luciferian development of science and technology"—CW 9ii, § 68), but it is only in *The Red Book* that science is placed under such a sustained attack. As we have just seen, in *The Red Book* it is science with its "awful magic" (RB, p. 279a) that has poisoned and lamed the god Izdubar, a god who wonders how it could be that Jung is "still alive even though [he] drink[s] from this poison every day" (RB, p. 279a).

It will be useful at this point to examine some of Jung's views on science as they were expressed both in *Liber Novus* and in his "scientific" writing during *The Red Book* period. Jung is clear that for him, science is a perhaps necessary evil. He says to the ailing Izdubar:

> We had to swallow the poison of science. Otherwise we would have met the same fate as you have: we'd be completely lamed, if we encountered it unsuspecting and unprepared. This poison is so insurmountably strong that everyone, even the strongest, and even the eternal Gods, perish because of it. If our life is dear to us, we prefer to sacrifice a piece of our life force rather than abandon ourselves to certain death. (RB, p. 279a)

It is unclear whether Jung is here even of the view that science has in some ways preserved and enhanced human life; Jung seems to hold that one accepts science to avert total disaster, but in the process one's life is robbed of at least some of its spirit and meaning. The effects of science are insidious as it causes men to be lamed, poisoned, and lacking without their being aware of its ill effects (RB, p. 283a).

Jung gives voice to a somewhat more generous view of science later in *The Red Book* when he encounters a "librarian" from whom he requests a copy of Thomas à Kempis's *The Imitation of Christ*, a fifteenth-century book of religious instruction and devotional piety. Jung says to the librarian, "You know that I value science extraordinarily highly. But there are actually moments in life where science also leaves us empty and sick. In such moments a book like Thomas's means very much to me since it was written from the soul" (RB, p. 292b).

Later, Jung takes up the subject of science in a conversation he has with his own soul, where he expresses doubt about abandoning science "for the sake of magic," which he finds "uncanny and menacing" (RB, p. 308a) In *Scrutinies*, Jung's soul tells him: "You should become serious and hence take your leave from science. There is too much childishness in it. Your way goes toward the depths. Science is too superficial, mere language, mere tools. But you must set to work" (RB, p. 336b). Ironically, given the charges by Karl Popper and others that Freudian psychoanalysis is non-scientific, the "science" that Jung most immediately "takes leave of", via *The Red Book*, is Freud's.

What is the "way that goes to the depths," if it is not science? Jung's answer, one that is implicit in *The Red Book* and explicit in *Psychological Types*, is that fantasy as opposed to reason is the road to the depths of the psyche. Indeed, *The Red Book* is built around what Jung would later call "active imagination." In *Psychological Types*, which was written during the same period as Jung's work on *Liber Novus*, Jung argues that creative fantasy is the bridge that unites thinking and feeling, and thus offers the means of uniting the *science of psychology* with a psychology of human *experience* (CW 6, § 84).

Jung maintains that if psychology insists on being a science, it must exclude the perspective of both feeling and fantasy. This is because, by definition, science is an "affair of the intellect" (CW 6, § 84). However, by excluding feeling and fantasy, a scientific psychology functions from a standpoint that cannot do full justice to its subject matter; indeed any science of psychology would itself be directed by feeling and creative fantasy in its practical application, i.e. when it is "placed at the service of a creative power and purpose" (CW 6, § 84). Jung sees "fantasy" as fulfilling the role of the "higher third" that unites the opposing principles of intellect and feeling, and which thereby brings psychology to life. Although Jung does not make this explicit either in *The Red Book* or *Psychological Types*, he is of the view that creative fantasy, as opposed, for example, to tradition or science itself, is what does and should provide psychology with its guiding values. Indeed, much of *The Red Book* can be understood as a sustained effort to arrive at such values through Jung's own creative and imaginative process. For Jung, these values are often opposed to those of conventional morality.

Jung asserts that acts of creative fantasy are exemplars of human freedom, a freedom that is, by definition, excluded by the very nature of the empirical scientific attitude (CW 6, § 532). Reading Jung's disdain for science in *The Red Book* through the lens of his comments in *Psychological Types*, we might arrive at the view that a natural scientific psychology has value but is woefully incomplete, as it can neither provide an account of nor impetus to the acts of creative imagination and freedom that lend meaning both to life and to science itself; the pretense that it can provide such meaning is the source of its "poison."

These ideas are given further expression in Jung's "Commentary on 'The Secret of the Golden Flower,'" which was written in 1929, and which, by Jung's own account, marked the abandonment of his work on *The Red Book* (RB, p. 360). In this commentary on an ancient Chinese text, Jung is far more charitable to science than he is in *The Red Book*, but continues to be cognizant of its limitations:

> Science is not, indeed, a perfect instrument, but it is a superior and indispensable one that works harm only when taken as an end in itself…Science is the tool of the Western mind and with it more doors can be opened than with bare hands. It is part and parcel of our knowledge and obscures insight only when it holds that the understanding given by it is the only kind there is. (CW 14, § 2)

Jung continues that "the East teaches us another, broader, more profound, and higher understanding—understanding through life" (CW 14, § 2). Such an understanding is higher because it is not limited to a single psychic function, the intellect, but includes feeling and intuition as well (CW 14, § 7). On the other hand, if the great scientific advances of the West were to be complemented by a full appreciation of these other psychic functions, "the West might expect to surpass the East by a very great margin" (CW 14, § 8).

Jung's views lead to a very broad definition of psychology, one that would include empirical science as just one of (and indeed not the highest of) its components. Within such a definition, philosophers, mystics, writers of fiction, and artists of all types, would be regarded as potentially making significant contributions to psychology, and, indeed, even the most cursory reading of Jung's own writings reveals this to be Jung's point of view. In an essay first published in 1946 and revised in 1954, Jung reflected upon his own career as an empirical scientist:

> I fancied I was working along the best scientific lines, establishing facts, observing, classifying, describing causal and functional relations, only to discover in the end that I had involved myself in a net of reflections which extend far

beyond natural science and ramify into the fields of philosophy, theology, comparative religion, and the humane sciences in general. (CW 8, § 421)

Interestingly, a similar view was early on expressed by Freud, who observed that his own case studies necessarily read like works of imaginative literature:

> [I]t still strikes me myself as strange that the case histories I write should read like short stories and that, as one might say, they lack the serious stamp of science. I must console myself with the reflection that the nature of the subject is evidently responsible for this, rather than any preference of my own. The fact is that local diagnosis and electrical reactions lead nowhere in the study of hysteria, whereas a detailed description of mental processes such as we are accustomed to find in the works of imaginative writers enables me, with the use of a few psychological formulas, to obtain at least some kind of insight into the course of that affection.[2]

Our own time has witnessed a progressive narrowing of the psychological gaze so as to exclude philosophy, literature, mysticism, art, and theology on the grounds that these are marginal to psychology's goal of creating a *science* of human cognition and behavior. In the process, Jungians, Freudians, and others who refuse to swallow what Jung described as the "poison" of a *scientistic* psychology have been marginalized, if not completely excluded from the field.

One further thought: We might ask if Jung is not too quick to turn to creative imagination as the *only* vehicle to a psychology that is true to life and the soul. Might there not be wider, indeed *non-natural scientific modes of reason* that can contribute to such a psychology as well (history, philosophy, and anthropology are disciplines that immediately come to mind). Jung, as we have seen (and will explore later in greater detail), was, in *The Red Book*, also quite critical of "reason," holding that while the ancients considered the Logos "an expression of divine reason" (*göttlicher Vernunft*) and a necessary corrective to the "unreason" (*Unvernunft*) that pervaded ancient times, in the end this Logos was transformed into a serpent, and rational men became serpent worshipers who spread its poison to others under the guise of "education" (RB, p. 280b).

HEALING A DYING GOD

Returning to our text, Jung is enthralled with the sick, blind, and dying God, describing him as "the beautiful and most loved one" who had come to him from the East (RB, p. 280a). Jung finds himself seized with compassion for Izdubar. He feels guilty for having further lamed the God with his own science and reason, just as the biblical God had once lamed man, when Jacob wrestled with an angel. Jung resolves to not let the God die: "If my God is lamed, I must stand by him, since I cannot abandon the much-loved" (RB, p. 281b). Jung feels that he has no other choice but to attempt to heal Izdubar, for otherwise Jung's life would be "broken in half." Here we find Jung's fascinating response to Nietzsche's "death of God." Nietzsche had declared:

> God is dead. God remains dead. And we have killed him. How shall we comfort ourselves, the murderers of all murderers? What was holiest and mightiest of all that the world has yet owned has bled to death under our knives: who will wipe this blood off us? What water is there for us to clean ourselves? What festivals of atonement, what sacred games shall we have to invent? Is not the greatness of this deed too great for us? Must we ourselves not become gods simply to appear worthy of it?[3]

For Jung, God, whether dead or only deathly ill, must be reborn or healed by man: "…our God is sick. We have seen him dead with the venomous gaze of the Basilisk on his face, and we have understood that he is dead. We must think of his healing" (RB, p. 281b).

Jung also takes up the themes of the sickness, healing, and rebirth of God in *Psychological Types*, where he references the poetic narrative work by Carl Spitteler, *Prometheus and Epimetheus* (1881), who writes: "And on the dark morning of that very day, in a still and solitary meadow above all the worlds, wandered God, the creator of all life, pursuing the accursed ground in obedience to the strange nature of his mysterious and grievous sickness" (CW 6, § 295). Jung writes: "The sickness of God expresses his longing for rebirth, and to this end his whole life-force flows back into the centre of the self, into the depths of the unconscious, out of which life is born anew" (CW 6, § 297). Jung here suggests that the healing and rebirth of God is a psychological process in which the self is given new life. The Gods cannot be permitted to die, for without the spiritual, mythological, and libidinous forces they represent, the self and humanity as whole would each be impoverished and sorely afflicted.

HEALING IMAGES

The chapter closes with two beautifully painted images. The first, **RB Image, p. 44,** depicts a silhouette of a lone man standing, arms outstretched, facing the last (or first) glimmer of light at sunset (or dawn) over what appears to be a modern city. Stars that fill the highest and darkest part of the sky appear to pour out of a faded ancient column. Perhaps this is a worshipper invoking the spirit of the depths to form an umbrella over the spirit of this time (RB, p. 229b), as it is the spirit of the depths that Jung must invoke to heal a dying God.

The legend of the next, full page painting (**RB Image, p. 45**) refers to *Atharva-veda* 4.1.4 (one of the four Hindu Vedas, or [Books of] Knowledge), which Shamdasani points out is a charm to promote virility, and is likely connected with Jung's efforts to heal the dying God, Izdubar (RB, p. 281, n. 110).

In his essay on Picasso, originally published in 1932, Jung distinguished between two types of art produced by his patients. *Neurotics* produce pictures that are synthetic, symmetrical, have a "unified feeling tone" and an "unmistakable meaning" (CW 15, § 208). *Schizophrenics* produce pictures characterized by fragmentation and "alienation from feeling," and which disturb or leave one cold by their "paradoxical, unfeeling, and grotesque unconcern for the beholder" (CW 15, § 208). While Jung takes pains to make it clear that he is not offering a psychiatric diagnosis, he states that Picasso's work falls into the latter group. I believe that Jung's paintings in *The Red Book* fall into his own "neurotic" classification. Symmetry, "unified feeling tone," and meaning are clearly evident in most of Jung's *Red Book* images, and many of them, including **RB Images, p. 44** and **p. 45,** are pleasing to and perhaps even "healing" for the viewer. Jung's use of color is particularly notable and his images are often symmetrical and unified. While a number of the images may well be thought of as "disturbing" (e.g. many in the **RB Images, pp. 80-97** series), they are by no means nearly as disturbing as some of the narrative passages in Jung's text. Even many of the images that involve dangerous serpents and beasts (e.g. **RB Images, p. 119, p. 129**) are extremely pleasing to the eye. It's as if these images serve as a counterpoint to the "accept all," hellish, chaotic, and "mad" imagery that dominates much of *The Red Book* narrative. Jung appears to be using the paintings as a means to organize both his fantasies and heal his "Self." This same trend towards organization, beauty, and harmony is evident in the calligraphy and the highly decorative drop-case lettering that begins many chapters and paragraphs. The *Atharva-veda* painting (**RB Image, p. 45**) is particularly illustrative of these trends, and has many of the harmonizing elements that are also present in Jung's mandalas (**RB Images, p. 105, p. 107, p. 364**).

"Chapter IX: Second Day," pp. 281-84

Jung is desperate to come to the aid of the dying God, and suggests that he will "risk everything" in a long and hazardous trek east in order to do so. It is interesting that after rejecting the Christian world view symbolized by Ammonius and the Red One, and claiming their ideas to be the "remains of earlier temples," Jung thinks to turn "east" and has compassion for the Babylonian God, Izdubar. However, Izdubar himself warns Jung that if he ventures east he will either be blinded or die[4] (RB, p. 282a), and in the end, Jung turns neither to the East nor the West for the remedy, but rather to his own thoughtful meditation (RB, p. 282a).

THE "REALITY" OF THE IMAGINATION

Jung's "medicine" for healing the ailing God, the "saving thought," is audacious in its formulation and radical in its implications: the God, Izdubar, must accept that he is a fantasy, as only in this way can he be renewed in his life. Jung fears that Izdubar will reject his proposal out of hand as "he will claim that he is completely real and that he can only be helped in a real way" (RB, p. 282a). Indeed, Izdubar's initial reaction to Jung's idea is that it is terrifying and "murderous" (RB, p. 282a). However, Jung succeeds in convincing the god to go along with his plan, suggesting to him, "I do not mean to say that you are not real at all, of course, but only as real as a fantasy" (RB, p. 282b). Jung explains that the tactic of calling Izdubar a "fantasy" is akin to giving the sick a "new name" in order to change his essence. Jung is here transitioning to a way of thinking, an epistemology, that will characterize all of his future thought. The imagination, the products of the psyche, especially those that emerge from the collective imagination/unconscious, are in their own manner every bit as "real" as the objects of the so-called objective world! Jung tells us straight away: "The tangible and apparent world is one reality, but fantasy is the other reality" (RB, p. 283a).

Izdubar is now prepared to acknowledge that he is a fantasy, if only on the pragmatic grounds that it might help to heal him. Jung then finds that he can carry the God, and indeed, without difficulty, squeeze him "into the size of an egg and put him in [his] pocket" (RB, p. 283a). Jung then proceeds with the god into a "welcoming house" where he is healed. Jung states: "Thus my God found salvation. He was saved precisely by what one would actually consider fatal, namely by declaring him a figment of the imagination" (RB, p. 283a). Jung declares that the God has become a "living fantasy" (RB, p. 283a). Having converted Izdubar into a such a figment, Jung now feels confident that he can carry the God "down into the Western land," as his "comrades will happily accommodate such a large fantasy" (RB, p. 282b). The renewed God can then plunge himself "into the flood of light of the East to resume his ancient cycle" (RB, p. 283a). Jung believes that he is providing a service to the West by bringing Izdubar in his new imaginal form. He warns: "If you do not have him with you in the Western lands, he will come running to you at night with clanking armor and a crushing battle ax," (RB, p. 283b) just as he had approached Jung (RB, p. 278a).

Shamdasani points out that years after he abandoned *The Red Book*, Jung told Aniela Jaffe that many of his fantasies in this section of *The Red Book*, including his imaginative solution to the sickness and death of a God were ridiculous (RB, p. 283, n. 114), and it is clear in the context of *The Red Book* that Jung abandoned this imaginative, mythological solution as unworkable. However, in many ways this "solution" comports with Jung's more general views on the role of fantasy, both in the individual and in the discipline of psychology. As we have seen, in *Psychological Types* Jung argues that creative fantasy is the bridge that unites thinking and feeling, and thus unites the *science* of psychology with a psychology of human experience (CW 6, § 84) and, as Jung puts it, "the springs of life" (CW 6, § 86). According to Jung, "every creative individual whatsoever owes all that is greatest in his life to fantasy" (CW 6, § 93). For this reason "fantasy" is far more "real" and significant than the words "fantasy" or "imagination" would normally suggest.

Further, in *Psychological Types*, Jung provides an account of the nature of God that is in essence a scholarly version of his healing and rebirth of Izdubar in *The Red Book*. Jung recites that for the 13th century German theologian, Meister Eckhardt, God and the soul are identical, and "God must be withdrawn from objects and brought into the soul, and this is the 'higher state' in which God is 'blissful'" (CW 6, § 421). Jung quotes Eckhardt to the effect that God created the world so that He might be born in man's soul, which in Jung's interpretation indicates that "God is dependent on the soul, and at the same time, that the soul is the birthplace of God" (CW 6, § 426). Indeed Jung notes that Eckhardt himself writes, "I know that without me God can no moment live; Were I to die, then He no longer could survive." (CW 6, § 432). In later sections of *The Red Book* Jung will meditate on the implications of his being the "mother" of his God, and of his having the power to either heal or destroy (RB, p. 285b) the race of Gods.

Jung's notion that humanity has, in the power of its imagination, the capacity to heal and give life to the gods recalls not only Eckhardt but also the Gnostic formula, "God created men, and men created God. So is it also in the world, since men created gods and worship them as their creations it would be fitting that gods should worship men."[5] Jung's concept of reality also echoes the Chabad Hasidic formula that both earth and the heavens partake in reality and illusion, being and nothingness:

> (Looking) upwards from below, as it appears to eyes of flesh, the tangible world seems to be *Yesh* [existing] and a thing, while spirituality, which is above, is an aspect of *Ayin* (nothingness). (But looking) downwards from above the world is an aspect of *Ayin* (nothingness), and everything which is linked downwards and descends lower and lower is more and more *Ayin* (nothing) and is considered as naught truly as nothing and null.[6]

Jung, with his concepts of the "Objective Psyche" and the reality of fantasy, provides philosophical content to these theosophical ideas.

Viewed from the perspective of Jung's desire to overcome Nietzsche's "death of God," the healing of Izdubar is a bold, if not shrewd move, for as Jung understood, it takes the greatest weakness of the theistic position (the argument that God is but a mere fantasy) and turns it into a strength (this "fantasy" is indeed God's "reality"). Just as Jung had absorbed the world's absurdity and evil into his conception of the deity, he now also absorbs God's "non-existence" into a renewed, imaginative conception of the divine. Later, in *Scrutinies*, Jung will do the same with the naturalist critique of theism by holding that Abraxas, the highest God, is to be identified with the cruel and contradictory natural world (RB, p. 350b). While some may regard these moves as an intellectual "sleight of hand," they can also be seen as bold efforts to radically transform our conception of both God and humanity.

"Chapter X: The Incantations," pp. 284-86

Jung imaginatively transforms the God Izdubar into an egg, which Jung carries in his hands as he proceeds to recite a series of "incantations for [the God's] incubation" (RB, p. 286a). In these incantations Jung declares himself to be the "mother" and "father" of the God, who "nurtures the seed of God" (RB, p. 284a) within himself. In language that reflects his preoccupation with pairs of opposites throughout *The Red Book*, and which anticipates his "Seven Sermons to the Dead" (which we encounter later in *Scrutinies*), the God is described as a coincidence of opposites, as "eternal emptiness and the eternal fullness...Eternal darkness and eternal brightness...Meaning in absurdity...Freedom in bondage...Yes in no" (RB, p. 284a, b). Jung implores the God to "rise up" and "break through the shell" for "We are wretched without you" (RB, p. 284b, p. 285a); yet at the same time, Jung remains conscious of his own role in the divine birth: "Come to us, we who will produce you out of our own body" (RB, p. 285a). Indeed, Jung claims to "have slain a precious human sacrifice" for this God, and the sacrifice appears to be Jung himself: "I have cut my skin with a knife. I have sprinkled your altar with my own blood" (RB, p. 284a, b).

IMAGES OF REGENERATION

The words of Jung's incantations are surrounded or flanked by a series of stylized paintings (**RB Images, pp. 50-61**). We are told by Shamdasani that these paintings are symbolic representations of Izdubar's regeneration (RB, p. 284, n. 122). The warmth of color in the first two images (**RB Images, p. 50, p. 51**) speaks to Jung's warmth and sympathy for the ailing deity, and their elements, structure, and symmetry give one the impression that they are a pictorial temple *within Liber Secundus*. The incantation that surrounds **RB Image, p. 50** begins, "Christmas has come. The God is in the egg," and indeed there is an egg-shaped form at the top center of the painting. In **RB Image, p. 51**, a serene figure meditates on a priestly throne, silently mastering the scene. In **RB Images, p. 52** and **p. 53**, the red deepens into burgundy and the focus is on smaller objects; we might here be witness to details within the imaginative temple of the mind. The mood is more serious, perhaps more introspective, and these images might themselves be stimuli to meditation. The colors are Persian and the forms Byzantine, suitable for the rebirth of a middle eastern deity. **RB Images, p. 54** and **p. 55** are less symmetrical, more pictorial, and the dominant color scheme shifts from red to blue. **RB Image, p. 54** is a snake or serpent that is surrounded by a glowing, fiery energy that arises from the dark depths. An abstract image of a tree with branches emerges and seems to grow into the cool light of the blue heights. The image legend *"Brahmanaspati"* refers to a vedic deity who is regarded to be the lord of prayer, the personification of piousness, and the god whose magical "word" destroys the enemies of the Gods.

RB Image, p. 55 is a stunning painting of a solar barge traveling on a blue green sea. Emerging from the sea's dark depths, just under the barge and essentially equal to it in size, is a terrible green, black, and gold sea creature. The painting clearly evokes the theme of surface and depth. We might surmise that the barge, directed by a dark masked and hooded figure, is the ego or persona that travels on the surface, hardly suspecting the monstrous forces that lie just beneath the plane of conscious awareness. Jung discusses the relationship of the hero to the sea-monster in *Transformations and Symbols of the Libido*, where he describes how the hero fights against the monster, is devoured by it, but then kills the monster by cutting a vital organ in the beast's belly (CW B, § 326; cf. CW 5, § 311). The hero, with the assistance of the fish, rises again to see the light of day. However, the hero, representing the conscious ego, must first be devoured by the unconscious before it re-emerges as what Jung will later call an individuated Self. In other places (CW B, § 393) the sea-monster is likened by Jung to the devouring power of the mother-libido, from which the hero/ego must free himself.

The legend underneath **RB Image, p. 59** reads "*hiranyagarbha*," from the *Hiranyagarbha Sukta* in the *Rig Veda*. It is the "golden egg," womb, or "universal germ" that in Indian philosophy gives rise to the cosmos, and even gives birth to the supreme spirit or Absolute, Brahman (cf. RB, p. 285, n. 130). Thus this image is particularly appropriate for Jung's re-birthing of the God Izdubar. In **RB Image, p. 61** a multi-legged monster stands over a small white egg that is itself poised upon a serpentine figure. This image occurs at the close of the incantations and seems to portend Jung's anxiety about the hazards of having contained the God in an imaginal egg, which now gives Jung the power to destroy it, and with it the entire race of Gods (RB, p. 285b), just as the monster stands in a position of power over the egg in the image. Perhaps this fearsome figure, which closely resembles the creature in **RB Image, p. 29** as well as the "devilish monster" in Jung's first mandala (the "*Systema Munditotius*", RB, p. 364), is Jung himself.

The caption of **RB Image, p. 64,** "*catapatha-brahmanam* 2, 2, 4" (RB, p. 286, n. 133), makes reference to the *Shatapatha Brahmana*, a prose text in the Vedic tradition. The image shows a figure, completely prostate before what appears to be a cracked egg, out of which a huge flame towers up to the room's ceiling and drips teardrop shapes of fire. A solar barge (see **RB Image, p. 55**) is subtly painted in the background. The chapter of the *Shatapatha Brahmana* that Jung cites in his caption to this image speaks of *Pragâpati* (*Parajapti*), a creator deity who presides over all procreation, and who generates *Agni*, the first of the Hindu gods. Shamdasani points out that in a manuscript, "Dreams," Jung had referred to this image as "the Opening of the egg," and that it was begun on February 4, 1917 (RB, p. 286, n. 132). The next chapter in *The Red Book* details the opening of Izdubar's egg, and describes how Jung kneels down on a rug in order to accomplish this feat, an act that is evidently portrayed in this painting. This is one of the few images in *Liber Secundus* that clearly illustrates an event described in the text.

JUNG'S AMBIVALENCE

In the end, Jung is ambivalent about his role in the divine birth, and is doubtful about his new conception of the godhead. While he is happy that his incantations have succeeded, he is troubled by a deity who is so pitiful and powerless that the God's fate is literally and figuratively in Jung's own hands. This is a God so devoid of power that one cannot even commit blasphemy against him, and Jung asks what value is there in a God that "one cannot even blaspheme" (RB, p. 285b). Jung toys with the idea that his imaginal transformation of the Gods is indeed their demise: "That is the demise of the Gods: man puts them in his pocket" (RB, p. 285b). Jung even considers deicide: "Perhaps I can eradicate this last one and with this finally exterminate the race of Gods" (RB, p. 285b). But Jung steps back from this thought, and asks himself in Gnostic fashion: "Are we not sons of the Gods? Why should Gods not be our children?" (Nietzsche had written, "Is man merely a mistake of God's? Or God merely a mistake of man?").[7]

In a final incantation, Jung declares that he loves this God "*as a mother loves the unborn she carries in her heart*" (RB, p. 286a). He is willing to trade in a powerful ruler God for one that provides "light and warmth" and "feeds the spirit" (RB, p. 286b). We will see that by the time our version of *The Red Book* ends with the "Seven Sermons to the Dead," an altogether different and more terrifying God emerges in the form of Abraxas.

Jung's Dialectical Journey

As we proceed through *The Red Book*, we discover that each stage in Jung's journey is superseded by a new stage, one that in effect critiques and incorporates the discoveries of each of the earlier stages. Jung himself describes this path in terms of the growth of a plant, in which each "new direction of growth is completely opposed to the previous one" but which nonetheless causes the plant to grow in a regular manner "without overstraining or disturbing its balance" (RB, p. 295b).

In the early chapters of *Liber Novus*, Jung comes to reject the notion of the hero and with that the hero-God, and he arrives at a stage in which he identifies with his own creative will. He later encounters the feminine, dark, and joyful aspects of his psyche, embodied in the figures of the simple maiden, Salome, and the Red One, and learns that there is more to his inner world than he had initially believed. After incorporating these "opposites", i.e. the hitherto ignored or rejected aspects of himself, he arrives at a point where he distances himself from the "old temples," i.e. Christianity, and rests content in a non-religious, natural "greening" of his own spirit. Yet, Jung does not remain long in this state before he encounters Izdubar and recognizes that he cannot live without a God, a God that he (along with his western counterparts) had nearly destroyed with science and reason. This God, who hails from the East, must be revived, and in order to do so, Jung reformulates the God as a "living fantasy" and makes him a function of the self. Yet this position too is unstable, and Jung expresses his doubts and ambivalence about a God that is only a function of human psychology. As will become clear, Jung's view of himself and his God takes several more turns before *The Red Book* comes to its abrupt end.

Jung's journey is a dialectic progression, one that echoes, on a psychological level, the dialectic of philosophy that Hegel had traversed in his *Phenomenology of Spirit*.[8] In that work Hegel attempted to trace the successive categories of human thought, knowledge, and desire, proceeding from the simplest, least adequate, and historically earliest categories, through more adequate forms, and ultimately to a conception of what he referred to as the Absolute. Hegel's approach was to begin with a concept or a theory which, on its face, appeared to provide an adequate account of its subject matter and to show that when such a theory is taken to its logical conclusion, it proves inadequate, ultimately yielding to an opposite conception. Jung, who was generally averse to Hegel (though he once called Hegel "that great psychologist in philosopher's garb" [CW 18, § 1734]), endeavors, like Hegel, to incorporate the opposites. However, unlike Hegel, the result of this is not a *higher conception* of man and the universe, but rather (as per Nietzsche), a *higher man*. *The Red Book* can be understood as Hegel's *Phenomenology* brought down to the level of concrete lived experience, and in this way Jung's project is again similar to that of the existentialists, who also sought to concretize Hegel's great work. The question we might ask is whether Jung hopes to arrive at an *endpoint*, for example, a fully *individuated* state that on the psychological level is akin to Hegel's Absolute; or is such an end state unsuited to work on the soul, which is perhaps better conceived as an unending dialectical journey? (Indeed, in one view Hegel's dialectic is itself without end, a rational process that indefinitely extends the contexts of knowledge and understanding without yielding a final philosophical truth).[9]

"Chapter XI: The Opening of the Egg," pp. 286-88

Jung describes how he opens the egg that brings forth the renewed God, who is now healed, transformed, and whole, and who emerges speaking as if he had awakened from a sleep. Izdubar relates that he "swam through a sea that wrapped him in living fire" (RB, p. 286b) and that in the process of rising and falling between the "heights" and the "depths," he has become "completely sun" (RB, p. 286b). Here we should recall that it was the sun that Jung found himself worshipping after the Christian anchorite, Ammonius, instructed him to recite his morning prayers, and that it was a verbal slip about Helios, the Sun God, that prompted Ammonius to accuse Jung of being the devil. We have also seen how, in *Transformations and Symbols of the Libido*, Jung identified the Sun God with the libido (CW B, p. 89, n. 27; cf. CW 5, § 324). Later in *The Red Book*, Jung will describe the Sun God as the "supreme lord of the world" (RB, p. 351b) but still only one amongst his Gnostic pantheon of deities.

THE INSTABILITY OF AN IMAGINED DEITY

Jung acknowledges that Izdubar is the sun, and begs the "most powerful" God's forgiveness for having carried him. Both Izdubar and Jung have quickly forgotten the God's former enfeebled condition, in which he was subject to Jung's power and whim. It seems that a psychologized understanding of God is inadequate and unstable, and either passes over into atheism or a renewed vision of an independent deity. Jung says as much when he writes that just as he thought he had held sway over the mighty one, he saw that "he [Izdubar] was the sun itself" (RB, p. 286b). Further, at the close of this chapter, Jung says, "The God of our work stands outside us and no longer needs our help," for "a created work that perishes again immediately once we turn away from it is not worth anything, even if it were a God" (RB, p. 288a).

The Red Book continually seesaws between the theological and the psychological. As Shamdasani (RB, p. 286, n. 137) points out, Jung, in *Psychological Types*, held that the renewed God symbolizes a recovery of life, a changed attitude, and an intensification of the libido (CW 6, § 301). Further, in that same work, Jung understood divine renewal as symbolic of a mediation or "middle way" between the opposites, especially between the opposing psychological types and functions, something he says that has long been known in the "East," in particular in Buddhism (CW 6, §§ 325-6).

CREATING GODS: THE PROJECTION OF LIBIDO

Jung seems to speak of the vicissitudes of the libido when he writes, "when I conquered the God his force streamed into me," but that with the God's rebirth all of Jung's force became possessed by Izdubar, who had "drunk the juice" out of Jung's life (RB, p. 287a). In later Jungian terms, we might say that Jung's individual libido has become completely invested in the God archetype; and once that archetype is projected outside of the ego, the ego is emptied of its life force. Confirmation of this is found in Jung's report that with the God's rebirth "the emptiness of the depths opened beneath [him]" (RB, p. 287a). Jung later relates that one who has created a God can become enamored of his creation and either attempt to follow this God into a higher world or end up preaching to others and even demanding to one's own and others' detriment that they follow this God as well (RB, p. 288a). We might understand the latter as a desperate effort on the part of an emptied ego to refill and reestablish itself.

With the externalization of a created God, human nature becomes filled with everything "incompetent...powerless...vulgar...adverse and unfavorable...exterminating...absurd" (RB, p. 287a). When the powerful, productive, good, and reasonable aspects of the self have been projected into (a created) all-powerful and all-good God, one is left only with the opposites of these virtues. Perhaps this is why so many atrocities and absurdities are committed by the devoutly religious. Indeed, we might go so far as to say that Jung's gestation and re-birth of Izdubar is itself an archetypal event that represents the psychological process through which the gods are created in general. Religion is then left with a paradox: if the God is consciously recognized as a projection of the Self, it can no longer function properly as a God, but if it is provided an independent life, human nature gravitates towards hell. Perhaps it is for this reason that Jung was later so adamant that we recognize the evil both in God and Self; if God is conceived as all-good, the Self runs the risk of being engulfed in its un-projected shadow elements. If, however, God is conceived of as balancing good and evil, the Self can retain such a balance as well.

ON THE SUFFERING OF GODS AND MEN

Jung provides some further comments on the subjects of God, man, good, and evil. He writes that "God suffers when man does not accept his darkness" (RB, p. 287a), and thus man maintains the image of a suffering god as long as he does not consciously accept his desire for evil but rather unconsciously remains in its grip. We might say that by sympathizing with a suffering God, one in effect feels sympathy with one's own depressed condition and thus avoids experiencing the hell of one's real darkness. Depression and other psychological suffering is the ego's means of avoiding its own repugnant desires and pleasures.

"FORMATION"

Jung introduces the concept of an individual's "formation" (*Gestaltung*), which he defines as the combining of one's "force" with "fullness." Combining one's force with "emptiness" always has "a dissolving and destructive effect" (RB, p. 287b), but, according to Jung, both combinations are necessary. By "formation" Jung seems to have in mind the structures of life and character that one comes to value and wishes to preserve. While such structures certainly do have meaning and value, they develop at the cost of the draining of one's life force, which is channeled into their maintenance. Those who are overly invested in their formations mistakenly believe that a "manifold increased formation will satisfy their desire" (RB, p. 287b), and the failure to receive such satisfaction only prompts them to enlist and even compel others to aid them in pursuit of their "form." At such point, one's desire increases but one's life force has been spent, and the only alternative is to enlist evil to dissolve the whole formation project. Formation is "good," and as such it can only be dissolved by evil. Too much good is inimical to life and, as such, we "are entirely unable to live without evil" (RB, p. 287b). Those who fail to dissolve their formations become selfish and ultimately "bad in their goodness" (RB, p. 288a). They find no lack of support for their formation projects as there are always those who are happy to become "alienated from themselves under a good pretext" (RB, p. 288a). The way out of this cycle is to "accept our evil without love or hate," thus depriving it of its power over us.

Jung's comments on desire in this chapter reflect a different aspect of human motivation than in his discussion of the subject in *Liber*

Primus ("Refinding the Soul," pp. 231-2), There Jung speaks of
desire (*Begierde*) as a genuine yearning for one's soul. However, for
Jung, desire has more than one face. In the present context "desire"
(*Sehnsucht*) becomes a futile effort to reify one's "good" and results
in an alienation from one's true self.

At the close of this chapter Jung writes that we must not remain
too attached to the Gods, and other products of our thought and
imagination, that we create. Just as our children eventually leave us to
live their own lives, our spiritual creations also separate from us and
"live their own fate" (RB, p. 288b). (Jung returns to this theme in
Liber Secundus, Chapter XXI, where he tells us that for this reason, he
must separate from his God, the sun, and turn towards animating the
emptiness of matter [RB, p. 288b]). The dialectic of the Self continues.

FROM GOD TO HELL

Several painted images serve as a transition between the end of
Chapter XI, "The Opening of the Egg," and Chapter XII, "Hell,"
and the progression of mood in these images reflects the change in
mood between these chapters.

RB Image, p. 69 is a cosmological painting in blues, violets, black,
crimson, and gold. While not perfectly symmetrical, it is suggestive
of tranquility and order. Quite reminiscent of **RB Image, p. 59,**
"*hiranyagarbha*," the primal seed of the cosmos, this image's cool colors
suggest that the creative forces of the cosmos are at least temporarily
in harmony and repose. The following painting, **RB Image, p. 70,** is
far more active, indeed explosive. It is a fiery image of regeneration,
though the result seems to be unbalanced and a bit chaotic—almost
like a juggler trying to keep too many objects in the air at once, some
of which are breaking apart as they fall. The rising energy in this
painting appears to be coming from a source that can be visually
interpreted as a green plant, an open hand, or two snake-like creatures.

Shamdasani provides evidence that the three snakes intertwined
in **RB Image, p. 71** were understood by Jung to represent his
triangulated struggles with his wife and Toni Wolff (RB, p. 288, n.
141). It is unlikely that Jung would have remained with such a
reductive interpretation, and here we should recall that for Jung, as
for the Greeks, the snake represents the soul, in part because it slithers

into the earth where the dead reside.[10] The symbol of (two) intertwined snakes in the caduceus appears on the staff of Hermes, the messenger of the Gods, who is also said to guide the dead into the netherworld. Intertwined snakes also appear on the heads of early sun deities in the Middle East and in early representations of Athena who, amongst other things, is the goddess of philosophy and wisdom.

RB Image, p. 72 is a highly symmetrical but rather disturbing picture. It is a mosaic composition in which a series of six conical beams of light (two green, two blue, one red, and one orange) point up and down over a largely black field, punctuated by small yellow lights. The viewer may have the sense that it is deep night, that his back is against the wall, and he is on the verge of being caught in one of these searching beams. In the text, Jung is about to journey into hell. The black background and the red veining in the drop case "D" of *Die hoelle* ("Hell") of **RB Image, p. 73**, which begins on the next page, continues this ominous feeling-tone. Brutsche has interpreted the juxtaposition of the cones of light in **RB Image, p. 72** as a "hymn to the coincidence of fundamental opposites,"[11] and indeed not only the structure of the image but also the juxtaposition of intense form and color, and the contrasts between the darkness and saturated colors, suggests a melding together of oppositions. Indeed, it is such a melding together that results from the journey into hell that Jung is about to undertake.

Chapter 6

The Descent into Hell

The Red Book: Liber Secundus

"Chapter XII: Hell," pp. 288-90

Jung reports upon a vision that made clear to him that two nights
after having created his God, he had entered the underworld. In
the midst of a nightmarish scene of ropes, axes, and a "tangle of
human bodies" (RB, p. 288b), Jung sees a young, red-golden-
haired maiden, with three devilish figures about her feet and body.
The maiden clasps a silver fishing rod, the end of which she has thrust
into the eye of one of the demons. Jung writes that the demons had
tried to torture and kill her but she successfully defended herself. Jung
hears a voice which tells him that the evil one "cannot sacrifice his eye,"
and that "victory is with the one who can sacrifice" (RB, p. 289a).
Indeed, in *The Red Book*, *sacrifice* is the path to individuation: sacrifice
of the "hero within," sacrifice of one's egoistic aspirations and desires,
sacrifice of the belief that certain things are essentially good and
necessary and must be obtained or achieved, and finally, as we are about
to learn, sacrifice of the quest for complete fulfillment.

Jung tells us that his soul had fallen prey to "abysmal evil" (RB,
p. 289a), and that this had occurred as a necessary by-product of his
desire to give birth to his God. One who desires "an eternal fullness
will also create eternal emptiness" (RB, p. 289a). Those who wish to

escape evil cannot create a powerful, happy and lustrous God, for all that they do will be "tepid and gray" (RB, p. 289a).

We may also be entitled to interpret Jung's comments in psychological terms: that one cannot forge a powerful, happy, and lustrous self without also creating an evil and empty one. The forging of such a radiant self will be followed by the imaginative unfolding of a nightmare. God, the world, and the self each require darkness and evil to serve as a foundation for meaning and value.

THE HOLINESS OF EVIL

Jung's comments about the evil one's eye provide us with some further insight into his views on the necessity of evil. Jung says of the evil one: "you should not harm him, above all not his eye, since the most beautiful would not exist if the evil one did not see it and long for it. The evil one is holy...we also need evil" (RB, p. 290a). Jung's comments here suggest that lust, avarice, and earthly desire, traditionally attributed to the influence of the devil, are actually the foundation for much, if not all, that is good. A rabbinic dictum, which I have already quoted in part, serves as an interesting comparison. In commenting on Genesis 1:31: "And God saw everything which He had made and behold it was very good," the rabbis proclaimed that "very good" refers to the *yetzer hara*, the evil impulse, for "were it not for that impulse, a man would not build a house, marry a wife, beget children or conduct business affairs" (Genesis Rabbah 9:7). The *Zohar*, the *locus classicus* of Jewish mysticism, held that the evil one is holy, and that the "very good" of Genesis 1:31 is "the angel of death." The *Zohar* says of death, "He should not be banished from this world. The world needs him...It is all necessary, good and evil."[1]

"...THE BRIDGE THAT COULD CONNECT US"?

For Jung, the evil one's eye is the vehicle through which his "emptiness [can] seize gleaming fullness" (RB, p. 289a). According to Jung, the evil one lies in wait in order to devour one who is beautiful, or one who is on the verge of birthing a God. Here, a comparison with the much later philosophy of Jean-Paul Sartre may be useful. In *Being and Nothingness* (1943) Sartre introduced the notion of "the look" as the vehicle through which the "emptiness" of human subjectivity endeavors to fill itself with being.[2] For Sartre, all concrete human relations—love, hate, sadism, masochism, indifference, etc.—involve an attempt to ensnare the other with one's gaze (or to be so *ensnared by the other's gaze*) in a futile effort to intuit a fullness in one's own identity or being. For Sartre, there is no real possibility of a genuine human encounter between or among equals; all human relations are modeled on the Hegelian notion of "master and slave."

Interestingly, Jung, in this very chapter, expresses his own pessimism regarding human relations. Acknowledging "the fearful devilishness of human nature" (RB, p. 289b), Jung goes on to say two things remain undiscovered, the "infinite gulf that separates us from one another" and "the bridge that could connect us" (RB, p. 289b). On the other hand, we should note that in his *Black Book*, on February 23, 1920, Jung wrote that while God originates in the solitude of the individual, the "fullness of the Godhead" occurs in the relationship between the lover and the beloved (RB, p. 307, n. 240). At the time, Jung seems to have been caught between a Sartrian notion of existential alienation and Martin Buber's view that it is in relationship with the other that we catch a glimpse of the "eternal thou."[3]

To reconcile these two opposing views we can perhaps turn to Jung's images rather than his words. The serpentine figures in **RB Image, p. 75** connect two spheres, and are suggestive of a reconciling principle. This painting may symbolize the harmonizing of two equal realms, perhaps a day world and a night world, perhaps Jung's conflicting views on human relations and their significance for God. Nothing, however, is completely resolved. The final line of text before this image is "for I still did not know what it means to give birth to a god" (RB, p. 290a).

"Chapter XIII: The Sacrificial Murder," pp. 290-91

"Nothing human is alien to me"

Jung now finds (or places) himself in an even deeper corner of hell, almost as if he is challenging himself to produce the most vile and repugnant thoughts and fantasies. The small painting that opens the chapter, **RB Image, p. 76**, is a drop case "D", and like the "D" that opens the previous chapter, it is red and black. In this painting many intertwined snakes produce an impression of chaos. Jung is about to engage in a highly disturbing inner adventure.

Entering a valley where the "air smells of crime, (and) of foul, cowardly deeds" (RB, p. 290a), Jung encounters the mangled and mutilated body of a small girl. Jung spares us nothing in his description, detailing that "The head is a mash of blood with hair and whitish pieces of bone, surrounded by stones smeared with brain and blood" (RB, p. 290a). A shrouded woman appears and asks Jung why he should become enraged at such a sight, for surely "these and similar things occur every day" (RB, p. 290b). When Jung responds that "most of the time we don't see them," the woman asks him if "knowing that they happen is not enough to enrage [him]" (RB, p. 290b). Jung echoes Hume's famous dictum that if he simply has *knowledge* of something, it is easier to ignore.

The woman beckons Jung to remove the child's liver, and Jung, who is repulsed at the thought of this "horrific and absurd deed" (RB, p. 290a), nonetheless complies when the woman, who informs him that she is the child's soul, asks him to do so for her sake. Jung balks, however, when he is asked to *eat* a piece of the liver, claiming that this is "madness…desecration, necrophilia," and that such an act would make him "a guilty party to this most heinous of crimes" (RB, p. 290b). The woman informs Jung that *as a man* he indeed shares in the guilt for this act and must atone for it, as it was a "man who committed this deed" (RB, p. 290b). Jung agrees; he curses himself for being a man and partakes of the child's organ.

One point so graphically made here is that as human beings we are all capable of and collectively responsible for the crimes of our fellow humans. Commenting on this scene in the *Black Book*, Jung writes "I realize: *Nil humanum a me alienum esse puto,*" a line from Terence's *Heauton Timorumenos* which Jung's translators render as "Nothing human is alien to me" (RB, p. 290, n. 149). Our human tendency, of course, is to distance ourselves from the criminal element, to sequester the criminal in the penitentiary, and to have him or her do penance for the chaos, hatred, and violence that is endemic to us all. We draw a sharp line between such evil and our image of both ourselves and God. Years later, speaking after the Second World War, Jung commented on these tendencies when he stated that if individuals seeking treatment,

> come from those "decent Germans" who want to foist the guilt
> onto a couple of men in the Gestapo, I regard the case as hopeless.

> I shall have no alternative but to answer the applications with a
> questionnaire asking certain crucial questions, like "What do you
> think about Buchenwald?" Only when a patient sees and admits
> his own responsibility can individual treatment be considered.[4]

Further,

> The only redemption lies…in a complete admission of guilt.
> *Mea culpa, mea maxima culpa*! Out of honest contrition for
> sin comes divine grace. That is not only a religious but also a
> psychological truth.[5]

RECLAIMING THE LIFE FORCE

Once Jung has consumed the dead child's liver, the woman, who
moments before had announced herself as the child's soul, throws back
her veil, appears as a beautiful maiden, and announces herself as *Jung's
own soul*. Jung comments that by eating of the "sacrificial flesh" of the
"divine child" (RB, p. 291a) he not only completes the genesis of his
God, but also permits the emergence of a restored and radiant human
Self. Stein refers to this episode as a second initiation rite within *The
Red Book*[6] (the first being the healing of Salome's blindness in *Liber
Secundus*, Chapter XI). By being complicit in the act of evil, Jung
"testifies that he is a man" (RB, p. 291a), and indeed restores to himself
the "primordial powers" that had initially flowed into the God that
he had re-created. Again, in Jung's view, one must descend into the
realm of evil in order to experience the radiance of one's soul. This is
indeed an age-old notion, one that Jung will later encounter in his
studies of European alchemy and, during the period of his writing
Answer to Job, in the Lurianic Kabbalah.

Interestingly, Jung holds that by partaking in the blood and flesh
of the divine child he (following an ancient belief) brings healing to
his soul and also "dissociates himself from the God" (RB, p. 291a). In
the *Black Book* he wrote that it took "this atrocity to destroy the image
of the God that drinks all my life force so that I could reclaim my life"
(RB, p. 291, n. 150). Here Jung seems to make an about-face with regard
to his project of healing the God who had been mortally wounded by
science. This healing now appears to be a stage in the development of
a fuller individuated and divinized Self. Indeed, Jung's thinking here

anticipates not only his own later views regarding evil within God and Self but also the "Death of God" theology of Thomas J.J. Altizer, who (inspired by Jung, Hegel, Nietzsche, Blake, and others) later held that the sacrifice of Christ resulted in the death of God and the birth of a renewed and now divinized man.[7]

As we have seen, *The Red Book* is a dialectical journey that moves beyond any static view of God, self, meaning, and truth, and while Jung, in this very chapter of *The Red Book*, tells us "there are not many truths...only a few" (RB, p. 291a), this phrase does not do full justice to the *movement* of truth and meaning, both in *The Red Book* and throughout Jung's entire oeuvre.

At the close of this chapter Jung offers some reflections that demonstrate his intense ambivalence regarding the God image and idea. The "primordial force" that was released from the God and returned to Jung after his partaking of the sacrifice is the "radiance of the sun" (RB, p. 291b), but it is not without its perils—for if the soul manages to dip into it, she develops a "holy affliction" (*heilige Krankheit*) and "becomes remorseless as the God itself" (RB, p. 291b). Perhaps this is because the soul becomes drunk with beauty and power.[8] In such instances one becomes captured by a "real God" from which there is no escape. Jung protests that while God may desire one's life, it is important for the individual to find his own path, life, and Self (RB, p. 291b).

Jung concludes that he is "ashamed" of his God, which appears to him to be "irrational craziness," a "sickness," "superfluous," and "an absurd disturbance of my meaningful human activity" (RB, p. 291b). Certainly Jung is not the first to think and feel each of these things. Like Jacob who wrestled with an angel, Jung continues to struggle with God, and at least at this point, no clear path to victory is at hand.

IMAGES OF HELL

Chapter XIII is followed by a series of 19 images, none of which are suggestive of a human form. **RB Image, p. 79** is another version of the mosaic "searchlight" painting of **RB Image, p. 72**, but now the beams are seen head on, as if the viewer is himself caught in their colored lights. This series of paintings contain, in my judgment, some of the most disturbing images in *The Red Book*. They are vaguely organic, and give one an impression of alien life forms, not quite plant and not quite insect. Many of them contain brown, black, and occasional red shard-like fragments that are sometimes enclosed within the main forms, but at other times seem to spill out of the forms or move about within them in chaotic fashion. In **RB Image, p. 85** a fish comprised of gold-colored shards hovers above the main image. Some of the paintings, beginning with **RB Image, p. 89**, contain Viking runes, glyphs from an old Norse/German alphabet that was in use prior to the Latinization and Christianization of Europe and used for magical and divinatory purposes thereafter. Runes were occasionally thought to have the power to bring the dead back to life.

Beginning with **RB Image, p. 93** the "organic" theme seems to give way to a more geometric motif, the two approaches being combined in **RB Images, p. 96** and **p. 97**. **RB Image p. 96** is an "art deco," almost "electrical" image, that resolves in the horizontal plane into tree branches and roots. This series of images is quite inhuman—indeed, with few exceptions, the most notable being **RB Images, p. 155** and **p. 169**, there are few real humans in any of Jung's *Red Book* paintings. However, the paintings in the current series, in contrast to many of the other *Red Book* images, have a cold, removed, alienated, even schizoid quality to them that may reflect Jung's extreme isolation and inwardness during this period and the difficulties that he seems to have had in bridging the gap to an actual other.[9]

Chapter 7

The Library, the Kitchen, and the Madhouse

The Red Book: Liber Secundus

"Chapter XIV: Divine Folly," pp. 292-3

A RETURN TO CHRIST?

Having struggled with the God of his own creation, and having subjected himself to an active imagination in which he descends into hell and partakes in "desecration" and "necrophilia" (RB, p. 290b), Jung, in reaction to or compensation for all this horror, imagines himself in a large hall, the reading room of a library, where he requests a copy of Thomas à Kempis's *The Imitation of Christ*, a 14th century devotional handbook that overflows with the adoration of God, and which reflects the ascetic/monastic world-view that Jung had earlier scorned in his dialogs with Ammonius, the anchorite. Jung explains: "When thinking leads to the unthinkable, it is time to return to the simple life" (RB, p. 293b). Jung tells the librarian that he has requested *The Imitation of Christ* for "devotional" as opposed to scholarly reasons, commenting that while he places a high value on science, there are moments when science leaves him sick and empty, and he is moved by a book such as Thomas' which is "written from the soul" (RB, p. 292b). Whereas earlier Jung had followed his denunciation of science with the very unorthodox plan to heal and give new life to an eastern God, Jung now leaves science and his own thanatic impulses for a very traditional immersion in the Christian religion. Indeed, we find Jung, who had earlier denounced traditional piety, defending religion, arguing that those who cast it aside do so in their undiscriminating youth and mainly on the dubious grounds that its contents "clash with natural science or philosophy" (RB, p. 292b). Jung adds, "You can certainly leave Christianity but it does not leave you. Your liberation is a delusion" (RB, p. 293a). In his response to the librarian who suggests that Nietzsche, Goethe, and others have provided a contemporary substitute for prayer, Jung says that Nietzsche is too agitated, provocative, and oppositional. In contrast to the sense of "superiority" offered by Nietzsche in *Zarathustra*, Jung suggests that there are those who require a "depressive truth," one that makes one inferior, "smaller and more inward" (RB, p. 293a). The librarian says, "I really had no idea that you take such a mediating position," to which Jung responds, "Neither did I—my position is not entirely clear to me" (RB, p. 293a).

It appears that we may be here witnessing another side of Jung, a side that appears to run against the grain of much that he has set forth since his encounter with the Red One in the second chapter of *Liber Secundus*, and suggests a return to the defense of Christianity that Jung proffered in his colloquy with the Red One on the Jews (RB, p. 260a). Indeed, the notion of "imitating Christ" appears to contradict Jung's earlier polemic against imitation of the hero (RB, p. 245a). Conscious of this contradiction, Jung makes yet another reversal and says, "If I thus truly imitate Christ, I do not imitate anyone. I emulate no one, but go my own way, and I will also no longer call myself a Christian" (RB, p. 293b).

ON IMITATION

Jung's ambivalence regarding "imitation" is clearly reflected in his public talks and writings during the period of *The Red Book*. In "The Structure of the Unconscious," first published in 1916 (CW 7, pp. 269-304), Jung writes: "Human beings have one faculty which, though it is of the greatest utility for collective purposes, is most pernicious for individuation, and that is the faculty of imitation" (CW 7, § 463). Jung here holds that imitation actually creates a false sense of difference, as individuals "ape some eminent personality, some striking characteristic or mode of behavior, thereby achieving an

outward distinction from the circle in which they move" (CW 7, §
463). However, most often such "specious attempts at differentiation
stiffen into a pose," and the imitator becomes "several degrees more
sterile than before" (CW 7, § 463). Jung holds that the "persona" is
essentially a product of this imitative process, whereby the imitator
puts on a mask and "*feigns individuality.*" In analysis the mask is stripped
away and the individual comes to see that what he thought to be
individual is fundamentally collective. However, in a second
manuscript, "Adaptation, Individuation and Collectivity," also written
in 1916 but unpublished during Jung's lifetime, he holds that it is
precisely through imitation that individuation is achieved; this is
because such imitation serves to "reactivate" the individual's own
values (CW 18, § 1100; cf. RB Intro, p. 209a). Jung writes:

> Through imitation, one's own values become *reactivated.* If the
> way to imitation is cut off, they are nipped in the bud. The
> result is helpless anxiety. If [however] the imitation is a
> demand made by the analyst, i.e., if it is a demand for the
> sake of adaptation, this again leads to a destruction of the
> patient's values, because imitation is an automatic process that
> follows its own laws, and lasts as long and goes as far as is
> necessary. (CW 18, § 1100)

Shamdasani has suggested that the "imitation" that Jung has in mind
in this essay is an imitation or conformity with the analyst or the
analytic process, in which individuation is itself the standard which
is to be copied.[1] Perhaps imitation of the analyst is like the
"Imitation of Christ," and we can reread Jung's *Red Book* dictum
about Christ as follows: "If I truly imitate Christ [read: "my
analyst," or "Jung"], I do not imitate anyone. I emulate no one,
but go my own way,[2] and I will also no longer call myself a Christian
[read: Jungian, Freudian, etc.]" (RB, p. 293b).

Jung acknowledges that he "did not succeed in uniting Christ with
the prophets of this time...the one commands submission, the other
the will" (RB, p. 293b). Jung asks himself how he might "think of
this contradiction without doing injustice to either?" (RB, p. 293b).
He suggests that while these ideas cannot be conjoined, they might
be lived "one after the other," and concludes that what cannot be
resolved by thinking is resolved by life (RB, p. 293b).

"Chapter XV: *Nox secunda*," pp. 293-98

THE "INTUITIVE METHOD"

We now enter into one of the more difficult chapters of *The Red Book*. Jung leaves the library and finds himself in a large kitchen where a fat woman, a cook, is attending the stove. Jung has nothing else to occupy him so he begins reading his copy of the *Imitation of Christ*. The cook asks Jung if he is a member of the clergy. She tells him that her own mother had left her a copy of Thomas' book, and they discuss the great merit of this work. Jung's eyes fall on a passage that implores one to base one's intentions on God's mercy rather than on one's own wisdom. Jung thinks to himself that this refers to Thomas' "intuitive method." A footnote to our text (RB, p. 294, n. 70) informs us that in the *Black Book*, Jung referred to the "intuitive method" of the French philosopher, Henri Bergson. Bergson distinguished between conceptual and intuitive thinking, noting that whereas the former understands *scientific reality* as being comprised of discrete, causally related events, the latter follows the flow of time and duration, grasping an underlying *metaphysical reality* that is creative and indeterminate.[3] Bergson held that conceptual and intuitive thinking can be combined to unify these divergent perspectives. These ideas mirror Jung's distinction between the scientific "spirit of the time," the more metaphysical "spirit of the depths," and the reconciling principle of creative imagination, which is certainly more intuitive than rational. Jung associates Christ with the "intuitive method," and writes, "I would like to imitate Christ" (RB, p. 294a).

THE "ANIMAL"

Suddenly Jung hears "swishing and whirring," a sound associated with the prophet Ezechiel (RB, p. 294a). He sees "many shadowlike human figures" and hears a "babble of voices," saying "Let us pray in the temple" (RB, p. 294a). A bearded man, who identifies himself as both Ezechiel and as an "Anabaptist," tells Jung that he and the others are "wandering to Jerusalem to pray at the most holy sepulcher" (RB, p. 294b). Jung wishes to join them, but Ezechiel informs him that he cannot do so because he has a living body and the wanderers are all dead. Jung learns that although these dead had "died in true belief," they "have no peace" as they "had not come to a proper end with life" because they had forgotten "something important that should have been lived" (RB, p. 294b). (We will again meet up with these same "dead" in *Scrutinies*, in the "Seven Sermons"). Ezechiel reaches towards Jung, imploring him to say what this "forgotten something" might be, and Jung responds, "Let go, daimon, you did not live your animal" (RB, p. 294b). In a footnote to the text, Shamdasani points out that four years later in 1918 in "On the Unconscious" (CW 10, § 31), Jung argued that the animal element was suppressed in Christianity, and Jung later held that Christ had committed the sin of failing to live "the animal side of himself" (RB, p. 294, n. 174). However, while we might feel justified in interpreting this to mean that in Jung's view Christianity had suppressed such natural instincts as sex and aggression, this interpretation does not do full justice to Jung's view of "living one's animal" in *The Red Book*.

Jung soon provides a description of animality that is at odds with, or at least complements the usual "unbridled instinct" account. Jung writes that animals do not "rebel against their own kind," are "well-behaved," "keep to the time-honored," are "loyal...to the land that bears them," and "hold to their accustomed routes" (RB, p. 296a). Further, they do not conceal their abundance, try to enforce their will on those of their own kind, nor imagine that they are something that they are not (RB, p. 296a, b). Jung then writes, "He who never lives his animal must treat his brother like an animal" (RB, p. 296b). One who abases himself and "lives [his] animal" will not only treat his brother well, but will be in a position to redeem the "roaming dead," the very dead that Jung had witnessed during his exchange with the prophet Ezechiel. Jung's meaning in all of this is not altogether clear, but he seems to suggest that because animals are true to their nature and do not engage in lies and deceit, they are in some ways "more civilized" than so-called "civilized man."

Jung in the Madhouse

Immediately after informing Ezechiel that he had failed to "live his animal," Jung finds himself being pushed through a crowd into a police van. There he opens his copy of *The Imitation of Christ* to a page which reads that all men, including saints, are subject to temptation. Jung interprets this to suggest that temptation is not only inevitable but necessary for life, and he quotes Cicero's dictum that when one no longer has desires "the time is ripe for death" (RB, p. 295a). Jung believes that his awareness of the importance of animality and desire "brought [him] into conflict with society" (RB, p. 295a), as he now finds himself flanked by policemen who will bring him to a mental ward. A small, fat professor sees him with the Thomas à Kempis volume and tells him that "nowadays, the imitation of Christ leads to the madhouse" (RB, p. 295a). The professor suggests that Jung suffers from religious paranoia, and, noting that Jung has wit, claims that Jung is "maniacally aroused" (RB, p. 295a). A mental status examination follows, during which Jung acknowledges not only that he has heard voices but that he "summoned them" (RB, p. 295a). The professor notes that Jung suffers from hallucinations. When Jung makes reference to the "intuitive method," the professor remarks, "The fellow also uses neologisms" (RB, p. 295a). While the professor suggests that Jung's diagnosis is clear, Jung insists that he is perfectly well, leading the professor to conclude that Jung lacks insight into his illness and has a poor prognosis.

Jung's clothes are inventoried, he is sent for a bath and then to bed in a large sickroom where to his right he sees a patient with a transfixed gaze and to his left a person whose brain is shrinking. Jung reflects, "The problem of madness is profound" (RB, p. 295a). He suggests that there is a "divine madness", which is "a higher form of the irrationality of the life streaming through us," but which "cannot be integrated into present-day society" (RB, p. 295a). Just before things grow dark, Jung asks, "What if the form of society were integrated into madness?" Here Jung intimates something of the course upon which his future work will tread: the path of transforming the individual and society through a re-integration of the myths and archetypes that the West had long since relegated to the garbage-bin of irrationality and madness.

FALLING INTO THE ABYSS

Jung speaks about his movement into "the space of feeling which was previously unknown to [him]" (RB, p. 295b). He associates this movement with the trust in divine mercy advocated in *The Imitation of Christ*, and he describes it as a state in which one entrusts oneself to one's neighbors with the mighty hope that all will work out for the best. On the other hand, his state of mind is such that all appears accidental, and everything that he once understood to be lawful and true is now seen as error. He has "fallen into the boundless, the abyss, the inanity of eternal chaos" (RB, p. 295b). While he speaks of a "quiet place in [the] soul" where everything is "simple and clear," he sees this as nothing more than a "polished crust over the mystery of chaos" (RB, p. 295b).

Spirits of the Dead

Jung next embarks on a lengthy discourse on "chaos" and the "dead." Chaos, we are told, is an "unending multiplicity" of the dead, and by this Jung means not only deceased human beings, but also all the discarded "images" of one's past and the entire "ghostly procession" of human history (RB, p. 296a). Jung tells his readers that the human "dead…look greedily through the empty sockets of your eyes" (RB, p. 296a), as if something that they did not fully live in the past can be lived and redeemed by the living in the present. These dead take the form of evil spirits that clamor for one's attention. A dead spirit "besieges you in sleepless nights…takes hold of you in an illness…[or] crosses your intentions" (RB, p. 296a). Jung reminds us that these dead "forgot only one thing: they did not live their animal" (RB, p. 296a).

Jung will have much more to say about (and to) the dead later on in *Scrutinies*, particularly in Philemon's "Seven Sermons," but here we should note that Jung's interest in the dead teetered on the boundary between a literal and metaphoric understanding of shades and spirits.

As a university student Jung attacked the materialism of his day and expressed an interest in spiritualism. In his lectures to the Zofinga Society Jung drew on Kant's speculative passages about the problem of spirits, to argue for the possibility of their existence (CW A, § 78).[4] Jung adopted a form of vitalism in which he held that an immaterial "soul," an "intelligence independent of space and time," survives bodily death. Indeed, at that time Jung felt that there was empirical proof for the soul's existence in photographic plates that purported to reveal its "materialization." Jung wrote, "man lives at the boundary between two worlds. He steps forth from the darkness of metaphysical being, shoots like a blazing meteor through the phenomenal world, and then leaves it again to pursue his course into infinity" (CW A, § 142). By 1899, however, Jung had made an about-face, reporting that he had never had an experience of God (CW A, § xiv, n. 3). He attributed religious experiences to unconscious processes and argued for a relationship between the sexual drive and religion.[5] However, while putting forward a causal explanation of mediumistic experiences in his medical thesis, Jung left open the possibility that paranormal phenomena were also involved. Indeed, during his years at the Burgholzi, and even later, Jung seemed to be preoccupied with poltergeist phenomena, and as is clear in *The Red Book*, he experienced the dead pressing upon and making demands of him.

Jung maintained a certain ambivalence about the paranormal throughout his career; at times proffering straightforward scientific explanations of what others might regard as supernatural phenomena (for example, comparing mediums to hysterics), and at times, both early and later in his career, placing stock in phenomena and principles, e.g. synchronicity, that are said to operate beyond the borders of the space-time continuum and which were largely rejected or ignored by normative science. While he most often voiced the view that *proof* of a non-spatial, non-temporal realm was impossible and maintained his focus on the *phenomenology* of spiritual and "parapsychological" *experience*, he left open the possibility of events and processes that transcend our modern, "enlightened" view of the world. Writing in 1934, Jung considered the "hypothetical possibility that the psyche touches on a form of existence *without* space and time" (CW 8, § 814), adding:

> The nature of the psyche reaches into obscurities far beyond the scope of our understanding. It contains as many riddles as the universe with its galactic systems, before whose majestic configurations only a mind lacking in imagination can fail to admit its own insufficiency. (CW 8, § 815)

Creativity as Destruction

Returning to our text, Jung writes that once one has been afflicted by the dead, one must withdraw into solitude and "dedicate the night to bringing about [their] salvation" (RB, p. 296b). While this may be an arduous task, one should not be dissuaded, as it is a "life branch from the tree of divinity (RB, p. 296b)." This involves a connection to "what was created and later subjugated and lost" (RB, p. 296b). One bears a certain responsibility for delivering the dead into freedom. There is something evil attached to what is new, for it "prepares the destruction" (RB, p. 296b) of what is now present. Here we see Jung's ambivalence, not only about the modern world and its lack of connection with the past, but also for the creative process. While, as we have seen, Jung held that creative imagination is the force that reconciles the opposites and thus leads to individuation, he here says that creative individuals, because they destroy the past, are afflicted with a "leprosy of the soul" (RB, p. 296b), a disease that casts them out from society.

Jung's albeit ambivalent notion that the new is damaging and evil because it "prepares the destruction" of the present anticipates Alfred North Whitehead's views in *Process and Reality* (1927-29).[6] A comparison with Whitehead's philosophy may provide us with some insight into Jung's thinking. Whitehead held that while "novelty" is the world's greatest craving, it is also the ultimate source of evil, for it entails a break with the past, a loss of the secure, the loved, and the familiar. "The ultimate evil in the temporal world," Whitehead wrote, "lies in the fact that the past fades, that time is a 'perpetual perishing.'"[7] Whitehead, who like Jung, was a Platonist enamored with the principle of *coincidentia oppositorum*, held that evil is a necessary by-product of the world's progression, and lies at the heart of what we know to be the Good.

Jung does not want us to "praise [the] leprosy" of the creative, as only Christ could violate society's laws in the name of something higher; for us to attempt to do so ourselves would be mere imitation. Our only transgression should be that we do not imitate Christ in his transgression of the law. It is better that we be like an animal that is "well-behaved in its herd and unwilling to infringe its laws" (RB, p. 296b). Here we again see Jung's unusual view of animality, which he understands to involve a connection with the past, the herd, and ultimately, biologically determined law. It is remarkable that *The Red Book*, which for many pages seems to proclaim a Nietzschean transvaluation of values, and which at other points asks us to imitate Christ by becoming uniquely ourselves, should, at least at this point in the text, arrive at what amounts to a very conservative reverence for the past and a commitment to natural, biological law. This is an ambivalence (or perhaps a *coincidentia oppositorum*) that also informs so much of Jung's later thought.[8]

Redeeming the Dead

One way to understand Jung's talk about the dead and our responsibility for their redemption is to see it in terms of his later call for contemporary man to rediscover within his own psyche the presence and value of the collective past. This interpretation is reinforced by Jung's proclamation at the close of this chapter that in spite of our contemporary refusal to accept the possibility of immortality, the dead "produce effects" in "the inner world" (RB, p. 298a).

Jung's call to redeem the dead goes so far as to ask us to do "penance" for "what fell victim to death for the sake of Christianity" (RB, p. 297a). Jung here may be alluding to the myths and polytheism of the pagan world, or perhaps the barbarism that was repressed in middle Europe when, according to Jung, Christianity was prematurely grafted upon it (CW 10, §§ 16-17).

Jung tells us that we must accept the dead because "the new will be built on the old," and because "a new salvation is always a restoring of the previously lost" (RB, p. 297a). An example of the latter is Christ's "restoration" of human sacrifice and the symbolic eating of the sacrificed body. However, here Jung points out that this restoration occurred under "the law of love," and if one does not accept what has *become*, one will destroy this law and become subject to "violent deeds, murder," etc. Again we see Jung's ambivalence regarding what *was* versus what has *become*: and, he now tells us we should revere the latter" (RB, p. 297b). As with Whitehead, Jung appears to advocate a dialectic between old and new, if by "new" one can include the revelation of Christianity, which Jung tells us involves "restoring what has existed since ancient times under the rule of love" (*Gesetze der Liebe*) (RB, p. 297b).

Jung closes this chapter with another call to seek atonement and work for the redemption of the dead. We should do this even though it goes against our grain to do such "hidden work that does not visibly serve man" (RB, p. 297b). We must "become accustomed to being alone with the dead," which, as we have seen, by its very nature involves "accepting the chaos."

Caring for the Departed

It may be helpful to briefly consider Jung's ideas in this chapter in connection with his later (1935, rev. 1953) "Commentary on *The*

Tibetan Book of the Dead," a book that contains "spells" that are designed to provide the dead with mystical insights, give them control over their underworld environment, protect them from evil forces, and offer them a guide through the nether-world. Jung focuses on the book's mystical philosophy which holds that at the moment of death the deceased are provided with the opportunity to attain the seemingly paradoxical insight that everything is both the creation of the Gods and a projection of their own consciousness (CW 11, § 834); in short, that the soul or consciousness is the Godhead itself (CW 11, § 840). Jung interprets this in terms of his theory of the archetypes of the collective unconscious. More pertinent in the present context, Jung interprets the "spells" of *The Tibetan Book of the Dead* in terms of "the psychological need of the living to do something for the departed" (CW 11, § 855), a need that is expressed in the Catholic Mass, and we might add, in the *Kaddish* and *Yizkor* ceremonies in Judaism. Jung's views on the dead in *The Red Book* accord well with this "psychological need," a need that perhaps requires no more explanation than the fact that we are grateful to those who have lived and died before us.

MANDALAS

Chapter XV contains two full page mandalas which, though not directly related to the text, symbolize the union of opposites (e.g. between life and death, past and future, madness and reason, meaning and chaos, creation and destruction, humanity and animality) that Jung is struggling with in this chapter and throughout *The Red Book*. **RB Image, p. 105** is one of the more beautiful and harmonious paintings in *The Red Book*, as well as being one of the most familiar. This image was reproduced by Jung in his 1930 essay "Commentary on 'The Secret of the Golden Flower'" and attributed to a male patient in treatment. Jung had a tendency to take his own dream and fantasy material and report upon it as if it derived from one of his analysands. The image was reproduced again in 1952 in his essay "Concerning Mandala Symbolism," as a "Picture by a middle-aged man" (CW 9ii, § 682). It can be argued that by attributing this mandala to a patient, as a presumably spontaneous untutored production, Jung showed a willingness to distort the facts in a manner that throws into question the evidentiary basis of the theory of the collective unconscious.

The painting itself is symmetrical, harmonious, and more pleasing than many of the images in the preceding chapter. Jung described it as containing two anima figures on the horizontal axis, a symbol of the Senex (Wise Old Man) at the top, and a chthonic/Luciferian figure at the bottom.[9]

RB Image, p. 107 is another beautiful mandala, following the phrase "I accepted the chaos, and the following night, my soul approached me" (RB, p. 298a). Then after the image, "My soul spoke to me in a whisper, urgently and alarmingly: 'Words, words, do not make too many words...'" (RB, p. 298a). Jung then follows his soul's importuning that he accept madness. In this drawing, the shards that are scattered through **RB Images, pp. 80-89** seem to be in harmonious order. Mandalas (meaning "circles" in Sanskrit) are utilized both in Hindu and Buddhist traditions as a means of focusing meditation, establishing a sacred space, inducing trance, and ultimately bringing the adept to a sense of oneness with the unitary Absolute that lies at the origin of the cosmos. Jung saw them as an expression of the unconscious Self and as a vehicle to the achievement of individuation and unity of the personality.

"Chapter XVI: *Nox tertia*," pp. 298-301

Accepting Madness

Jung's soul speaks to him, urging him to be silent and listen, and to recognize that his foundations are all in *madness*. Jung's soul tells him that if he wishes to be truly open to everything, he must accept madness as well (RB, p. 298a). Madness is to be neither feared nor despised; rather it has a light that must be permitted to shine, and Jung "should give it life." Jung's soul continues to discourse on madness, proclaiming as we saw earlier, that madness is associated both with philosophy and daily life (RB, p. 298a), which is fundamentally crazy and illogical. Life is an unknown mystery with no rules, and what we call knowledge is an effort to "impose something comprehensible" (RB, p. 298a) on what is without fixed meaning.

Constructivism: "We create the truth by living it"

Jung again finds himself in the madhouse speaking with the professor who the night before had diagnosed him with "religious paranoia" (RB, p. 295a). The professor tells Jung that his speech is incoherent and Jung acknowledges that he is "completely lost," confused, and has "gone crazy" (RB, p. 298b). Jung soon finds himself conversing with a fellow patient who he refers to, perhaps ironically, as "the fool." The fool informs Jung that he is "Nietzsche, only rebaptized," and also "Christ the Savior" (RB, p. 298b), and complains that the professor is the devil who has prevented him from marrying the mother of God and saving the world. Shamdasani points out (RB, p. 298, n. 192) that Jung had encountered delusions similar to this during his days on the medical staff of the Burgholzi. When Jung tells the patient that what he has said is "pure mythology," the fool calls him crazy and ignorant. Jung's assessment involves a double entendre; on the one hand conveying utter skepticism regarding the fool's *mythical claims*, and on the other hand conveying a fascination with the fool's *mythological experience*. Indeed, the fool's claims (that he is Nietzsche only re-baptized, that he has a special connection with the mother of God, and that he is destined to be humanity's savior) closely parallel the myth Jung constructs for himself in *The Red Book*. Indeed, Jung here again suggests that he himself is the "crucified one" (RB, p. 299a). But Jung, at this point as elsewhere in *The Red Book*, is in a rather existential, constructivist mood, and is not quite ready to travel the road of finding collective meanings in universal archetypes and myths. While he has a vision of a tree rising from the sea, its crown in heaven and its roots in hell, this philosophical tree (which as we have seen represents Jung's view that the individual is rooted in both good and evil) offers him no comfort. Jung reflects that there is no formula, no "paved road" to salvation; the only roads are those that we ourselves build. "Our life is the truth that we seek...We create the truth by living it" (RB, p. 299a). One route out of the "night of the soul" is to turn for comfort to a book like the *Imitation of Christ*, another is to face the abyss with the realization that there is no meaning other than that which one creates and affirms for oneself. Ultimately, Jung will find neither of these routes satisfactory.

"...THE WORD IS AN IMAGE OF GOD"

Jung now raises a new question about language, asking whether the descriptions he provides of his hellish visions are merely a "web of words," and he inquires about the nature of words in general. Jung concludes that words have meanings that "pull up the underworld" (RB, p. 299b). Words are both paltry and mighty, great and small, empty and full, and for this reason, he says, "the word is an image of God" (RB, p. 299b). We have already seen how Jung had described God as the "eternal emptiness and the eternal fullness," and the "meaning in absurdity..." (RB, p. 284a, b). He now tells us that language (which, according to scripture, is God's instrument for creating the world) is the very vehicle of this *coincidentia oppositorum*. Jung, who earlier in *Liber Secundus* had described how words were a sort of rampart against the flux (RB, p. 270a), now associates words with the sea, chaos, and the arbitrary—at the same time writing that this sea of chaos "is our way, our truth, and our life" (RB, p. 299b). Jung's meaning here is difficult to fathom, and it may not be fully expressible in discursive, rational terms. However, what he seems to be saying is that both life and language present themselves as empty and full, as meaningful and absurd, and that any honest confrontation with our experience and discourse must embrace this duality if we wish to avoid the false and the incomplete. There are moments in each person's life when one's experience is meaningless and one's words are empty—we must accept, embrace, and (as we shall see momentarily) love these moments if we are to discover our soul and find our God. Indeed, as Jung is about to suggest, the discovery of one's soul is at the same time the discovery of God.

GOD IS BORN THROUGH RADICAL ACCEPTANCE

Jung now returns to a theme he had introduced with his vision of the rebirth of the god Izdubar, and which he will later develop in such works as *Answer to Job*: God longs to be incarnate in and completed by man. Indeed the God of the present era "can be born only through the spirit of men as the conceiving womb of the God" (RB, p. 299b). Yet this "birth of God" can only occur if man accepts the lowest within himself (i.e. the meaningless, the false, and the evil), "under the law of love according to which nothing is cast out" (RB, p. 299b). Jung is here advocating a path of *pure* radical acceptance, as he states that one who accepts the lowest within himself out of selfishness or greed, out of anything but love, is damned—but one must also strive to accept this damnation as, under the law of love, "None of the damnation is cast out either" (RB, p. 300a).

Jung is of the view that by taking upon ourselves and showing mercy to the mad, the base, the chaotic, the sick, and the contemptible within ourselves, God is healed and finds completion. Just as Christ suffered for the salvation of mankind, each individual must suffer for the sake of God (RB, p. 300a). One's suffering must be total. Just as one must love what is despicable within oneself, one must also "hate that which he loves in himself" (RB, p. 300b). By accepting the lowest within oneself, one lowers an invisibly small "seed into the ground of Hell" (RB, p. 300b), from which grows one's life, thereby conjoining the Above with the Below. One who "strives for the highest finds the deepest" (RB, p. 300b), and Jung suggests that the highest is only realized when one plants one's seed in hell, as it is from this seed that the "the tree of life" will emerge (RB, p. 300b). This may not quite be a Sabbatean "redemption through sin," but it is a view in which one only finds redemption through an acceptance of the chaos and evil within oneself and the world.

The Shadow

In his later writings Jung described the "shadow" as the archetype that embodies those aspects of the self that the ego rejects as evil, damaging, or reprehensible. According to Jung, the ego acts as if the "persona," which is comprised of the "acceptable" aspects of one's personality, those aspects that one presents to the world (CW 9i, § 43), is coextensive with the self, and as a result one's shadow can emerge without warning and wreak havoc upon the self and others. Jung held that one's shadow is frequently projected onto others (CW 9ii, § 16), and he developed the view that psychotherapeutic treatment always entails the patient's discovery of his shadow (CW 10, § 440), which has positive ("bright shadow") as well as negative aspects. For Jung, the process of individuation involves the acceptance and incorporation of one's shadow into the personality, and the forging of a self that is far wider and deeper than one's ego or persona.

Jung does not specifically describe the "shadow" as an archetype or primordial image in *The Red Book*. Nevertheless, Jung's struggle with his own shadow as well as with the ideas behind the shadow concept are evident throughout *Liber Novus*. As we have seen, he writes that we are "entirely unable to live without evil" (RB, p. 287b), that we must submit to and "love" what horrifies us within ourselves (RB, p. 235b), and that we must comprehend our own darkness (RB, p. 272b). The encounter with our dark, aggressive, and thanatic impulses provides not only a wider awareness of our own possibilities, but an important basis for empathy with others.

In *The Red Book*, Jung suggests that a confrontation with our dark side is necessary for psychological transformation: "You will need evil to dissolve your formation, and to free yourself from the power of what has been, to the same extent which this image fetters your strength" (RB, p. 287b). The idea here is that an incursion from our shadow self can break apart the limiting structures of our persona or ego and open us to creativity and change.

Only by accepting the evil within us can we prevent it from harming and controlling us. Jung writes:

> Thus we probably have to accept our evil without love or hate, recognizing that it exists and must have its share in life. In doing so we deprive it of the power it has to overwhelm us. (RB, p. 288a)

We should not work to suppress or eliminate the darker aspects of ourselves. This is because, "the more the one half of [our] being strives toward the good, the more the other half journeys to Hell" (RB, p. 314b). Jung adds, "Because we know that too far into the good means the same as too far into evil, we keep them both together" (RB, p. 315a). Jung is here developing the notion that the psyche unconsciously compensates for a one-sided diet of ideas, feelings, and actions.

Jung's comments on the dark side of the self also apply to the "personality" of God which, as we have seen, Jung came to believe was an archetype that is equivalent to the self:

> the God I experienced is more than love; he is also hate, he is more than beauty, he is also the abomination, he is more than wisdom, he is also meaninglessness, he is more than power, he is also powerlessness.... (RB, p. 339a)

Indeed, God's completeness and the fact that the divine is the template for the human personality necessitate the existence of the divine shadow (RB, p. 243a).

As we have seen, God "suffers when man does not accept his darkness" (RB, p. 287a). It is for this reason that "men have a suffering

God" (RB, p. 287a). Presumably God's suffering would end once mankind accepted the evil within itself. This is one reason why Jung says, "Because I wanted to give birth to my God, I also wanted evil" (RB, p. 289a). God suffers (or remains unborn) because of the individual's failure to accept his own darkness. One might translate this in psychological terms as follows: the failure of the ego to integrate the shadow results in a deeper suffering of the individual and a failure to actualize the Self. While in *Psychological Types* Jung seems to suggest an equivalence of the individual's shadow and the unconscious (CW 6, § 268), Jung's more considered view was that it is possible, even imperative, for an individual to attain consciousness of his shadow self.

So much of *The Red Book* is propaedeutic to Jung's later ideas about integrating the shadow that one can almost become impatient with the repetition. We must appreciate, however, that *The Red Book* is not a finished theoretical treatise, but rather records Jung's struggle with certain key experiences, intuitions, and ideas that he returns to from a variety of angles in order to more fully comprehend and work them through *for himself.* Perhaps this is one reason why he was so hesitant about *The Red Book's* publication.

THE OTHER

Jung makes an interesting comment about the "other" in the context of his musings about "radical acceptance." One must not treat the other as an enemy over against oneself, but must understand that "the other is also in you" (RB, p. 301a). In an article that originally dates from *The Red Book* period, Jung writes:

> We discover that the "other" in us is indeed "another," a real man, who actually thinks, does, feels, and desires all the things that are despicable and odious. (CW 7, § 43)

From *The Red Book* we learn that one who recognizes that the other is also within himself "quarrels and wrangles no more, but looks into himself and keeps silent" (RB, p. 301a). Like one who accepts the lowest within himself, he who accepts the other within "sees the tree of life whose roots reach into Hell and whose top touches Heaven" (RB, p. 301a). Such an individual is freed "from the old curse of the knowledge of good and evil," and therefore stops projecting his evil onto others, as he no longer seeks to deny the evil within himself. Jung explains that one who denies evil within himself or projects it onto others can no longer provide "dark nourishment [to] the depths," and this causes his tree of life to become "sick and withered" (RB, p. 301b); the same fate which, according to an ancient legend, befell the tree in Eden after Adam partook of its fruit (CW B, § 375; cf. CW 5, § 368). Because the knowledge of good and evil prompts us to reject the dark aspects of our nature, such knowledge is a curse.

Jung returns to the question of the other in *Liber Secundus*, Chapter XVII.

On Doubt

Jung concludes this chapter with some comments on "doubt," which he says characterizes both "the strongest and the weak" (RB, p. 301b). The strong take hold of and possess their doubt, while the weak are possessed by it. One can only affirm and possess his doubt, if "he endures wide-open chaos" (RB, p. 301b). Jung acknowledges that he cannot speak with any certainty: "My speech is neither light nor dark, since it is the speech of someone who is growing" (RB, p. 301b).

The import of this entire chapter, indeed of much of *The Red Book*, can be understood in terms of Jung's quite postmodern efforts to reclaim the value of hitherto debased terms of a series of polarities: madness/sanity, evil/good, chaos/order, doubt/certainty, empty/full, etc. This is a project that was initiated by Nietzsche and reached further expression in such later European philosophers as Jacques Derrida. Jung's role in the development of this postmodern sensibility has often been ignored, and *The Red Book* bears witness to the extent to which he anticipated philosophical ideas that were to become *au courant* half a century later.[10]

Images of Destruction and Rebirth

As we move deeper into *Liber Secundus* we find that the paintings, which were completed years after the text, begin to have little apparent connection to Jung's narrative. Indeed, in the next chapter we will see that the images create a narrative of their own, which serves as a counterpoint to *The Red Book* text.

RB Image, p. 109 represents the "man of matter," who, along with an accompanying serpent, is destroyed by a golden ray when he ascends into the world of spirits. Jung's caption for this image states that the golden ray originates in the "spirit of the heart" and that the material man falls and disintegrates with joy (p. 298, n 193). The evil serpent is also unable to remain in the world of spirits. Here we might speculate based upon Jung's annotation in the *Black Book* (RB, p. 299, n. 201) that the material man is Jung himself, who having married into great wealth and enjoyed the material success of his profession, takes pleasure in the disintegration of this persona when he turns from science and the pursuit of prestige to the pursuit of "knowledge of the heart." Jung's own mortal criticism of his worldly ego/persona becomes a major theme in *Scrutinies* (RB, p. 334 ff)

The caption of **RB Image, p. 111** reads: "The serpent fell dead unto the earth. And that was the umbilical cord of a new birth" (RB, p. 299, n. 201). This is the same evil serpent depicted in **RB Image, p. 109**. It too is killed by the golden ray. For Jung, the serpent is an *iridescent* image, a sign of evil and the herald of a new birth, and indeed a new birth is depicted in **RB Image, p. 113**. Jung's caption describes this image as "Phanes," the "divine child." Phanes is the primeval deity in Orphic cosmogony who is said to have emerged from the "world egg" and is considered the first ruler of the cosmos. In *Transformations and Symbols of the Libido*, Jung describes Phanes as "the 'shining one,' the first created, the 'father of Eros'" (CW B, § 223; cf. CW 5, § 198). According to Jung, Phanes is bisexual and the God of Love (CW B, § 223; cf. CW 5, § 198). Jung also compares this God to the "world soul" or "One" in Plotinus. We will see that this image (of Phanes) reappears in a subsequent painting (**RB Image, p. 117**) where it is identified as TELESPHOROS, a Greek God of healing. In the *Black Book* Phanes is described in superlative terms as "the smile of dawn......the resplendent day...the immortal present...the light that illuminates every darkness...loves embrace and whisper...the warmth of friendship...the promise of life...the benevolent and gentle..." (RB, p. 301, n. 211). He is the messenger of Abraxas, but in contrast to Abraxas, who Philemon will describe in cruel and frightening terms in the "Seven Sermons" (RB, p. 350b), Phanes appears to be something very close to Jung's version of the all good, beautiful, and illuminating deity that he frequently struggles against.

"Chapter XVII: *Nox quarta*," pp. 302-5

THE RED BOOK: DREAM, VISION, OR LITERATURE?

Jung himself now confirms his interest in breaking down the barriers between the terms of traditional polarities. Jung's soul tells him: "The door should be lifted off its hinges to provide a free passage between here and there, between yes and no, between above and below, between left and right" (RB, p. 302a). Jung himself is caught in several polarities: "Is it day or night? Am I asleep or awake? Am I alive or have I already died?" We may here again wonder about the state of consciousness that produced the "visions" in *The Red Book*. Are they psychotic productions, hysterical hallucinations, dreams, conscious fantasies, intentional literary productions, or the result of a free play of Jung's imagination? As we have seen, Jung later advocated that his patients engage in "active imagination," a quasi-meditational technique in which one allows images and figures to emerge into consciousness and then observes rather than controls how they develop. While *The Red Book* narratives read as if they have been consciously elaborated, and they were commented upon by Jung in a wakeful, conscious state, Jung himself denied that his visions were anything but "real", and he adamantly refused to speak of them as art (MDR, pp. 185-6). In the current chapter he suggests that at least the experiences he relates about the madhouse were the result of an *incubation dream* (RB, p. 302b), a dream that elaborates upon a topic or theme that one focuses upon prior to falling asleep.

Regardless of the general nature of his *Red Book* experiences, Jung now relates that he has awakened from one vision into another. The fat cook, with whom he had discussed *The Imitation of Christ* before he was taken off to the mental ward, tells him that he has awakened from an hour's sleep. Jung says that he has "certainly dreamed," and he asks himself if he is in the "realm of mothers," a reference to the descent of Faust into a region that Jung would many years later equate with the collective unconscious (RB, p. 302, n. 217). Jung next reencounters the librarian, to whom he returns his copy of the Thomas á Kempis volume. He now agrees with the librarian that "for people like us" *The Imitation of Christ* is boring, again reversing himself and reverting to his early negative view of the spiritual guidance and comfort afforded by traditional piety.

PARSIFAL

Jung soon finds himself in a performance of Wagner's opera, *Parsifal*. He is in the magic garden of Klingsor, a villainous sorcerer who seeks to steal the Holy Grail—the plate or cup used by Jesus at the last supper. Two of the characters in the opera, the Christian knight Amfortas (the knight who protects the grail) and the seductress Kundry (who seduces Amfortas at Klingsor's behest), are played respectively by the librarian and the cook, from whose library and kitchen Jung has just exited. Jung is surprised to see that Klingsor closely resembles him. Parsifal, the young, naïve hero of the story, enters the scene and "Klingsor venomously throws the feather at Parsifal...[who] catches it calmly" (RB, p. 302b). Suddenly the scene shifts to the final act where Jung sees Parsifal, who is now adorned with Hercules' lion skin, modern trousers, and a helmet. Jung suddenly recognizes that he himself is Parsifal. At this point Jung takes off his armor, which is "layered with history and chimerical decoration" (RB, p. 303a). He is now wearing the white shirt of a penitent, and he goes to a spring where he washes his feet and hands. Jung then removes his penitent's shirt and dons his civilian clothes, walks out of the scene, encounters himself "kneeling down in prayer as the audience" (RB, p. 303a), and merges with himself.

The strangeness of this account is certainly suggestive of a dream, but we must recall that in Jung's narrative he has just awakened from the dream in which he is brought to the madhouse. Further, Jung's splitting and then re-merging with himself has the earmarks of a dissociative fantasy. However, within *The Red Book's* subjectivist epistemology, in which fantasy has a reality that equals or exceeds that of the so-called objective world, the transitions between dream, dissociative vision, active imagination, and theater may be of limited importance. What is significant here is Jung's identification with the characters in Wagner's opera: first with Klingsor, the villainous seeker of the Holy Grail, and then with Parsifal, the Grail's holy protector. The entire *Red Book* can and has been understood as the quest for the "Holy Grail of the Unconscious"[11] and the grail has been a favorite theme of Jungian interpreters. Though Jung himself ceded the interpretation of the Holy Grail to his wife Emma Jung and Marie-Louise von Franz,[12] he does comment on the Parsifal legend in

Psychological Types, where he describes Parsifal as "free from the opposites and…therefore the redeemer, the bestower of healing and renewed vitality who unites the bright, heavenly, feminine symbol of the Grail with the dark, earthly, masculine symbol of the spear" (CW 6, § 371). This is indeed an apt characterization of Jung's own project in *The Red Book* and beyond.

Jung further suggests that each character in the Parsifal legend represents an aspect of a single collective personality (CW 6, § 371). Klingsor, the power hungry, manipulative magician; Kundry, the seductive witch (who for Jung symbolizes the "instinctive life force"); Amfortas, the knight who falls and is wounded after allowing himself to be seduced; and Parsifal, the naïve youth who ultimately matures into the healing savior and king ("and rescues the libido from the state of restless, compulsive instinctuality"—CW 6, § 371), can each be understood as moments in Jung's, and by extension, the individual's development. Each are archetypes under whose influence the ego successively falls.

Jung's identification with the Parsifal legend has also been interpreted as representing his relationship to Freud. One interpretation by J.R. Haule[13] views Amfortas as representing Jung's championing of psychoanalysis and Klingsor as Jung's personal ambition and grab for power. However, the narrative can readily be understood in reverse fashion: Klingsor, who is often considered a Jewish stereotype, can be seen as representing Jung's identification with Freud and the Freudian effort to develop a non-Christian view of the soul's depths (i.e. steal the Holy Grail) through the power of sexuality (represented by Kundry). Amfortas would then represent Jung's identification with traditional Christian piety and the everlasting wound inflicted on that piety by sexuality/psychoanalysis. Finally, Parsifal (who in the end baptizes the seductress Kundry) represents that aspect of Jung that endeavors to reconcile these opposites, heal Jung's wound, and, in effect, "Christianize", or at least spiritualize, the Freudian libido.

On Logic

Jung enters into a discussion that touches upon the nature of logic, a logic that is close to the four-valued "Buddhist" logic of Nagarjuna and which today might be spoken of as a version of "dialetheistic" reasoning.[14] Like Nagarjuna, dialetheists hold that logic should not be limited to the true and the false, but should also consider the values of "both true and false" and "neither true nor false." While given his critique of reason Jung might have regarded many of his statements in *The Red Book* as non-logical or *trans-logical*, he provides several examples in this chapter of what might also be considered dialetheistic reasoning, for example, when he calls the "way of life/nameless one...neither clever nor stupid...man and woman...poor in meaning yet so rich...the chosen one since he was the most rejected...full of drunkenness while sober" (RB, p. 304a, b). Further, Jung affirms that the "unreal is real, what was real is unreal" (RB, p. 304b), and in the name of the "nameless one" (*Namenlose*), he asserts, "I, who I am, am not it...I divided myself into two and in that I united myself with myself...*I have bathed myself with impurity and I have cleansed myself with dirt*" (RB, p. 304b). Some of these paradoxes may be said to illustrate an even closer relation between opposites than dialetheistic co-existence. For example, when Jung speaks of "the chosen one since he was the most rejected" (RB, p. 304b), we have two poles of a dichotomy that not only co-exist but which are understood as interdependent. Such interdependence might be said to be the logical form of *coincidentia oppositorum*.

Jung's descriptions in this chapter of the "way of life" and of the "nameless one" (RB, p. 304b) bring to mind the paradoxical descriptions of the "Pleroma" (the infinite divine essence) found in Gnostism, with which Jung was generally familiar by the time he composed *The Red Book*, and which, as we will see, he mirrored in his "Seven Sermons to the Dead." Subsequent discoveries of original gnostic writings only underscore the paradoxical and dialetheistic nature of gnostic thought. For example, in the Nag Hammadi text, *Thunder, The Perfect Mind*, Sophia, who represents the duality of both the Pleroma and man's soul,[15] declares:

> I am the first and the last.
> I am the honored and the scorned one.
> I am the whore and the holy one...
> I am the bride and the bridegroom,
> > and it is my husband who begot me.
>
> ...You, who tell the truth about me, lie about me,
> > and you who,

have lied about me, tell the truth about me.
...For I am knowledge and ignorance
...I am the one whom they call Life,
and you have called Death.
...I am a mute who does not speak
and great is my multitude of words.[16]

Later in *Liber Secundus* Jung provides an excellent example of dialetheistic reasoning when he writes, "The magical is good and evil and neither good nor evil" (RB, p. 314a). Multi-valued logic is implicit not only in Gnosticism but in nearly all mysticism, and, as I have mentioned, it was explicitly advocated by Nagarjuna and the early Buddhist logicians. It has only occasionally been accepted in the West, which, with the exception of the several decades when Hegelian logic rose to prominence, has been largely dominated by Aristotelian, either/or, linear thinking. Western philosophy has generally been suspicious of any "reasoning" that violates or appears to violate the "law of non-contradiction," and as we will see when we come to examine Jung's "critique of reason," Jung later turned to the East as a foundation for his view that "either-or" logic should give way to a more encompassing form of thought (CW 11, § 833).

THE "NAMELESS ONE," JUNG'S NEW MAN/NEW GOD

Jung's thinking takes a decidedly Gnostic turn in his description of the "nameless one," which he intimates is a new God and moreover a new man who is capable of bringing the opposites into conjunction and unifying diverse aspects of the psyche and soul. This new man and new "way of life" is the "secret teacher of nature," "the great sage who has superhuman knowledge", who "prophesizes the future" (RB, p. 304a) and completes the Christ. The nameless one "expands the realm of Christ with Hell," but has no name, since he has "not yet existed, but [has] only just become" (RB, p. 304b).

Jung's consideration of the various paradoxes that constitute the healing "way of life" and the "nameless one" (RB, p. 304b) who completes Christ occurs in the context of his discussion of the dividedness of the self. Jung writes, "He who wants to accept himself must also really accept his other" (RB, p. 303a). While we desire to see ourselves as "one," as a unified personality (for example, by identifying ourselves with a particular skill or talent), we are actually divided between a self and an "other," the latter serving as a container for all that is dark, avoided, or rejected in the psyche. "Growth" only begins when you have "reached that freedom through the suffering of your spirit to accept the other despite your highest belief in the one, since you are it too…" (RB, p. 303b). One cannot escape the other. If one attempts to do so, "the other would suffer great need and afflict us with his hunger" (RB, p. 303a). Further, "Nothing should separate me from him, the dark one. If I want to leave him, he follows me like a shadow" (RB, p. 305a). For Jung, it is only through one's embrace of the other within oneself that the new God/man can arise.

IMAGES OF THE JOURNEYING SELF

Several full page images adorn Chapter XVII, and these paintings, starting with **RB Image, p. 117**, take on a narrative of their own, which runs through **RB Image, p. 127** in the next chapter of *Liber Secundus*.

Jung's caption for **RB Image, p. 115** reads, "the golden fabric in which the shadow of God lives" (RB, p. 302, n. 219). In *Liber Primus* Jung had spoken of God's shadow as the "nonsense" which is the unavoidable complement to the supreme meaning (RB, p. 230a). The figure in this painting is quite nonsensical: it is both cat and human-like, and the position of its feet and body make it hard to understand how it can stand erect in the square-patterned room. A sun in the center, perhaps an image of the supreme meaning, casts its rays on this shadow/nonsense figure.

RB Image, p. 117 is a beautifully drawn and detailed image of a young man, "Atmavictu" who Jung described as a "supporter" who had aided him in the murder of the hero Siegfried (RB, p. 304, n. 226; cf. *Liber Primus*, Chapter VII). In these images, however, Atmavictu is depicted as a hero, and, as will be discussed momentarily, Jung's understanding of the hero archetype (which as we have seen was "post-heroic" in *Liber Primus*) seems to harken back to the position he had taken earlier in *Transformations and Symbols of the Libido*.[17] Atmavictu attempts unsuccessfully to dissuade a multi-armed dragon from reaching up to devour the sun. Also present is Telesphoros, who closely resembles the divine child in **RB Image, p. 113,** and a tiger, which Jung terms an evil spirit that exists in some men (RB, p. 303, n. 222). In

Memories, Dreams, Reflections, we learn that in 1930 Jung carved two wooden figures, one of which he reproduced in stone for his garden in Kusnacht (MDR, p. 23) and which essentially replicated a small figure he had carved as a child (MDR, p. 21). Jung says that his unconscious supplied him with the name for this figure: "Atmavictu," which he says means "breath of life." The derivation of this name is most likely "Atma," from the Sanskrit, *Atma* or *Atman* for "breath" or "soul," and "victu" from the Latin for "nourishment" or what "sustains life." In Hindu, especially Vedantic thought, Atman is one's "true self," the self that is identical with the transcendent self of the universe. Telesphoros is a Greek deity whose name means "bringer of completion," and who is associated with healing and recovery.

In **RB Image, p. 119**, which can be seen on the cover of this volume, Atmavictu has slain and is in the process of dismembering the dragon, which is now bleeding profusely. Jung writes that the dragon must not surrender the sun along with its blood (RB, p. 305, n. 226). He relates that Atmavictu is now cutting into the dragon's belly to retrieve the sun, but multiple suns are already falling out of the wounds left from the severed limbs. Obviously, the sun in **RB Image, p. 117** is not the first one that the dragon has swallowed. This is a wonderfully rich and dynamic image. Recall that Jung, in *Liber Primus*, Chapter VII, identified Atmavictu as the youthful supporter who had assisted him in the terrible, if necessary, murder of the hero, Siegfried, who Jung regarded both as a symbol of the vicissitudes of libido (CW B, § 628) and of his own intellect/superior function (RB, p. 242, n. 115, citing *Black Book* 2). In *Transformations and Symbols of the Libido*, Jung spoke of a universal myth of the battle of the hero with the dragon, and identified the dragon with the son's longing for the mother (CW B, § 585; cf. CW 5, § 575). For Jung, the sun's being swallowed by the dragon is symbolic of the libido's regression (CW B, § 610). The hero's victory over the dragon symbolizes the separation from the mother (CW B, § 589; cf. CW 5, § 580) and the triumph over the regressive pull of the unconscious. Both "sun" and "dragon" are polyvalent in Jung's thinking; the "inner sun" represents man's true nature (CW B, § 652) and the dragon is the guardian of a treasure (CW B, § 398; cf. CW 5, § 395). Interestingly, Siegfried (who had been "murdered" by Jung and Atmavictu) is said to gain immortality by drinking the blood of the slain dragon (CW B, § 550; cf. CW 5, § 541). We might say that the dragon swallowing the sun symbolizes a stage in the process of individuation in which the conscious ego regresses into the unconscious, remains for a time in its grip, and emerges as a fully individuated self after it has been released. The suns pouring out of the dragon's body in **RB Image, p. 119** are Selves (or aspects of one self) that have been liberated after traversing this course. While these images seem to recapitulate the view of the hero in *Transformations and Symbols of the Libido*, there is a difference, since Atmavictu, the slayer of the dragon, has already killed the hero; consequently, the result of his regression into the unconscious cannot be the triumph of a hero/ego, but is better understood as the emergence of an individuated Self, for whom the ego, if it is has not actually died, is no longer center stage. Indeed, Jung's journey in *The Red Book* might be said to exemplify this very process, one in which the individual regresses into and integrates elements of the personal and collective unconscious in the service of creating a wider "Self." In this way Jung's journey serves as a general model for our own individuation. A parallel to this idea is found in the Lurianic Kabbalah, where sparks of human and divine energy entrapped in the negativity of the "husks" of the "other side" must, like the suns in the dragon's body, be discovered, liberated, and reintegrated by the individual in order for the self, world, and God to be restored and complete.[18] The narrative of **RB Images, p. 117** and **p. 119** is resumed with **RB Image, p. 123**.

RB Image, p. 121 is Jung's depiction of the *Lapis Philosophorum* or "philosopher's stone." Jung describes it as the "incorruptible seed that maintains a separation between the father and mother" (RB, p. 305, n. 230). In alchemy the stone is conceived as the substance that can transform base metal into gold and serve as an elixir of life, rejuvenation, and even immortality. Jung later interpreted its transformative properties in psychological terms as a vehicle for the formation of the self. Jung identifies **RB Image, p. 122** with the reverse side or shadow of the stone depicted in **RB Image, p. 121**. It depicts Atmavictu in his old age, after having withdrawn from creation. The image is also identified with Izdubar, Philemon, and Ka ("spiritual essence" in ancient Egyptian thought) (See RB, p. 305, n. 231 and n. 232).

In **RB Image, p. 123** the slain dragon from **RB Images, p. 117** and **p. 119** can be seen lying face up at the bottom of the painting. Jung informs us that the Cabiri (chthonic Gods who Jung encounters later in *Liber Secundus*, 320a ff) grow from the flowers that emerge from the body of the dragon (RB, p. 306, n. 233). Jung describes the Cabiri as misshapen, shriveled, elemental dwarflike spirits who possess "ridiculous wisdom" and bear the "secret arts" (RB, p. 320a). Atmavictu, standing on an orb in the sky across from a temple, pours "holy water" from a jug onto the flowers below.

RB Images, pp. 117-127 constitute a fairly cohesive narrative that can be interpreted in terms of Jung's later conceptions regarding the individuation process. We will continue this narrative with **RB Image, p. 125**, after our discussion of the text of Chapter XVIII.

"Chapter XVIII: The Three Prophecies," pp. 305-7

ACCEPTING ALL

Jung has another encounter with his soul, an encounter he records as having occurred on January 22, 1914. Again, his soul raises the question of Jung's capacity to "accept" all things, and she reels off an increasingly morbid litany of historical artifacts, acts, and events in an effort to test Jung's capacity to absorb the ills and evils of mankind. Jung's soul begins rather lightly with such weapons as "worm-eaten lance shafts, twisted spears (and)...rotten shields" (RB, p. 305b), which Jung says that he can accept with ease, admonishing his soul that she "know(s) better" than to query as to whether he can accept such trifles. Things escalate a bit with "dirty pouches filled with teeth, human hair, and fingernails" and "all the superstitions hatched by dark prehistory" (RB, p. 305b), but Jung has no problem accepting these as well. Jung's soul now ups the ante: "fratricide...torture, child sacrifice, the annihilation of whole peoples...epidemics...razed cities, frightful feral savagery, famines..." (RB, p. 305b), and Jung resigns himself to accepting these as well. Curiously, it is when his soul moves on to the positive products of human civilization—"the treasures of all past cultures, magnificent images of Gods, spacious temples, paintings...books full of lost wisdom, hymns and chants of ancient priests..."—that Jung protests, exclaiming, "That is an entire world—whose extent I cannot grasp. How can I accept it?" (RB, p. 305b). Jung's soul responds, "But you wanted to accept everything? You do not know your limits. Can you limit yourself?" to which Jung replies that he must limit himself as no one could ever comprehend such wealth (RB, p. 306a). Jung's soul, now satisfied with Jung's humility, tells him to "Be content and cultivate your garden with modesty" (RB, p. 306a).

Jung's diffidence here is all the more curious because it is precisely the whole of human culture and civilization that he will later pack into the "Self" through his conception of the archetypes of the collective unconscious, a project which he had already begun in 1912 with *Transformations and Symbols of the Libido*. Here, in *The Red Book*, Jung seems to have paused, if only briefly, in the face of the enormity (and perhaps hubris) of this task. Recall that in the previous chapter, after identifying himself with the hero/savior Parsifal, Jung removed his armor "layered with history and chimerical decoration," did penance, and returned to his "civilian" self (RB, p. 303a). For at least a moment in *Liber Secundus* Jung sees the wisdom of laying down his historical armor and limiting himself and his imagination as he takes to heart his soul's admonition to "take shears and prune your trees" (RB, p. 306a). In the remainder of this chapter we find Jung struggling with this limiting process.

THE "RELIGION THAT IS STILL TO COME"

Jung now reverses direction and states that his soul presented him with three ancient things that point to the future: "the misery of war, the darkness of magic, and the gift of religion" (RB, p. 306a). Notably, these are three things that those with a liberal, scientific bent (and Freudians) might ordinarily attempt to overcome. According to Jung, these three things have in common the unleashing and binding of chaos. While he provides little in the way of elaboration of this idea he makes some intriguing comments about the "Religion that is still to come." These comments shed light both on Jung's understanding of chaos and the relationship between his thought and postmodernism. In an almost uncanny presentiment of ideas on religion and the messiah that will be put forth by the French philosopher, Jacques Derrida, more than sixty years later, Jung describes the future religion as "monstrous" (*Ungeheure*) (RB, p. 306a). Derrida will later write that we must be open to a future (and a "messiah") that is so unanticipated that it cannot in any way be circumscribed and can only be described as "monstrous" from our current perspective.[19] Here in *The Red Book*, Jung expresses a quite similar view: "no word can grasp it, no will can conquer it" (RB, p. 306a)..."the future should be left to those of the future" (RB, p. 306b). By being open to such an unarticulable vision of a future religion, a religion that from the present point of view is chaos rather than order, we maintain an open economy of thought and free ourselves from the religious dogmatism of those who "know" what God is and will be.

Before returning to his "small garden," Jung makes the claim that "Little good will come to you from the outside. What will come to you lies within yourself. But what lies there!" (RB, p. 306a). As we have seen, Martin Buber later criticized Jung for his locating God and truth within the self, rather than understanding it as arising out of encounter between distinct subjects. Here Jung insists that knowledge is indeed limited to knowledge of the self. Jung asks, "How can you know what you are not" (RB, p. 306b), and he answers, "Remember that you can know yourself, and with that you know enough." Jung avers, "you cannot know others," in effect taking a skeptical position on the philosophical problem of "other minds." He concludes, "A knower may know himself. That is his limit" (RB, p. 306b). This appears to be an early and very broad version of Jung's claim that "Metaphysical assertions…are *statements of the psyche* and are therefore psychological" (CW 11, § 835), another claim for which Buber later took him to task, on the grounds that "all statements, if they are considered not according to the meaning and intention of their contents but according to the process of their psychic origin could be described as 'expressions of the soul' ['statements of the psyche']"[20] Later, when Jung fully articulates his conception of the collective unconscious, he will in effect argue that one knows others, in fact the whole of humanity, through a deep knowledge of oneself, and indeed Jung had already hinted at this idea in the early pages of *Liber Primus* when he wrote that "you are an image of the unending world, all the last mysteries of becoming and passing away live in you" (RB, p. 230a). Yet the view that a knower can only "know himself," or knows others only through himself, renders Jung subject to the criticism that his thinking and experience, at least in *The Red Book*, is one that is too introverted and even borders on a form of solipsistic idealism. A reader may be inclined to ask, where in *The Red Book* is there an encounter with the concrete, living other? As we have seen, earlier in *The Red Book* Jung had proclaimed that we have (perhaps we should read, "he had") yet to discover both the "gulf that separates" and "the bridge that could connect us" (RB, p. 289b). In *The Red Book*, we certainly see Jung struggling to find a place for the "other" within his experience, and, as discussed earlier, in *Memories, Dreams Reflections,* he records that he abandoned work on *The Red Book* as he re-emerged into a more public life (MDR, p. 197). We might understand Jung's *Red Book* period as a retreat from the inflated and inauthentic public persona he had evolved during the years of his association with Freud, and as a time during which intense self-reflection and self-scrutiny permitted him to "live with himself" and thus re-emerge into more authentic relations with others.

FURTHER DOUBTS

Jung now enters into a mood of self-doubt that is Cartesian in scope: "With painful slice," he says, "I cut off what I pretended to know about what lies beyond me …And my knife cuts even deeper…until I know only that I am without knowing what I am" (RB, p. 306b). Jung is here in a humble frame of mind that contrasts markedly with his expansive claims to heal and give birth to a God, as well as his claim to understand the collective psyche of humanity. He writes, "I want to be poor and bare…naked before the inexorable" (RB, p. 306b). Jung now says that he wants to discard his "divine and devilish" burden, explaining that it is not up to him to "prove the Gods and the devils and the chaotic monsters, to feed them…and to protect them with belief against disbelief and doubt" (RB, p. 307a). In *The Red Book* we see an intellect that yearns passionately to be completely open to doubt and at the same time to be certain that it knows, that wishes to accept the burden of prophesizing a new religion and who shuns that task. Small wonder that Jung developed the idea that the Self is a *coincidentia oppositorum.*

IMAGES OF THE COMPLETED SELF

We have seen how in **RB Images, pp. 117-123** Jung depicts the battle and triumph of the hero/antihero Atmavictu over the dragon, which symbolizes the regressive forces of the unconscious. Atmavictu eviscerates the dragon and thereby releases the sun (the libido) which had been swallowed by the dragon in **RB Image, p. 117**. Now in **RB Image, p. 125** Atmavictu, having slain the dragon and released the sun/libido from its belly, is suspended above the earth and holds a quadrated *blazing sun* over a town comprised of various medieval and modern elements (RB, p. 306, n. 237, and MDR, p. 100). This sun, we might surmise, represents the liberated libido and self. **RB Image, p. 127** (which appears in Chapter XIX but will be considered here) was completed on January 9, 1921. In this image Jung depicts what he describes as four kinds of human sacrifice that correspond to the four psychological functions of thinking, feeling, sensation, and intuition, which he wrote about in *Psychological Types*, published in 1921. The four quadrants also appear in the brilliant sun-image in **RB Image, p. 125,** suggesting that the full liberation of the personality must traverse all four functions, in spite of the sacrifices and travails this may mean for the individual.

Chapter 8

Magic, Symbols, and the Critique of Reason

The Red Book: Liber Secundus

"Chapter XIX: The Gift of Magic," pp. 307-9

Jung is well known for his receptive attitude toward such "discredited" disciplines as alchemy and astrology, which he generally interpreted in psychological terms as manifestations of the archetypes of the collective unconscious. In *The Red Book*, Jung takes a favorable view of another presumably discredited discipline, "magic," but he does so without obviously interpreting it in psychological terms. Jung's interest in magic is meant to serve as a corrective or compensation for the excesses of science and reason, and it would thus defeat his purpose to provide a rational explanation of magical practices and beliefs.

It is Jung's soul that introduces him to "magic," and she informs him that he must accept both the fortune and misfortune that this will bring. Jung inquires about the nature of the misfortune that accompanies the gift of magic, and his soul states that he must sacrifice both the giving and receiving of "solace" if he is to possess magic's "black rod." Jung protests that such a sacrifice "means the loss of a piece of humanity" (RB, p. 307b), and his soul's response is to ask rhetorically whether nature offers solace? Jung hesitates to take the misfortune of magic upon himself, stating that he is "happy with the warmth of life" and he is reluctant to make such a sacrifice (RB, p. 307b). He believes that by taking on magic his humanity will be replaced by "severity," both to himself and others. As Shamdasani points out, Nietzsche, in *Ecce Homo*, held that "Every acquisition, every step forward in knowledge....is the result of courage, of severity toward oneself" (RB, p. 307, n. 239).

Jung's soul advises him not to struggle against magic, and moreover to surrender the enlightened scientific attitude that interferes with his belief in the black rod. Jung asks his soul to be patient, for his "science has not yet been overcome" (RB, p. 307b), and to do so "for the sake of magic...[is] uncanny and menacing" (RB, p. 308a). Yet it is too late for Jung to reject magic, for he has already made the commitment to accept "everything," especially all that is darkest in humanity. Jung accepts "the black rod because it is the first thing the darkness" has granted him (RB, p. 308a), yet he continues to wonder what "magic" will bring. He asks, "Will you bring bad weather, storms, cold, thunder and lightning, or will you make the fields fruitful and bless the bodies of pregnant women?" (RB, p. 308a).

AN "EXISTENTIAL" FORM OF MAGIC

Jung's attention now shifts to a nameless, formless god or redeemer who arises from the acceptance of magic and is one of the "gifts of darkness." A stunning image of a man who appears to be summoning a demonic serpent-deity (**RB Image, p. 129**) accompanies Jung's exhortation that one should raise one's hands in both prayer and despair but not gaze upon the God to come (RB, p. 308a, b). One must recognize that the future God is not only created by "inhuman forces" but also arises from each individual (RB, p. 308b). Such creation is a highly personalized affair, as one must gaze into oneself, as each individual's path is unique to him or her.

The task of creating the future, and presumably the new God and new religion, is magical. It is also "existential," as in the process the "dead will besiege you to live your unlived life" (RB, p. 308b). Jung strikes the same existential note when he asks, "Time is of the essence, so why do you want to pile up the lived and let the unlived rot?" (RB, p. 308b). One again has the impression that the God/redeemer that is to come is indistinguishable from a unique, highly individuated Self.

Jung's description of the magical "way" to redemption involves the familiar *Red Book* themes of the merging of heaven and hell and the union of the opposites (RB, p. 308b, p. 309a). Jung provides a poetic description of *"A solitary cooking up healing potions"* that clearly anticipates his later interest in the alchemical work. Jung writes, *"I took old magical apparatuses and prepared hot potions and mixed in secrets and ancient powers ...I watched over the cauldron through many starry nights...Just a little longer and fermentation will be complete"* (RB, p. 309a). However, the "solitary" who involves himself in this magical activity refrains from being a savior because his way has been blocked by the one who was "nailed to the cross" and "one [savior] is truly enough" (RB, p. 309b). Even more importantly, each must prove his worth by living his own life (RB, p. 309b). By refraining from being a savior so that each may find salvation for him or herself, the solitary appears to be at odds with the Mahayana bodhisattva who refrains from entering Nirvana for the sake of remaining on earth and teaching the way of salvation to others.

IMAGES OF MAGIC

In **RB Image, p. 129,** one of *The Red Book's* most stunning paintings, the spirit of a serpent conjured by a dark figure below, rises over a sleeping town. A brilliant star glows through the serpent and illuminates the center of the scene. As noted above, this image of summoning or divination may reflect the magical conjuring of a nameless God. This painting and the image to follow (**RB Image, p. 131**) depict a brilliant cool night star/ sun that complements the fiery "day sun" in **RB Image, p. 125.** After traversing the four functions, the Self now assimilates the dragon and shadow elements of the night. In **RB Image, p. 131** what was barren below blossoms into a warm tropical evening under the rays of the night sun. The text prior to this image speaks about the union of the poles of "Heaven and Hell" and "Above and Below" (RB, p. 308b, p. 309a).

In **RB Image, p. 133** a mysterious stone hangs over a cold, forbidding, and morose mosaic man, whose eyes radiate solar light. The text suggests that this is an image of the "Solitary" (RB, p. 309a), whose "runes" and magical potions are for the sake of man. Jung suggests that there is something "inhuman" about magic, and the figure painted here, cold and stone-like (drawn, as Jay Sherry points out, in an "Aztec" style[1]) is very much lacking in human qualities.

Jung describes **RB Image, p. 135**, which was completed on November 25, 1922, as a fire that emanates from "Muspilli," which, as depicted in an early medieval German epic poem by that name, is the divine abode from which emanates a cataclysmic world-ending fire (cf. RB, p. 309, n. 248). The fire takes hold of the tree of life, and all takes place in the world egg incubated by the solitary's "unnameable God" (RB, p. 309, n. 248). Jung relates that a "cycle is completed" and the smoke and ash (of the tree of life?) give rise to new creatures. As Jung plunges himself into the world of "magic" and the new God of the solitary, something indeed "monstrous" may emerge.

"Chapter XX: The Way of the Cross," pp. 309-12

Jung has a vision of a serpent creeping into the body of the crucified Christ and emerging from his mouth. As Jung watches in confusion, a white bird on his shoulder speaks: "Let it rain, let the wind blow, let the waters flow and the fire burn. Let each thing have its development. Let becoming have its day" (RB, p. 310a). Through the juxtaposition of these gruesome and sublime images Jung conveys the thought that living one's own life, i.e. having one's "development," is a grim task. "Truly," Jung tells us, "the way leads through the crucified" (RB, p. 310a). Entering into one's own life not only requires enormous humility but the overcoming of aversion and even disgust. A person "would rather devise any trick to help him escape, since nothing matches the torment of one's own way" (RB, p. 310a). Some fall in love and others commit crimes as a means to avoid becoming themselves. Jung is again in an existential frame of mind, one that draws on Nietzsche's *Zarathustra* and anticipates the notions of "authenticity" in Heidegger and Sartre, and, of course, Jung's own notion of "individuation." Jung suggests that the endeavor to gain power over others and to make them be, act, and think like oneself is actually a means of avoiding one's own path. Indeed, one should make demands upon no one save oneself, since when one makes demands upon another he avoids responsibility for his own life.

THE NATURE OF THE SYMBOL

We are now treated to a discourse on the meaning and nature of the "symbol," which Jung sees as the key to inner freedom, and presumably to individuation as well. Anticipating a distinction he will make in *Psychological Types*, Jung writes: "If the word is a sign it means nothing. But if the word is a symbol it means everything" (RB, p. 310b). Harkening back to his vision of the serpent emerging from the mouth of Christ, Jung says that "the way rises in the darkness and leaves the mouth as a saving symbol" (RB, p. 310b). The symbol, Jung writes, involves a human struggle with darkness, it "rises out of the depths of the self...and places itself unexpectedly on the tongue" (RB, p. 311a). Indeed, one can recognize the symbol because it is "alien to the conscious mind" (RB, p. 311a). By accepting the symbol one gains access to a new "room" in one's psyche, and enters into a gate leading to salvation. There are many such gates and each are comprised of symbols. Jung is here framing his notion of the "transcendent function," which unconsciously and imaginatively produces symbols that unite opposites and reconciles conflicts that cannot be resolved through conscious thought (RB, p. 311b). Jung writes that "good and bad must first be united if the symbol is to be created" (RB, p. 311a). The symbol "becomes;" it is "neither thought up nor found. Its becoming is like the becoming of human life in the womb" (RB, p. 311a). According to Jung, the symbol is "born from the mind, as befits a God" (RB, p. 311a).

We catch a glimpse of Jung's theory of archetypes in nascent form when he tells us that what arises via the symbol is "always something ancient" (RB, p. 311b) and "To give birth to the ancient in a new time is creation" (RB, p. 311b). Jung compares the "soul of humanity" to the repeating wheel of the zodiac, and, in an echo of Plato's theory of reminiscence, he says that everything that comes to the soul "from below to the heights was already there" (RB, p. 311b).

The symbol, meaning, and salvation can never, according to Jung, arise out of will and intention. One cannot act as if one were a charioteer, guiding the forces of one's psyche so as to preserve one's aims. Instead, one must let go of intention altogether if one is to enter into progress and the future. "Futurity grows out of me...against [my] will and intention" (RB, p. 311b). Jung will later speak of abandoning the direction of "ego consciousness" in favor of the deeper, more profound voice that emanates from the "Self." Here, after noting that the "ancients devised magic to compel (outer) fate" (RB, p. 311b), Jung says that one must now seek magic "to determine inner fate" (RB, p. 311b). He is about to take upon himself the task of becoming an apprentice to a magician.

SYMBOLS OF THE SELF

Here again, it will be useful to momentarily depart from our text in order to provide a general picture of Jung's understanding of the nature of the symbol and its relation to the "Self" during the period of *The Red Book*'s composition. For Jung, "symbols" rather than "facts" or "ideas" are the "royal road" to both psychological insight and wisdom. In *The Red Book* we learn that "there are not many truths, there are only a few. Their meaning is too deep to grasp other than in symbols" (RB, p. 291a). Indeed, one of Jung's greatest contributions to the intellectual dialog of the 20th century was to help establish the symbol as a vehicle for knowledge, insight, and personal transformation. While "the ancients lived their symbols" (RB, p. 236a), in our own time, when the world has become all too real, in the sense of "reality" as it is defined by science and reason, we are in danger of losing our connection to symbolic meaning, and this, for Jung, amounts to a loss of human meaning.

In *Psychological Types*, Jung explains that symbols, in contrast to signs, are the best possible expression "of a relatively unknown thing, which…cannot be more clearly or characteristically represented" (CW 6, § 815). In that work Jung repeats and expands upon his *Red Book* claim that a symbol cannot be produced through conscious mentation, but must always be created through unconscious activity, an activity that has both rational and irrational elements (CW 6, § 822). Jung called the psychic function that produces symbols the "transcendent function," and he writes that it produces psychological transformation by facilitating "a transition from one attitude to another" (CW 6, § 828).

As we have seen, Jung holds that symbols are the means through which the psyche reconciles or unites opposites. For Jung, "The raw material shaped by thesis and antithesis, and in the shaping of which the opposites are united, is the living symbol" (CW 6, § 828). In this Jung is later echoed by the French structural anthropologist Lévi-Strauss, who held that myths reconcile contradictions that cannot be resolved through reason.[2] By holding that opposites can only be reconciled via symbols, Jung consciously opposed himself to Hegel, who held that contradictions could be overcome through dialectical *reason*.

In *Psychological Types* Jung explains that a symbol is "born of man's highest spiritual aspirations." It arises "from the deepest roots of his being…from the lowest and most primitive levels of the psyche" (CW 6, § 824). If we reflect upon these ideas for a moment we realize that the contradictions that symbols reconcile must always involve a conflict between good and bad (RB, p. 311a), civilized and primitive, or at least between "accepted" and "rejected;" otherwise, there would be little need for their reconciliation. In *Psychological Types* Jung describes how the symbols of the great religions reconcile spirituality with sensuality (CW 6, § 825). One need look no further than the symbol of communion, where the Catholic initiate consumes the body and blood of Christ, or the symbols of Jewish ritual, where blessings are recited over sensual pursuits such as food, drink, wine, and fragrances.

Jung makes the bold claim that symbols provide one with true freedom. In *The Red Book* he states, "Our freedom does not lie outside us, but within us…One can certainly gain outer freedom through powerful actions, but one creates inner freedom only through the symbol" (RB, p. 311a). How can we understand this claim? First, we should note that Jung relates how "in the symbol there is the release of the bound human force struggling with darkness" (RB, p. 310b, p. 311a). Further, the symbol, by reconciling good and evil, enables one to integrate the dark aspects of self and the world and frees one from the grip of one's shadow. Finally, by reconciling conflicts that would otherwise produce depression, anxiety, or other psychological symptoms, the symbol has the potential to free us from our neurotic inhibitions.

Jung was not the only 20th century thinker to hold that the *imagination* is the key to human freedom. In his 1940 work, *The Psychology of the Imagination,*[3] Jean-Paul Sartre argued that the imagination, by enabling consciousness to negate, transcend, and ultimately transform what is presented to it as "real," is the source of man's ontological freedom. However, in contradistinction to Jung, who held that fantasy and symbols emerge from an "other" (i.e. the collective psyche) over which one has no conscious control, Sartre held that "the image…is a consciousness that aims to produce its object,"[4] and that the image contains nothing other than that which consciousness puts into it.[5] Indeed, for Sartre, the constructed nature of the image is precisely the source of human freedom. Here we find another source of the distinction between Jung and the existentialists, a distinction that results in a contrast between the "existential" and "archetypal" man, the former asserting his freedom through conscious decision, the latter through an attunement with forces and symbols that are beyond his conscious control.

Amongst the symbols discussed by Jung, those pointing to the "Self" are of paramount importance. To take just a few examples, for Jung, the "Primordial Man" (CW 15, § 548), the philosopher's stone (CW 9ii, § 426), mandalas (CW 9i, §§ 542, 717; CW 15, § 717), Christ (CW 9ii, pp. 36-71), Buddha (CW 9ii, § 304), and God (CW 9ii, §§ 116, 304) are all symbols of the union of opposites that constitutes the Jungian Self. Indeed, like its symbols, the Self points to something that is familiar yet, because it is largely unconscious, very imperfectly known. For Jung, the symbol is paradoxically both *determined* by our heredity, history, and collective humanity, *and* is the source of our *free will*.

For Jung, a symbol, if it is to function as such, can never be completely understood. As he famously puts it in *Psychological Types*:

> So long as a symbol is a living thing, it is an expression for something that cannot be characterized in any other or better way. The symbol is alive only so long as it is pregnant with meaning. But once its meaning has been born out of it, once that expression is found which formulates the thing sought, expected, or divined even better than the hitherto accepted symbol, then the symbol is dead, i.e. it possesses only a historical significance. (CW 6, § 816)

One suspects that this "death of the symbol" contains Jung's understanding of Nietzsche's proclamation of the death of God. In *The Red Book* Jung suggests that science, presumably by explaining clearly and rationally so many things that God had hitherto been invoked to explain, had killed the gods, or at least made them mortally ill. We might say that for Jung, the symbol of God was no longer pregnant with meaning, and was in need of a new influx of mystery—something he sought to provide through his notions of fantasy, the archetypes, and the collective unconscious.

Today we might ask whether the symbol of the Self is itself threatened with death, either by the mechanistic view of the person that is emerging from biological psychology and cognitive science, or the fragmentation brought about by contemporary society and the expression of this fragmentation in post-modern art, thought, and culture. Further, we can inquire into what would comprise human "self-understanding," if the very symbol/concept of the Self were no longer viable or interesting. This is not a result that Jung found particularly palatable. As we will see, he held that the Self must remain an impenetrable mystery if it is not to die.[6]

"Chapter XXI: The Magician," pp. 312-330

In this long, winding, and difficult chapter of *Liber Secundus* we are introduced to Philemon (**RB Image, p. 154**), the "magician" who in *Scrutinies* will speak of the Gnostic mysteries in his "Seven Sermons to the Dead." Jung tells us that Philemon's "magical rod lies in a cupboard together with the sixth and seventh books of Moses and the wisdom of Hermes Trismegitsus" (RB, p. 312a). Interestingly, Jung himself kept *The Red Book* in his kitchen cupboard at Kusnacht, where it remained even after his death. Of further note, the *Sixth and Seventh Books of Moses* is reputedly a book of Kabbalistic magical spells that was published in 1849 by Johann Schiebel, who claimed, without adequate justification, that the spells were derived from ancient Talmudic and Kabbalistic sources.[7]

Philemon, as here represented by Jung, is the character described in Ovid's *Metamorphoses* who with his wife, Baucis, welcomed Jupiter and Mercury into their homes after the Gods had been turned away by a thousand others, and who were rewarded not only by their being permitted to survive a devastating flood, but by being anointed as priest and priestess in the Gods' temple. Jung, who believes that Philemon holds the secret of magic, makes a concerted effort to get him to explain its nature and workings; but Philemon is quite coy in response, stating, "there is nothing to tell" (RB, p. 312b). Still, we manage to learn that magic is conducted with "sympathy," by which Philemon means both "compassion" and "sympathetic," or imitative, means. We also learn that for Philemon magic "is inborn in man," an idea that Jung reinforces with his observation "that all people in all times and in all places have the same magical customs" (RB, p. 313a), again touching upon a line of thinking that accords with his developing notion of the collective unconscious. While Jung expresses a certain skepticism about magic, calling it "one of the vain tools of men" (RB, p. 313a), the introduction of "magic" provides him with the opportunity to discuss the role of reason and unreason in the search for one's soul.

REASON AND MAGIC

Philemon tells Jung that magic is outside the category of knowledge, and is "the negative of what one can know" (RB, p. 313b). Indeed, when it comes to magic "there is nothing for you to understand," as "Magic happens to be precisely everything that eludes comprehension"[8] (RB, p. 313b). When Jung protests that this must mean that "magic is nothing but deception" (RB, p. 313b), Philemon admonishes him for *reasoning* about the matter. Philemon explains that the difficulty with magic is precisely the difficulty of existing without reason. This is why most magicians are advanced in years—since reason declines with old age. Perhaps, Philemon explains, Jung should wait a few years until his "hair has gone grey" and his "reason has slackened" (RB, p. 313b).

Reflecting upon his encounter with Philemon, Jung makes a number of further observations about magic and reason. We learn that "It is an error to believe that there are magical practices that one can learn. One cannot understand magic. One can only understand what accords with reason. Magic accords with unreason, which one cannot understand." Further, "The world accords not only with reason but with unreason" (RB, p. 314a), a claim that Jung must have at least vaguely intended as his response to Hegel's assertion (made in the *Philosophy of Right*) that only the rational is real. Jung has already told us that there is a "reality" that corresponds to the imagination, and he is here adamant that there is an element of reality that is not comprehensible by reason. Indeed, there is a form of understanding, i.e. "magical understanding," that "one calls noncomprehension" (RB, p. 314a). There is something akin to "negative theology" at work here. I am reminded of the assertion by the Italian-Jewish philosopher and Kabbalist, David ben Judah ha-Hasid (1470-1526), that because of God's hiddenness and incomprehensibility, "forgetting" is the mode of comprehending the deity.[9] Jung takes this sort of paradox a step further when he says of magic that it makes "what is not understood understandable in an incomprehensible manner" (RB, p. 314b). Stein has interpreted "magic" in *The Red Book* not as a power, but as an attitude that is receptive to the unconscious and the irrational, and which endeavors to make it intelligible.[10]

The Great Mystery

While Jung entertains the idea that "only those without reason [need magic] to replace their lack of reason" (RB, p. 314a) and that we are therefore no longer in need of magic, he very quickly returns to the idea "that the greater part of the world eludes our understanding," and this leaves open the door to magic even in our own time. While he acknowledges that at least a portion of what we currently find incomprehensible may be rationally comprehended in the future (RB, p. 314b), Jung holds that the deepest, most interesting layers of the soul present themselves as insuperable mysteries that are essentially impenetrable to human reason, and further that it is only through a confrontation with such mysteries that one can fully encounter one's soul and become individuated as a self. This, for Jung, is the "magic" of Philemon, and indeed the foundation of a true depth psychology. In a letter to Hans Schmid, dated Nov 6, 1915, Jung writes:

> The core of the individual is a mystery of life, which is snuffed out when it is 'grasped'… Therefore, in the later stages of analysis, we must help people towards those hidden and unlockable symbols, where the germ lies hidden like the tender seed in the hard shell. There should truly be no understanding in this regard, even if one were possible.[11]

During the period of *The Red Book's* composition Jung was not alone in regarding the self and the meaning of life an impenetrable mystery. Six months after Jung's letter to Schmid, a young philosopher, Ludwig Wittgenstein, who would soon become the darling of logical positivism, wrote in his notebooks, "The I, the I is what is deeply mysterious,"[12] and less than three years later: "We feel that even when all possible scientific questions have been answered, the problems of life remain completely untouched."[13] According to Wittgenstein, "There are, indeed, things that cannot be put into words. They make themselves manifest. They are what is mystical."[14]

Jung relates magic to the production of chaos and disarray: "If one opens up chaos, magic also arises" (RB, p. 314b), and, "Where reason establishes order and clarity, magic causes disarray and a lack of clarity" (RB, p. 314b). In his draft to *The Red Book*, Jung states that the practice of magic involves the translation of chaos into something which can be understood (RB, p. 314, n. 271), but as we have seen, for Jung, "magical understanding" is a form of "non-comprehension." Jung states that "One can teach the way that leads to chaos, but one cannot teach magic. One can only remain silent about this, which seems to be the best apprenticeship" (RB, p. 314b). Again, the comparison to the early Wittgenstein is apt. At the close of his *Tractatus*, speaking about the "mystical," those aspects of the world that cannot be articulated in language, Wittgenstein writes: "Whereof one cannot speak, thereof one must remain silent."[15]

Jung suggests (but does not state outright) that magic arises when one achieves access to unconscious aspects of the self. He writes, "Magic is a way of living," and it appears when one senses that a "greater other is actually steering" one's chariot (RB, p. 314b). Magic then occurs, but its effects cannot be predicted. It must, however, be accepted totally if one's "tree" is to grow, and such acceptance can involve a certain "stupidity" and "tastelessness." This suggests a parallel to the analytic process, where one must suspend one's rational, moral, and aesthetic judgment in order for unconscious contents to emerge.

Magic can also be understood in religious or theological terms. After all, Philemon and Baucis serve as priest and priestess to the Gods, and, as we have seen, Jung's notion of an *essential unknown* places him in close proximity to mysticism and negative theology. For example, according to the Jewish mystics, the infinite God, *Ein-sof* (literally, "Without End")

> cannot be an object of thought, let alone of speech, even though there is an indication of it in everything, for there is nothing beyond it. Consequently, there is no letter, no name, no writing, and no word that can comprise it.[16]

Jung later equated the infinite God with the unconscious, since the two were, for him, psychologically indistinguishable, and he regarded the unconscious as containing an element of the essential unknown.

In his "The Relations between the Ego and the Unconscious" (1928), Jung later wrote, "There is little hope of our ever being able to reach even approximate consciousness of the self, since however much we make conscious there will always exist an indeterminate and indeterminable amount of unconscious material which belongs to the totality of the self" (CW 7, § 274).

JUNG'S CRITIQUE OF REASON

We have already witnessed how Jung, in *The Red Book*, is highly critical of *science*, holding it responsible for the sickness of both the Gods and the human psyche, and we now see how Jung, in his discourse on "magic," turns his critical gaze upon *reason* as well. Indeed, much of *The Red Book* can be understood as an effort to create a counterweight to the modern tendency to rationally understand all things.

According to Jung:

> The ancients called the saving word the Logos, an expression of divine reason. So much unreason was in man that he needed reason to be saved…[But] in the end [the Logos] poisons us all…We spread poison and paralysis around us in that we want to educate all the world around us into reason. (RB, p. 280b)

For Jung, reason is not only present in thinking but in feeling as well (we are all familiar with those whose emotions tend to be "appropriate" and "reasonable"). However, those who are always intellectually and emotionally rational are, in Jung's view, secretly "worshipers of the serpent" (RB, p. 280b), since reason should always simply be a servant to other ends.

Jung is skeptical even regarding reason's ability to provide a basis for knowledge:

> Whenever I want to learn and understand something I leave my so-called reason at home and give whatever it is that I am trying to understand the benefit of the doubt. I have learned this gradually, because nowadays the world of science is full of scary examples of the opposite. (RB, p. 313a)

Jung observes "that the world comprises reason and unreason," adding, "and we also understood that our way needs not only reason but unreason" (RB, p. 314a). This is an idea that Jung would maintain throughout his career. For example, in his essay, "Psychological Aspects of the Mother Archetype," originally written in 1938 and revised in 1954, Jung wrote that one "ought never to forget that the world exists only because opposing forces are held in equilibrium. So, too, the rational is counterbalanced by the irrational..." (CW 9i, § 174). In the 1954 revised version of this essay, Jung expressed dire concern about the consequences of science, technology, and reason. Alluding to the development of nuclear weapons, he stated that the time had come

> when the achievements of science and technology, combined
> with a rationalistic and materialistic view of the world,
> threaten the spiritual and psychic heritage of man with
> instant annihilation. (CW 9i, § 195)

In *Psychological Types* Jung took a more sober position with respect to reason and clarified that he used the term "irrational" "not as denoting something contrary to reason, but something beyond reason, something, therefore, not grounded on reason" (CW 6, § 774). This, he informs his readers, includes "elementary facts;" for example, "That the earth has a moon, that chlorine is an element, that water reaches its greatest density at forty degrees centigrade."[17] Jung includes chance and the accidental features of objects and events under the heading of the "irrational." Yet in *The Red Book*, Jung acknowledges that certain things that are beyond reason today may not be so tomorrow: "One can be certain that the greater part of the world eludes our understanding...a part of the incomprehensible, however, is only presently incomprehensible and might already concur with reason tomorrow" (RB, p. 314a, b). This, however, may not be possible, for example, for the objects of religious experience, which reason tells us are an illusion or an illness. Jung tells us that it is "quite easy for our reason to deny the God and speak only of sickness," yet "the fiery brilliance of the God [is] a higher and fuller life than the ashes of rationality" (RB, p. 339a).

Jung's difficulty with reason is in part rooted in his belief that it is associated with only two of what he considered to be the four psychic functions. As we have seen, according to Jung, reason is associated with thinking and feeling, which he regarded as the rational functions. In Jung's typology, sensing and intuition are "irrational," largely because, unlike thinking and feeling, they are grounded in perception rather than judgment. Jung held the symbol in such high regard because he saw it as a product of all four psychic functions. In *Psychological Types* he says of the symbol:

> It certainly has a side that accords with reason, but it has another side that does not; for it is composed not only of rational but also of irrational data supplied by pure inner and outer perception. (CW 6, § 823)

One might readily suppose that based upon this definition, the irrationality of the symbol, and the irrational in general, are not functions that necessarily contradict reason or science (after all, sensation and intuition are also involved in the rational scientific process). However, in other writings, Jung suggests that the irrational is pre-rational, illogical, and associated with madness. In *Psychological Types* he says that a symbol "must derive equally from the lowest and most primitive levels of the psyche" (CW 6, § 824). As we have seen, in *The Red Book*, irrationality (like madness) is a form of the spirit that is part of all teachings, philosophies, and life (RB, p. 298a). One who refuses to enter into the irrational, illogical world of madness has, according to Jung, failed to comprehend the full nature of the psyche and, moreover, has remained outside of life itself.

There is, from Jung's perspective, yet another problem with reason. According to Jung, "the laws of reason are the laws that designate and govern the average, 'correct,' adapted attitude…Everything is 'rational' that accords with these laws, everything that contravenes them is 'irrational'" (CW 6, § 786). Since Jung regards "creative fantasy" to be the road to the soul, it follows from Jung's view that reason can never bring us to the soul, because reason, by itself, can never contravene the norm or "ruling discourse." As Stein suggests, for Jung reason (and intention) repeat the past but do not create a future.[18] It is an interesting question as to whether this is actually so—whether, for example, the revolution in the development of computers proceeded at least in part on an irrational basis.

Reason is often associated with a logic of "consistency," and as we have seen, the question of "consistency" and "contradiction" has already been raised in some of Jung's *Red Book* pronouncements, and is indeed an important question for Jungian psychology in general. We should note that Jung came to regard strict consistency as a limitation of the European mindset, pointing out, for example, in his "Commentary on *The Tibetan Book of the Dead*" that the "unspoken assumption (of Eastern thought) [is] the antimonian character of all metaphysical assertions…not the niggardly European 'either-or', but a magnificently affirmative 'both-and'" (CW 11, § 833). Late in his life, Jung stated,

> I should be prepared to make transcendental statements, but on one condition: that I state at the same time the possibility of their being untrue. For instance "God is," i.e., is as I think he is. But as I know that I could not possibly form an adequate idea of an all-embracing eternal being, my idea of him is pitifully incomplete; thus the statement "God is not" (so) is equally true and necessary. (CW 18, § 1584)

I am here reminded of the Kabbalist Azriel of Gerona's conception of God as the "Union of all contradictions," including those of faith and unbelief.[19]

We might again ask, however, whether the acceptance of contradiction necessarily requires an abandonment of reason, which Jung, in *The Red Book* and elsewhere, seemed to assume. As we have seen, a contrary view is held by Buddhist, Hegelian, and "dialetheistic" logicians, who have each suggested that it is perfectly rational to speak of propositions (such as the "Liar's paradox," e.g. "This statement is false") that are both true and false (or neither true nor false) and/or which logically imply their own contradictions. Hegel, for example, held that logic must be dialectical in order to reflect the essential oppositions that are prevalent in the world:

> every actual thing involves a coexistence of opposed elements. Consequently to know, or, in other words, to comprehend an object is equivalent to being conscious of it as a concrete unity of opposed determinations.[20]

THE DANGERS OF "UN-REASON"

Jung's celebration of the irrational appears to have figured into his early enthusiasm for National Socialism. At the Tavistock Clinic in London in 1935 Jung described how Nazism not only had a hypnotic effect upon the German people, but even, when he was in Germany, upon Jung himself:

Would you have believed that a whole nation of highly intelligent and cultivated people could be seized by the fascinating power of an archetype? I saw it coming, and I can understand it because I know the power of the collective unconscious. But on the surface it looks simply incredible. Even my personal friends are under that fascination, and when I am in Germany, I believe it myself, I understand it all, I know it has to be as it is. One cannot resist it. It gets you below the belt and not in your mind, your brain just counts for nothing, your sympathetic system is gripped. It is a power that fascinates people from within, it is the collective unconscious which is activated...We cannot be children about it, having intellectual and reasonable ideas and saying: this should not be...An incomprehensible fate has seized them, and you cannot say it is right, or it is wrong. It has nothing to do with rational judgment, it is just history. (CW 18, § 372)

While this statement is meant to be *descriptive*, and indeed provides insight into the advent of the Nazi era, it comports too closely with Jung's *Red Book* critique of reason and conventional morality (RB, p. 280b, p. 313a), with Jung's later claim that "We should never identify ourselves with reason..." (CW 7, § 111), and with his admission that he was initially optimistic about Hitler and the Nazis[21] for us not to be concerned about its theoretical implications. In 1939 Jung told H. R. Knickerbocker, an American journalist, that Hitler's "unconscious has exceptional access to his consciousness" and that it was this that made him a "true leader."[22] The problem with this is that it was just such access to the collective unconscious, and the consequent taming of the ego's "virtue" and "reason," that Jung had prescribed for the modern soul. Indeed, the same year as the Knickerbocker interview, Jung published a paper in English, "The Meaning of Individuation" (published in CW 9i, pp. 272-89, in somewhat modified form as "Conscious, Unconscious and Individuation"), in which he stated that "unconscious influences...are often truer and wiser than our conscious thinking" (CW 9i, § 504), and that what "in Indian philosophy is called the 'higher' consciousness, corresponds to what we in the West call the 'unconscious'" (CW 9i, § 506).

After the war Jung would say that he could not bring himself to believe that a civilized European state could act so irrationally:

> When Hitler seized power it became quite evident to me that
> a mass psychosis was boiling up in Germany. But I could
> not help telling myself that this was after all Germany, a
> civilized European nation with a sense of morality and
> discipline. (CW 10, § 472)

However, Jung's pre-war optimism regarding the Nazis and Hitler
raises serious questions about any psychology, philosophy, or theology
that fails to hold the non-rational psychic functions accountable to
reason. While in *The Red Book* and many of his subsequent writings
prior to World War II, Jung was adamant that reason cannot dominate
the psyche or our understanding of it, later, in reflecting upon the
irrational psychic forces that in his view produced the events that
occurred in Nazi Germany, he came close to modifying his thinking
and recalibrating the relationship between unconscious contents and
rational understanding:

> As a psychiatrist, accustomed to dealing with patients who are
> in danger of being overwhelmed by unconscious contents, I
> knew that it is of utmost importance, from the therapeutic point
> of view, to strengthen as far as possible their conscious position
> and powers of understanding so that something is there to
> intercept and integrate the contents that are breaking through
> to consciousness. (CW 10, § 473)

In a late life interview, first published in 1958,[23] Jung went even further
in his assessment of the relationship between the unconscious and
conscious reason:

> Since everybody believes or, at least, tries to believe in the
> unequivocal superiority of rational consciousness, I have to
> emphasize the importance of the unconscious irrational forces,
> to establish a sort of balance. Thus to superficial readers of my
> writings it looks as if I were giving the unconscious a supreme
> significance, disregarding consciousness. As a matter of fact the
> emphasis lies on consciousness as the *conditio sine qua non* of
> apperception of unconscious contents, and the supreme arbiter
> in the chaos of unconscious possibilities. (CW 18, § 1585)

Stein points out that Jung kept a bust of Voltaire in his study,
which Stein interprets in terms of the conclusion of *Candide* which
espouses a philosophy of cultivating one's own garden.[24] Might it not

also be that this bust of Voltaire, who himself symbolized the Enlightenment, was a reminder for Jung of the value of reason and even a compensation for Jung's own fascination with the non-rational?

Even during his *Red Book* period Jung had doubts about the vehemence with which he had critiqued rational thinking. Shamdasani quotes from an unpublished letter to J.B. Lang, dated January 17, 1919, in which Jung writes,

> It is the devil who says: Disdain all reason and science, mankind's highest powers. That is never appropriate even though we are forced to acknowledge [the existence of] the irrational. (RB Intro, p. 207)

I am here reminded of the Hasidic parable of the "two pockets." In one pocket a man should keep a piece of paper on which is written, "I am but the dust of the earth," and in the other pocket a paper with the phrase, "For me the entire world was created." Wisdom is knowing which pocket one must reach into on any given occasion. It seems that for Jung, one pocket should hold a paper with the phrase, "We should never identify ourselves with reason..." (CW 7, § 111), while "It is the devil who says: Disdain all reason and science, mankind's highest powers" (RB Intro, p. 207) should be held in the other.

THE THREE TYPES OF LOVERS

Returning to our text, Jung now recites an ode to Philemon, whose very name suggests that he is a lover (RB, p. 315a). Philemon's survival of the flood indicates that "he remained alive when chaos erupted," and Jung reflects, "Truly it is the lover who survives" (RB, p. 315a). In a revealing passage Jung states that there are three types of lovers, "those who love men, those who love the souls of men, and those who love their own soul" (RB, p. 315b). Philemon, Jung tells us, exemplifies the third type of lover, and Jung asks whether one is not a man "until one is a lover of one's own soul" (RB, p. 315b). It is telling that Jung would choose such an inner-facing "lover" as his spiritual guide, especially a lover who, as Jung now says, has a "cold" wisdom, "with a grain of poison, yet healing in small doses" (RB, p. 315b). Jung praises Philemon for his not having lecture halls and students, and for providing only words that left Jung with "nothing" and "doubt." Jung tells Philemon: "you are no Christian, since you nourish yourself from yourself and force men to do the same"

(RB, p. 315b). Indeed, Philemon appears to leave Jung to his own devices, both in his assessment of Philemon's character and in discerning the nature of the "magic" that Philemon represents. Whereas Christ has led men to "expect gifts from their saviors" (RB, p. 316a), Philemon is wise because he withholds gifts, expecting "everything to grow from within itself" (RB, p. 316a), a notion that anticipates Jung's later ideas regarding the psychotherapeutic conditions for individuation.

Philemon is the "father of all eternal wisdom" (RB, p. 315b), but his wisdom is paradoxical, for it is invisible, and Philemon's "truth is unknowable, entirely untrue in any given age, and yet true in all eternity" (RB, p. 316a). (We are here brought back to the distinction between the "spirit of this time" and the "spirit of the depths" with which *The Red Book* began.) Further, Philemon is a "vessel of fables," and would be seen as a "liar and a swindler" if he "went to men as a man" (RB, p. 316b). Another paradox involves the fact that Philemon teaches only the dead (RB, p. 316b), as only false teachers teach the living, and the living receive truth from teachers only by killing them (RB, p. 317a). At this point in *The Red Book,* Philemon appears to be little more than a blank screen upon which Jung projects his fantasies about magic, and who thereby forces Jung to rely upon himself in his search for wisdom and truth. However, Jung's path to wisdom will not be direct nor easy, for "only he who knows the darkest error knows what light is" (RB, p. 317a).

Chapter 9

Philosophical and Theological Reflections

The Red Book: Liber Secundus

"Chapter XXI: The Gift of Magic," cont.

Dialog with the Serpent/Soul

Jung emerges from his encounter with Philemon as a magician, and he now proceeds to play a magic flute and seduce the serpent into believing that she is his soul (RB, p. 317a). Jung then engages in a series of encounters with a figure that is alternately identified as a serpent, Jung's soul, and a bird. Jung asks his "soul" for some words of wisdom or advice, and she responds that she lets "grass grow over everything" Jung does (RB, p. 317a). Jung finds this somewhat banal, and his soul explains, "Banality is my element," adding, "the more uncommon you are the more common I can be" (RB, p. 317a), suggesting that a man who is outwardly preoccupied with the esoteric and the beyond is *compensated* by a soul that is quite down to earth and ordinary.

In his dialog with his serpent/soul Jung returns to his preoccupation with the coincidence of the opposites, which now emerges as the major theme of his *Red Book* quest. His soul informs him that a "last supper" is being prepared and Jung concludes that he is to be "both guest and dish at this meal," a thought that he finds both sweet and horrifying (RB, p. 317b). With this there is a merger of "madness and reason," "tears and laughter," "morality and immorality," and "joy and pain" (RB, p. 318a). Further, where there is love (as with Christ) there is also the serpent, and one who wants to "become" stands in the middle of a battle between the serpent and the bird (RB, p. 318b).

JUNG'S "INNOVATION," THE MERGING OF OPPOSITES

Jung inquires about the consequences of his "innovation," the unification of the opposites. "How will it be," he asks, "now that God and the devil have become one?" (RB, p. 318b). Will this merger bring life to a standstill? Is it not the case that strife between the opposites (as opposed to their unification) is the very condition of life? The serpent/soul answers that this is indeed the case (RB, p. 318b), and adds that Jung's "innovations" have deprived her of a source of power (RB, p. 319a). Jung pleads that he is not the guilty one, as it was his serpent/soul that led him "carefully along the way," to which the serpent responds "you might have rejected the apple" (RB, p. 319a), intimating that the coincidence of opposites is the very knowledge that was forbidden to mankind. Jung thus suggests that the forbidden fruit not only provided knowledge of the distinction between good and evil, but of their essential unity as well.

Jung now has a complex vision, one that involves the throne of God, the holy trinity, heaven, and Satan. He informs Satan, "we have united the opposites" and indeed "bonded you (Satan) with God" (RB, p. 319a). Satan responds cavalierly that this idea is a "hopeless fuss" and asks, "Why such nonsense?" Jung insists that his coincidence of opposites is "an important principle," as "We have to put a stop to never-ending quarrelling, to finally free our hands for real life" (RB, p. 319a). Satan's devilish retort is that Jung's theory "smells of monism," and "special chambers have been heated" in hell for its advocates. Jung replies that he is no monist, as he has "no single correct truth" (RB, p. 319b).

Jung states that with the union of opposites a strange and incomprehensible thing occurred: "nothing further happened," and "life turned into a complete standstill" (RB, p. 319b). Jung, in a bit of a panic, asks Satan what should be done, and Satan admonishes him for getting involved in "the order of the world" to begin with. However, Jung observes that the "holy trinity" (which remains on the scene) is "taking things cooly" and "does not seem to dislike the innovation"

(RB, p. 319b). Satan responds that the holy trinity's reactions are not to be trusted and that the "standstill" Jung has produced with his presumptuousness "closely resembles the absolute," and "the absolute was always adverse to the living" (RB, p. 319b). In contrast to the absolute, who is boring and vegetative, Satan claims to be "ambition, greed for fame, lust for action....the fizz of new thoughts...", and he advises Jung to "completely revoke [his] harmful innovation as soon as possible" (RB, p. 319b).

Jung and Satan then debate the true nature and value of life; whether the personal life of ambition and desire is preferable to the life of divinity with its "forbearing patience" and "eternity" (RB, p. 320a). The question is not resolved, neither here in *The Red Book*, nor, I would hazard, in our own lives. Should the goal of life be the intensification of desire and the efforts at its fulfillment, or the death of desire with its attendant repose and relief from the suffering of unsatisfied wants? Jung, with his "innovation" of the unity of opposites, arrives at the threshold of a mystical (quite Eastern) solution to the problem of life, but then hesitates at the precipice. "This time," he tells Satan, "you have counseled me well" (RB, p. 320a). Later Jung will declare that while those in the West can learn much from the wisdom of the East, we cannot wholeheartedly adopt its spiritual path (CW 11, § 902). The thinking that entered into this conclusion is percolating in these *Red Book* dialogs.

THEOSOPHICAL NOTIONS

The narrative shifts again and Jung addresses himself to the Gods. He enters into a wide-raging theosophical monologue that commences with the question of whether he should begin in "suffering or in joy, or in the mixed feeling lying between" (RB, p. 320a). Jung speaks of the "little drop of something that falls into the sea of nothingness" prior to the world's creation, and which widens into "unrestricted freedom" (RB, p. 320a). He harangues and curses the devil, praying "that the gold of the Gods will spray out of [his] body" (RB, p. 320b). In a theosophical metaphor that parallels images in gnosticism, alchemy, and the Kabbalah, Jung speaks of the devil's casings bursting asunder so that the divine seed or golden one can be freed from the "slithery mud" (RB, p. 320b). Certainly, at the time of *The Red Book*, Jung was already familiar with the Gnostic notion of a divine spark entrapped in the material world, and he will later speak about the alchemical process of extracting gold from base metal as a metaphor for the individuation of the Self. Late in his life Jung will encounter the Kabbalistic metaphor of extracting a seed or spark of divine light trapped in the casings or husks (*Kellipot*) of the "Other Side,"[1] a metaphor for the repair and restoration of the soul and world.

Jung encounters the Cabiri, early Greek gods who Jung regarded as "elemental spirits" and chthonic deities who "still have roots in the soil like plants" (RB, p. 320b). He says that the Cabiri are "the first formations of the unformed gold" that arise from the devil's body, and he asks them if they are the "earthly feet of the Godhead" (RB, p. 320b), demanding that they reply.

The Cabiri greet Jung, who they respectfully term "the master of the lower nature," and they inform him that they "know the unknown and the inexplicable laws of living nature" (RB, p. 320b). Indeed, they describe themselves as responsible for the slow, lethargic process through which dead matter "enters into the living" (RB, p. 321a). They have brought Jung a gift, a "flashing sword" with which he "can cut the knot which entangles [him]" (RB, p. 321a). It turns out that this knot is nothing other than "the great snarled ball" which mother nature has woven as Jung's *brain*, and the Cabiri inform Jung that since man is entangled in his brain, Jung, as the "master of lower nature," must "cut through the entanglement" (RB, p. 321a). Indeed, the Cabiri tell Jung that this very entanglement with the brain constitutes his madness. Jung is incensed by the insinuation that he is mad, and he hurls some select words at the Cabiri, calling them "roots of clay and excrement" and "polyp-snared rubbish." He adds that the Cabiri are themselves the "root fibers" of his brain, to which the Cabiri respond that they require destruction as they are the entanglement (RB, p. 320a).

The Cabiri inform Jung that they are willing to die for him and when they die Jung "will no longer be his brain, but will exist beyond [his] madness" (RB, p. 321b). One who is ensnared within the brain is "wild" and puny, but one who rises above his brain "gain(s) the form of a giant" (RB, p. 321b). Jung finally agrees to strike the mortal blow, the Cabiri declare that what they both feared and desired has come to pass, and Jung asserts that he now stands above his brain, has built a tower out of the "lower and upper beyond" (RB, p. 332a), and is the "master of [his] own self" (RB, p. 321b).

What can we make of this encounter with the Cabiri, their destruction, and the consequent transcendence of the brain? At least three possibilities come to mind, which are not mutually exclusive: *humanly*, transcending the brain suggests a rising above one's animal or material nature; *philosophically*, it suggests surpassing the naturalism or "soulless materialism," which holds the mind to be identical with and determined by the brain; and *psychologically*, it suggests a going beyond mere thinking in favor of feeling and other psychic functions. The latter interpretation is supported by Jung's statement that his tower has "not arisen from the patchwork of human thoughts" (RB, p. 321b, p. 322a), but all three interpretations make sense in the context of both *The Red Book* and Jung's later psychology. Jung comments: "Just as a tower surmounts the summit of a mountain on which it stands, so I stand above my brain, from which I grew...I am master of my own self" (RB, p. 321b). This suggests a philosophical view in which the psyche is causally and naturally produced by the brain and nervous system, but attains its independence by virtue of the individual's capacity to take the brain and its products as an object to be judged, rejected, or in Jung's case, sliced through and disentangled (RB, p. 321a).

ARCHETYPE, MIND, AND BRAIN

There are certainly strains of spiritualism (e.g. the notion that "spirit" is independent of matter) and vitalism (the idea that living things, particularly humans, contain a non-physical element or are governed by non-mechanistic laws) in Jung's thinking.[2] However, at times Jung speaks as if the archetypes of the collective unconscious are identical (or at least conceptually interchangeable) with instinctual behavior CW 9i, § 91) and rooted in the brain. In his earliest (1916) reference to the "collective psyche" prior to his use of the term "collective unconscious," Jung wrote: "The universal similarity of human brains leads to the universal possibility of a uniform mental functioning. This functioning is the *collective psyche*" (CW 7, § 456). Later, in his 1928 edition of "On the Psychology of the Unconscious," Jung referred to images of the collective unconscious being "laid down in the brain," but, as Marilyn Nagy[3] points out, this reference was deleted from Jung's fifth and final edition of this essay (CW 7, § 151).

In his 1936 essay, "Concerning the Archetypes" (CW 9i, pp. 54-74), Jung, without adopting a specifically spiritualist or vitalist position, divorced himself from the idea that the psyche should be understood as reducible to the brain. He argued that there is

> no ground at all for regarding the psyche as something secondary or as an epiphenomenon; on the contrary, there is every reason to regard it, at least hypothetically, as a factor *sui generis*, and to go on doing so until it has been sufficiently proved that psychic processes can be fabricated in a retort. (CW 9i, § 117)

Further, Jung described the psyche as "an autonomous reality of enigmatic character [that]...appears to be *essentially different* from psychochemical processes" (CW 9i, § 118).

It will be worth our while to inquire briefly into the implications of Jung's *Red Book* and later ideas about the mind's autonomous nature for his concepts of the archetypes and the collective unconscious. While these terms do not make a direct appearance in *The Red Book*,[4] the work certainly contains a wealth of material that can be regarded as archetypal in nature. Apart from the numerous mythological characters, events, and motifs that fill its pages, *The Red Book* provides the conceptual basis for such Jungian archetypes as the anima, shadow, persona, Senex, hero, maiden, Self, God, etc. On the other hand, there is little, if anything, in *The Red Book* that supports a conception of the archetypes of the collective unconscious as *instinctual* or *hereditary* categories, motifs, or images that appear spontaneously in the dreams and fantasies of individuals of diverse eras and cultures and which cannot be explained on the basis of previous learning. One reason for this is that by the time Jung began composing *The Red Book* he himself had already made a systematic study of world mythology, and indeed, many of the mythical images, characters, and motifs he describes in *The Red Book* had already made their appearance in his earlier, published works, most notably *Transformations and Symbols of the Libido* (1912). Indeed, as Giegerich has pointed out, *The Red Book* is "steeped in learnedness,"[5] and for this reason provides us with little or nothing in the way of a window into anything *a priori* or innate.[6]

There is, however, an important sense in which *The Red Book* does provide us with a window into the "collective psyche," and this in spite of Giegerich's claim that *The Red Book* is an essentially opaque work in which an interiorized factual ego replaces "mind" or "mythic cosmos" as the arena of truth.[7] *The Red Book's* path to the collective psyche is the same taken by any other masterful introspective work of philosophy, theology, or literature—through its exploration of themes of universal and enduring interest. The proof of this, of course, is in the *reading*, and my goal in this work has been to demonstrate that *The Red Book* is filled with such enduring material. Here, however, I would like to reflect for a moment on the ideas of "archetypes" and the "collective psyche," in the hope of arriving at a formulation of these concepts that is perhaps in better accord with Jung's notion of the Self "standing above" the brain.

The question that we should ask ourselves is whether the archetypes of the collective unconscious are necessarily rooted in inherited innate ideas, or might rather have a different foundation, in *the invariants of human experience*? In other words might the archetypes have a *phenomenological* as opposed to a strictly *biological* basis? The explanation for the fact that certain symbols (for example, the "sun" as a symbol of psychic energy, power, knowledge, God, or enlightenment) appear in widely separated cultures or eras need not appeal to either heredity or dispersion, but may simply reflect the fact that most human beings respond to the world in similar ways. Indeed, the majority, if not all, of the archetypes that play a significant role in Jungian theory can be understood in precisely this way, as representations or symbols of trans-cultural, trans-historical, and perhaps universal situations, experiences, and values—that derive from the experience of *being human*. It is in this sense that we may find "archetypes" in *The Red Book*: in its discussions of God and hell, the devil, the evil within man, the feminine and the masculine, the terror and value of death, reason versus emotion, the experience of chaos and madness, magic, the search for meaning and soul, etc.; each of these are archetypal themes, regardless of whether they emerge spontaneously from Jung's unconscious or are the product of consciously articulated imagination, reflection, and study.

THE HEREAFTER

Returning to *The Red Book* text, Jung again approaches his serpent/soul and queries if she can provide him news of "what is happening in the beyond" (RB, p. 322a). The serpent hesitates but then disappears, and soon Jung hears her say that she has reached Hell and has encountered a "hanged man," who Jung presently sees before him. The man tells him that he was condemned for poisoning his wife and parents, but that he did so in order to "honor God" (RB, p. 322a), hoping to transport them into a life of "eternal blessedness." Jung briefly interrogates the man, and his queries ("What went through your mind?" "Did your wife agree to the murders?"—RB, p. 322a) might be asked by a forensic expert assessing a defendant's level of criminal responsibility.[8] But Jung's interest soon shifts to the question of life in the hereafter. The hanged man tells Jung that he has not seen his relatives but from time to time he seems to be able to speak with his wife, but only about trivial matters and in a completely impersonal fashion. When Jung asks how he spends his time in the hereafter, the man replies that he has *no time to spend* and that "Nothing at all happens" (RB, p. 322b). Jung finds it hard to believe that one who comes from the beyond has virtually nothing to report, and the man responds that when he was alive and had a body he would have found it interesting to communicate with the dead, but now this means nothing to him. He doesn't even care whether or not he is in hell.

The hanged man disappears and Jung again speaks with his serpent/soul, asking her if things are indeed so boring and colorless in the beyond. The serpent responds that from what she has seen there is only shadowy motion, and "nothing personal whatsoever" (RB, p. 322b). Further, according to the serpent, there is no possibility of reconciling personal and absolute life; these are not opposites that can be united, but rather "simple differences," like "day" and "year," and "bushel" and "cubit" (RB, p. 322b). Jung finds this "enlightening but boring," and the serpent says that with the balancing and marriage of the opposites the dead may actually become extinct. (Given what Jung has said elsewhere about the dead, it may be that those who die having grasped the coincidence of the opposites die in peace and have no further needs).

While in *Liber Secundus* Jung borders on a "dissolution" view of the afterlife, later in his career he developed a more optimistic stance on the question of immortality, devoting an entire chapter to the question in *Memories, Dreams, Reflections* (MDR, pp. 299-326), where he stated that he was "convinced that at least part of our psychic existence is characterized by a relativity of space and time" (MDR, p. 305). Jung described how after his heart attack in 1944, he had beatific visions of what might be termed a disembodied existence, and stated that he had "never since entirely freed [himself] of the impression that this life is a segment of existence..." (MDR, p. 295). In one of his first letters after recovering from his heart attack, Jung wrote: "What happens after death is so unspeakably glorious that our imagination and our feelings do not suffice to form even an approximate conception of it."[9]

ON THE DEVIL AND THE DEAD

Jung commences a rather difficult monologue about the devil and the dead. He defines the devil as "the sum of darkness of human nature" (RB, p. 322b), and describes himself as one who wanted to live in the light, in God's image. However, because of this desire "the sun went out" (RB, p. 322b) for him when he entered the depths. In order to escape the devil's grasp Jung united himself with the serpent, which in effect drew the darkness from the beyond into the daylight, saved what was immortal within him, and satisfied the demands of the dead. In doing this, Jung says, he has taken something of the dead and death into himself, an act which provided him with solidity and durability, since death "is the most enduring of all things" (RB, p. 323a). By taking on death and the demands of the dead, Jung surrenders his "personal striving" and is taken for a dead man. It is here that Jung holds that a recognition of "death" serves to distance one from ambition and desire, overcome one's ego strivings and bring one to a rich and beautiful life in which one becomes oneself (RB, p. 323a). Such an "individuated" person is contrasted with one who, out of presumed altruism, "always wants only the fortune of others" (RB, p. 323a). Such a person, Jung writes, is a murderer, because in the process of attempting to force blessedness on others "he kills his own growth" (RB, p. 323a).

LOVE

Jung again converses with his serpent/soul who informs him that his reconciliation of the opposites and the satisfying of the dead is no real accomplishment, as "the living must first begin to live" (RB, p. 323b). Nevertheless, Jung's soul tells him that he has made a good beginning and is deserving of a reward, which comes in the form of the images of Elijah and Salome.

Salome demands that Jung answer why he has refused her love, and Jung responds that he is brought to tears by her words, as "One can never hear enough of love..." (RB, p. 323b). When Salome says that she wants their love to be more than words, Jung says that whenever he thinks of love he recalls a dream in which his body lies on sharp needles and his chest is crushed by a bronze wheel (RB, p. 324a). Jung soon suggests that being entangled with love is a great burden. For Jung, "simply thinking about it is dreadful" (RB, p. 324a), as he lacks the strength "to hoist another fate onto (his) shoulders" (RB, p. 324a). When Salome says that she will help him bear the burden, Jung responds that each should bear the burden of himself, and Elijah agrees: "May each one carry his own load. He who wants to burden others with their baggage is their slave" (RB, p. 324a). Jung wants Salome to give to him "out of [her] fullness, not [her] longing" (RB, p. 324b). This is certainly sage advice, which for any would-be lover is easier to satisfy in theory than in practice. Jung, however, wants to emphasize the point, and he tells Elijah that he should set his daughter, Salome, on her feet, as he, Jung, longs for men's "fullness and freedom, not their neediness" (RB, p. 324b).

Elijah now informs Jung that he has been gloomy ever since he has lost his serpent. Jung responds that *he* now has Elijah's serpent, having "fetched her from the underworld" (RB, p. 324b) in order to provide "hardness, wisdom, and magical power" and to balance the upper and nether worlds (RB, p. 324b). Elijah curses Jung for being a thief, but Jung responds that this curse will have no effect, because one in possession of the serpent cannot be affected by curses.

Jung now has some further reflections on love, saying that he has accepted Salome as pleasure but has rejected her as love (RB, p. 324b), for "love...belongs to others" (RB, p. 325a) while his love desires to remain with himself. Jung is aware that there is something strange about his desire for isolation, as "something should join men together" (RB,

p. 325a), and here is yet another place in *The Red Book* where it is arguable that Jung fails to leave the orbit of the self for an authentic encounter with the other. As if anticipating the merits of this criticism and experiencing guilt in relation to it, Jung soon enters into a period of great suffering.

JUNG'S TORMENT: "LOVE NEVER ENDS"

Reencountering the serpent, Jung wants to be credited with the "sacrifice" of having rejected Salome's love, to which his serpent/soul responds that this was hardly a sacrifice for Jung. Jung asks what he can do, to which the serpent responds that it is not a matter of action but rather of thought, and shortly the serpent is transformed into a small white bird that soars and disappears into the clouds. From high in the sky the bird reports to Jung that she has found for him a gift from heaven, a "golden royal crown" (RB, p. 325a) incised with the inscription "Love never ends" (I Corinthians 13:18). (We now begin a section of *The Red Book* that is not in Jung's calligraphic volume but is rather culled from Jung's *Red Book* draft). Jung inquires into the crown's meaning, but the bird turns back into the serpent, and Jung, who sees that Salome continues to weep, finds himself "hovering" or "hanging" from a tree for her sake and his own. We should note that the Norse God Odin hung for nine nights from the "World Tree" as a sacrifice to his divine self in order that he might gain wisdom and power (CW B, § 400).

Jung says that first he was crucified and now he is experiencing the equally agonizing fate of hanging, and he asks Salome if he must be decapitated (like her "earlier friend"—John the Baptist) as well. Salome assures Jung that she has "utterly forsaken" him (RB, p. 325b), and Jung then asks her to cut the cord of his noose. She protests that he is hanging too high on the "Tree of Life" for her to reach and he must devise his own help. Jung asks Salome if she can at least tell him her thoughts about the "golden crown," and Salome, now shocked into ecstasy tells Jung that this means that he is to be crowned, thereby bringing great blessedness to the two of them. Jung protests that he is "suffering unspeakable torment," swaying on the "branch of the divine tree," which he now regards as the tree for the sake of which his ancestors committed the original sin (RB, p. 326a).

The serpent is again transformed into a bird and flies off to seek assistance, and Jung contemplates whether the phrase inscribed on the crown, "Love never ends," actually means eternal hanging and torment. He reflects that he is hanging between sky and earth, and he asks himself if it is indeed true that love is eternal. Suddenly, an old raven appears and tells him that this depends on one's "notion of love and the other" (RB, p. 326a), which Jung interprets as referring to the distinction between heavenly and earthly love. Jung praises the beauty of heavenly love but says that since he is a man, he has set his sights on "being a complete and full-fledged man" (*ein ganzer und rechter Mensch*) (RB, p. 326a), which presumably refers back to his dialog with Salome in which he said that love must remain with himself (RB, p. 325a, b). The raven calls Jung an "ideologue" (RB, p. 326a). Jung dismisses him and the serpent reappears coiled around a branch. She informs Jung that she is only half of herself, and that while this "magical" half can be of use to him in life, she is powerless to provide assistance to one who is hanging.

Suddenly, Satan appears before Jung and "with a scornful laugh" informs him that his hanging is the result of his "reconciliation of the opposites" (RB, p. 326a). If Jung will only recant of this notion (and presumably renew the division between God and the devil), he will be returned to the "greening earth" (RB, p. 326a). Jung refuses to recant and says he is willing to come to his end for this idea, and Satan, scoffing at Jung's intellectual integrity, asks: "Where is your inconsistency?" reminding him that this is one of life's important rules (RB, p. 326b). Jung protests that he has been inconsistent *ad nauseum*, to which Satan responds that he has not been inconsistent in the right places. Jung holds out the hope that perhaps he can be assisted by his white bird. Satan continues to scoff: "Reconciliation of the opposites! Equal rights for all! Follies!" (RB, p. 326b).

Jung's white bird reappears and informs Jung that he will fly if he strives for what is above, but will continue to hang if his desire remains with what is below. The "riddle of the crown" (RB, p. 326b) is that it is one with the serpent, and, what's more, Jung must understand that he and Salome are one as well. All Jung must do is "fly" and both he and Salome will grow wings. Jung glides down to earth in the glow of a sunset reminiscent of the third day of creation. The opposites are reconciled as Jung resists the torture and logic of the devil.

Jung's resolution of his dilemma is not wholly satisfying. "Love," while now spiritualized, is again subordinated to individuation ("being a complete and full-fledged man"—RB, p. 326a) and the coincidence of opposites. The recognition that he and Salome are one is an intrapsychic event for Jung, rather than an act or experience of love between two distinct individuals. Perhaps nothing more can be expected in a deeply introspective work in which all "others" are interior objects—and, in one sense, aspects of the self. As we are about to see, Jung recognizes this, but does not find a way clear of his isolation.

On the other hand, the relationship between individuation and love is certainly more complex than "mutual exclusion."[10] Indeed, the capacity to be individuated to be able to "live with oneself" may be a condition for loving an other in a manner that does not attempt to force one's "formation" (RB, p. 288a), "blessedness" (RB, p. 323a), or projections onto them. Indeed, as I observed earlier, Jung's profound turn inward may have well been the condition for his later emergence into more authentic relationships with his students, colleagues, and the world at large.

SELF, LIFE, AND LOVE

Jung now remembers the Cabiri, who he believes started him on this perilous adventure by urging him to cut through his entanglement with his brain. He reflects that he has become "condemned within himself" and that he has become his own "priest and congregation, judge and judged, God and human sacrifice" (RB, p. 327a). Giegerich refers to this passage when he writes of the "totalitarianism" of interiorization,[11] which he believes to be characteristic of the entire *Red Book*, and, indeed, Jung himself appears to be struggling with the very question of a nearly solipsistic encounter with nothing but himself.

Jung describes his work as a "secret operation" (RB, p. 327a) that is now nearing completion, and he suggests that although the words he has used to describe this operation may not be "beautiful", he questions whether "truth [is] beautiful and beauty true" (RB, p. 327a). He now enters into a discourse about life and love. "Life stands above love," and while "love is pregnant with life," once life has been born love becomes an empty shell that expires. Jung is here echoing and deepening a theme that appears in his 1912 work, *Transformation and Symbols of the Libido*, where he interpreted various heroic myths as illustrating the need for the child to separate itself from the mother (RB, p. 327, n. 339; cf. CW B, Ch. 6, pp. 266 ff). In *The Red Book*,

Jung writes that the individual must achieve the even more difficult task of cutting him/herself loose from *love*. "Love," he writes, "seeks to have and to hold, but life wants more" (RB, p. 327a). Indeed, Jung goes so far as to coin (the decidedly unchristian) aphorism that "whoever loves does not live and whoever lives does not love," which he feels forced to assert by the "spirit of the darkest depths" (RB, p. 327a).

The Gospels say, "God is love. Whoever lives in love lives in God, and God in him" (1 John 4:16), and Jung is now disturbed, even repulsed, by the fact that everything he utters seems to be "backwards." He asks, "Should everything be turned into its opposite?" a question he will later answer by invoking the principle of "enantiodromia," the idea of "the emergence of the unconscious opposite in the course of time" (CW 6, § 709). We have already seen this notion at work earlier in *The Red Book*, when Jung's feeling function emerges over and against his dominant thinking function. As the principle of *compensation* (CW 6, § 693-5), this idea will become one of the bedrocks of Jung's thought. The question to be asked here, however, is whether Jung's compensation for the Christian view of love that he was taught in his youth has gone too far to the other extreme.

Indeed, Jung is repulsed by his having "broke love and life in twain" (RB, p. 327b) and feels deceived by the Cabiri, and even by Philemon. Jung accuses Philemon of being a charlatan who "aped the mysteries" (RB, p. 327b), caused "a…basilisk to be housed in the nest of the dove" (RB, p. 327b), and instigated Jung's hanging from the tree. Jung is even distressed that his soul who, having become "pregnant" with these ideas, caused him to become the father of the Antichrist.

It would seem that Jung's relationship to and views about love remain unresolved in *The Red Book*. This problem is tied to Jung's self-preoccupation during the period of this work, and may in part account for Jung's abandonment of *The Red Book* project, as he moved into a phase of his life in which he became increasingly engaged with others. In discussing "The Secret of the Golden Flower," which Richard Wilhelm sent him in 1928 and which Jung suggests inaugurated the end of his work on *The Red Book*, Jung says: "That was the first event which broke through my isolation. I became aware of an affinity; I could establish ties with something and someone" (MDR, p. 197).

THE KING'S SON

Jung's soul/serpent now tells him a story, which Jung, in his *Black Book* says is told to him because his ambition has prevented him from being able to resume his work (RB, p. 327, n. 344). A childless king who desires to have a son is told by a wise woman that although he has sinned, he should bury a pound of otter lard in the earth for nine months and wait to see what happens. Nine months later the king finds an infant boy sleeping in the pot that had contained the pound of lard. He and his wife raise the child as their son, and at twenty the son informs the father that he knows he was born not of a woman but through sorcery and the king's repentance for his sins. The son, who is more powerful than any man, demands the throne, and the king, surprised and outraged by the son's demands, desires to have him killed. However, he fears his son and returns to the sorceress who tells him that although he is confessing a desire to commit yet another sin, he should again place a pot with a pound of otter's lard in the earth for nine months. The king again follows her instructions and over the next nine months his son grows progressively weaker and dies, and the king buries his son near the now-empty pot.

However, the king is filled with remorse over his son's death and he again returns to the sorceress, who tells him to once more go to his son's grave, fill it with otter lard, and return in nine months. For a second time an infant son is born of the earth, but this time he grows to maturity in 20 weeks and once again demands the king's crown. At this point, the king, knowing how things will most surely develop, embraces his son "with tears of joy" (RB, p. 328b) and crowns him king. The son is grateful and holds his father in high esteem for the remainder of the old king's days.

LETTING GO OF ONE'S WORK

The serpent interprets this "fairy tale" (RB, p. 328b) in terms of Jung's dissatisfaction with his own "son," i.e. Jung's *work*. (Indeed the *Black Book* version of the story makes this very explicit by substituting "work" for "son" in key phrases of the serpent's interpretation—RB, p. 328, n. 346). Further, the serpent admonishes Jung for his desire to be "a man in every way," and insists that Jung accept both his inner mother and inner child. According to the serpent, as a creator, Jung needs a mother, since he himself is not a woman. He must also accept his role as a child, which means that he must surrender his own ambition and power. Indeed, Jung is "smaller and weaker" than the son/work he has produced, and he should simply "Let everything grow. Let everything sprout; [as] the son grows out of himself" (RB, p. 328b).

Jung's struggle here is paradigmatic of the author or artist's struggle with his own work—the desire to maintain control over it and to forestall any unwanted or negative ramifications. To that end Jung had tied himself into a knot, speaking out against longing and love, advocating a manliness and independence verging on total isolation, then cursing his creation for leading him into such an extreme rupture between life and love. In relating the story about the king and his son, Jung's soul disabuses Jung of the notion that he must seek such radical independence, and also frees him from the idea that he can control the implications of his own work. Having brought together the opposites of good and evil, heaven and hell, etc., Jung must allow the *coincidentia oppositorum* to develop in their own manner. Jung decides to allow himself to submit to the son, the myth, and the work so that it is lived and "sings itself" (RB, p. 328b).

Jung now takes his meditation on the opposites a step further. He reflects that in the past while he "loved the beauty of the beautiful…the strength of the strong," and "laughed at the stupidity of the stupid," etc., he "must now love the beauty of the ugly…admire the stupidity of the clever…(and) honor the goodness of the bad" (RB, p. 329a). Jung's thoughts here provide a new, psychological step in his *Red Book* quest to accept all, as well as a further development of his still nascent ideas regarding the shadow, compensation, and individuation. We might again say that the possibility of personal growth requires an acknowledgment and even acceptance of both that which is acceptable and unacceptable within oneself and others. On the other hand, the danger in this point of view is that it can ultimately lead to a moral relativism, and, as we have seen, to the kind of thinking that Jung himself engaged in when he held out hope that something good might come out of National Socialism. Indeed, this is the *shadow side* and worst danger of the entire *coincidentia oppositorum* idea.

In spite of the serpent's interpretations, Jung is resentful and outraged that his "son" has taken his crown. Indeed, his son (who he refers to as his soul in the *Black Book*—RB, p. 329, n. 48) emerges from the "water, great and powerful" (RB, p. 329a) and demands Jung's life. Jung asks the son if he has become a God, implying that Jung's own work is in a sense deified. The son replies that while he will rise into eternity, Jung has "been in immortal company long enough" (RB, p. 329a) and must now remain on earth among men. Further, Jung is now a woman,[12] pregnant with (another) child, suggesting that Jung's work is far from complete.

Jung's son, the son produced by the sorcery of his work, is now polyvalent: he is Jung's soul, Jung's work, the "magically produced boy," the coincidence of opposites, and a God who speaks in "gruesome riddles" (RB, p. 329b). This God will be "present and not present," heard and not heard, existent and non-existent. Further, he will be Jung's God alone—as he informs Jung, "No one besides you has your God" (RB, p. 329b) and Jung will be alone among men, in "solitude in multitude" (RB, p. 329b). Jung pleads with his son/soul/God to remain, but the God's wings grow and he ascends to the eternal light, leaving Jung lamed and "utterly empty" (RB, p. 329b). Jung is left alone, with only his "self" as a companion. He reflects that he requires an "opus," one that he can "squander decades on" and through which he "must catch up with a piece of the middle ages—within [himself]" (RB, p. 330b). Perhaps this is the new child that he carries within himself. *Liber Secundus* ends with Jung staking out the terms of his journey back in time, beginning when "asceticism, inquisition, torture [were] close at hand" (RB, p. 330b). In order to do this, he says, he must be alone with himself, paradoxically preaching "the gospel of godforsaken solitude" (RB, p. 329b).

Solitude has a double meaning for Jung in *The Red Book*. On the one hand, it suggests the need to distance oneself from others in the pursuit of one's work, one's individuation, and one's soul. On the other hand, it suggests the capacity to "live with oneself," after scrutinizing and critiquing oneself in the most honest and direct manner (as Jung is about to do in *Scrutinies*). For Jung, the two meanings are connected as he will relate that after angrily critiquing himself, he "noticed that [he] began to bear being alone with [himself]" (RB, p. 334b). "The touchstone, Jung writes, "is being alone with oneself" (RB, p. 330b). So concludes *Liber Secundus*, and we would be wise to understand this "being alone" in both the psychological sense of a retreat from the world and the moral sense of the capacity to bear one's own beliefs, attitudes, and actions.

IMAGES OF WHOLENESS

In addition to the painting of Philemon (**RB Image, p. 154**), Chapter XXI contains several other major images. In 1951 Jung published **RB Image, p. 155** anonymously and described it as a painting of a dream about the Anima appearing to the Christian Church (RB, p. 317, n. 283; cf. CW 9i, § 369). What is remarkable about this image is that it and **RB Image, p. 169** are the only two paintings in *The Red Book* to clearly depict actual, non-mythological human figures. In **RB Image, p. 155**, several dozen churchgoers are depicted quite naturalistically. We know that at the close of his *Red Book* period Jung felt a need to return to the real world, and these pictures may mark the beginning of that return.

RB Images, p. 159 and **p. 163** depict two mandalas that were reproduced anonymously by Jung in "Commentary on 'The Secret of the Golden Flower'" (CW 14, pp. A6, A10). Mandalas, which are images of wholeness, begin to make their appearance as Jung manages to integrate *The Red Book* materials into a more conscious and balanced picture of his psyche. We should note that these images were produced in 1927 and 1928 respectively, after the chaos and visions that generated *The Red Book* had likely ended. In **RB Image, p. 169**, which was evidently also painted at a late date, rays from a mandala, quite similar to the mandala depicted in **RB Image, p. 159**, emanate into a multi-ethnic mass of human faces, a portion of which look toward the radiant star, while the majority gaze in other directions. A number of human skulls are depicted in the periphery. Sherry points out that the image is reminiscent of the caricatures Jung drew as a small boy, and the faces which continued to appear to Jung late in life as hypnogogic images "of people who soon afterward died" (MDR, p. 30).[13] This parade of living and dead humanity, *The Red Book's* final painting, is perhaps a fitting symbolic conclusion—as Jung molds his search for his own soul into a psychology that charts the path towards individuation and wholeness for the living, while at the same time maintaining a deep reverence for the dead.

Chapter 10

I, Self, Prophet, Soul, and God

The Red Book: Scrutinies

Scrutinies, pp. 333-59

The first two parts of *The Red Book, Liber Primus* and *Liber Secundus*, contain Jung's fantasies and visions from October 1913 to February 1914, originally recorded in Jung's *Black Books* 2-5. Sometime in the winter of 1917 Jung began work on a new manuscript that reported upon and interpreted a series of other fantasies that Jung experienced at a mainly later period, from April 1913 to June, 1916. These fantasies are recorded in *Black Books* 5-6 and effectively constitute the third part of *Red Book,* entitled *Scrutinies.* (RB Intro, p. 207, Editorial Note, p. 225).

RAGE AGAINST THE "I"

Scrutinies begins with a series of Jung's reflections on his "I" that rapidly develop into a barrage of merciless self-criticism. Like Wittgenstein, who during this same period was baffled by the very existence of the human subject ("The 'I', the 'I', is what is deeply mysterious!"[1]), Jung asks "What is my I? What is my I?" (RB, p. 333a). Yet Jung quickly passes beyond metaphysics to the psychological question regarding the unity and value of the ego. He speaks to his "I," telling it that it has "no correct self-esteem" and that it "must think about improving" if "they" are to live together. Jung cautions his "I" against claiming that it is his "soul," and calls his "I" an "empty nothing" and a "disagreeable being," one that is self-righteous, overly ambitious, power hungry, cowardly, dishonest, pompous, and "a horror to live [with]" (RB, p. 333a). Jung rages against his "I" and says that he plans to pull off its skin, pin its unjust words to its body, and pull out its tongue (RB, p. 333b). He suggests that his "I" will "derive pleasure from this torment," and he plans to increase this pleasure until his "I" "vomits with joy." Jung warns his "I" that he cannot call on God's mercy and help, for the "dear old God has died" (RB, p. 333b) and the new god that has arisen is neither loving nor forgiving, but is rather "a magnificent frightful entity" inclined to "burn you with fire for the forgiveness of your sins" (RB, p. 333b). Jung calls his "I" an "idiot," who childishly wants to be "understood" by others, but who is rather in need of a dose of self-comprehension.

Jung is ruthless in his self-deprecation, and while his language might suggest that his "I" is an entity different from his criticizing self, the overall effect, as Shamdasani and Beebe point out, is more honest and direct than it would have been had Jung directed it against an abstraction like the "ego" or "shadow."[2] As Beebe puts it, "Psychologically there's an integrity to owning negative aspects as belonging to an 'I' who is myself, rather than characterizing them as traits of my shadow."[3] Indeed, as we have seen, while a concern with the characteristics of the "shadow" are pervasive throughout *The Red Book*, Jung had yet to formulate the shadow as an archetype or aspect of the self.

Still, Jung's self-criticism is *both personal and general*. On the one hand, we should note that it was written on the very day, April 20, 1914, that he resigned as president of the International Psychoanalytic Association (RB, p. 333, n. 6), and clearly reflects Jung's dejected and depressed state that followed upon his final break with Freud. Jung focuses upon his own inordinate ambition, vanity, self-interest, false modesty, and need for recognition (RB, p. 334a). On the other hand, Jung's harangue against his "I" also reflects his more sober criticisms of the ego in general, with its practical, rational, and self-aggrandizing goals. Indeed, Jung's critique is not far from the biblical cry against the vanities of the world (Ecclesiastes 1:2) nor from the Buddha's call for a de-identification with, and ultimate dissolution of, the self. Jung says to his "I," "If I tame you, beast, I give others the opportunity to tame their beasts" (RB, p. 334b). Indeed, who among us can say that we are immune from the criticisms that Jung levies against himself? Then again, it is unclear whether such damning self-scrutiny always has a positive psychological effect. While Jung would continue to be highly critical of any complete identification with the "ego," he developed more subtle methods for helping his patients transcend the ego's ambitions and narcissism.

Jung writes that as a result of his self-criticisms, he found it easier to be alone with himself (RB, p. 334b). He now re-communes with his "soul," who tells him that his current state of "uncertainty" is a good one, full of creative possibilities (RB, p. 335a). Jung again hears Ezechiel's "rushing of wings" (Ezechiel 1:22), which he attributes to his soul, now in the form of a bird, rising toward "the fiery brilliance of the outspread Godhead" (RB, p. 335a). Turning to his "I," Jung tells it that it "will be crucified for the sake of life" (RB, p. 335a). With this, Jung's soul rises higher and declares that she has achieved happiness. However, Jung, now identifying with his crucified "I," becomes bitter and tells his soul that she lives "from the blood of the human heart." Further, "The divine consumes the human" and were it not for the fact that Jung recognizes the necessity of his soul's ascent to "the eternal realm," he would call her "the most terrible scourge of men" (RB, p. 335a). His soul responds that "the way of life is sown with fallen ones" (RB, p. 335a), suggesting that the ego must suffer and fall if the soul is to ascend, i.e. if the individual is to become centered in the Self.

THE (IN)COHERENCE OF THE SELF

With all of Jung's talk about his "I" and "soul," and given the number of inner figures that populate *The Red Book*, the question arises as to who is the "I" of Jung's narrative? Jung says such things as, "But I did not understand my I and therefore spoke to him" (RB, p. 335b). What are we to make of all of this? On the one hand, *The Red Book* is witness to what might be called an extreme refinement in the capacity for *self-reflection*, a capacity that was also evident in Nietzsche and Freud. On the other hand, one might surmise that Jung's self-reflection (and self-division) in *The Red Book* is extreme to the point of being pathological, and Jung himself recognizes that in writing *The Red Book* he verged on the brink of psychosis (RB, p. 360). As we have seen, Jung all but acknowledged his own capacity for dissociation—for example, in *Memories, Dreams, Reflections,* he describes how in early adolescence he came upon the idea that he was "actually two different persons" (MDR, p. 33). On the other hand, he believed that his own dissociation (MDR, p. 45), and the phenomena of dissociation in general, were by no means always pathological, and that the capacity for the unconscious to generate an autonomous center in contradistinction to the ego was a general tendency (CW 9i, § 496, MDR, p. 45).

I have considered Jung's "dissociation" elsewhere[4] and will not enter into an extended discussion of it here. However, it is important to recognize that the "dissociation" and "multiplicity of the self" that we find in *The Red Book* may be as much a reflection of the modern, and especially post-modern, psyche as it is of Jung's personal psychology. While the narrative "I" of *The Red Book* (as opposed to the "I" that is subject to Jung's critique), may reflect a sort of master, observing ego or subject, or hold a place for Jung's evolving Self (which in Jung's later view is centered between the conscious ego and the unconscious), it may, on the other hand, be nothing more than a *narrative device* that temporarily keeps the author and reader in place, but which is not necessarily reflective of a metaphysically or psychologically coherent subject. It is perhaps ironic that Jung, who spoke so often about forging a coherent and individuated "Self," should, in *The Red Book*, do so much to deconstruct the very notion of a coherent person. One of the questions we must ask in reading *The Red Book*, with its multiple "egos," multiple Gods, and multiple spiritual pathways, is whether a coherent self or spiritual path is possible or even desirable.

BELIEF

Jung now enters into questions regarding "knowledge" and "belief." Whereas in past times belief was the best means to lead men to what is reasonable and good (RB, p. 335b), reliance on belief in our own time would mean a return to a "childhood" that we have outgrown. There is an emptiness to belief that fails to involve the "whole man," and for this reason "our life with God" cannot be solely grounded in belief. While one "should wrestle for knowledge" (RB, p. 336a), one cannot eliminate belief in favor of knowledge altogether—one must strike a balance between them.

ENTERING SOLITUDE

It is in this context of balancing knowledge with belief that Jung is confronted with his soul's prediction that he must and will enter into solitude. Jung doubts the wisdom of this prediction as he "dread(s) the madness that befalls the solitary" and fears "committing an injustice to men" if he goes his "own way" (RB, p. 336a). Jung's soul informs him that he need not fear madness and that his "greatness" requires his solitude. He need not concern himself with others, since in contrast to them he has "laid [his] hand on the divine" (RB, p. 336a). It is useless for Jung to resist his solitude because it is required for his "work" (RB, p. 336b), the full nature of which is about to be clarified.

"RIPENESS COMES…LATE…IN THE SPRING"

Jung is confronted by "an old man with a white beard", who describes himself as "a nameless one, one of the many who lived and died in solitude" (RB, p. 336b). This figure informs Jung that he must "bleed for the goal of humanity," and in order to do so he must [once again] "take [his] leave from science" (RB, p. 336b). While science is childish and shallow, "mere language, mere tools," Jung must go to the "depths" and "set to work." Jung does not understand what his work must be. The poem that issues from the mouth of the old man, which says, amongst other things, that "Nonsense streams from the deepest wells" and "Ripeness comes as late as possible in the Spring," provides no assistance as Jung finds the poem "dreadfully meaningless." However, he gains a certain insight into it when a month later (June 24, 1914) his soul recites, "The greatest comes to the smallest" (RB, p. 336b). Jung says that it was these words that granted him the "courage" to write the earlier parts of *The Red Book*. We should note that Jung was nearly 39 years old when he had these transformative experiences, which he later attributed to "a sin of [his] youth" (CW 18, § 1501).[5] In Jung's case it would seem that "ripeness" indeed came late in the "spring."

PHILEMON: TEACHER

A year passes before Jung again hears from "the voices of the depths" (RB, p. 336b). In the summer of 1915 he saw an osprey plunge into the water, snatch a fish, and fly off into the skies. Jung's soul informs him that this is "a sign that what is below is borne upward" (RB, p. 337a), and it is not long before he again hears the voice of Philemon. In contrast to their last encounter, when Philemon was reticent to answer Jung's queries about magic, the old magician now tells Jung that he wants "to do business" with Jung, master him, and "emboss [him] like a coin" (RB, p. 337a). Jung is told that like gold, he "should pass from hand to hand" and express "the will of the whole." Later in his career, Jung will make much of both "fish" (as a symbol of the collective unconscious) and "gold" (as a symbol of the Self).

Philemon still expresses some ambivalence about teaching Jung, stating, "If I do not teach, I do not have to disavow" (RB, p. 337a), and that "the best truth is also such a skillful deception" (RB, p. 337b), but in the end Philemon says that the burden of silence is greater than the weight of not unloading his burden. He warns "the listener" to "defend himself" against his ruse. Jung is undeterred, telling Philemon that while many have deceived themselves about him, "he who fathoms Philemon fathoms himself" (RB, p. 337b).

The Sin of (the Virtue of) Self-forgetting

Jung is left to his own thoughts, and he reflects upon the "mutual enchantment" of Christian morality in which the ethics of "self-surrender" results both in the renunciation of one's self and the effort to selfishly master the other, presumably by insisting upon his/her self-surrender as well. Jung prefers a Nietzschean individualism, in which each accepts himself, lives his own life, and "bears his own burden" (RB, p. 337b). Jung calls the Christian "self-forgetting" virtue a sin and an "unnatural alienation from one's own essence" (RB, p. 337b). Indeed, one who enters upon the path of self-surrender and makes a virtue of self-forgetting harbors a sense of "Bitterness, injustice, and poison" (RB, p. 338a). One should submit only to oneself, and the work of redemption is self-work that requires self-love (RB, p. 338a). Still, one cannot strive after self-redemption; one enters into it only when one has abandoned the need to have it.

It is interesting that Jung's celebration of self-love and the value of the self should follow so closely upon his devastating critique of his own ego, and the reader may wonder about what appears to be a complete about-face in Jung's thinking. Indeed, Jung, who had just scorned his "I" as a useless vanity, is about to tell us that the union with the Self allows one to reach God (RB, p. 338b). I do not believe that there is a single path out of this paradox, but there are several considerations that help explain it. First, we have seen that for Jung, the human subject is initially anything but a unified whole, and Jung in *The Red Book* is not only divided between his narrative "I," the "I" or ego he scrutinizes, and his soul (which takes the form of both a serpent and a bird), but is also dispersed amongst the various inner figures he encounters in his "visions." Thus the "I" that Jung mercilessly criticizes need not be the "Self" that he must love in order to find redemption. Indeed, we know from Jung's later writings that he makes a sharp distinction between the conscious "ego" and the partly unconscious "Self" (CW 6, § 706), and holds that the individuated "whole man" is centered much closer to the Self than to the ego. It is this "Self" that Jung will later hold to be indistinguishable from the God archetype. Second, there need not be a paradox between honest, even merciless self-scrutiny and self-love. Indeed, self-love may at times require such criticism if the individual is to awaken from his/her narcissistic slumbers into a more fulfilling life. Jung says as much in his 1941 essay, "Transformation Symbolism of the Mass," where he holds that "the integration or humanization of the self is initiated from the conscious side by our making ourselves aware of our selfish aims..." (CW 11, § 400; cf. RB, p. 338, n. 32). Finally, I am again reminded of the Hasidic parable of "the two pockets," where the self is regarded *both* as the dust of the earth *and* the reason for the world's creation.

The Work of Self-Redemption

Jung tells us that one only "blunders into the work of self-redemption unintentionally," that this work "is neither beautiful nor pleasant," and that it is largely accomplished alone (RB, p. 338a). One who seeks such redemption must endure great torment and should count oneself amongst "the sick", if he feels the impulse to impart redemption to others. For this reason, one should not use others as vehicles for one's own redemption. While the need for self-redemption often expresses itself in a desire to love another, we should not deceive ourselves into believing that we love others to make them happy, nor lie to ourselves that we love the other "selflessly."

We love others to "alter our own condition" (RB, p. 338a), and the latter is something that we should do on our own.

We are here again confronted with the problem of Jung's introversion. Jung will later describe psychotherapy as a "dialectical relationship between doctor and patient...an encounter, a discussion between two psychic wholes," which brings about self-transformation (CW 11, § 904). However, here and throughout *The Red Book* there is little, if any reference to the psychotherapeutic or any real *relationship*. Indeed, in *The Red Book*, Jung is on a path that involves interactions only with figures of Jung's individual, and the collective, imagination. *The Red Book* is almost completely sealed off from the external world, which impinges on it only at a very few points, for example, through Jung's vague references to "the war." However, we should again note that the self-absorption of Jung's *Red Book* (and related writings) is not necessarily a fault. For Jung in *The Red Book*, love of another is only possible after one has taken responsibility for, and learned to live with oneself, and refrained from imposing oneself on others. *Liber Novus* involves a period of interiorization in which Jung, in effect, "incubated" a new manner of relating to himself, the Gods, and the other. Here, we might well note that the two major forms of psychotherapy to arise in the early years of the 20th century, psychoanalysis and analytic psychology, *began with self-analysis* and only *evolved* into dialogic procedures.

SELF AND GOD

Jung enters into a discussion of Self and God, saying that apart from any prior opinions on the matter, he knows from *experience* that "through uniting with the self we reach the God" (*Durch die Vereinigung mit dem Selbst erreichen wir den Gott*) (RB, p. 338b). As we have seen, Jung relates that this realization was unwanted and unexpected, yet so powerful that he writes, "if it is a deception then deception is my God" (RB, p. 338b). While Jung says that he could provide rational arguments against the truth of this claim himself, such arguments would have no impact on his knowledge that he experienced God through union with the Self. Jung does not want to believe this insight; he recites that "Only a sick brain could produce such deceptions," and he likens himself to one who is "overcome by delusion" (RB, p. 338b). Yet this delusion is the very essence of his knowledge, as "a living God afflicts our reason like a sickness," and fills one with intoxication and chaos. Indeed, one must "wrestle with the God for the self" and God "appears as our sickness from which we must heal ourselves" (RB, p. 338b). These paragraphs in *The Red Book* provide the kernel for Jung's later notion of the God archetype. While Jung will later insist that he can say nothing about a metaphysical God *per se* (CW 14, § 781; CW 12, § 15), he will, especially in *Aion*, adopt the view that the God image or archetype (i.e. the phenomenological "God" that is manifest in the psyche) is identical with the "whole man" or "Self" (CW 9ii, § 73, § 116, § 170).

It is worthwhile to consider Jung's views on the relationship between Self and God in some detail. Few of Jung's ideas have enlisted as much interest and controversy both within and beyond psychology as Jung's equation of the God archetype with the Self. Especially in his later works, Jung is careful to point out that this equation is purely psychological in nature, and he means to imply nothing about the nature of an actual metaphysical deity, the existence of which, Jung says, is beyond the scope of his purely empirical inquiry (CW 9ii, § 311). Such disclaimers, however, have not deterred others from reading into Jung the view that in our own time the transcendent God has died and divinity has been reborn in mankind (Altizer[6]), that Jung adopted a form of modern Gnosticism in which God is discovered through an immersion in the self rather than through an "I-thou" encounter with others (Buber[7]), or even that Jung created an oral tradition, parallel to his writings, in which he set himself up as a spiritual prophet and incarnation of the deity (Noll[8]). Readers of *The Red Book* may find support for and against each of these positions, as the relationship between Self and God is a pervasive theme in this work.

We have just seen how Jung states in no uncertain terms that one reaches God through a union with one's Self (RB, p. 338b). Stein argues that by stating that we "reach" God through uniting with the Self, Jung maintains a distinction between God and Self.[9] While this may be so, the distinction is quite slender; at times Jung holds that God is born out of the Self and at other times suggests that God is identical with it.[10] The notion that God is discovered through a journey into one's own soul is expressed in multiple ways throughout *The Red Book*. Early in *Liber Primus*, Jung asserts that he discovered that "…the depths in me was at the same time the ruler of the depths of world affairs" (RB, p. 231a). Later on, Jung affirms that a god is born out of an embrace with oneself (RB, p. 245b):

> If you desire yourself, you produce the divine son in your embrace with yourself. Your desire is the father of the God, your self is the mother of the God. But the son is the new God, your master. (RB, p. 245b)

At another point, Jung asks if we are born of the Gods, why should the Gods not also be born of us? (RB, p. 286a). According to Jung, with the death of the hero (and the passing of the old God), one must descend into one's "worst and…deepest" (RB, p. 250a) and become one's own creator (RB, p. 249b). In the process one becomes a Christ oneself (RB, p. 253b). Further, "The new God is his own follower in man. He imitates himself" (RB, p. 245a).

Jung makes a number of other varied remarks in *The Red Book* on the connection between the Self and God. While he had not as yet conceptualized the "Self" as an archetype, it is clear that in *The Red Book* he understands the "Self" as something wider than the personal ego or conscious "I." In the majority of Jung's remarks, however, the fate of God or "the gods" is in the hands of humanity, or literally in the hands of Jung himself. As we have seen, Jung describes himself as healing the wounded god by having him recognize that he is indeed a fantasy in the mind of man, a fantasy that, in Jung's view, is paradoxically, the true "reality" of the divine (RB, p. 282b). In describing this, however, Jung speaks of the tremendous power implied by the notion that the fate of the gods is in the hands of man, as he can either heal or destroy them (RB, p. 285b). Unlike Nietzsche, however, who decided, in effect, to let the gods die, Jung chooses to give the gods new life, first with a series of "incantations" over the ailing God Izdubar, and later through a series of divine gestations in the womb of Jung's own psyche.

At times in *The Red Book* Jung speaks in almost Hegelian fashion of the "new God" being born through the spirit of mankind:

> Just as the disciples of Christ recognized that God had become flesh and lived among them as a man, we now recognize that the anointed of this time is a God who does not appear in the

> flesh; he is no man and yet is a son of man, but in spirit and not
> in flesh; hence he can be born only through the spirit of man as
> the conceiving womb of the God. (RB, p. 299b)

As we proceed through *Scrutinies* and read the "Seven Sermons to the
Dead," we will see that, according to Philemon, man is not only a
"gateway" for the appearance of the Gods, but that the dead know that
"man even creates its Gods," and as such "the Gods were of no use"
(RB, p. 354b). This, of course, sounds like the modernist/rationalist
position which Jung later criticized as resulting in neurotic complexes.
However, Jung's view is that while man might be said to create the gods,
such creation is not a fabrication in order to fulfill an infantile psychological
wish or atone for one's guilt (Freud) but rather a spontaneous creative act
stemming from the deepest, and thus most meaningful, recesses of the
collective psyche. The gods are, in one view that can be developed from
Jung, an archetypical collective fantasy of humanity, and for this reason
are as psychically real as the so-called objective world.

Jung's views on the relationship between Self and God during the
period of *The Red Book* were given more scholarly expression in
Psychological Types. In the context of his discussion of the theology of
the German mystical philosopher, Meister Eckhart, Jung writes:

> The 'relativity of God,' as I understand it, denotes a point of
> view that does not conceive of God as 'absolute,' i.e., wholly
> 'cut off' from man and existing outside and beyond all human
> conditions, but as in a certain sense dependent on him; it also
> implies a reciprocal and essential relation between man and
> God, whereby man can be understood as a function of God,
> and God as a psychological function of man. From the
> empirical standpoint of analytical psychology, the God-image
> is the symbolic expression of a particular psychic state, or
> function, which is characterized by its absolute ascendancy
> over the will of the subject, and can therefore bring about or
> enforce actions and achievements that could never be done
> by conscious effort. (CW 6, § 412)

Jung quotes Eckhart's expression, "For man is truly God, and God is
truly man" (CW 6, § 416), as well as the philosopher's formulation:

> I know that without me/God can no moment live; Were I to
> die, then He/ No longer could survive/...I am God's child,

His son/ And He too is my child;/ We are the two in one,/
Both son and father mild./ To illuminate my God/ The
sunshine I must be;/ My beams must radiate/ His calm and
boundless sea." (CW 6, § 432)

Jung writes that for Eckhart, "God is dependent on the soul, and…the
soul is the birthplace of God" (CW 6, § 426). According to Jung, "God
and the soul are essentially the same when regarded as personifications
of unconscious content (CW 6, § 421).

Jung again takes up the theme of Self and God in his 1934-9
seminar on Nietzsche's *Zarathustra,* where he says, "The self is by
definition the totality of all psychical facts and contents…it contains
all the archetypes…it is like a personification of nature and of
anything that can be experienced in nature, including what we call
God."[11] Nevertheless, Jung also hesitates to completely identify God
with the Self, stating:

> the term *self* is often mixed up with the idea of God. I would
> not do that…[this] borders on impertinence…The experience
> of the self is so marvelous and so complete that one is of course
> tempted to use the conception of God to express it. I think it is
> better not to, because the self has the peculiar quality of being
> specific yet universal…so it is a relatively universal being and
> therefore doesn't deserve to be called God.[12]

Nevertheless, in *Aion,* Jung returns to expressing the Self archetype/
God Archetype equivalency, stating, for example, that "…the
spontaneous symbols of the self, or of wholeness, cannot in practice
be distinguished from a God-image" (CW 9ii, § 73), and that "Jesus
is…the 'spiritual inner man'" (CW 9ii, § 118). On the other hand,
the Antichrist "is just as much a manifestation of the self, except
that he consists of its dark aspect" (CW 9ii, § 79). In the end,
"psychology…is not in a position to make metaphysical statements"
and "can never prove that the God-image is God himself, or that the
self takes the place of God" (CW 9ii, § 308).

The view that man discovers God through an encounter with the
Self, and even that *man creates God,* has its precedent in several mystical
traditions. For example, amongst the Gnostics, with whose writings
Jung was deeply involved during the period of *The Red Book,* we
find the claim that God and man reciprocally create one another.[13]

A similar point of view is expressed in the classical Kabbalistic text, the *Zohar*, where we read "He who 'keeps' the precepts of the Law and 'walks' in God's ways, if one may say so, 'makes' Him who is above."[14] Late in his career, Jung stated, "The Hasidic Rabbi Baer from Mesiritz, whom they called the Great Maggid... anticipated my entire psychology in the eighteenth-century."[15] While Jung does not explain his assertion, in all likelihood he made it partly because Maggid held that the Godhead has a hidden life within the mind of man.[16]

Jung provides a rather sophisticated theological formulation of the relationship between Self and God in a letter written on February 19, 1919 to Joan Corrie and quoted in an editorial footnote to *The Red Book*.

> The primordial creator of the world, the blind creative libido, becomes transformed in man through individuation & out of this process, which is like pregnancy, arises a divine child, a reborn God, no more (longer) dispersed into the millions of creatures, but being one & this individual, and at the same time all individuals, the same in you as in me. (RB, p. 354, n. 123)

While there are passages in *The Red Book* that might be said to support Noll's charge that Jung sought to deify himself, as when Salome tells him, "You are Christ" (RB, p. 252b), on the whole, in *The Red Book*, as elsewhere, Jung speaks of a divine image or archetype which is accessible to all who make the requisite interior journey. Jung recognized the close relationship between psychology, philosophy, and religion, and in a 1943 article, "Psychotherapy and a Philosophy of Life," went so far as to call psychotherapy a "religion *in statu nascensdi*" (CW 16, § 181)[17], and while he may have been tempted during *The Red Book* period to see himself as that religion's "prophet," he ultimately rejected this role.[18] In a talk, translated in Jung's *Collected Works* as "The Structure of the Unconscious" and first delivered in 1916 (see CW 7, p. 269, n. 1), Jung states:

> [Psychotherapy] is an art, a technique, a science of psychological life, which the patient, when cured, should continue to practice for his own good and for the good of those amongst whom he lives. If he understands it in this way, he will not set himself up as a prophet, nor as a world reformer; but, with a sound sense of

the general good, he will profit by the knowledge he has acquired during treatment, and his influence will make itself felt more by the example of his own life than by any high discourse or missionary propaganda. (CW 7, § 502)

"The Gods Have Become Diseases"

Jung's view that God is "our sickness" (RB, p. 338b) can be profitably juxtaposed with a similar claim in his 1929 "Commentary on 'The Secret of the Golden Flower,'" where he famously states, "The gods have become diseases; Zeus no longer rules Olympus but rather the solar plexus and produces curious specimens for the doctor's consulting room" (CW 13, § 54). At that time Jung developed the view that modern, "rational and enlightened" man, having lost all belief in and experience of the gods and having suppressed the archetypal forces that produced such belief and experience in past eras, suffers from a spiritual malaise in which these suppressed forces, unrecognized as "divine," return to produce psychical ills (in much the same manner that, according to Freud, repressed sexuality produces neurotic symptoms). It is unclear whether at the time of *The Red Book* Jung had framed such a theory, and in contrast to his later formulation that the *absence* of God produces pathology, he asserts in *Scrutinies* that the *presence* of God produces illness and that God is manifest in the illness he produces. Regardless, the connection between God, chaos, psychical disease, and the irrational had certainly been well established in Jung's mind by the time he wrote *Scrutinies*. Jung tells us that if we treat God as an illness and then endeavor to heal it, we "lose part of life," as where once God's "fire blazed," now only "dead ashes lie" (RB, p. 339a).

Jung's Hesitation

We are next treated to a brief reflection on the "ashes of rationality," which Jung regards as "suicide," inimical to the fullness of life and inferior to the "fiery brilliance of God" (RB, p. 339a). While Jung says that he cannot cut himself off from experiencing this God, he must nonetheless free himself from it as it is both love *and* hate, beauty *and* abomination, wisdom *and* meaninglessness, power *and* powerlessness, omnipresence *and* "my creature" (RB, p. 339a). While Jung's desire to liberate himself from such a deity is understandable, as life would be impossible if one continually embraced both poles of each of these oppositions, Philemon immediately advises him to the contrary, beckoning him to enter into a deeper immersion in the divine. Indeed, Philemon informs Jung that his work is in "the grave of God" (RB, p. 339a).

Jung now reflects on the changes he has observed in Philemon's character since the conclusion of *Liber Secundus* when Jung's son/soul/God ascended to the upper realms. Jung suggests that he had in some manner been fused with Philemon and was intoxicated by his language and sensitivity (RB, p. 339a). Indeed, Jung states that the majority of what he had written in *The Red Book* proper was probably given to him by Philemon, but now he and Philemon have become distinct (RB, p. 339a).

THE STRUGGLE WITH THE DEAD

Several weeks later, Jung is approached by three "shades" who demand from him a symbol, a mediator or a sign. While Jung is baffled as to what this might mean, he is soon astonished to find that a sign placed in his hand reads "HAP" (a phallic deity), which the shades refer to as "God's other pole" (RB, p. 339b) and which they describe as the spirit of flesh and blood, sperm, entrails, genitals, head, feet, hands, sputum, excretion, etc. Jung is horrified by this "night God" and queries whether the shade speaking to him is the devil. He receives the response, "The enlightening thought comes from the body" (RB, p. 339b). We soon learn that the dead need a meal of the "life juices of men" (RB, p. 339b) and believe that Jung can provide them with it, as they want to share in his life.

Jung continues the struggle with the dead that will preoccupy him through much of the remainder of *Scrutinies*. He experiences a strong ambivalence towards the departed. On the one hand, he calls the shade his "beloved," asking her to open him to the "darkness of the spirits" (RB, p. 340a); on the other hand, he is repulsed by her, calls her a "sinister womb," and fears that she wants to "suck the life out of [him] for the sake of the shadow" (RB, p. 340b). What is clear is that the dead one wishes to return to life and requires Jung's "blood" in order to do so. She is willing to take any "animal form," even if it means becoming Jung's "dog." While Jung is initially taken in by her, and despairingly offers her his blood ("drink...drink so what should be will be" RB, p. 340a), he is soon exhausted and challenges the shade's demands, asking her why he should devote himself to the dead instead of the living. "Did you not have your time to live?" he asks. "Should a living person give his life for your sake…?" (RB, p. 340b). The shade responds that the living fritter their life away (RB, p. 340a), and in seeking love are continually running from themselves (RB, p. 341a). What's more, they are hypocrites, who on the one hand preach divine and human love but then use the gospel to justify war and "murderous injustice" (RB, p. 341a). The shade suggests that the dead are much closer to Jung than the living, that they belong to his "invisible following and community" (RB, p. 340b), and that Jung need not die in order to enter their darkness, he need only allow himself to be "buried" (RB, p. 341a). Finally, communion with the dead is suited to Jung, whose work involves solitude and the capacity to "bear and endure oneself" (RB, p. 341a).[19]

Jung is not convinced. He responds, "I see only graves before me," and he asks by whose will is he commanded to commune with the dead. The shade responds that it is the "will of God," a god who "knows no pity" (RB, p. 341a), only "power and creation" (RB, p. 341b). This God commands and Jung must dispense with his anxieties and act: "There is only one road, the military road of the Godhead" (RB, p. 341b). Jung concludes that in spite of the fact that he is averse to obeying anyone, he has no ground for refusing to obey this voice. In doing so Jung learns that he must not seek joy. Joy cannot be pursued but only comes as a byproduct of fulfilling a task. Jung fears that he may not be up to the task before him and that the shade will destroy him, but she responds in Darwinian fashion: "I am life that destroys only the unfit" (RB, p. 341b).

Jung does not know where to begin, and the shade tells him that he requires a "church." Jung protests that he is not a prophet to have a church, and is "not entitled to know any better than others" (RB, p. 341b). The shade, however, continues that the church is required and adds, cryptically, that the "holy ceremony must be dissolved and become spirit," and that a "bridge" will "lead out beyond humanity" (RB, p. 342a). Jung is baffled, but the shade continues by reciting a prayer and invocation to the dead in Jung's name, stating that Jung will refresh the dead with his blood, that he will form a community in which the images of the living and the dead will unite, and that "the past will live on in the present" (RB, p. 342a).

We will soon have occasion to discuss the full significance of Jung's communion with the dead, but we should here note clues which suggest that, from a psychological perspective, the union of the dead with the living and the past with the present is propaedeutic to (or perhaps a metaphor for) Jung's notion of the collective unconscious. The shade tells Jung, "The history of humanity is older and wiser than you" (RB, p. 342a), and, further, it has only been in recent times that people have "begun to forget the dead and to think that they have now begun the real life" (RB, p. 342a). Jung's great task will be to show contemporary men and women that the images, myths, and wisdom of the past (i.e. the dead) cannot be forgotten, and that they remain within the collective psyche as a boundless source of spiritual and existential meaning. It is this realization that serves as the "bridge" that leads "beyond humanity" (RB, p. 342a), turns the holy ceremony (i.e. the old religious forms) into spirit, and produces a *new man*.

AMBIVALENCE TOWARDS CHRISTIANITY

Jung relates that he became gloomy and confused after hearing the dead one's invocation (RB, p. 342b). He looks up and sees his soul irradiated by the godhead, and he tells her that in spite of his confusion he has accepted the dead one's charge on his own and her behalf and will endure the bitterness of being "crucified on the tree of life" (RB, p. 342b). Yet, he asks his soul why he should be the one "to drink the cess of humanity that poured out of Christendom" (RB, p. 342b). Here, in a single phrase, Jung crystalizes the negative view of Christianity that he has expressed intermittently throughout *The Red Book*; yet at the same time he makes allusions to the "last Supper" (RB, p. 342a) and "Christ's cup" (RB, p. 342b; cf. n. 62), which again suggest his own identification with the Christian messiah.

PHILEMON'S WARNING

Philemon appears and addresses Jung, taking a position that is opposed to, and which perhaps compensates for the message he has received from the shade and his soul. Philemon warns Jung against his soul's and the dead's efforts to arrogate power over him. Jung must have a mixture of love, hate, fear, and contempt for his soul, and above all must keep her in his sight (RB, p. 343a), as she is disloyal, heinous, and cunning! Philemon tells Jung that he must see his soul in himself; if not, he will see her in his fellow man and this will drive him mad, intimating a dynamic (later articulated by Jung) in which a man projects his anima onto others, at times with disastrous results (CW

9ii, § 19). Jung's soul, according to Philemon, is "only distantly related to humankind" (RB, p. 343a), and she must be imprisoned and shielded from others. Most importantly, Jung should not burden others with what his soul (in its devilish or Godly form) leads him to believe. Indeed, unless specifically requested to do so, Jung should not offer advice or act upon others at all, as he has no claim to understanding others, just as they have no claim to understanding him. Jung should attend to the weeds in his own garden instead of pointing to the shortcomings in his fellow man. By acting upon and thinking about others, Jung fails to distinguish himself from his own soul and runs the risk of acting as a *daimon* or playing God (RB, p. 343a, b). One who, even with the best of intentions, forces himself on the other, increases the others' blindness by setting a bad example. Jung must "draw the coat of patience and silence" over his head (RB, p. 343b). He should not be seduced by his soul and the daimons into doing their work.

We might say that in all of this Philemon is urging Jung to adopt a position that is quite close to what the Kabbalists spoke of as *Tzimtzum* (contraction/concealment) with respect to the other. Indeed, according to the Kabbalistic and Hasidic view, just as God contracted and concealed himself to allow a world to emerge in its own essence and freedom, human beings should contract and conceal themselves to enable those around them to blossom fully as themselves. This is an important, if somewhat paradoxical principle, that is often relevant in psychotherapy—the therapist fosters transformation by getting out of the client's way.

Jung is not so sure, however, whether to accept Philemon's advice about his relationship to his own soul, and he asks his soul whether the advice strikes her as good. His soul admits to him that she desires everything that Jung might give to others, his love, even his hate, as she will require these on the "great journey" she will begin after Jung's death (RB, p. 343b). She also agrees that Jung should throw her in prison, where she can collect herself and reflect upon her journey.

JUNG'S STRUGGLE WITH HIS SOUL

Jung responds that his soul is "divinely beautiful," but then enters into a tirade in which he rebukes her for tormenting him. His soul sobs, pleads for compassion, and is horrified by Jung's accusations. In a play on words, Jung tells his soul that she has *no soul* because she is "the thing itself" (RB, p. 344a). Turning the tables on her, Jung asks his soul if perhaps she would like him to be her "earthly soul." At this point Philemon steps forward to praise Jung's soul in Jung's name, telling her, amongst other things, that she lives in the "golden temple" and that "we, your vassals, wait on your words" (RB, p. 344a). He then says, "Let this be a festival celebrating joy and life—the day upon which you, blessed one, commence your return journey from the land of men where you have learned how to be a soul" (RB, p. 344a). Jung's soul looks both "saddened and pleased" at Philemon's words, and prepares for her re-ascent into the heavens, but Jung is now suspicious that she is hiding something from humanity. Jung's soul tries to bluff her way through, but Jung detects her lie, and she breaks down and admits that indeed she has stolen "love, warm human love…the holy source of life, the unification of everything separated and longed for" (RB, p. 344b).

Jung lectures his soul on the immoderation, greed, hunger for power, and insatiability of daimons, souls, and gods, and he tells his soul that if she wants love she will have to "crawl in the dust" and learn humility (RB, p. 345a). Philemon reappears and says that both Gods and men have been "victims of deception," and Jung, after reprimanding his soul for her failure to honor humankind (RB, p. 345a), implores her to devote herself to the salvation of man. She agrees and instructs Jung to "set to work" building a furnace where the old, broken, and ruined will be thrown into a "melting pot" and renewed. She describes for Jung, "a custom of the ancients…to be adapted for new use," which involves "incubation in a smelter, a taking back into the interior" (RB, p. 345b), and which clearly anticipates Jung's later interest in alchemy. Like the alchemists, Jung's soul proposes a "holy ceremony" that involves the formation and shaping of matter. Matter, according to Jung's soul, "strengthens thought" (RB, p. 345b) and shapes salvation.

Jung does his soul's bidding by forming into matter the thoughts she has provided him (an act he will later concretize by building his castle in Bollingen). But soon his soul announces that "the breath of fire" is descending upon him and that Jung must therefore be brought before the "ruler of this world" (RB, p. 345b) who demands Jung's fear. Jung hesitates, stating that he wishes to avoid the world's ruler, but his soul insists that he possesses a "word" that should not be concealed. Jung has a vision of the world on fire, and of himself going about in a "burning robe with singed hair, a crazy look in [his] eyes," proclaiming the agony that this fire will bring (RB, p. 346a). Jung asks his soul to explain, but she simply responds that he must look up and see the skies reddened by the flames (RB, p. 346a).

In these preliminaries to the *Septem Sermones ad Mortuos* (Seven Sermons to the Dead), we have a case study of the inner life, the conflicts, urges, and doubts of a reluctant prophet. Jung's reluctance remained as he addressed his prophesy only to the dead and refused to publish the Sermons during his lifetime or to have them included in his *Collected Works*. Jung eventually abandoned the prophetic mode of expression altogether and re-cast his ideas within the idiom of science, but the "Sermons" and *The Red Book* as a whole show us how close he came to seeing himself as a prophetic figure.

Chapter 11

The Seven Sermons to the Dead

The Red Book: Scrutinies, cont.

Jung reports that his soul was silent for many days, but that eventually he was visited by a "dark crowd" (RB, p. 346b), and his soul hastily informed him that they would tear down his door. Jung curses the crowd, but his soul bids him to let them speak. At this point Philemon, who is garbed in a white priestly robe, places his hand on Jung's shoulder, and Jung tells the dead to have their say. In unison they cry out, "We have come back from Jerusalem where we did not find what we sought" (RB, p. 346b), and they ask Jung, not for his blood, but for his light. Philemon is about to deliver the "Seven Sermons to the Dead," which in the printed versions that Jung circulated privately during his lifetime, bears the subheading, "The seven instructions of the dead. Written by Basilides in Alexandria, where the East touches the West. Translated from the original Greek text into the German language" (RB, p. 346, n. 81). We should here recall that according to the New Testament, Christ's "gospel was preached even to those who are now dead" (I Peter 4:6).

I will not labor long on the question of why Jung attributes the "Sermons" to Philemon in *Scrutinies* and to Basilides in the printed editions that Jung distributed during his lifetime (RB, p. 346, n. 81). As the "Seven Sermons" have now been available to all for more than 50 years, much has been written on them and their connection to

Gnosticism.[1] Basilides was a second-century Christian Gnostic whose ideas are known almost exclusively through the writings of Christian authors who reported his ideas as heresies. Jung, who by the time of *The Red Book* had made a certain study of Gnosticism (which he says intensified between 1918 and 1926), chose the pseudepigraphic attribution as a means of linking the Sermons to this ancient cult, and indeed the "Seven Sermons" contain many Gnostic themes. It also appears clear that Jung is presenting his version of "Gnosticism" as an alternative, indeed a superior alternative, to Christianity, and that the dead, who complain of not finding what they sought in Jerusalem, are about to be provided instruction, emanating from Alexandria, where "East meets West" (RB, p. 346, n. 81), and which is meant to enlighten them to a non-Christian (or at least non-traditional Christian) form of wisdom.

Did Jung believe that he was somehow "channeling" ancient ideas? He suggested as much in a letter to Maeder,[2] and in *Memories, Dreams, Reflections* he said that in writing the "Seven Sermons," he "was compelled from within, as it were, to formulate and express what might have been said by Philemon" (MDR, p. 190). While, as we have seen, at a certain point in his career Jung seemed to dismiss the "Sermons" as a "sin of [his] youth" (CW 18, § 1499), late in his life he said that they formed a "prelude to what [he] had to communicate to the world about the unconscious" (MDR, p. 192). Indeed, he informed Aniela Jaffe that all of his work and creativity derived from the fantasies and dreams that began in 1912 and eventuated in *The Red Book* and "Seven Sermons" (MDR, p. 192). In 1957 Jung stated that the period during which he was involved with the inner images of *The Red Book* was the most important of his life and that his entire life consisted in elaborating on this material which flooded him from the unconscious and "threatened to break" him. He writes that everything he did since this "numinous beginning" was simply the "outer classification, the scientific elaboration, and the integration into life" (RB, p. vii).

THE FIRST SERMON: THE PLEROMA

The "Seven Sermons" are philosophical and theosophical in content, and while they can (and have) been interpreted in psychological terms, I will initially examine them as the metaphysical discourses that they appear to be on their face. The first sermon begins: "Now hear: I begin with nothingness. Nothingness is the same as fullness. In infinity full is as good as empty" (RB, p. 346b). Philemon states that one can say anything or nothing about nothingness because the infinite or "Pleroma" has "no qualities, since it has all qualities" (RB, p. 346b; cf. RB, p. 370a). The word "Pleroma," which is used a number of times in the New Testament by Paul (e.g. Colossians 2:9), has the meaning of "fullness" and generally, especially among the Gnostics, refers to the sum of divine powers. By equating the Pleroma with both fullness and nothingness, Jung is tapping into a tradition that is reminiscent not only of Gnosticism but also of Hinduism, Neoplatonism, and the Kabbalah, and which was later adapted by Hegel in his philosophy of the Absolute. In Indian thought, *Brahman*, as the supreme truth of the cosmos, is everything, but since it is without attributes, it is also *Sunya*, nothingness or the void. For Plotinus, the "One" seeks, needs, and has nothing and therefore overflows itself into the All. The Kabbalists held that the Infinite, *Ein-sof*, was also *Ayin*, "nothingness." Hegel would give philosophical expression to these mystical notions with his view that absolute being, because it is bereft of all distinctions and determinations, is "nothingness."[3] Jung will later compare the Pleroma to the unconscious, as an infinite but indeterminate (and thus being-less) realm, but here his focus appears to be on the nature of being in general.

There is a sense in which all inquiry begins with Leibniz's famous question, "How is it that there is something rather than nothing?"[4] and Jung/Philemon appears to be addressing this very mystery. On the one hand, the equation of something-ness with nothingness seems to solve, or at least eliminate the question, since in this view, Being (the world) proceeds from nothingness out of necessity, as the two are *identical*. Indeed Jung asks how it is that creation came into being (RB, p. 347a) and answers that while individual creatures have a beginning, creation—like death—is "ever-present" (RB, p. 347a). However, we might sharpen our inquiry by noting that being "ever-present" is itself a state of affairs, and this leads to the question of how it is that any "state of affairs at all" arises. Why is there "no state of affairs" whatsoever? It would seem the question is unanswerable, but by pressing against it we are humbled and awed, and this awe is not only the beginning of a mythical and religious outlook, but is the foundation of the mystery that Jung held to be central to the enigma of the Self.

We learn from Philemon that the Pleroma is to be distinguished from creation and is indeed its "beginning and end" (RB, p. 347a), pervading creation like "sunlight pervades the air." Still, creation "has no share" in the Pleroma, and at least from a certain perspective this applies equally to humanity, which is part of creation but "infinitely removed" from the Pleroma because it is "confined within time and space" (RB, p. 347a). In all of this Jung seems to echo the ancient Gnostic view that material creation is alienated from the divine essence and that man as a corporeal entity is completely profane, containing within his soul only a spark of the Pleroma, which must be recognized so that the individual can ascend on high, leaving the corporeal self and world behind.

"…THE PLEROMA IS ALSO IN US"

However, Philemon/Jung goes on to say that in spite of our infinite distance from the Pleroma, "we are…the Pleroma itself," "the Pleroma is also in us," and "We are also the whole Pleroma" (RB, p. 347a). This paradox is related to the familiar mystical notion that the macrocosm or "absolute" is mirrored or contained in the microcosm or "soul," an idea that readily gives rise to the view that God is contained within the Self.[5] One way to make sense of the paradox of man's distance from, yet identity with, the Pleroma is to recall Jung's early interest in Kant's distinction between the phenomenal and noumenal orders, the former the realm of space, time, and matter, and the province of knowledge and science, and the latter the transcendent atemporal, acausal, non-spatial realm that is the domain of ethics and religion. When Jung places an infinite distance between humanity and the Pleroma, he is speaking of the *phenomenal* order; and, when he identifies humanity *with* the Pleroma, he is speaking about the *noumenal* realm in much the same way that Kant argued that phenomenally man is determined but noumenally ensouled and free. On the other hand, we can also understand Jung's paradoxical pronouncements about the Pleroma as referring to a single all-encompassing reality that exists in *unio oppositorum*, and which reveals its dual or multiple aspects only when it is described in language.

It is only in language that the Pleroma is "everything and nothing," both separated from and contained within man, differentiated and non-differentiated, the smallest point and the "boundless firmament" (RB, p. 347a).

We can gain insight into the paradoxes involved in our efforts to *represent* the Pleroma through a consideration of the difficulties involved in representing a three-dimensional globe in a two-dimensional space; all efforts to create a map of the entire world fail in one or more crucial ways. Think of the various methods of mapping the whole earth—the rectangular "Mercator" projection, which distorts the size of land masses near the poles; the dual polar projections, which distort the world by representing it as *two* circular discs (each centered upon one of the poles); and the "equal areas", or so-called "orange-peel" projection, which represents the size of land masses fairly accurately but at the expense of producing disturbing gaps on the earth's surface. Each of these projections are valid and "true" in spite of their apparent inconsistency with each other. Ultimately, the effort to map the world results in the development of a number of useful but inadequate flat projections that seem to contradict, but actually complement, one another.

Our cartographic analogy helps us to see how *representation* causes a rupture in an essentially un-representable whole. Support for this as an interpretation of Jung's view is forthcoming in his claim that his statements about the Pleroma are "figurative" (RB, p. 347a), which suggests that its paradoxes may be a function of figurative *language*, and that it is a "delusion" (RB, p. 347b) to believe that we can think about the Pleroma, suggesting that the process of thought/language distorts the Pleroma's essence.

ALL IS RELATIVE AND NOT RELATIVE

Philemon asks why it is that Jung speaks about the Pleroma at all. Jung's answer is quite interesting and suggests a relativistic, even postmodern mode of thought. He says that he speaks of the Pleroma "in order to begin somewhere" and to free one from the delusion that "there is something fixed or in some way established from the outset" (RB, p. 347a). Indeed, "Every so-called fixed and certain thing is only relative. That alone is fixed and certain that is subject to change" (RB, p. 347a).

We should not be surprised that Jung will soon contradict himself on this very matter, when he says, for example in the very next paragraph, "Creation is ever present and so is death" (RB, p. 347a), suggesting that these things are somehow fixed and established! Again, Jung's (and our) problem is one of representation—once a philosophical claim is put into language its opposite comes in its wake. Later in his career Jung will express a similar idea when he says that even the notion of the coincidence of opposites must be complemented by its opposite, i.e. "absolute opposition" in which the opposites don't coincide![6]

DIFFERENTIATION

Philemon now proclaims that "differentiation" is the essence of creation, and because man is a created entity, his essence compels him to differentiate "qualities of the Pleroma that do not exist" (RB, p. 347b), but rather reflect his own nature. Indeed, differentiation of qualities is vital to humanity's very existence—were man to stop making distinctions, he would "fall into the Pleroma itself" (RB, p. 347b), cease to exist as a separate, created being, and, in effect, dissolve into nothingness. Borrowing a term from Schopenhauer and Eduard von Hartmann (RB, p. 347, n. 85), Jung tells us that the *principium individuationis* expresses man's nature to struggle "against primeval, perilous sameness" (RB, p. 347b). Jung will, of course, later make "individuation" the goal of analytic treatment and the mark of the fully actualized human being. He will hold that while the collective unconscious (i.e. the Pleroma) is the source of human vitality and inspiration, one must integrate this source into consciousness *and become sufficiently differentiated from it* so as to creatively express oneself as a unique individual.

Jung treats us to examples of qualities that man differentiates in the Pleroma (or in the world) as pairs of opposites. These include fullness and emptiness, living and dead, good and evil, beautiful and ugly, "the one and the many," etc. (RB, p. 347b). Strictly speaking, these qualities "do not exist" (RB, p. 347b) but cancel each other out in the Pleroma, which Jung conceives as a *unio oppositorum*. However, the pairs of opposites are *effective in us,* and, while on the one hand, they mark us as distinct from the Pleroma and give us life, they also victimize us, as "the Pleroma is rent within us" (RB, p. 348a). Jung's thinking here is difficult to grasp; he holds that if we strive after a particular quality and neglect its opposite, e.g. "good" as opposed to "evil" or "beautiful" as opposed to "ugliness," we "forget our essence" as differentiation and fall under the spell of the Pleroma. This is because in the Pleroma the qualities are united, and thus one who, for example, strives after the good will necessarily also be seized by evil, and the same for each of the other pairs of opposites. Jung suggests that the only way to remain true to our essence as differentiation and to avoid dissolution in the Pleroma is to maintain our distance from the pairs of opposites, to differentiate ourselves from both good *and* evil, beautiful *and* the ugly, etc.

Jung is of the view that striving after good to the exclusion of evil, or after any one pole to the exclusion of its opposite, is like trying to seize the circle without also taking in its boundary, or attempting a flight to the crescent moon while avoiding the full one.[7] As the opposites are "phenomenally" distinct but "noumenally" identical, it is an illusion to think that we can have one without the other. Here again *metaphysical* speculation serves as a foundation for Jung's *psychological* idea that the Self is a coincidence of opposites, and that psychic wholeness can only be achieved when one consciously integrates both poles of an opposition, e.g. *persona* and *shadow* into one's personality. It is not so much that one distances oneself completely from both good and evil or beauty and ugliness, but that one recognizes the illusion of accepting one while rejecting the other. As we have seen, it is not just the "Seven Sermons" but also much of *The Red Book* that is devoted to this very theme.

ON DIFFERENCE

Jung's views on "differentiation" bear comparison with those that the French philosopher, Jacques Derrida, put forth half a century later. With his 1968 paper "Différance,"[8] Derrida introduced a notion that was to have ramifications in philosophy, literature, and political thought. Derrida produced a "difference" in the spelling of his term by substituting an "a" for an "e" in such a manner that this difference cannot be heard in French but can be discerned graphically. He introduced "*difference*" in order to make oblique reference to the spaces between letters, phonemes, and words that allow them to be distinguished from one another, and hence produce language and meaning. Derrida went on to suggest that *différance* is "older than being itself," and he indicated that while *différance* itself can never be "presented", it makes possible the very gesture or presentation of being present. An implication of this is that without differentiation there could be no experience, meaning, or being whatsoever. One ramification of Derrida's ideas on difference is that the search for a unitary philosophy, absolute truth, singular vision of self and the world becomes a chimera, as any unity, singularity, or absolute must rest upon the foundation of that which is different from itself. This leads to a respect for differences in culture, art, thought, and religion, and the abandonment of any Hegelian-like effort to integrate all ideas and things. A further implication of this view is that things and ideas are integrally related to, and indeed dependent upon their polar opposites, and that the effort to exalt one pole of a binary opposition (good, being, presence, reality) and debase its opposite (evil, nothingness, absence, illusion) is a fruitless endeavor. With this highly truncated account of the role of *différance* (difference) in late 20th century thought, we are, I believe, in a position to appreciate Jung's own thoughts on difference in *The Red Book*. Five decades prior to Derrida's seminal essay, Jung appreciated the significance of difference for all things human and otherwise. From the "Seven Sermons" we learn:

> Differentiation is creation. It is differentiated. Differentiation is its essence, and therefore it differentiates. Therefore man differentiates since his essence is differentiation. (RB, p. 347a, b)

Jung recognized that an important implication of difference is that we are unwise to think we can ally ourselves with one pole of a binary opposition:

> When we strive for the good or the beautiful, we forget our essence, which is differentiation. And we fall subject to the spell of the qualities of the Pleroma. (RB, p. 348a)

Jung further appears to have held that another implication of differentiation is a call to allow the world to develop in all of its varied manifestations. As we have seen in *Liber Secundus*, Jung's soul, in the form of a white bird, declares that each thing should have its own time, becoming, and development (RB, p. 310a).

Jung/Philemon again expresses the view that a primal unity is torn asunder in the human subject (RB, p. 348a). However, while Jung is adamant that man's "very nature is differentiation" (RB, p. 347b), he does not abandon the notion of transcending difference. According to Jung,

> ...he who accepts what approaches him because it is also in him, quarrels and wrangles no more, but looks into himself and keeps silent. He sees the tree of life, whose roots reach into Hell and whose top touches Heaven. He also no longer knows differences. (RB, p. 301a)

We might say that the possibility of (psychologically, philosophically, and mystically) transcending difference lies in the fact that it too is a pole of a binary opposition with unity, and in accord with Jung's approach to the opposites, this pole must also be embraced. For Jung, differentiation is a function of our conscious mental life; in the unconscious the opposites are non-distinct (CW 6, § 179). The process of individuation involves the differentiation of psychic functions (e.g. sensation and intellect), ego from non-ego, positive from negative, good from evil, and then their re-integration in the formation of a Self.

According to Jung, differentiation is necessary for direction and purpose (CW 6, § 705), and to prevent an arbitrary identification with one pole of an opposition and "a violent suppression of its opposite" (CW 6, § 174). In *Scrutinies* Jung describes on the psychological level what Derrida and others were to declare on a philosophical level fifty years later: the importance of acknowledging the so-called "inferior" poles of various oppositions (e.g. evil, the imaginary, absence, the irrational) and bringing them into the experience and discourse about the self and the world. However, for Jung, it is not only differentiation, but ultimately a *reintegration* of the opposites that is necessary to prevent the ego from falling prey to one or the other poles of an opposition. Indeed, it is a fundamental principle of Jungian psychology that the opposites must each be both differentiated *and* united, for "when the individual consistently takes his stand on one side, the unconscious ranges itself on the other and rebels" (CW 6, § 175). Indeed, this is one idea behind Jung's concepts of the shadow and compensation and a major source of his interest in the principle of *coincidentia oppositorum*.[9]

Jung's reflections on "difference" in *The Red Book* are relevant to the question of whether the psychotherapeutic and individuation process results in a unitary Self, or is better understood as resulting in a condition in which the Self's multiplicity is acknowledged and permitted to flourish. Jung is sometimes seen as unduly valorizing "wholeness," and his *Red Book* thoughts on difference, along with his interest in polytheism (which as we will see is quite clearly articulated in *Scrutinies*), suggest that just as there is no single, unified God (or single understanding of God), there can be no authentic notion or experience of a singular, unified Self, an idea that has been put forth most forcefully by James Hillman.[10] This is an idea that has been, and will continue to be, debated both within and outside Jungian circles.

THINKING ALIENATES

We learn in the first sermon that it is *thinking* that produces the distinctions between qualities and thus alienates us from our essence (RB, p. 348a). It is thinking that leads us to strive after "the non-existing qualities of the Pleroma" (RB, p. 348a), and which therefore causes us to fall back into the Pleroma itself. This is because by thinking one pole of an opposition, we are unsuspectingly seized by the other pole and suddenly find ourselves plummeting back into the vortex of non-differentiation. This occurs even if we think "differentiation," since doing this inevitably leads us into its opposite, "sameness" (RB, p. 348a). Jung seems to suggest that our essence as distinctiveness should not and cannot be *thought*, but should rather be *lived*, as a "striving for one's own essence" (RB, p. 348a). While it may be impossible to think unity and difference, good and evil, or beauty and ugliness together, these dichotomies can be symbolized, and moreover, lived. Indeed, it is precisely this "double" mode of living that is one of the *sine qua non's* of psychotherapy, for example, when the patient comes to both "love" and "love and hate" those with whom he/she is closest.

One who achieves such a mode of life need know nothing at all about the Pleroma, and the only reason that one teaches these ideas is so one can learn to "bridle [one's] thoughts" (RB, p. 348a). Here the theosophy of the "Seven Sermons," like the Buddhist's ferryboat, is a vehicle that one discards after it conveys one to one's destination. In this connection we should note that after composing the "Seven

Sermons," Jung discarded both the theosophical and aesthetic mode of expression that is evident throughout *The Red Book* (MDR, p. 188).

WHO ARE THE DEAD?

At this point the dead grumble and fade away. Jung asks Philemon why it is that he instructs the dead on these strange and ancient teachings. Philemon answers that he does so because their "lives were incomplete" and that they must now be fulfilled so they "can enter into death" (RB, p. 348b). In *Black Book* 5, a portion of which is printed as "Appendix C" of *The Red Book*, we learn that the "dead who besiege us are souls who have not fulfilled the *principium individuationis*" (RB, p. 370b). Moreover, while the dead were once Christians, they have repudiated, and have in turn been rejected by this faith, and the doctrine of the "Seven Sermons" is precisely the teaching that was once "discarded and persecuted" (RB, p. 348b) by Christianity.

According to Stein, the dead addressed in the "Seven Sermons" are the heirs of the Enlightenment who died without faith and thus had no way to continue their soul's journey after their demise. Because they lived their lives solely within the confines of the "time-bound ego," they had no taste of the timeless in life, and thus failed to enter eternity in death.[11] As we will see, in the seventh sermon Philemon informs the dead that each individual has a connection to a divine, guiding star—the God within, which is his eternal home and resting place.

On the one hand, the "Seven Sermons," like *The Tibetan Book of the Dead*, is meant as a guide to the dead in completing their unfinished work, achieving their peace, and making the transition into eternity. By addressing the Sermons to the dead, Philemon/Jung signals an acknowledgment of the continued presence and humanity of the departed that has become increasingly rare in Western, "civilized" cultures. Indeed, the dead have bequeathed to us not only their wealth and accomplishments but also their unresolved concerns and problems, and it behooves us to treat them with both honor and reverence. On the other hand, as Jung himself was to later suggest, the dead also represent the unconscious aspects of the living, as they are "the voices of the Unanswered, Unresolved, and Unredeemed" (MDR, p. 191).

We might say that in spite of Philemon's declarations to the contrary (RB, p. 349b), the "Seven Sermons" are therefore addressed as much to the living as to the dead. They are, in effect, Jung addressing himself, but they are also ultimately, like *The Tibetan Book of the Dead*, addressed to a wider audience. The "Sermons" are meant for the "living dead" who, having rejected traditional Christianity, find themselves spiritually and psychologically incomplete.

"...THINGS ARE AS I KNOW THEM"

Jung asks Philemon if he "believes" what he teaches, to which Philemon responds that he does not *believe* what he teaches but rather teaches what he *knows*. In a supposed clarification that only adds to the confusion, Philemon says,

> I do not know whether it is the best that one can know. But I know nothing better and therefore I am certain these things are as I say. If they were otherwise I would say something else, since I would know them to be otherwise. But these things are as I know them since my knowledge is precisely these things themselves. (RB, p. 348b)

This suggests that Philemon/Jung, in spite of his earlier assertion that knowledge is relative (RB, p. 347a), claims to have a direct apprehension of truth. This claim can be contrasted with Jung's own more modest pronouncement on the same topic approximately three years before his death:

> If I call something true, it does not mean that it is absolutely true. It merely seems to be true to myself and/or to other people. If I were not doubtful in this respect it would mean that I implicitly assume that I am able to state an absolute truth. This is an obvious hybris. (CW 18, § 1584)

However, as Shamdasani points out, in 1959 when a BBC television interviewer asked Jung if he now believes in God, Jung responded that this was difficult to answer, but then proceeded to state, "I know. I don't need to believe. I know" (RB, p. 348, n. 89). Yet, as Stanton Marlan suggests,[12] even here there is a certain ambiguity in Jung's knowledge claim. Is Jung claiming knowledge of the *God experience* or knowledge of a *metaphysical deity*? The former claim would be consistent with virtually all of Jung's other post *Red Book* pronouncements, the latter would constitute a radical departure.

Remarkably, Philemon's claim to direct apprehension of the real comes just a few paragraphs after he has declared that it is a delusion to think that "there is something fixed or in some way established from the outset" and that, "Every so-called fixed and certain thing is only relative" (RB, p. 347a). As I have suggested earlier, in connection with our discussion of "Knowledge of the Heart" (in Chapter 2), an ambivalence regarding the nature of knowledge is not only present in *The Red Book* but runs through Jung's later writings as well, and continues to pervade much of Jungian thought. This is a topic that deserves further inquiry and development, but as Papadopoulos has pointed out, one finds in Jung two very different attitudes,[13] and I believe that these attitudes have led to two quite different versions of Jungianism. The first is an attitude of uncertainty, multi-perspectivism, revisionism, and suspension of judgment, coupled with the view that the unconscious is an "essential unknown" and that *unknowing* is a preferred mode of apprehension. The second is an attitude, perhaps rooted in Jung's interpretation of Gnosticism and certainly part and parcel of his Platonism, in which Jung claims to possess, or at least pursue knowledge about real and invariant archetypes, meanings, etc. that presumably lie at the foundation of the human psyche. This attitude is not only apparent in Jung's comment about his "knowledge" of God, but is also evident, for example, whenever Jung provides an apodictic interpretation of a fantasy or dream, or makes general pronouncements about national and ethnic modes of consciousness.[14] At times these two attitudes merge in Jung's thinking, as when in his "Commentary on *The Tibetan Book of the Dead*", Jung suggests that the book's authors saw their Gods both as projections of the human mind and as absolutely real (CW 11, § 833), but at other times, as Papadoupolos[15] notes, they remain quite distinct.[16]

THE SECOND SERMON: ON THE DEATH OF GOD

The dead reappear and now demand knowledge of God, asking "Where is God? Is God dead?" (RB, p. 348b). In response to their queries, Philemon responds that "God is not dead. He is as alive as ever. God is creation" (RB, p. 348b). Like humanity and the rest of creation,

God is both distinct from, and identical with the Pleroma. However, in contrast to (the rest of) creation, God is less differentiated since "he is the manifestation of the effective fullness of the Pleroma" (RB, p. 348b). In the paradoxical or *iridescent* language that is characteristic of mysticism, Jung states that we must identify God with, and differentiate God from, the Pleroma in order to have "effective fullness" (RB, p. 348b). As "effective fullness," God is here distinct from the Pleroma, because the latter, being infinite, also includes "effective emptiness," which Jung will identify with the devil (RB, p. 349a). However, like all other things, God is also the Pleroma itself.

In speaking about God as a second order emanation or manifestation of the Pleroma, Jung is in accord with much of Gnostic thought, which indeed regarded the God of the Bible rather pejoratively as a lower level demiurge who fashioned the material world. A similar, though by no means derogatory distinction is made by the Kabbalists between *Ein-sof* (the Infinite) and the more accessible, personal God towards whom one directs one's praise and prayers. Jung's "God" in the "Seven Sermons" is also free of the negative connotations of the Gnostic's demiurge, but as we will see, Jung's God is not the omnipotent being of traditional faith. Jung contrasts "God," which he describes as "effective fullness," with the devil, whose essence is "effective emptiness" (RB, p. 349a). In making this contrast Jung appears to come close to adopting the very *privatio boni* doctrine of evil that he was to later famously reject on the grounds that by making evil a privation, the church had diminished evil's living psychic reality and ignored its power (CW 11, § 247).

Like all the distinctions that arise out of the Pleroma, the distinction between God and the devil is presumably made by us. However, like the Tibetan Gods, who are both *samsaric* projections and real (CW 11, § 833), the assertions about, and distinctions we make between God and the devil are both psychic and objective: "We need no proof of their existence. It is enough that we have to keep speaking about them" (RB, p. 349a). However, unlike the later Wittgenstein, who might have said that "god" and the "devil" are a function of the "language game" in which these terms/figures appear, Jung seems to hold that God and the devil have "essences" (RB, p. 349a) that necessarily emerge in *any language* whatsoever. He will later call these essences "archetypes."

God and the devil are, according to Jung, the "first manifestations of nothingness, which we call the Pleroma" (RB, p. 349a). They stand very close to the Pleroma, and represent "fullness and emptiness, generation and destruction" (RB, p. 349a). They have "effectiveness" in common, by which Jung seems to mean that unlike the Pleroma, which is totally remote from human life, God and the devil have actual effects in our lives and world.

However, standing above God and the devil is another forgotten God, who Jung calls Abraxas and identifies with "effect in general" (RB, p. 349a). Abraxas, who Jung in his 1932 Visions Seminar described as the Gnostics' supreme deity and a "time God" (RB, p. 349, n. 93[17]), unfolds freely as "force, duration [and] change," since its opposite, "the ineffective neither exists nor resists." It is interesting, given Jung's earlier gyrations about the sun god in *Liber Secundus* (RB, p. 271b ff), that he distinguishes Abraxas from the traditional God, by calling the latter "Helios." Recall that it was a verbal slip that the anchorite Ammonius made about the sun god, Helios, that prompted him to call Jung a pagan "devil" (RB, p. 272b). The "Seven Sermons" mark Jung's clearest moment of pagan polytheism. The dead realize this and since they were Christians, we now find them raising "a great tumult" (RB, p. 349a).

Philemon is not distressed by the dead's outrage, as he continues to insist that in spite of their nominal Christianity they have rejected their Christian faith. This is because, without knowing it, they entered an era "where one should believe only what one knows" (RB, p. 349b). Philemon's teaching is about a God to whom one does not pray, and in whom one does not believe, but who one nevertheless "knows." Jung now makes the charge that Philemon teaches about "a terrible and dreadful God" (RB, p. 349b) who has no concern for human joy or suffering, to which Philemon responds that the dead have already rejected a god of love. The God that Philemon teaches about is both creator and destroyer, without particular qualities, and about whom "nothing can be attributed" (RB, p. 349b), as this is the only God that can be known. This is a God, Philemon tells Jung, "who dissolves unity, blasts everything human, who powerfully creates and mightily destroys" (RB, p. 349b). Perhaps Philemon can make the claim to *know* such a God, the God Abraxas, who is "force, duration, change" and "the effectual itself" (RB, p. 349a) because it is virtually indistinguishable from the blind forces of nature that comprise the universe. The closer one's definition of God comes to the universe itself, the more certain one can be of God's existence! "Abraxas," we are told, "is the world, its becoming and its passing" (RB, p. 350a).

THE THIRD SERMON: ABRAXAS

The dead, however, wish to know more about this "highest God," and thus the third sermon begins. We are told that Abraxas draws the *summum bonum* from the sun and the *infinum malum* from the devil. Now, in clear distinction to the doctrine that evil is a privation of the good and thus not part of the divine essence, we learn that Abraxas himself is *LIFE*, "the mother of good and evil" (RB, p. 350a). Abraxas is both the sun and "the eternally sucking gorge of emptiness," both "life and death... truth and lying, good and evil, light and darkness" (RB, p. 350a). Shamdasani calls Abraxas "the uniting of the Christian God with Satan" (RB Intro, p. 206).

Abraxas, Jung avers, "is terrible," and we have now, in typical Gnostic fashion, been treated to an account of Abraxas' attributes that appears to contradict the earlier claim that "nothing can be attributed to him" (RB, p. 349b). However, this list of attributes, by virtue of their inclusiveness and generality (e.g. "He is the saint and his betrayer"), tells us very little, if anything, specific about the supreme God. One thing is clear: We must accept the devil if we are to have the good lord: "Everything that you create with the Sun God gives effective power to the devil" (RB, p. 350a).

The characterization of Abraxas as "terrible" and as "the monster of the underworld, a thousand-armed polyp, a coiled knot of winged serpents, frenzy" (RB, p. 350a), invokes comparison not only with the unconscious, but with the broad conception of the "monstrous," unforeseeable future that will later appear in the thought of Jacques Derrida,[18] and which we have already discussed in connection with Jung's view of a future that "no word can grasp...[and] no will can conquer..." (RB, p. 306a). Like Derrida's "monstrous," Abraxas can be understood as the awesome future that can neither be anticipated nor circumscribed by words: "Before him is no question and no reply" (RB, p. 350b).

Jung nevertheless queries Philemon if he should "understand this God," to which the master responds that Abraxas "is to be known but

not understood" (RB, p. 350b). A god that can be understood can be held
"in the hollow of your hand" and must thus be thrown away—a reference to
Jung's earlier dealings with the god Izdubar (RB, p. 285b). Abraxas is
no Izdubar, and we have yet another turn in the dialectical wheel of Jung's
spiritual journey in *The Red Book*. Unlike Izdubar, the mythic god who was
made ill and nearly killed by the advent of science, Abraxas is the "chaos," the
"utterly boundless," "eternally incomprehensible…cruel contradictoriness
of nature" (RB, p. 350b).[19] When asked why he calls this unfathomable
chaos "God," Philemon responds that if the universe were "lawful" he
would call this lawfulness "God," but as it is in fact "chance, irregularity,
sin, error," etc., it is this which must be given the name of the deity
(RB, p. 350b). Philemon adds that humans have always "named the
maternal womb of the incomprehensible God" (RB, p. 351a), and this
is the God about which he teaches. It is a God who having emerged
from both being and non-being, both "is and is not" (RB, p. 351a).
Here we see Jung in one of his more "unknowing" moods, a mood that
seems at odds with the Platonism implicit in his theory of the archetypes
and the collective unconscious. Yet this is not a perspective that Jung
would soon, if ever, discard. As we see in his *Seminar on Nietzsche's
Zarathustra*, nearly two decades after writing the "Seven Sermons," Jung
says that the purpose of life is unknown and that we are safe in holding
that our lives are mere chaos, meaninglessness, and chance.[20]

We have seen how, early in *Liber Novus*, Jung declared that the
Supreme Meaning is the union of meaning and absurdity, of sense and
nonsense (RB, p. 229b). As Stanton Marlan points out in his Foreword
to this volume, Jung was by no means the only one of his
contemporaries to be preoccupied with this tension; indeed, James
Joyce described this structure in *Finnegan's Wake* with the term
"chaosmos" as a way of expressing the coincidence of chaos and cosmos,
multiplicity and unity, and absurdity and meaning that characterizes
this work. Jung himself seems to have recognized this in Joyce, and,
indeed understood that part of the value of Joyce's *Ulysses* resided in
its "creative destruction" (CW 15, § 180).[21]

THE FOURTH SERMON: POLYTHEISM

The fourth sermon is delivered the following night in response to
the dead's demand that Philemon, "the accursed one," speak to them
"about Gods and devils" (RB, p. 351a); and, it is in this sermon that

Philemon/Jung makes his case for polytheism. We learn of two devil Gods, the "Burning One," which is Eros, and the "Growing One," which is the "Tree of Life," and how "good and evil" unite in each. Here, as well as in the next sermon, we find a hint of Jung's understanding of Eros, which in contrast to the Freudian view, attributes the erotic to *both* the "drive nature of man" and "the highest form of spirit" (RB, p. 351, n. 4; CW 7, §§ 32-33).

The Gods are as innumerable as the stars in the heavens; indeed, "each star is a God, and each space that a star fills is a devil" (RB, p. 351a). But the principle Gods are four, and each is under Abraxas, "the effect of the whole." "One the... Sun God," two is Eros, which "binds two together," "three is the Tree of Life," and "four is the devil" (RB, p. 351a). (Here we see an early example of Jung's fascination with the quaternity, which he will elaborate upon in relation to Gnosticism in *Aion*, Chapters XIII and XIV [CW 9i, pp. 184-265].) One who "recognize[s] the multiplicity ... of the Gods" (RB, 351a) is happy, but those who substitute for this divine diversity a single deity not only produce "the torment of incomprehension" (RB, 351b), but damage the very aim and foundation of creation, the essence of which is differentiation. As the self is multiple, so must be the Gods.

Jung/Philemon goes so far as to say that "the multiplicity of Gods corresponds to the multiplicity of men" (RB, p. 351b), and although he does not claim a one-to-one correspondence between men and their Gods, this claim, in concert with the highly individualized views of "my God" earlier in *The Red Book,* might suggest that each individual has his or her own deity.[22] However, regardless of the number and nature of the Gods, there is no value in divine worship. This is especially true for Abraxas, since our worship and prayer add nothing to nor take anything from the highest of the Gods (RB, p. 351b). Presumably prayer would have no impact on a God who is identified with chaos, contradiction, and cruelty (RB, p. 350b).

We learn, amongst other things, that "Man shares in the nature of the God" (RB, p. 351b), that there are "bright heavenly" Gods and "dark earthly Gods," and that the latter "form the earthly world" (RB, p. 351b). While the "Sun God is the supreme lord of the world," the heavenly and earthly Gods are equal to one another in power (RB, p. 351b).

The dead interrupt Philemon's sermon, laugh angrily, and mock him. Upon their withdrawal, Jung gently admonishes Philemon for making the error of adopting a polytheism that results from the mind being chained to the world of sensory manifestations, a tendency that had been overcome by the Christian Fathers (RB, p. 351b). Philemon responds that the dead have taken a purely practical approach to their world, weighing and counting horses, sheep, and parcels of land, and have failed to acknowledge the material world in its sacred aspect. They have not, for example, atoned for the cattle they slaughtered or done penance for the "sacred ore that they dug up from the belly of the earth" (RB, p. 352a). Philemon protests that he has not invented a polytheism, but that many powerful Gods have raised their voices in protest and bloody vengeance at a humanity that has "weighed, numbered, apportioned, hacked, and devoured" (RB, p. 352a), and which has failed to worship the "holy tree" or make peace with the soul of the golden-eyed frog. At the end of his oration, Philemon bends down to kiss the earth and says, "Mother may your son be strong." Then turning his gaze upwards to the heavens he states: "how dark is your new light" (RB, p. 352a).

While one need not adopt multiple Gods in order to intuit a spark of divinity in nature (Kabbalah and Hasidism do this in a monotheistic context), Philemon's polytheism reflects an awe and reverence for nature that was part of the pagan world-view and that began to dissipate as humanity forgot its many nature deities and asserted its mastery over the environment. Such reverence is refreshing, especially now in our environmentally conscious era.

THE FIFTH SERMON: SPIRITUALITY, SEXUALITY, COMMUNITY

The following night the dead beseech Philemon to teach them "about the church and holy communion" (RB, p. 352a), and we arrive at the fifth sermon, which begins as follows: "The world of the Gods is manifest in spirituality and in sexuality. The celestial ones appear in spirituality, the earthly in sexuality" (RB, p. 352b). As we have seen, Jung rejected Freud's purely biological "drive" view of the erotic, and he came to regard the sexual and the spiritual as interdependent forces (cf. RB, p. 252, n. 12). Jung is now in accord with certain Gnostic sects who held sexuality to be a sacred act, as well as with the Kabbalah, which understood the creation and redemption of the world in cosmic, erotic terms.[23] Here Philemon equates spirituality with the embrace and creativity of the celestial mother, and sexuality with what he calls

"PHALLOS," the earthly father, which is also a cosmic creative power. Both are "superhuman daimons that affect us more than the Gods since they are closely akin to our essence" (RB, p. 352b). Because sexuality and spirituality are daimons, they are not qualities of a person that one can possess or control, but rather exist in themselves and encompass and possess the individual.

Philemon moves on to the question of community. He says that the absence of community produces sickness and suffering—perhaps, we might here interject—the very suffering that Jung's isolation brings him in *The Red Book*. According to Philemon, the Gods impose community on man, and a certain amount of community is necessary. Any excess, however, is to be avoided. A proper balance must be struck between man's independence, which in Jung's *Black Book* is associated with the future and the father, and his immersion in the community, which is associated with the "source" and the mother (RB, p. 353, n. 117). It is noteworthy that Jung develops this theme in articles[24] that were written in 1916, the same year as the composition of the "Seven Sermons." In "The Structure of the Unconscious," he argues that a unity of the individual and collective must be achieved, but not through subordinating the one aspect to the other (CW 7, §§ 489-90). However, what Jung means by the "collective" is not so much the external social order, but rather the intrapsychic realm that he is now beginning to conceptualize as a collective unconscious, which in the *Black Book* is referred to as the "mother" and the "source" (RB, p. 353, n. 117). Jung holds that in analytic treatment the "dissolution of the persona" gives rise to fantasies that reflect "all the treasures of mythological thinking and feeling" (CW 7, § 468), which on the one hand, can produce flashes of creative genius but, on the other hand, can be overwhelming to the individual and lead to a condition that is analogous to the mental derangement of schizophrenia. Individuation is the process through which one assimilates aspects of the collective, uniting them with, and marshaling them for a unique life.

THE SIXTH SERMON: ADDING UNREASON TO REASON

In the sixth sermon, Philemon continues on the theme of the daimons of sexuality and spirituality. Whereas the former comes to one's soul as a serpent, the latter enters the soul as a white-bird. Philemon describes the daimon of sexuality in feminine and highly pejorative terms, describing her as a mischievous tyrant, whore, and tormentor. The daimon of spirituality is masculine, solitary, and chaste—he is the messenger of the mother. In all of this Philemon appears to be restating the biblical and gnostic view of women as the source of temptation and evil, and the dead implore him to "cease this talk," claiming they "have known this for a long time" (RB, p. 353a). They tell Philemon that in all of his talk of Gods, daimons, and souls he has been overcome by a "childish delusion" (RB, p. 353a). The dead, on the other hand, are proud of their reason and mock what they see as Philemon's "superstition." (Here we have evidence that the "dead" of the "Seven Sermons" are also the living who have "died" to all but science and reason). Philemon, for his part, implores the dead to add his "folly to [their] cleverness" (RB, p. 353b), and his unreason to their reason (RB, p. 353b), as this will lead them "from the eternal whirl onto the unmoving stone of rest" (RB, p. 353b). The dead are unconvinced and they accuse Philemon of "want[ing] to turn the wheel back" (RB, p. 353b), by which they seem to mean reversing the progress of the rational age. Philemon, however, speaks of a renewal of the earth that will arise from his teaching. He recites an incantation: "Fruit of the earth, sprout, rise up—and Heaven, pour out the water of life" (RB, p. 353b).

The following night Jung asks Philemon: "What fires have you kindled? What have you broken asunder?" (RB, p. 353b), to which Philemon responds cryptically that everything remains as it was before except for the occurrence of "a sweet and indescribable mystery" (RB, p. 353b). When Philemon says that he has "stepped out of the whirling circle" (RB, p. 353b), Jung asks if this means that he and Philemon are one and the same: "Are you I, am I you?" (RB, p. 353b). Philemon does not answer, but concludes by suggesting that he has ended the cycle of rebirths and endless happenings that plague the dead and the living.

THE SEVENTH SERMON: THE DOCTRINE OF MAN

The dead return the next day and say that they have forgotten to ask Philemon to teach them about man, and the seventh sermon begins with the declaration that "man is a gateway" (RB, p. 354a) from the great world of Gods, daimons, and souls to the small, inner world of the individual psyche. In this microcosm, man encounters a lonely star, his own Pleroma and divinity.[25] Here, in this "inner infinity" man stands as Abraxas, his own God, "the creator and destroyer of his own world" (RB, p. 354a). This is the "one guiding God" (RB, p. 354a), and the one interior God to whom man should pray. Philemon avers that "prayer increases the light" of the inner star and "throws a bridge across death" (RB, p. 354a). As long as man turns away from the greater world and "flaming spectacle of Abraxas" (RB, p. 354a), nothing separates him from his one God.

The idea that "man is a gateway…through which the procession of the Gods passes" (RB, p. 354a) again heralds Jung's notion that the time-honored myths (CW 7, § 468) emerge in man's dreams and fantasies. Philemon says that the dead understood that the Gods pass through man, but were convinced that human life is "nothingness and transitoriness," and that since man "creates its Gods," the Gods "were of no use" (RB, p. 354b). However, for Jung, the consequence of these ideas is that in the contemporary world where the (transcendent) Gods have been debunked and even declared dead, the Gods must be rediscovered in the psyche of man. The Gods, as Jung stated with conviction earlier in *Scrutinies*, can only be discovered through an encounter with oneself; it is this "Self" that one must turn to in prayer for spiritual strength; for it is man, understood as a gateway of divine powers, who both creates and destroys himself. Philemon intimates that one who recognizes this transcends time and becomes "eternal in each moment" (RB, p. 354b). Here in the Seventh Sermon Jung presents a gnostic/existentialist faith, in which the individual, fortified and inspired by the Gods within, assumes responsibility for his own existence, and in the process somehow transcends time and escapes the cycle of life and death. Man must seek his own *inner* "star" which is "the God and goal of man…his lone guiding God" (RB, p. 354a) and to whom the soul goes to rest after death. Upon hearing this the dead were lifted from their burden and "ascended like smoke above the shepherd's fire, who watches over his flock by night" (RB, p. 354b).

In his 1928 essay, "The Relations between the Ego and the Unconscious," Jung provided what might be termed a psychological interpretation of the seventh sermon, when he wrote: the "Self" might equally well be called the "God within us…The beginnings of our whole psychic life seem to be inextricably rooted in this point, and all our highest and ultimate purposes seem to be striving towards it" (CW 7, § 399).

The "Seven Sermons" thus offer a dialectic that is not very different from the one Jung travels in the main body of *The Red Book*: the one transcendent God is fragmented into innumerable manifestations of divinity which are then interiorized in the human psyche. In the Sermons, the transcendent God is said to exist, but he is identified with the incomprehensible, boundless chaos and cruelty of nature (RB, p. 350b). One cannot pray to or expect anything from such a God; it is only the inner God, the "lonely star" (RB, p. 354a) or "procession of the Gods" within (RB, p. 354b), that makes any difference in an individual's life. As Jung declared early in *The Red Book*, science effectively rendered the traditional gods useless, and it is only by acknowledging that they are a product of man's collective mythological imagination that they can be re-empowered for humanity and (paradoxically) again made real.

On the one hand, the Gods must be interiorized in order to become effective for humanity, but on the other hand, it is this interiorization that enables man to reach beyond himself once again towards a transcendent divine. This is clearer in the *Black Book* (of September 1916) than it is in the "Seven Sermons." In the *Black Book* Jung's soul informs him that "the individual is a mere plant without flowers and fruit, a passageway to the tree of seven lights" (RB, p. 354, n. 125), which Jung enumerates as the Pleroma, Abraxas, the Sun, the moon, the earth, the phallus, and the stars, in short, the basic elements of his Gnostic theosophy. Thus the process by which the Gods are interiorized leads back to the possibility of again intuiting them as transcendent beings, and what's more, enables the individual to reach beyond himself to a divinity that is of collective significance and value. Again, we see a dialectic and balance between the individual and the collective.

The "Seven Sermons" as Psychology

We might ask, to what extent is the "Seven Sermons" actually a treatise about metaphysics, about the infinite, being and non-being, the parade of Gods, and the spirits of the dead, and to what extent is it fundamentally a psychological treatise that uses Gnostic and neo-Gnostic metaphors to express ideas about the human ego, the reality of the unconscious, and the nature of the Self? As we have seen, Jung will later disclaim any interest or capacity to make theological and metaphysical statements. He will even provide a psychological interpretation of certain Gnostic motifs in their connection with the psychology of the Self (CW 9ii, pp. 184-221). Nevertheless, given the full context of the material within which the Sermons are embedded and a fair reading of *The Red Book* materials as a whole, it is difficult to justify the assertion that Jung had no metaphysical or theological intentions in the "Seven Sermons." What seems to me far more likely is that, at least at this point in his career, Jung did not make the distinctions between psychology, theology, and metaphysical philosophy that he felt compelled to make later on, distinctions which were *certainly not made* by the Gnostics themselves. The idea that the origin and ground of the cosmos is identical to, or at least mirrored in the human soul is one that was not only present in Gnosticism, but also in a wide range of spiritual traditions, including Hinduism, Vedanta, Buddhism, and the Kabbalah—each of which speak in terms that ignored our current disciplinary boundaries between metaphysics and psychology. Indeed, one of the "compensatory" functions that the "Seven Sermons," and *The Red Book* as a whole, can serve for us today is to reopen psychology to ideas, experiences, and influence from such other disciplines—not to conflate psychology with metaphysics, theology, philosophy, and art or to confuse these disciplines with one another, but rather to keep the boundaries between them semi-permeable, as they clearly were for Jung during the period when he authored *The Red Book*.

Jung's views on the relationship between psychology and theology appear to have changed over time, and it is unclear that he ever adopted a single point of view on their connection. James Heisig has argued that Jung's understanding of this relationship went through three distinct stages: in the first (from roughly 1900-1921), Jung understood religious experience to be a function of human emotion; in the second (from approximately 1921-1945), he understood religious myths and ideas to be a projection of the archetypes of the collective unconscious; and, in the third (after 1945), he suspended judgment regarding the objective correlates of archetypal/religious experience.[26] With the publication of *The Red Book*, this sequence loses any plausibility it may have once had, as *The Red Book* materials on their face do not support either an emotional or an archetypal projective hypothesis about religion. Instead, religious objects, even if they are a function of the imagination, are taken to be absolutely real. Having said this, a psychological interpretation of the "Seven Sermons" is most easily grasped in the context of the archetypal projection hypothesis, the view that in formulating ideas about the ultimate nature of the cosmos, humanity projects experiences of the psyche that it understands implicitly and intuitively. The underlying notion is that human consciousness has gone through a series of phases. Initially, the contents of the unconscious, the archetypes, are projected onto the world, and humanity is immersed in a world of daimons, spirits, and archetypal meanings. Over time, the projection of these archetypes is confined to the heavens, and the great mythologies and transcendent religions take form. With the further passage of time, and owing to humanity's identification with the rational powers of the ego, the projections are withdrawn, the Gods die or become irrelevant, and individuals completely fail to recognize the action of the archetypes of the collective unconscious. This, according to Jung, was the modern condition, the condition responsible for the spiritual malaise of his own time. This was also the condition he referred to when he said "the gods have become diseases" (CW 13, § 54), for in a state in which the archetypes are ignored, where spiritual experience is completely crowded out by reason, the collective unconscious will wreak havoc on the human psyche. Jung ultimately held that his psychology could provide individuals with a direct awareness of the archetypes within their own psyches; this could be achieved through an openness to and comprehension of the effects of these archetypes in dreams, fantasy, and art, in concert with a new psychological appreciation of the spiritual traditions that reason had found wanting and which had thus been discarded or ignored.

With this background in mind we can understand the "Seven Sermons" as a discourse on the human psyche. As we have seen, in this view, the "dead" are not so much those who have literally died, but rather the living, who having completely identified with reason and the material life, have become dead to their souls. When Jung/Philemon speaks to the dead about the Pleroma and Abraxas, it is not only to awaken them to the infinite and terrifying foundation of the cosmos, a foundation that can neither be "rationalized" nor "explained," but, more importantly, to awaken us to the ineffable ground of our own being in an unconscious that is infinitely wider than any of our individual selves and about which nothing definite can be said or understood. Talk about the infinite Pleroma and its transcendence yet immanence within the human psyche is designed to awaken us to the great mystery of our own being and shake us from our rational/scientific and skeptical slumbers. For Jung, something of the mystery of the origins of the cosmos remains alive within each of us, and it is the experience of this mystery that Jung is attempting to impart to the dead and his readers in the early "Sermons." Further, in describing the effects of the Pleroma, Jung conveys the notion that the great, original fullness is the unconscious origin of all specific psychical functions, as well as the goal towards which the individual, once he is adequately differentiated, can return to for his/her sense of personal meaning and wholeness. The psychological goal is to become permeable to the unconscious and its secondary spiritual, satanic, and archetypal manifestations without being swallowed up by it in a *unio mystica* that would obliterate all individuality and conflict. Rather, one must accept that the human psyche is "rent apart" and come to recognize, experience, and accept this divided condition, one that involves both good and evil, reason and unreason, fullness and emptiness, sameness and difference, life and death, truth and falsehood, beauty and ugliness, God and the devil, consciousness and unconsciousness, etc. Since the unconscious ground and source of our spiritual and psychological wholeness involves a coincidence of each of these opposites, one cannot hope to latch onto one pole of any of these dichotomies without being ensnared by the other. It is better that one accept each pole, e.g. both reason and unreason, both good and evil, into one's life, experience, and world-view, as only then can one experience the differentiated wholeness that will give rise to the individuated self. However, this cannot be accomplished via thought, but as we have seen throughout our discussion of *The Red Book*, must be arrived at through creative fantasy—hence the imaginative nature of the "Seven Sermons." When such differentiated wholeness is achieved, the individual becomes the gateway for the "procession of Gods," as the archetypal forces that had been projected in earlier times, then suppressed by reason, are rediscovered and reignited within the human mind.

Years after concluding his work on *The Red Book*, Jung provided an interpretation of certain Gnostic myths and symbols that reinforces the notion that the "Seven Sermons" are from one perspective highly psychological in nature and intent. In "Gnostic

Symbols of the Self," Jung compared the relationship of the unconscious (Self) to the conscious ego with the relationship between the Gnostics' "blessed, nonexistent God" and the "demiurge" (CW 9ii, § 297), whom the Gnostics disparaged as being ignorant of its pleromatic origins. The demiurge, which, as we have seen, the Gnostics identified with the creator God of the Bible, represents the conscious, rational ego, which in its arrogance believes that it is both the creator and master of the human personality.

As Jung points out in several of his later works (e.g. CW 9ii, § 344, CW 14, §§ 46-7, § 700), the Gnostic spark, or scintilla, which is placed in the human soul, represents the possibility of the psyche's reunification with the unconscious. Jung wrote that in working with neurotics his "aim is to create a wider personality whose centre of gravity does not necessarily coincide with the ego," but rather "in the hypothetical point between conscious and unconscious" (CW 9ii, § 297), in Gnostic terms between the demiurge and the Pleroma.

Jung's interest in Gnosticism served as an interpretive basis for his later understanding of alchemy, the commencement of which effectively brought an end to Jung's work on *The Red Book* (RB, p. 360). As Jung concluded his work on *Liber Novus*, he surrendered metaphysical language and prophetic pronouncements in favor of a more scientific idiom. Still, astute readers were able to discern the metaphysics and philosophy that lay behind, and were coordinated with his psychology. The "Seven Sermons" and *The Red Book* as a whole provide a clear window into the philosophical and theological underpinnings of Jung's later work.

Chapter 12

Final Encounters, Final Reflections

The Red Book: Scrutinies, cont.

Encounters with Death and the Celestial Mother

The "Seven Sermons" are complete and Jung now has a series of encounters that reaffirm his spiritual quest. He first meets "a dark form with golden eyes" (RB, p. 354b), who we soon learn is none other than "death" (RB, p. 355a), a figure that, as we have seen, Jung had earlier dialogued with in *Liber Secundus*, Chapter VI. Death now informs Jung that he must enter into his "stellar nature" (RB, p. 355a) (recall the "lonely star" as the individual's inner infinity) by abstaining from interaction with men, and by relinquishing human suffering and joy. Jung must practice abstinence, renounce longing and fear, and while he may show pity toward others and "love the whole" (RB, p. 355a), he must forego compassion, for it leads to alienation. This final directive is a curious condition in what otherwise sounds like an almost Buddhist call to non-attachment.

Death tells Jung that he is present to "lay the cover of protection" on him, and this means that death must be present "in the midst of life" (RB, p. 355a). Jung feels that death's prescriptions will lead to "grief and despair" as he wished to "be among men" (RB, p. 355a), but he is informed that he must be veiled in his relationship with others, surrender his solar nature, and turn to his inner star. In Gnostic terms, this star is the "spark" of the Pleroma, the identification with which enables the adherent to escape his material condition and realize his godly Self. Such an escape, however, is not really commensurate with Jung's focus on "this life" (RB, p. 232a), and his charge that one should live one's life to the full (RB, p. 308b).

Death vanishes and Philemon tells Jung that it is time "to fulfill what the dark one prophesied for [him]" (RB, p. 355a). Philemon touches Jung's eyes and opens his gaze, after which Jung beholds the figure of a woman in the night sky ensconced in a mantle of stars. Philemon prays that the (celestial) mother accept Jung as her child and that she take him into the sun's abode. However, a voice from afar, "like a falling star" (RB, p. 355b), declares that Jung must first purify himself from the "commingling" with others that has caused him to retain human joy and suffering. Jung must enter into a period of solitude and abstinence before the celestial mother will accept him as her child.

JUNG'S TEMPTATION

Jung accepts his charge, but in the fourth night of his solitude he sees a strange man in a turban and a long coat whose eyes are both kind and clever. This man, who in the *Black Book* is referred to as an Islamic Turk (RB, p. 355, n. 131), tempts Jung with the joy, love, and "healing fire" of women. In the *Black Book* this "Turk" cleverly informs Jung that the "*houris*" (the voluptuous and alluring women that lead the faithful to paradise) will bring Jung into a paradisiacal world of ideas (RB, p. 355, n. 132). Like Christ, who was tempted during his 40 days and nights of fasting in the desert (Matthew 4:1-11, Luke 4:1-13), Jung is tempted in his period of purification and solitude. However, unlike Jesus, who is offered all the world's kingdoms (Luke 4:5-7) in return for his worship of the devil, Jung is tempted with women, books, and ideas.

Jung's temptation is brief, as he quickly sees that it is Philemon, disguised as the dark man, who was tempting him. Philemon informs Jung that he has yet to experience the "dismembering," and that he must be "blown apart and shredded and scattered to the winds" (RB, p. 355b), to the point that he has his own "Last Supper" and nothing remains but his shadow. Then Jung "will hold the invisible realm in his trembling hands" (RB, p. 355b). Jung understands that he must replace the bondage of commingling (with men) with a "voluntary devotion" and "whole love" (RB, p. 356a) so that he can bond with "the great mother" and attain his "stellar nature." On the way, death will begin in [him] and bring him into a new life. In the process, Jung will willingly accept his pain and suffering and overcome his sin (RB, p. 356a). The teachings of the "Seven Sermons" have brought Jung further along the path of solitude that will lead him to his inner nature and the Gods within. It is this turning inward that will enable him to be a light to others.

THE EXISTENTIAL MEANING OF CHRIST

Philemon now approaches Jung with a silver fish, which the old magician says he has brought so that Jung can be comforted. A shade, wearing a "robe of grandeur" (RB, p. 356a), stands in darkness by the door—it is none other than Christ himself. Philemon launches into a monologue directed at Christ, praising him for his "divine patience" and for having made men out of animals. However, men have failed to grasp Christ's essential message. They have not loved their neighbor but have instead coveted his possessions. More significantly, they have failed to learn from Christ's "awe inspiring life" (RB, p. 456b), as they have imitated Christ and sought redemption in him, rather than living their own lives as Christ had lived his. Christ's life shows how individuals must take their lives "into their own hands, faithful to their own essence and their own love" (RB, p. 356a). Instead of childishly imitating and making demands upon Christ, men need to mature, find a place for Christ in their hearts, and then find a way to carry on his work on their own (RB, p. 356b). Philemon tells Christ "your work would be completed if men managed to live their own lives without imitation" (RB, p. 356b).

Jung reprised this "existential" view of Christ in 1936, where in a lecture entitled "Is Analytic Psychology a Religion?" he stated:

> We all must do what Christ did. We must make our experiment.
> We must make mistakes. We must live out our own vision of
> life…When we live like this we know Christ as a brother, and
> God indeed becomes man.[1]

If, as Philemon suggests, Jung is to be a prophet (RB, p. 355b), he is to be an *existential* prophet, one who, as we have seen, cannot be imitated, but who must guide each person on the path to his own self-realization. Jung was clearly influenced by Nietzsche in his view that man can no longer imitate the Gods and heroes, but that each individual must instead forge his own unique identity and self. However, in contrast to Nietzsche, Jung believed that in the process of forging a unique self, one, in effect, participated in the (re)creation of the Gods as well. Nietzsche, of course, was skeptical of any passage from the self to the Gods, writing in *Thus Spake Zarathustra*:

> Could you create a God? Then do not speak to me of any gods. But you could well create the overman...you could re-create yourselves: and let that be your best creation.[2]

Man's Inhumanity to Man

Philemon's next visitation produces a somewhat different and rather confusing turn. Jung overhears Philemon speaking, evidently to the dead, about man's inhumanity to man, how "he saw that they were slaying each other and...sought grounds for their actions" (RB, p. 356a). A sage bids them to stop this insanity, but men cannot stop killing one another because of their stupidity and their willingness to surrender their lives to serve the "serpent of God." However, since the serpent is from God, one who refrains from murder deceives and denies God, because "The God grows strong through human murder" (RB, p. 357a). The audacious suggestion here is that one who refrains from evil denies God, as evil is part of the divine essence. Jung writes that he could not understand Philemon's words, but that he was "horrified by the atrocities that attend the rebirth of a God" (RB, p. 357a). Here again, we see Jung exploring the basis for his later conception of the shadow or evil aspect of God, a conception that has a foundation in world mythology (e.g. Saturn's eating of his children, the wrath of Yahweh, the demonic deities of Buddhism), and which Jung will later explore in his *Answer to Job*.

The Death of the One God

Jung dreams of Elijah and Salome, and the following night he summons them to answer his queries. Elijah relates that he has grown weak because much of his power has gone over to Jung, and further, he has been distressed after hearing a "malicious word" (RB, p. 357a), apparently originating from or associated with Jung, which declared the death of the one God. Jung is astonished that Elijah has not heard that "the world has put on a new garb" (cf. MDR, p. 306), and that the one God has gone and has been replaced with many Gods and daimons. (Here Jung again echoes Nietzsche's Zarathustra, who asked, "Could it be possible? This old saint in the forest has not yet heard anything of this, that *God is dead.*"[3]) Elijah acknowledges that he had indeed heard a "thunderous pagan roar…full of horror yet harmonic" (RB, p. 357b), and Jung, gladdened that Elijah has heard this sound, explains that the one God has "truly died," that "he disintegrated into the many, and thus the world became rich overnight." Unlike Nietzsche, who celebrated the death of the one God as the demise of them all,[4] Jung rejoices in the renewed proliferation of deities and announces that as a result, there has also been a corresponding transformation and enrichment of the individual soul (Jung's soul), an idea that will later become the basis of Hillman's thinking regarding the diversity within the Self.[5] While the soul has retained her unity, she has also become multiple, having divided into a serpent and bird, father and mother, and Elijah and Salome (RB, p. 357b). However, Jung says that he must now separate Salome and Elijah from his soul and situate them as daimons, as they "know nothing of the being of men" (RB, p. 357b).

Elijah objects that he dislikes this "multiplicity," and Salome adds that only the simple is pleasurable. Jung disagrees—"In truth the multiple captivates you" (RB, p. 357b), and Salome, now convinced that Jung is correct, turns to Elijah to tell him that the one, being too simple, is less pleasurable than the many. Elijah is saddened and asks whether the one might still exist in the face of the many, to which Jung responds in part that the many derive from "one multiple God from whose body many Gods arise" (RB, p. 358a). Elijah asks if this God is new and then proceeds to doubt the possibility of the new, as he believes (and here Jung again echoes Nietzsche) that all things are a recurrence of what has happened before. Elijah bids Salome to depart with him, but as she leaves she whispers to Jung that multiplicity appeals to her, regardless of whether it is new or eternally valid.

DISOBEYING THE GODS

After Elijah and Salome depart, Jung's dreams become anguished and he is visited by his soul, who informs him that the reason for his anguish is that she and the Gods are tormented and suffering. Jung, she says, must intercede on the Gods' behalf, and help them through his "wits" (RB, p. 358a) and "obedience" (RB, p. 358b). Jung, however, says that man is no longer willing to obey the Gods unconditionally; man is no longer a slave but "has dignity before the God," as man "is a limb that even the Gods cannot do without" (RB, p. 358b). Jung's view here, that the Gods cannot do without the help of man, is a theme that we have seen earlier in *The Red Book* (cf. RB, p. 281ff), and which will feature prominently in Jung's later thought, most prominently in his *Answer to Job* (CW 11, pp. 355-470). Here, however, at the close of *The Red Book*, Jung declares that the Gods need man, but he is not yet ready to establish a cooperative relationship with them. He declares that the Gods have been so insatiable in their demands for human service that they blinded humanity into believing that there was either a single loving heavenly father or no Gods at all. The result was that today one "who struggles with the Gods is even thought to be crazy" (RB, p. 358b).

Jung's soul is astonished that he refuses to obey the Gods, but Jung tells her to ask the Gods themselves what they think of his refusal. His soul divides herself into a bird and a serpent; the bird flies up to query the heavenly Gods and the serpent descends to inquire of the Gods below (RB, p. 358b). The Gods are all outraged by Jung's refusal to obey them, but Jung remains defiant, stating that he has done everything he can to placate the Gods and that their outrage now barely disturbs him. Jung's soul now devises a trick, crafting a dream in which Jung is depicted as a horned devil. Jung's soul wants this dream to frighten him, but, Jung sees through the ruse and his soul finally conveys to him that the Gods have relented—he has "broken the compulsion of the law" (RB, p. 359a). Jung is now painted as a devil, as the devil "bows to no compulsion" (RB, p. 359a). Indeed, the devil is accepted by the Gods out of the realization that "it would be bad for life if there were no exception to eternal law" (RB, p. 359a).[6] Jung's soul announces that the Gods have "accepted [his] sacrifice" (RB, p. 359a), and Jung celebrates the fact that the devil has aided him in the release from his bondage.

It is worth noting that here, at the close of *The Red Book*, Jung frees himself from obedience to the Gods, but insists that they retain a place in the world and human order. By way of contrast, Nietzsche, who also longed to be liberated from divine control, held that only God's utter demise could provide the requisite freedom. Nietzsche writes:

> Indeed, we philosophers and 'free spirits' feel as if a new dawn
> were shining on us when we receive the tidings that 'the old
> God is dead': our heart overflows with gratitude, amazement,
> anticipation, expectation. At last the horizon appears free again
> to us, even granted that it is not bright: at last our ships may
> venture out to face any danger; all the daring of the lover of
> knowledge is permitted again: the sea, *our* sea, lies open again;
> perhaps there has never yet been such an 'open sea.'[7]

Like Nietzsche, Jung desired freedom from the Gods, but, as we have
seen, he was not ready to surrender the notion that man is responsive
to something higher than himself: In his 1934 seminar on Nietzsche's
Zarathustra, Jung stated:

> ...to Nietzsche God is dead...he assumes that the judge is
> himself. But the self as a whole that is greater than the
> individual... is the judge and the avenger, not the part; the part
> is the thing that is judged...We should always be conscious
> of the fact that we are merely instrumental. I don't know why
> Nietzsche was not able to realize this quite simple thought
> of the self's being the total and himself only a part, an atom
> in a molecule. This is not my original idea of course. I got the
> formula from the east. Nietzsche unfortunately had not
> studied eastern philosophy.[8]

Murray Stein holds that in *The Red Book* Jung sought to create a
"level ground" between the Gods and humanity as the basis for a
"dialogic relationship" between the Self and that which is beyond it.[9]
For Stein this is more than just a channel between the ego and the
collective unconscious, but is rather (as it is for Buber) a bridge to a
transcendent divine other. According to Stein, Jung's view on this
dialogic relationship culminated in *Answer to Job*, where Jung spoke
of a relationship between God and humanity that is "mutually
transforming." Stein sees this view as having connections with Alfred
North Whitehead's "process theology." As I have argued previously,[10]
it is also deeply resonant with the Kabbalistic conception of *Tikkun
ha-Olam*, the notion that humanity completes both the world and
God through ethical, spiritual, and other meaningful action. Indeed,
late in his life Jung recognized this connection, writing in 1954 to
the Reverend Erastus Evans:

In a tract of the Lurianic Kabbalah, the remarkable idea is
developed that man is destined to become God's helper in the
attempt to restore the vessels which were broken when God
thought to create a world. Only a few weeks ago, I came across
this impressive doctrine which gives meaning to man's status
exalted by the incarnation. I am glad that I can quote at least
one voice in favor of my rather involuntary manifesto.[11]

IN PHILEMON'S GARDEN

Jung next sees Philemon strolling in his garden, speaking to a shade,
who in the *Black Book* is again identified as Christ (RB, p. 353, n.
153). Philemon tells the shade that man's sins have "straightened" him
and brought him beauty (RB, p. 359a). The shade identifies Philemon
as Simon Magus, who in the Acts of the Apostles (8:9-24) is the
sorcerer who offered Christ money in exchange for the power of "laying
on hands," and whose name is associated both with "simony," the sin
of purchasing power or influence in the Catholic Church, and the early
Gnostic Simonian sect. Philemon informs the shade that Simon, and
his female companion, Helena, have been transformed into Philemon
and Baucis, who in Ovid's *Metamorphoses* are the old couple who showed
hospitality to Zeus and Hermes.[12] Philemon further informs the shade/
Christ that he is now in Philemon's and Baucis' garden in the "world
of men" and that men are no longer slaves and swindlers of the Gods,
but rather grant the Gods hospitality. Further, the "worm," the Satan,
who Christ dismissed after his temptation in the desert, is also in the
garden. Christ asks if he has fallen prey to the power of a trick, but
Philemon, drawing a number of comparisons between Christ and the
devil (noting for example that they both practice the arts of healing),
responds that Christ must recognize that his own "nature is also of
the serpent" (RB, p. 359b). The shade responds that Philemon has
spoken the truth, and asks Philemon "do you know what I bring you?"
Philemon knows only that one who "hosts the worm also needs his
brother," and says that the worm has brought "lamentation and
abomination" (RB, p. 359b). The shade replies, "I bring you the
beauty of suffering. That is what is needed by whoever hosts the worm"
(RB, p. 359b), and with that *Scrutinies* and our edition of *The Red
Book* comes to an abrupt end—in the middle of a sentence.

"Epilogue," p. 360

In 1959 Jung wrote in the calligraphic volume of *The Red Book* that he had worked on this volume for 16 years and that its contents may seem like madness and "would also have developed" (RB, p. 360) into madness had he not "with the help of alchemy" been able to contain and organize these experiences. Jung soon came to understand alchemy as a system of thought that deals with "psychic processes expressed in pseudochemical language" (CW 12, § 342). As alchemy treated the symbols of chaos, the soul, evil, and the merging of opposites, Jung found a ready container for his *Red Book* experiences and ideas. The alchemist's efforts to bring about a union of opposites in the laboratory and to perform what they spoke of as a "chymical wedding" were understood by Jung as antecedents to his own "innovation" of merging the opposites and his attempts to distinguish, but at the same time forge a unity, e.g. between the masculine and feminine, and the good and evil aspects of the psyche. We might say that for Jung, this "unity in difference" was *The Red Book's* major theoretical and personal achievement.

Chapter 13

The Red Book and Contemporary Psychology

According to Jewish tradition, there are four levels of biblical interpretation, corresponding to the four consonants of the Hebrew word PaRDeS, which means "orchard" and is etymologically related to our word, "paradise." The four levels are: (1) "p'shat," the "plain" meaning of the text, (2) "remez," allegorical interpretation, (3) "derash," the text's metaphorical significance, and (4) "sod," the mystical meaning, known only through revelation. Jung himself makes oblique reference in *The Red Book* to this tradition when he asks the anchorite, if like "a few Jewish scholars" (RB, p. 268b) he holds that scripture has both an exoteric and esoteric meaning. This approach, however, was not limited to Jewish exegetes. Medieval Christianity also developed a fourfold scheme that interpreted the New Testament in terms of its literal, typological (i.e. Old Testament), moral, and anagogical or prophetic significance. Without according *Liber Novus* the status of "scripture," it too has levels of meaning that may be open to hermeneutic inquiry. We have, in the course of the present volume, understood *The Red Book* in terms of each level of the PaRDeS scheme—examining the text's literal meaning, and in many cases inquiring into its allegorical, metaphorical, and mystical/theological significance. Here I would like to pursue a metaphorical interpretation that I introduced at the outset of this work, and which I promised to return to at its close.

As I stated in the Introduction, *The Red Book* can be metaphorically understood as a dream, not the dream of an individual person, but the dream of the discipline and practice of psychology. Indeed, *The Red Book* has many characteristics that are typically associated with dreams: it is filled with strange, haunting, and at times frightening images, its narrative is surreal, and, most importantly, it arrives into our awareness in a manner that is completely discontinuous and indeed disruptive of our business (as psychologists) as usual. Even Jungians find *The Red Book* jarring. For example, in an interview appearing in the Fall, 2010 issue of the *Jung Journal*, Murray Stein, a prominent training analyst with the International School of Analytical Psychology in Zürich, stated:

> This book is going to take a long time to digest. There is, as has been said by many others already, much in *The Red Book* that is familiar to us from things Jung said in MDR and in some of the Seminars. Nevertheless, I have to say that most of the material in *The Red Book* is brand new to me—completely unfamiliar.[1]

There is good reason to believe that *The Red Book* would have seemed more familiar to readers had it been published during the era in which it was written. As Shamdasani has pointed out, the style and tone of *The Red Book* echoes not only Nietzsche's *Zarathustra* but also various other experiments on the border between psychology, art, and literature that were current during the late 1800s and the early years of the 20th century (RB Intro, p. 204). That *The Red Book* comes to us out of psychology's treasured past, like a time capsule that has been sealed from both our view and the exegetical and critical ravages of time, adds to the impression that it is like a dream, for, as we know, dreams often contain feelings, attitudes, and thoughts revived from a bygone era as if they were (to use Freud's analogy) recently excavated from Herculaneum or Pompei. As Shamdasani describes in his Introduction to *The Red Book*, Jung certainly had his reasons for withholding *The Red Book* from publication, and I have no reason to suggest that he did so with the purpose of preserving its message and impact for a future era. Jung's keeping *The Red Book*, his strangest and perhaps the most important work in his entire oeuvre, in his kitchen cupboard for so many years, and its remaining unpublished for many years thereafter, has the effect of giving us the experience of awakening from a dream in which Jung has spoken to us from beyond the grave.

Jung himself once stated that one would need "almost divine knowledge of the human mind" to formulate a general theory of dreams. However,

> dreams are always about a particular problem of the individual about which he has a wrong conscious judgment. The dreams are the reaction to our conscious attitude in the same way that the body reacts when we overeat or do not eat enough or when we ill-treat it in some other way. *Dreams are the natural reaction of the self-regulating psychic system.* This formulation is the nearest I can get to a theory about the structure and function of dreams. (CW 18, § 248)

It is for this reason that Jung often spoke of dreams as compensating for a one-sided conscious standpoint, and in *Memories, Dreams, Reflections* Jung states, almost as a matter of fact, "Dreams are, after all, compensations for the conscious attitude" (MDR, p. 133). While dreams may not *always* serve as a *compensation* or balance to conscious thoughts and perspectives,[2] sometimes they do fulfill this function. Continuing with our metaphor of *The Red Book* as *psychology's* dream, we are entitled on Jungian grounds, to ask what conscious attitude on the part of psychology does *The Red Book* challenge or serve as a compensation for?

To answer this question we need to think in a rather broad historical manner about the developments in psychology since Jung's death in 1961. In the past 50 years psychology has become increasingly scientized, far more so than in Jung's own time, and the practice of both psychiatric and psychotherapeutic treatment has become increasingly medicalized. In the twenty years that I was on the psychology staff of Bellevue Hospital in New York (1984-2003), the Dept. of Psychiatry went from being dominated by psychoanalysts to becoming almost exclusively "psychopharmacological." University departments of psychology have completely purged Jung, and even Freud, from the academy, and to a significant extent this has occurred in hospitals and clinics as well, where they have been replaced by so-called "empirically supported" (largely pharmacological and cognitive-behavioral) treatments. We have arrived at the point where, with few exceptions, the only places where one can seriously study psychoanalytic or Jungian theory are in a few academic departments in the humanities and in specialized analytic training institutes. Psychology, as I stated earlier, has essentially become separated from its philosophical, literary, and theological roots, and has carved itself out as a specialized science with clear boundaries from other social sciences and much sharper ones from the humanities and such disciplines as anthropology and history. "Cognitive science" has emerged as a discipline that endeavors to model human thought and emotion within a computational framework, and the project of "reducing" human consciousness to its neurophysiological and/or "information processing" substrate is considered by many to be within reach. What Jung, in *The Red Book*, referred to as the "spirit of this time" (the scientific, hyper-rational mode of thinking) is, within the discipline of psychology, gaining a stranglehold on the academy and profession. Philosophically, existentially, psychoanalytically, and archetypally minded thinkers and practitioners, most of them advanced in years, hang on, almost like relics of a bygone age, and the shift in paradigm may well be complete when the majority of these retire or die.

While perhaps a bit of a caricature (though I daresay hardly an exaggeration), the above describes the "conscious attitude" that would encounter the "*Red Book* dream", if contemporary psychology awakened to its compensating messages. What would those messages be?

The compensations afforded to psychology by *The Red Book* are many. I will focus here on those that are broad and general, and not necessarily dependent on Jungian theory. The odd character of the book, surprising even to those very familiar with Jung's public life and oeuvre, underscores the uniqueness and depth not only of Jung's mind, but of the individual psyche in general. We may think that we know others or that we know ourselves, and yet there are depths and dimensions to their (or our own) personality that we have never seen or even considered possible. That Jung should turn out to be an artist of considerable skill and vision, as evidenced by his beautiful paintings in *The Red Book*, and that he should have wandered in and out of territory that by even his own account bordered on insanity, warns us against placing arbitrary limits on who we are and what we and others are capable of. The depth of the soul revealed in *The Red Book* materials serves as a compensation for the tendency in contemporary psychology to conceive of the psychotherapeutic process in simple cognitive, pragmatic, and manualized terms, and reminds us that psychological exploration has the potential to open worlds as well as treat symptoms. Further, the experimental and dialectical nature of Jung's quest for soul and meaning warns us against the tendency to believe that psychological knowledge and wisdom is somehow straightforward and cumulative. Rather, the search for such knowledge and wisdom will in all likelihood involve numerous changes of direction, many dead ends, and the re-examination of discarded paths and ideas.

As we have seen in connection with our discussion of Jung's notion that the "supreme meaning" is a melting together of sense and nonsense, in much of *The Red Book* Jung is working and writing in the "chaotic forest" that lies beyond the clearing of conventional meaning, and it was only by first entering this forest of nonsense that he was able to generate the "sense" that came to inform his later psychology. We can take this as an important compensation for psychology's contemporary concern with research methodology, operational definitions, and clarity. Both Jung and Freud produced their epoch-making psychologies by transgressing the boundaries of what the scientific establishment of their day regarded as good sense, and it appears that one reason why Jung refused to publish *Liber Novus* during his lifetime was precisely because of its transgressive nature. As the beneficiaries of the decision by Jung's heirs to release *The Red Book* for publication in our own time, we should take heed of its transgressive, "non-sensical" qualities and not be afraid to enter into them ourselves, in our lives, with our clients, and in our psychological theorizing.

The very notion of "psychological knowledge" is brought into question by *The Red Book*. The journey it describes involves a search for meaning and wisdom rather than knowledge *per se*, and it might best be understood in terms of the old philosophical quest for "the good life." Whether or not we believe that Jung's *Red Book* quest was successful (and there are good reasons to think that at least in some ways it was not), his pursuit of what it means to lead the good life and actualize oneself as a human being is, from the perspective of contemporary psychology, refreshing and illuminating. Jung speaks of attaining "knowledge of the heart," and the quest for such knowledge serves as a compensation for our cotemporary fascination with knowledge of and by the brain. The chapter in *Liber Secundus*, where the Cabiri insist that Jung must cut through his entanglement with the brain (RB, p. 321a), is a graphic metaphor for this compensation.

Jung's *Red Book* critiques of science and reason are hardly palatable to the contemporary psychological mind-set, within which they are likely to be viewed as reactionary, and as a call to return to medieval ignorance. Jung's Nietzschean critique of virtue is also likely to be rejected, but for very different reasons. I have felt that in his (however important) critiques of reason and virtue, Jung at times went too far, and stumbled into dangerous territory from which his rational ego might have saved him. Nevertheless, his critiques of science and reason provide some of the most valuable compensations that "*The Red Book* dream" can offer. If psychology involves the pursuit of the good life, of the actualization of the whole person and his/her full relatedness to others, then it must also involve those human functions—feeling, sensation, intuition, as well as creative imagination—that are neither scientific nor completely rational. Psychology, of course, protests that it indeed *studies* these "non-rational" functions, but does so rationally and scientifically, and that this is the only justifiable way to investigate them. *The Red Book's* compensatory message, however, is that while the pursuit of a rational, scientific psychology is important and justified, it risks leaving out other of the psyche's voices that must be heard. This point, *made discursively* in *Psychological Types*, is made narratively, artistically, and experientially in *The Red Book*. Jung's idea is that our quest to attain a full perspective on the psyche or soul must be initiated from positions that are not only rational and scientific, but also experiential, intuitive, imaginative, and, in short, inclusive of the whole man. A psychologist, one might be inclined to say, must not only pursue psychological knowledge, but must also be open to the lived experience, imaginative possibilities, and artistic and spiritual pursuits that complement and give life to that knowledge. This not only means that psychology should reopen its boundaries to other disciplines, including those that are artistic and literary, but that it should also consider the possibility that things of great psychological significance can be better or only expressed in modalities such as music, art, and literature that are neither scientific nor rational in the narrow sense of the term. Jung's use of mandalas and other paintings as a vehicle for achieving and expressing "wholeness" is a case in point.

The Red Book's confrontation with the chaos, madness, vanity, and evil inherent in the human psyche serves as a compensation for contemporary psychology's emphasis on "positive thinking." Indeed, *Liber Novus* might be a virtual *nightmare* for the new and growing field of "positive psychology," which is itself a reaction to clinical psychology's and psychiatry's focus upon the abnormal and pathological. Passages in which Jung relates his fantasy of eating the liver of a young murdered girl (RB, p. 290b), engages with his soul about accepting the evils of history—famines, torture, child sacrifice, genocide, and epidemics (RB, p. 305b)—identifies the supreme God with that which is cruel, contradictory, and incomprehensible in nature, and in which he rages against and promises to torment his "I," remind us not so much of the pathology of the human psyche, but of the *normal aggressive and thanatic elements within it. The Red Book's* insistence on the value of chaos, the reality of meaninglessness, and the soul-making potential of madness serve as a counterweight to the emphasis upon coherence, meaning-making, and adjustment that pervades much of today's clinical thinking. Of course, many of these themes are familiar from Jung's later writings, as well as from the work of many psychoanalysts and existentialists, and *The Red Book's* arrival may simply serve as a reminder from psychology's past that such ideas should remain part of the discourse of a field that has become increasingly "current" and dismissive of its history. Further, *The Red Book's* "soul-finding" journey suggests that the goal of psychology should not simply be the pragmatic one of achieving normality and health, but the creative one of actualizing ourselves in ways that may deviate from the ruling discourse. *The Red Book* at least raises the question of whether the aim of our discipline should be the production of "well-adjusted" men and women or the development of perhaps less "adjusted" but more creative and fulfilled individuals.

Several of *The Red Book's* "compensations" are as relevant to a "theological dreamer" as they are to a psychological one. The reader of *The Red Book* cannot help but be struck by Jung's preoccupation with the question of God; hardly a page goes by without some indication of the deity, his/her absence, multiplicity, demands, horrific nature, sickness, death, rebirth, or revival. Surely, many will see in *The Red Book* one of God's last dying breaths within the Western intellectual tradition, or perhaps the mere stirrings of a corpse that only seems animate because it is being pulled by Jung like a marionette on strings.

Yet, there will be others (and I include myself among them) who, while acknowledging the problematic nature of traditional conceptions of God, continue to maintain, as did Jung, that just as there are material, ethical, and aesthetic dimensions to our lives, there is a spiritual dimension to our existence, one that moves at least some of us to experience, or at least pursue, a spiritual object, wholeness, or absolute, and/or feel deeply troubled by its absence. *The Red Book* prompts us to ask how the spiritual dimension of life is manifest in our own time. Has this dimension, as some have suggested, been completely absorbed by the material, ethical, aesthetic, and psychological aspects of life, so that the question of "God" has become irrelevant to educated, cultured, and mature men and women, and the God symbol emptied of its meaning,[3] or does something remain of the deity, the divine, or the absolute that is essential, even in our scientific, pragmatic, and materialistic age?

Jung's views of God and Gods in *The Red Book* change and multiply at such a rate that one almost gets the impression that he is desperately flailing about for a "God" to fill the vacuum left by the faith that he himself lost when he perceived the emptiness of his father's religion. In the process he nevertheless enters into several fascinating conceptions of the divine that radically depart from traditional theological discourse (e.g. God as an imaginary yet real being, God as the chaos, cruelty, and contradictoriness of nature, God as the melding together of the meaningful and the absurd, God as arising from a confrontation with the Self), each of which highlight an aspect of the psychology of religious experience. *The Red Book* dream prompts us to at least consider the God question, as its narrative and painted images flood us with the vicissitudes of the divine spirit. That Jung's conceptions were so radical for his time (and perhaps even for our own) suggests that psychologically the divine is everywhere the ruling discourse is not, and as each new conception of the divine itself becomes a ruling or routinized discourse, we may require a new language and new experience to go beyond it. Indeed, this may be true today for Jung's once radical equivalence of the God archetype with the Self. The point isn't that we either accept or reject Jung's *Red Book* conceptions or images of God or the Gods but rather that we take heed of his willingness to go beyond "the received" views of his own day (both theistic and atheistic) and, as he says of Christ, go his own way in his pursuit of God in a manner that is non-imitative but faithful to his own being.[4] In *The Red Book* we see the origins of Jung's later intimation that a full conception of the deity must even traverse the conceptions that God *is* and *is not* (CW 11, § 833), a view that in some ways follows from what he presents as *The Red Book's* main "innovation," the *coincidence of opposites.*

The *Red Book* reader/dreamer will certainly be struck by Jung's fascination with the *coincidentia oppositorum* idea, an idea that continued to absorb Jung throughout the remainder of his life and career. What, we might ask, does this idea compensate for? To answer this, we should first note that the very notion of compensation is rooted in the idea of the coincidence and interdependence of the opposites. As we learn from the first "Sermon to the Dead," one cannot pursue one pole of an opposition to the neglect of its opposite, because these poles are united in the Pleroma and unconscious, and the pursuit of one quality will necessarily bring on its opposite (RB, p. 348a). Jung's main interest in *The Red Book* is reconciling such value opposites as good and evil, sense and nonsense, madness and sanity, thought and emotion, beauty and ugliness, etc. As he was to make fully explicit in *Psychological Types*, Jung sees imaginatively generated symbols as the vehicle through which these opposites that are "rent" within the human psyche can be reconciled. However, it is important to remember that in spite of his reference to it as his "innovation," Jung did not originate the notion of *coincidentia oppositorum*, and that, as he himself recognized, his views on the opposites are heir to a long tradition that includes Heraclitus, the Gnostics, the Kabbalah, Nicholas of Cusa, and Hegel in the West, and virtually all spiritual traditions and schools of philosophy in the East. However, Jung can and should be credited for bringing this tradition into 20th century thought.

While Jung insisted that the opposites could only be brought together through imaginative symbols, and that rational efforts to bridge the opposites were misplaced psychology, his "innovation" can and should help reawaken psychology to the entire *coincidentia oppositorum* tradition. Indeed, we might ask if psychology might not make use of the coincidence of opposites idea not only in its understanding of the personality, psychopathology, and psychotherapy of the individuals it studies, but also reflectively in comprehending the fragmentation within psychology itself. By psychology's "fragmentation," I mean the multiplicity of theories and paradigms (e.g. neurobiological, behavioral, cognitive, systems, depth psychological, existential, etc.) that, particularly within the clinical field, compete for hegemony (or at least a place) within the discipline. Currently, paradigms within psychology and psychiatry rise and fall on the basis of factors that are as much economic and socio-cultural as they are scientific and philosophical, and the efforts to achieve supremacy for a single paradigm (whether it be psychoanalytic, or more recently, biological or cognitive-behavioral psychology), while at times institutionally successful, have been conceptually unsatisfying.

Jung's view, as expressed in *Psychological Types,* was that each of the perspectives in psychology current in his day contained partial truths that reflected the personality types of their creators (CW 6, § 89ff). Stimulated by *The Red Book's* understanding of the coincidence of opposites, we might ask if differing psychological paradigms, both in Jung's and our own time, reflect imbalanced efforts to pursue one pole of one or more critical psychological dichotomies to the neglect of their opposites.[5] Amongst these dichotomies, each of which Jung considered explicitly or implicitly in *The Red Book*, are introspection and public observation, elementism and holism, individualism and collectivism, free-will and determinism, empiricism and hermeneutics (facts and interpretations), knowledge and essential mystery, etc. We might, for example, observe that biological psychology is generally grounded in a publicly observable, elemental, deterministic, and empiricist view of the human mind, while existential psychology is far more introspective, holistic, non-deterministic, and hermeneutic in its foundations and approach. However, seen through the lens of the *coincidentia oppositorum* idea, we might expect to find an interdependence between these two psychological perspectives, one that is rooted in the interdependence of the poles of the philosophical dichotomies upon which these very perspectives are based. If introspection and public observation, determinism and free will, facts and interpretations, etc. are interdependent ideas, then the psychological paradigms that are founded upon the acceptance of certain poles of such oppositions and the rejection of others must be complementary and interdependent as well. In this view, for example, the more psychologists strive for a brain-based, deterministic explanation of the psyche, the more radically they will be confronted with the realities of lived experience, indeterminism, and freedom of the will (and vice versa). Jung himself began to turn in this direction late in his life when in his essay on synchronicity he took up the problem of the relationship between depth psychology and quantum physics (CW 8, pp. 417-519). Part of Jung's genius resided in his ability to discover deep connections where others could only see differences, and, amongst the great psychologists of the twentieth-century, he was virtually alone in holding that he had no corner on the truth, and that psychology could be narrated from a variety of different points of view. In line with his *Red Book* view that in order to pursue one's "essence" one must differentiate oneself from each pole of the critical dichotomies, Jung even went so far as to suggest that one must abandon the pursuit of a single, comprehensive theory altogether

> In our dreams we are just as many-sided as in our daily life, and just as you cannot form a theory about those many aspects of the conscious personality you cannot make a general theory of dreams. Otherwise we would have an almost divine knowledge of the human mind, which we certainly do not possess. We know precious little about it, therefore we call the things we do not know unconscious. (CW 18, § 248)

Following Jung's lead, and remaining with our metaphor of *The Red Book* as a compensating dream for contemporary psychology, we might say that its compensations are indeed "many sided," and it would be impossible to detail even the majority of them here without recapitulating the entirety of this book. However, amongst those compensations we have yet to consider in this chapter we might well include the singular importance of the *imagination* in the phenomenology of lived experience, as a transformative factor in individual's lives, as a vehicle for psychological understanding, and as an equilibration for psychology's focus on cognition and emotions. In addition, *The Red Book*'s charge to "accept all" that is human serves as a compensation for the field's emphasis on pathology, on the one hand, and "character strengths and virtues", on the other. *The Red Book*'s understanding of the multiplicity and fragmentation of the normal self serves as a corrective for psychology's view that such fragmentation is a sign of mental disorder; and Jung's insistence upon the value of interiority and difference (of both the individual and the psychologist) serves as a compensation for psychology's tendency to rely upon publicly observable behavior, group data, and group norms. However, as I have suggested, the inward, especially solitary journey of *The Red Book* is also not without its limitations and dangers.

As I have already intimated, not all of the compensations of the "*Red Book* dream" will, or should come to us as a shock. Indeed, many, if not the majority of them, have been with us even during the years when Jung kept his illuminated manuscript hidden away in his kitchen cupboard in Kusnacht, as they were for the most part present in Jung's *Collected Works*, seminars, and letters that have been in plain sight for years. However, what is so different about *The Red Book* is its dramatic, visionary tone and the concentrated impact of its narrative and images. The work is completely unvarnished by Jung's later need to integrate his vision into a scientific psychology and the practice of medicine. Further, while Jung's *Collected Works* and other writings have been exposed to the eroding elements of interpretation and criticism, *The Red Book*, like some prehistoric insect preserved in amber, has the power to strike us as virtually "new," and perhaps for this reason, shake us from our routinized ways of thinking and living.

Of course, in spite (and even because) of its scriptural and prophetic presentation we need not, and should not, take anything in *The Red Book* as if it were holy writ, just as one need not and should not blindly incorporate the literal message of a dream into one's wakeful consciousness and behavior. If one dreams that one has committed a murder, this does not mean that one should kill someone in waking life, or that one should even accept that one is a killer; what it may mean, however, is that one has failed to be consciously aware of one's angry, aggressive, and even murderous impulses. Similarly, if in *The Red Book*, Jung's soul exhorts him to abandon science or reason for magic, this hardly means that we ourselves should literally follow this advice. What it might mean, however, is that we have failed to even consider, let alone integrate, non-scientific and non-rational aspects of and perspectives on the psyche into our understanding of ourselves and the total person. As I stated at the outset, *The Red Book* raises more questions than it answers, and I am of the view that at least several of its *apparent* views, including its denigration of science and reason, its attitudes towards love, the willing of evil, and its repeated suggestion that the search for the soul is an inner, solitary journey, warrant careful scrutiny and criticism. One should wrestle with one's dreams not be blindly guided by them; a field should take its history seriously and neither ignore nor feel chained to it, and this, I believe, is the spirit with which we should read and receive this most remarkable work from psychology's past.

Notes

NOTES TO INTRODUCTION

¹ Some interesting observations on *The Red Book* paintings can be found in Jay Sherry's "A Pictorial Guide to *The Red Book*", downloaded from: http://aras.org/docs/00033sherry.pdf, and Paul Brutsche, "*The Red Book* in the Context of Jung's Paintings," *Jung Journal: Culture & Psyche* 5/3 (Summer, 2011): 8-24.

² The variety of perspectives that can be taken in reflecting upon *The Red Book* material can be seen in the Summer 2011 (5/3) issue of *Jung Journal: Culture & Psyche* where ten authors bring psychological, literary, aesthetic, theological, and even geometric perspectives to *The Red Book* narrative and paintings.

³ This, for example, is the position James Hillman held with respect to the interpretation of dreams. See James Hillman and Laura Pozzo, *Inter Views: Conversations Between James Hillman and Laura Pozzo on Therapy, Biography, Love, Soul, Dream, Work, Imagination and the State of the Culture* (New York: Harper & Row, 1983), p. 53.

⁴ C.G. Jung, *The Red Book, Liber Novus*, ed. Sonu Shamdasani, trans. Mark Kyburz, John Peck, and Sonu Shamdasani (New York: W.W. Norton & Company, 2009).

NOTES TO CHAPTER 1

¹ V. Walter Odajnyk, "Reflections on 'The Way of What is to Come,'" *Psychological Perspectives* 53:4 (October 2010): 437-454.

[2] Jewish law is also described with the term "the way" (*halakha*—literally, "the path that is walked").

[3] Murray Stein, "Carl Jung's Red Book," vidoetaped lecture, Asheville Jung Center (Asheville, NC), January 22, 2010.

[4] Richard Noll, *The Jung Cult: Origins of a Charismatic Movement* (Princeton, NJ: Princeton University Press, 1994), and Richard Noll, *The Aryan Christ: The Secret Life of Carl Jung* (New York: Random House, 1997). For a sober critique of Noll's thesis, see Sonu Shamdasani, *Cult Fictions* (New York: Routledge, 1998).

[5] Sonu Shamdasani, *Jung and the Making of Modern Psychology: The Dream of a Science* (Cambridge: Cambridge University Press, 2003).

[6] Laurens van der Post, *Jung and the Story of Our Time* (London: Penguin, 1975), p. x, cited in Shamdasani, *Jung and the Making of Modern Psychology,* p. 348.

[7] James L. Jarrett, ed., *Jung's Seminar on Zarathustra,* abridged edition (Princeton, NJ: Princeton University Press, 1997), pp. 199-200.

[8] I am indebted to Stanton Marlan for highlighting the notion that in *The Red Book* Jung enters into an initially outrageous "excess of meaning."

[9] See Richard Rorty, "Unfamiliar Noises: Hess and Davidson on Metaphor," in his *Philosophical Papers* (Cambridge: Cambridge University Press, 1991), Vol. 1, pp. 162-172.

[10] Sigmund Freud, *The Standard Edition of the Complete Psychological Works of Sigmund Freud,* ed. and trans. James Strachey (London: Hogarth, 1957), Vol. 12, pp. 1-82.

[11] Jung does make reference to Schreber in *Transformations and Symbols of the Libido*, where he states that Schreber correctly and rationally understood that reality is a product of the libido. C.G. Jung, *Collected Works of C.G. Jung, Supplementary Volume B,* trans. Beatrice M. Hinkle [1912] (Princeton: Princeton University Press, 1991), § 599. Further references to this work will be abbreviated "CW B" followed by paragraph or page number.

Jung also refers to Schreber in the revision of *Transformations and Symbols of the Libido* (1912), referenced above. This revision was retitled *Symbols of Transformation* and published in English in 1956 as Volume 5 of Jung's *Collected Works.* Jung writes that Schreber "gave God, sadly uninformed about the affairs of humanity, notice of his existence." C.G. Jung, *Collected Works of C.G. Jung,* trans. R.F.C. Hull (Princeton, NJ:

Princeton University Press, 1956), Vol. 5, § 144. Further references to Jung's *Collected Works*, are abbreviated "CW," and will be followed by the volume number and paragraph or page number.

¹² James Hillman, *On Paranoia* (Dallas, Texas: Spring Publications, 1988), p. 55 ff.

¹³ Michael Vannoy Adams, *The Fantasy Principle: Psychoanalysis of the Imagination* (New York: Brunner-Routledge, 2004), pp. 76-130.

¹⁴ Shamdasani points out that Jung, in his conversations with Aniela Jaffe, indicated that he was surprised that the experiences that culminated in *The Red Book* had not broken him in the way that such experiences had broken others, like Schreber. Sonu Shamdasani, Introduction to C.G. Jung's *The Red Book, Liber Novus*, ed. Sonu Shamdasani, trans. Mark Kyburz, John Peck, and Sonu Shamdasani (New York: W.W. Norton & Company, 2009), p. 219, n. 239, citing the Protocols of Aniela Jaffe's Interviews with Jung for his *Memories, Dreams, Reflections*, recorded and edited by Aniela Jaffe (New York: Vintage Books, 1989). [**Author's note:** Further references to Jung's *Memories, Dreams, Reflections* are abbreviated to MDR, followed by page number.]

¹⁵ Edmund Husserl, *Ideas Pertaining to a Pure Phenomenology and to a Phenomenological Philosophy—First Book: General Introduction to a Pure Phenomenology*, trans. Fred Kersten, rev. ed. (The Hague: Nijhoff, 1982. Originally published in 1913.)

¹⁶ On Dilthey, see Rudolf A. Makreel and Frithjof Rodi, eds., *Understanding the Human World: Selected Works of Wilhelm Dilthey* (Princeton: Princeton University Press, 2010) and Rudolf A. Makreel, *Dilthey: Philosopher of the Human Studies* (Princeton: Princeton University Press, 1993).

¹⁷ Jung to Hans Schmid, 6 November 1915, C.G. Jung, *Letters*, Volumes I and II, eds., Gerhard Adler, Aniela Jaffe, and R.F.C. Hull (Princeton, NJ: Princeton University Press, 1973), Vol. I, p. 31.

¹⁸ In *Memories, Dreams, Reflections* Jung writes:

> When I was writing down these fantasies, I once asked myself, 'What am I really doing? Certainly this has nothing to do with science. But then what is it?' Whereupon a voice within me said, 'It is art.' I was astonished. It had never entered my head that what I was writing had any connection with art. Then I thought,

'Perhaps my unconscious is forming a personality that is not me, but which is insisting on coming through to expression.' I knew for a certainty that the voice had come from a woman. I recognized it as the voice of a patient, a talented psychopath who had a strong transference to me. She had become a living figure within my mind...I said very emphatically to this voice that my fantasies had nothing to do with art, and I felt a great inner resistance... 'No it is not art! On the contrary, it is nature...' (MDR, pp. 185-186).

[19] Wolfgang Giegerich, "*Liber Novus*, that is, The New Bible: A First Analysis of C.G. Jung's *Red Book*," *Spring: A Journal of Archetype and Culture* 83 (Spring 2010): 361-411, p. 367.

[20] *Ibid.*, p. 368.

[21] *Ibid.*, p. 369.

[22] We might say that this paradox is of vital significance for what Giegerich himself might call the "logical life of the soul."

[23] Aristotle, *Posterior Analytics*, Book I, Part I, trans. and ed. R. McKeon, *The Basic Works of Aristotle*, rev. ed. (New York: Random House, 1941), p. 110.

[24] This phrase in its fuller context ("a bloody laughter and a bloody worship. A sacrificial blood binds the poles") suggests a connection with Jung's 1913-14 visions, to be discussed *infra*, of a sea of blood and a terrible cold that freezes all in its wake. C.G. Jung, *The Red Book, Liber Novus*, ed. Sonu Shamdasani, trans. Mark Kyburz, John Peck, and Sonu Shamdasani (New York: W.W. Norton & Company, 2009), p. 231a. [**Author's note:** As the great majority of the pages in Shamdasani's Introduction and the English translation of Jung's *The Red Book* work are printed with two columns on each page, most of my references to these pages are made with the modifiers "a" and "b" referring to the left and right hand sides of the page, respectively.]

[25] Mircea Eliade, "Eliade's Interview for 'Combat,'" *C.G. Jung Speaking*, eds., William McGuire and R.F.C. Hull (Princeton, NJ: Princeton University Press, 1977), p. 234.

Notes to Chapter 2

[1] There was even an unsubstantiated family tradition that Jung's paternal grandfather had been Goethe's illegitimate son, a tradition that Jung says "at once corroborated and seemed to explain [his] curious reactions to *Faust.*" (MDR, p. 234).

[2] Jung to Erastus Evans, C.G. Jung, *Letters*, Volumes I and II, eds. Gerhard Adler, Aniela Jaffe, and R.F.C. Hull (Princeton, NJ: Princeton University Press, 1973), Vol. I, p. 175.

[3] Clearly, Jung sensed a strong connection between desire and the imagination. While he states that desire is an image of the soul, one might also understand the imagination as a *product* of desire.

[4] Renos Papadopoulos, "Jung's epistemology and methodology," in Renos Papadopoulos, ed., *The Handbook of Jungian Psychology: Theory, Practice and Applications* (New York: Routledge, 2006), pp. 7-53, pp. 45-6. Papadopoulos describes this as a distinction between Jung's "Socratic openness," which yields "hypotheses" subject to doubt and revision, and Jung's "Gnosticism", which leads him to a steadfast conviction in the correctness and transformative power of his theories.

[5] C.G. Jung, "Diagnosing the Dictators," *C.G. Jung Speaking*, eds., William McGuire and R.F.C. Hull (Princeton, NJ: Princeton University Press, 1977), p. 119.

[6] Friedrich Nietzsche, *Thus Spake Zarathustra,* Part I, in *The Portable Nietzsche,* ed. and trans. Walter Kaufmann (New York: Viking Press, 1968), p. 129.

[7] C.G. Jung, "Commentary on 'The Secret of the Golden Flower'", CW 13.

[8] Gershom Scholem, *Major Trends in Jewish Mysticism* (New York: Schocken, 1941), p. 217.

[9] C.G. Jung, *Letters*, Vol. II, p. 157.

[10] Richard Noll, *The Aryan Christ: The Secret Life of Carl Jung* (New York: Random House, 1997), p. 274.

[11] Nietzsche, *Zarathustra*, Part I, *Portable Nietzsche*, ed. Kaufmann, p. 138.

[12] The question of our capacity to "move beyond language" is a difficult one in a post-Heideggerean and post-Wittgensteinian context. See, Sanford L. Drob, "James Hillman on Language: Escape from the

Linguistic Prison," in Stanton Marlan, ed., *Archetypal Psychologies: Reflections in Honor of James Hillman* (New Orleans, LA: Spring Journal Books, 2008), pp. 153-170.

[13] Nietzsche, *Zarathustra*, Part I, *Portable Nietzsche*, ed. Kaufmann, p. 174.

[14] In *Memories, Dreams, Reflections* Jung specifically denies that his childhood division into personality 1 and personality 2 involved pathological dissociation and says that such a "split" is "played out in every individual" (MDR, p. 45).

[15] Rudolph Otto, *The Idea of the Holy* (Oxford: Oxford University Press, 1923).

[16] Nietzsche, *Zarathustra*, Part I, *Portable Nietzsche*, ed. Kaufmann, p. 153.

[17] *Ibid.*, p. 174.

[18] Wolfgang Giegerich, "*Liber Novus*, That is, The New Bible: A First Analysis of C.G. Jung's *Red Book*," *Spring: A Journal of Archetype and Culture* 83 (Spring 2010): 361-411, p. 411.

[19] *Ibid.*, p. 393.

[20] In 1946 Jung wrote of the importance of strengthening the conscious position so that the individual is able to integrate unconscious contents breaking into awareness (CW 10, § 473).

[21] In this I am indebted to Rabbi Adin Steinsaltz, who says, "We live in the worst of all possible worlds in which there is yet hope, and that is the best of all possible worlds." Adin Steinsaltz, "The Mystic as Philosopher," *Jewish Review* 3:4 (March 1990): 14-17 (reprinted online at www.newkabbalah.com "Jewish Review"); cf. S. Drob, *Symbols of the Kabbalah* (Northvale, NJ: Jason Aaronson, 2000), p. 340.

[22] Nietzsche, *Zarathustra*, Part I, *Portable Nietzsche*, ed. Kaufmann, p. 136.

[23] See Sonu Shamdasani and John Beebe, "Jung Becomes Jung: A Dialogue on *Liber Novus* (*The Red Book*)," *Psychological Perspectives*, 53 (2010): 410-436.

[24] *Ibid.*, p. 417.

[25] Walt Whitman, *Song of Myself: The First and Final Editions of the Great American Poem* (Charleston, SC: Create Space, 2004), p. 51.

[26] C.G. Jung, "Analytical Psychology: Notes of the Seminar given in 1925," in *Analytical Psychology*, ed. William McGuire (Princeton: Princeton University Press, 1989), p. 57.

[27] E. A. Bennet, *Meetings with Jung: Conversations Recorded by E.A. Bennet During the Years 1946-1961* (Zürich: Daimon Verlag, 1982), pp. 61-62.

[28] Hilda C. Abraham and Ernst L. Freud, *A Psycho-Analytic Dialogue: The Letters of Sigmund Freud and Karl Abraham, 1907-1926,* trans. B. Marsh and H.C. Abraham (New York: Basic Books, 1965), p. 34.

[29] Murray Stein, "Carl Jung's Red Book," videotaped lecture, Asheville Jung Center (Asheville, NC), January 22, 2010.

[30] W. McGuire, ed., *The Freud/Jung Letters: The Correspondence between Sigmund Freud and C.G. Jung,* trans. R.F.C. Hull (Princeton: Princeton University Press, 1974), p. 492. While Freud responded that he fully agreed with the quotation from Nietzsche, he made a slip and wrote "why" instead of "when," when he wrote: "a third party...would ask me why I had tried to tyrannize you intellectually." Jung's Nietzsche quotation is from Nietzsche, *Zarathustra*, see Part I, *Portable Nietzsche,* ed. Kaufmann, p. 190.

[31] Of particular interest in this regard is the work of Wolfgang Giegerich, a Jungian analyst whose work is essentially a dismemberment of Jung and his ideas. Giegerich's review of *The Red Book,* "*Liber Novus,* that is, The New Bible: A First Analysis of C.G. Jung's *Red Book,*" published in *Spring: A Journal of Archetype and Culture* 83 (Spring 2010): 361-411, is a case in point. We might say that Giegerich is indeed a good (*Red Book*) Jungian in his murderous review of this very book.

[32] James L. Jarrett, ed., *Jung's Seminar on Zarathustra,* abridged edition (Princeton, NJ: Princeton University Press, 1997), p. 199.

[33] *Ibid.*, pp. 203-4.

NOTES TO CHAPTER 3

[1] Robert N. Linrothe and Marilyn M. Rhie, eds., *Demonic Divine: Himalayan Art and Beyond* (Chicago: Serindia, 2004).

² On the *Sitra Achra,* see Sanford Drob, *Symbols of the Kabbalah* (Northvale, NJ: Jason Aaronson, 2000), Ch. 8.

³ Wolfgang Giegerich, "*Liber Novus,* That is, The New Bible: A First Analysis of C.G. Jung's *Red Book,*" *Spring: A Journal of Archetype and Culture,* Vol. 83 (Spring 2010): 361-411, p. 394.

⁴ Georg Wilhelm Friedrich Hegel, *Hegel's Logic,* trans. William Wallace (Oxford: Clarendon Press, 1975), par. 48, Zusatz (note).

⁵ Rabbi Dov Baer, Ner Mitzvah ve-Torah Or, II, fol. 6a, quoted in R. Elior, *The Paradoxical Ascent to God: The Kabbalistic Theosophy of Habad Hasidism,* trans. Jeffrey M. Green (Albany, NY: State University of New York Press, 1993), p. 64.

⁶ I have examined the notion of *coincidentia oppositorum* in Jewish mysticism in my book, *Kabbalah and Postmodernism: A Dialog* (New York: Peter Lang, 2009), Ch. 6. See also, Sanford L. Drob, *A Rational Mystical Ascent: The Coincidence of Opposites in Kabbalistic and Hasidic Thought,* www.newkabbalah.com (2003-2005).

⁷ Niels Bohr, "Discussion with Einstein on Epistemological Problems in Atomic Physics," in *Great Books of the Western World,* ed. Mortimer J. Adler, Vol. 56 (Chicago: Encyclopedia Britannica, Inc. 1990), p. 354.

⁸ On Jung and National Socialism, see *Lingering Shadows: Jungians, Freudians, and Anti-Semitism,* ed. Aryeh Maidenbaum and Stephen A. Martin (Boston: Shambhala, 1982). I have considered Jung's attitude towards National Socialism in Chapter 10 of my book, *Kabbalistic Visions: C.G. Jung and Jewish Mysticism* (New Orleans, LA: Spring Journal Books, 2010). As an example of Jung's optimism regarding the Nazi state, James Kirsch wrote in 1982 that Jung had expressed in 1933 that "he had some hopes there would be a positive outcome of [the] Nazi movement," and he could not accept Kirsch's "decision to leave Germany as soon as possible." James Kirsch, "Carl Gustav Jung and the Jews: The Real Story," reprinted in Maidenbaum and Martin, *Lingering Shadows,* pp. 51-87, at p. 64.

⁹ For example, in *Answer To Job,* Jung makes a brief reference to the Lurianic *Sitra Achra* ("Other Side") when he says: "The new factor is something that has never occurred before in the history of the world, the unheard of fact that, without knowing it or wanting it, a mortal man is raised by his moral behaviour above the stars in heaven, from which position of advantage he can behold the back of Yahweh, the

abysmal world of the 'shards'" (CW 11, § 595). Jung himself notes that the shards (which represent the evil but still divine counterparts to the ten *Sefirot* or archetypal virtues) is an allusion to later Kabbalistic philosophy (CW 11, p. 381, n. 8).

[10] *Sefer ha Bahir*, par. 109, as cited in Gershom Scholem, *Origins of the Kabbalah*, trans. R.J. Zwi Werblowski (Princeton: Princeton University Press), p. 149-150.

[11] *Zohar*, III 63a-63b, in I. Tishby & F. Lachower, *The Wisdom of the Zohar: An Anthology of Texts, I, II, & III*, arranged and rendered into Hebrew, English trans. David Goldstein (Oxford: Oxford University Press, 1989), Vol. 2, p. 523.

[12] *Zohar*, II, 183b-184a, in H. Sperling, M. Simon, and P. Levertoff, eds. (London: Soncino Press, 1931-4), Vol. 4, p. 125; cf. Tishby & Lachower, *Wisdom of the Zohar*, Vol. 2, p. 534.

[13] See Adin Steinsaltz, "The Mystic as Philosopher," *Jewish Review* 3:4 (March 1990): 4-17, reprinted at www.newkabbalah.com, "Jewish Review"; cf. Drob, *Symbols of the Kabbalah*, p. 340.

[14] Jung to Kirsch, February 16, 1954, *The Jung-Kirsch Letters: The Correspondence of C.G. Jung and James Kirsch,* ed. Ann C. Lammers (London: Routledge, 2011), pp. 195-6.

[15] "Salome" is unnamed in the New Testament but is described as the stepdaughter of Herod Antipas. She is named by Josephus in his *Jewish Antiquities* (Book XVIII, Chapter 5, Sec. 4).

[16] Sigmund Freud, *The Standard Edition of the Complete Psychological Works of Sigmund Freud*, ed. and trans. James Strachey (London: Hogarth, 1957), Vol. 2, pp. 160-1.

[17] In his later writings, Jung makes his view clear that while we in the West can learn a great deal from Eastern spiritual thought and practices, we cannot adopt its solutions to our own problems (CW 11, § 902).

[18] A Hindu Goddess, the consort Shiva, and associated with energy, blackness, death, and destruction.

[19] Georg Christoph Lichtenberg, *Aphorisms*, trans. R.J. Hollingdale (London: Penguin, 1990), p. 168.

[20] G.E. Moore, "Wittgenstein's Lectures in 1930-33", in G.E. Moore's *Philosophical Papers* (London: Allen and Unwin, 1959), p. 309.

[21] Richard Noll, *The Aryan Christ: The Secret Life of Carl Jung* (New York: Random House, 1997).

[22] Jung himself would later suggest that thought "appears" to the primitive man: "he does not think it" (CW 10, § 15). Such a man can hardly be said to be a subject or a "Self" in the modern, Cartesian sense of the term.

[23] Linrothe and Rhie, eds., *Demonic Divine*.

[24] *Ibid.*, p. 9.

[25] See Sanford L. Drob, "Kabbalah, Jungian Psychology, and the Challenge of Contemporary Atheism," *Psychological Perspectives*, in press.

[26] In a later revision of Jung's "Draft," which Shamdasani estimates to have been made in the mid-1920s, Jung substituted the term "idea" (*Idee*) for "forethinking" (*Vordenken*). Sonu Shamdasani, Introduction to C.G. Jung, *The Red Book, Liber Novus*, ed. Sonu Shamdasani, trans. Mark Kyburz, John Peck, and Sonu Shamdasani (New York: W.W. Norton & Company, 2009), p. 214, n. 195.

[27] See Patrick L. Miller, "Aristotle's Pure Thought," downloaded November, 2011 from http://www.unc.edu/plmiller/Aristotles_Pure Thought.pdf.

[28] Plotinus, *Aeneid,* trans. Stephen MacKenna (Whitefish, Montana: Kessinger Publishing, 2005), Book 4, Ch. 8, Sec. 1.

[29] Jonathan D. Jacobs, "An Eastern Orthodox conception of theosis and human nature," *Faith and Philosophy*, 2009, 26(5): 615-627, downloaded November, 2011 from (http://web.mac.com/jonathandjacobs/Site/Papers_files/Jacobs-Theosis.pdf). Jacobs writes:

> What was hinted at in Scripture became explicit in the early Church. Irenaeus of Lyons claimed that God "became what we are in order to make us what he is himself." Clement of Alexandria says that "he who obeys the Lord and follows the prophecy given through him . . . becomes a god while still moving about in the flesh." "God became man," Athanasius famously tells us, "so that men might become gods." Cyril of Alexandria says that we "are called 'temples of God' and indeed 'gods,' and so we are." Basil claims that "becoming a god" is the highest goal of all. Gregory of Nazianzus implores us to "become gods for his sake, since he became man for our sake." Such quotations are a small selection of the many and varied appeals to theosis in the early church.

³⁰ *Sefer ha Yichud*, in Moshe Idel, *Kabbalah: New Perspectives* (New Haven: Yale University Press, 1988), p. 188.

³¹ "Irene Champernowne Interview, December 19, 1969," C.G. Jung Biographical Archives, cited in Richard Noll's *The Aryan Christ*, p. 276.

NOTES TO CHAPTER 4

¹ Murray Stein, "Carl Jung's Red Book," videotaped lecture, Asheville Jung Center (Asheville, NC), January 22, 2010.

² Jung to James Kirsch, May 26, 1934, cited by Michael Vannoy Adams and Jay Sherry, in "Significant Words and Events," *Lingering Shadows: Jungians, Freudians, and Anti-Semitism,* ed. Aryeh Maidenbaum and Stephen A. Martin (Boston: Shambhala, 1982), p. 374.

³ Frederick Nietzsche, *Zarathustra*, Part II, *The Portable Nietzsche,* ed. and trans. Walter Kaufmann (New York: Viking Press, 1968), p. 200.

⁴ *Jung's Seminar on Zarathustra,* abridged edition, ed. J.L. Jarrett (Princeton, NJ: Princeton University Press, 1997), p. 77.

⁵ Martin Buber, *Tales of the Hasidim* (New York: Schocken, 1947). Although Buber has been criticized for selectivity in his approach to Hasidism, the stories he presents amply demonstrate the role of joy in Hasidic spirituality.

⁶ Jung himself apparently advised his patient Christina Morgan to do just that, make her own "Red Book." Sonu Shamdasani, Introduction to C.G. Jung, *The Red Book, Liber Novus,* ed. Sonu Shamdasani, trans. Mark Kyburz, John Peck, and Sonu Shamdasani (New York: W.W. Norton & Company, 2009), p. 216a. Morgan's drawings and dreams were analyzed by Jung in his "Vision Seminars." C.G. Jung, *The Vision Seminars* (Zürich: Spring Publications, 1976).

⁷ Luigi Zoja, *Ethics and Analysis: Philosophical Perspectives and Their Application in Therapy* (No. 13, Carolyn and Ernest Fay Series in Analytical Psychology) (College Station, TX : Texas A & M University Press, 2007). On the development of a "depth-psychological", individually oriented ethic, see Erich Neumann, *Depth Psychology and a New Ethic* (New York: Harper Torchbooks, 1973).

[8] Nietzsche, *Zarathustra*, Part I, *The Portable Nietzsche*, ed. Kaufmann, p. 129.

[9] Jung, *Seminar on Nietzsche's Zarathustra*, p. 52.

[10] Martin Heidegger, *Being and Time,* trans. John Macquarrie & Edward Robinson (London: SCM Press, 1962).

[11] "Notes," *Portable Nietzsche*, ed. Kaufmann, p. 458.

[12] Ludwig Wittgenstein, *The Tractatus Logico Philosophicus*, trans. David. F. Pears & Brian F. McGuinness (London: Routledge & Kegan Paul Ltd., 1961).

[13] Ludwig Wittgenstein, *Philosophical Investigations*, trans. G. Elizabeth M. Anscombe (New York: Macmillan, 1953).

[14] Murray Stein, "Carl Jung's Red Book," videotaped lecture, Asheville Jung Center (Asheville, NC), January 22, 2010.

[15] Nathan Schwartz-Salant, "The Mark Of One Who Has Seen Chaos: A Review of C.G. Jung's *Red Book*," *Quadrant: The Journal of the C.G. Jung Foundation*, 40:2 (Summer 2010): 11-40.

[16] Thomas Kuhn, *The Structure of Scientific Revolutions* (Chicago: University of Chicago Press, 1962, 2nd ed., 1970).

[17] Martin Buber, "Religion and Modern Thinking," in his *Eclipse of God: Studies in the Relation Between Religion and Philosophy* (Amherst, New York: Humanity Books, 1988), pp. 63-92. Buber's dialog with Jung receives a thorough and sympathetic analysis by Barbara D. Stephens in her "The Martin Buber-Carl Jung disputations: protecting the sacred in the battle for the boundaries of analytical psychology," *Journal of Analytical Psychology* 46 (2001): 455-91. In his book, *On Behalf of the Mystical Fool: Jung on the Religious Situation* (New York: Routledge, 2010), John Dourley takes Buber to task for his claim to know and set the boundaries of a "legitimate experience of the deity" (p. 72).

[18] In *Transformations and Symbols of the Libido*, Jung noted that in Mithraism, Helios is the visible representative of the divine (CW B, § 307).

[19] Jung's interaction with the anchorite is reminiscent of certain events in Goethe's *Faust*, which Jung had considered several years earlier in *Transformations and Symbols of the Libido*. Like Faust, the anchorite is preoccupied with the meaning of the "Logos" in the opening sentence of the Gospel of John. Interestingly, Faust's understanding of "Logos"

as "deed" is echoed by the anchorite's rejection of Logos as a mere "word," and his desire to set the Logos within the context of the *life of man*. Further, the description of both Faust's and the anchorite's interest in the Logos is soon followed by an encounter with the devil; for Faust, the devil takes the form of Mephisto, and for Ammonius, it takes the form of Jung. Both Faust and the anchorite are simultaneously attracted to and repulsed by sun-worship. As we have seen, the anchorite's attraction to Helios is revealed in a verbal slip, while his rejection of this attraction is manifest in his resultant fury at Jung for having prompted him to make this parapraxis. In *Symbols of Transformation,* Volume 5 of the *Collected Works,* and in the earlier *Transformations and Symbols of the Libido*, Jung quotes a passage that reveals Faust's attraction to Helios ("And now at length the sun-god seems to sink, Yet stirs my heart with new-awakened light"—CW 5, § 117; cf. CW B, § 133), but also notes Faust's rejection of this "solar" impulse ("Spurn this terrestrial sun, Leave, resolute, its loveliness"—CW 5, § 118; cf. CW B, § 134). Jung concludes that it was precisely such sun/nature worship that was so threatening to the medieval Christian. Like Faust, the anchorite as a medieval Christian is caught in the conflict of what Jung in *Transformations and Symbols of the Libido* termed Faust's "Scylla of world-renunciation and the Charybdis of its acceptance" (CW B, § 141; cf. CW 5, § 121). It would not be an exaggeration to say that in *The Red Book* this is a conflict for Jung himself.

[20] Murray Stein, "Carl Jung's Red Book," videotaped lecture, Asheville Jung Center (Asheville, NC), January 22, 2010.

[21] *Ibid.*

NOTES TO CHAPTER 5

[1] The name "Izdubar" was introduced in 1872 as a result of initial difficulties which scholars had in reading the cuneiform writing in which this God was named and described.

[2] Sigmund Freud and Joseph Breuer, *Standard Edition of the Complete Psychological Works of Sigmund Freud,* ed. James Strachey (London: Hogarth Press, 1955-67), Vol. 2, pp. 160-1.

[3] Nietzsche, *The Gay Science,* Section 125, *The Portable Nietzsche,* ed. Walter Kaufmann (New York: Viking Press, 1968), pp. 95-6.

[4] Jung will later describe the origin of the "Seven Sermons" in "Alexandria" with the phrase "where the East touches the West" (C.G. Jung, *The Red Book, Liber Novus,* ed. Sonu Shamdasani, trans. Mark Kyburz, John Peck, and Sonu Shamdasani (New York: W.W. Norton & Company, 2009), p. 346, n. 81), and throughout his life will have an open but cautious attitude toward Eastern psychology and spirituality—holding that there are dangers in its being wholeheartedly adopted by the Western mind.

[5] Kurt Rudolph, *Gnosis: The Nature and History of Gnosticism,* trans. R.M. Wilson (San Francisco, CA: Harper, 1987), p. 93.

[6] Schneur Zalman, *Likutei Torah, Devarim,* fol. 83a, quoted in R. Elior, *The Paradoxical Ascent to God: The Kabbalistic Theosophy of Habad Hasidism,* trans. J.M. Green (Albany, NY: State University of New York Press, 1993), pp. 137-8.

[7] Nietzsche, *Twilight of the Idols 7, Portable Nietzsche,* ed. Kaufmann, p. 467.

[8] G.W.F. Hegel, *The Phenomenology of Mind,* trans. J.B. Baille (New York: MacMillan, 1931).

[9] For example, Robert Solomon, *In the Spirit of Hegel* (Oxford: Oxford University Press, 1983).

[10] On the symbol of the snake in *The Red Book,* see Eleonóra Babejová, "She Will Wind Herself Around You," *Jung Journal: Culture & Psyche* 5/3 (2011): 94-115.

[11] Paul Brutsche, "*The Red Book* in the Context of Jung's Paintings," *Jung Journal: Culture & Psyche* 5/3 (Summer, 2011), p. 13 ff.

NOTES TO CHAPTER 6

[1] *Zohar,* III 63a-63b, *Raya Mehemna,* Isaiah Tishby & Fischel Lachower, *The Wisdom of the Zohar: An Anthology of Texts, I, II, & III,* arranged and rendered into Hebrew, trans. David Goldstein (Oxford: Oxford University Press, 1989), Vol. 2, p. 523.

[2] Jean-Paul Sartre, *Being and Nothingness,* trans. Hazel Barnes (New York: Washington Square Press, 1966).

³ Martin Buber, *I and Thou*, trans. Robert G. Smith (New York: Charles Scribner's & Sons, 1937).

⁴ C.G. Jung, "The Post-War Psychic Problems of the Germans," *C.G. Jung Speaking*, eds. William McGuire and R.F.C. Hull (Princeton, NJ: Princeton University Press, 1977), p. 150.

⁵ *Ibid.*, p. 153. I will not here take up the question of Jung's facing of his *own* guilt with respect to the patently anti-Semitic comments he made during the Nazi era. I have dealt with this question at length in Chapter 10 of my *Kabbalistic Visions: C.G. Jung and Jewish Mysticism* (New Orleans, LA: Spring Journal Books, 2010), pp. 161-206.

⁶ Murray Stein, "Carl Jung's Red Book," videotaped lecture, Asheville Jung Center (Asheville, NC), January 22, 2010.

⁷ See, for example, the following works by Thomas J.J. Altizer: *The Gospel of Christian Atheism* (Philadelphia: Westminster Press, 1966), *History as Apocalypse* (Albany, NY: State University of New York Press, 1985), and *Living the Death of God: A Theological Memoir* (Albany, N.Y.: State University of New York Press, 2006).

⁸ In his 1916 paper, "The Structure of the Unconscious", Jung made use of the term "Godlikeness" (CW 7, § 454); cf. Sonu Shamdasani, Introduction to C.G. Jung's *The Red Book, Liber Novus*, ed. Sonu Shamdasani, trans. Mark Kyburz, John Peck, and Sonu Shamdasani (New York: W.W. Norton & Company, 2009), p. 208b to denote a condition in which the ego "annexes the unconscious heritage of the collective psyche" (CW 7, § 457), resulting in "a hypertrophy of self-confidence, which in turn is compensated by an extraordinary sense of inferiority in the unconscious" (CW 7, § 457). This appears to be Jung's psychological understanding of the "holy affliction" he here alludes to C.G. Jung's *The Red Book, Liber Novus*, ed. Sonu Shamdasani, trans. Mark Kyburz, John Peck, and Sonu Shamdasani (New York: W.W. Norton & Company, 2009), p. 291b.

⁹ Additional information on these paintings is provided in Shamdasani, Introduction to C.G. Jung's *The Red Book, Liber Novus*, pp. 291-2, n. 155-157.

NOTES TO CHAPTER 7

¹ Sonu Shamdasani, *Jung and the Making of Modern Psychology: The Dream of a Science* (Cambridge: Cambridge University Press, 2003), p. 307.

² Interestingly, Jung writes that the individual can go his own way but is first obliged by the collective demands to purchase his individuation at the cost of an equivalent work for the benefit of society (CW 18, § 1099).

³ Henri Bergson, *The Creative Mind: An Introduction to Metaphysics* (New York: Kensington Publishing Corp, 1946).

⁴ C.G. Jung, Supplementary Volume A to Jung's *Collected Works*: The Zofinga Lectures, trans. R. Jan Van Heurck (Princeton, NJ: Princeton University Press, 1983).

⁵ See Francis X. Charet, *Spiritualism and the Foundations of C.G. Jung's Psychology* (Albany, NY: State University of New York Press, 1993), p. 141.

⁶ Alfred North Whitehead, *Process and Reality: An Essay in Cosmology*, eds. David R. Griffin and Donald W. Sherburne (New York: Free Press, 1979. Original year of publication, 1929).

⁷ *Ibid.*, p. 340.

⁸ An example of Jung's respect for "animality", in the sense of "keep(ing) to the time-honored" and being "loyal...to the land that bears [one]" (RB p. 296b), is evident in his 1930 essay, "Your Negroid and Indian Behavior" where he writes that a Pueblo Indian, by being embedded in myth and cosmos, has none of the European's spiritual poverty, as he is fully rooted to his place. The original article, written in English, was published in *Forum* (New York), LXXXIII: 4 (April, 1930): 193-99. The article was retitled "The Complications of American Psychology" and appears in CW 10, pp. 502-14.

⁹ In his notes to *The Red Book*, Shamdasani provides a detailed description of the drawing's significance based upon Jung's writings, including his 1930 "Commentary on 'The Secret of the Golden Flower'" (CW 13) and his 1952, "Concerning Mandala Symbolism" (CW 9i). Sonu Shamdasani, Introduction to C.G. Jung's *The Red Book, Liber Novus*, ed. Sonu Shamdasani, trans. Mark Kyburz, John Peck, and Sonu Shamdasani (New York: W.W. Norton & Company, 2009), p. 297, n. 186.

[10] Stanton Marlan provides interesting insights into the connection between Jung and Derrida in his *The Black Sun: The Alchemy of Art and Darkness* (College Station, Texas: Texas A & M University Press, 2005). On Jungian psychology and deconstruction, see also Michael Vannoy Adams's 1983 article, "Deconstructive Philosophy and Imaginal Psychology: Comparative Perspectives on Jacques Derrida and James Hillman," in *Jungian Literary Criticism*, ed. R.P. Sugg (Evanston, IL: Northwestern University Press, 1992), pp. 231-48.

[11] Sara Corbett, "The Holy Grail of the Unconscious", *New York Times Magazine*, September 16, 2009.

[12] Emma Jung and Marie-Louise von Franz, *The Grail Legend* (Princeton: Princeton University Press, 1998).

[13] John Ryan Haule, "Jung's 'Amfortas' Wound': Psychological Types Revisited", *Spring: A Journal of Archetype and Culture*, Vol. 53 (1992): 95-112, http://www.jrhaule.net/wound.html, retrieved August, 2011.

[14] "Dialetheism," see *Stanford Encyclopedia of Philosophy*, from http://plato.stanford.edu/entries/dialetheism/, retrieved May 2011.

[15] Kurt Rudolph, *Gnosis: The Nature and History of Gnosticism*, trans. R.M. Wilson (San Francisco, CA: Harper, 1987), p. 81.

[16] From the Gnostic text, "Thunder: The Perfect Mind," in *The Nag Hammadi Library*, ed. James M. Robinson, 3rd ed. (San Francisco: Harper & Row, 1988), pp. 295-303.

[17] Indeed, Jung never seems to have completely abandoned his understanding of the hero as reflecting the individual's emancipation from the regressive libidinal forces that maintain merger of the ego with the mother. This is evident in the fact that Jung retained this model of the hero when he revised *Transformations and Symbols of the Libido* in 1952. See Sonu Shamdasani and John Beebe, "Jung Becomes Jung: A Dialogue on *Liber Novus* (*The Red Book*)," *Psychological Perspectives*, 53, 2010, p. 422-3.

[18] Sanford Drob, *Symbols of the Kabbalah* (Northvale, NJ: Jason Aaronson, 2000), Ch. 9; Sanford Drob, *Kabbalistic Metaphors* (Northvale, NJ: Jason Aaronson, 2000), Chs. 7, 8.

[19] On Derrida's notion of the "monstrous", see, for example, Jacques Derrida, "Deconstruction and the Other," in *Dialogues with Contemporary Continental Thinkers,* ed. Richard Kearney (Manchester:

Manchester University Press, 1984), p. 123; see also Jacques Derrida, *Points...Interviews, 1974-94,* ed. Elizabeth Weber, trans. Peggy Kamuf et. al. (Stanford: Stanford University Press, 1995), where Derrida writes that the "future is necessarily monstrous: the figure of the future, that is, that which can only be surprising, that for which we are not prepared, you see, is heralded by species of monsters. A future that would not be monstrous would not be a future." (pp. 386-7). On Derrida's views on the messiah, see his *Spectres of Marx: The State of the Debt, The Work of Mourning, & the New International,* trans. Peggy Kamuf (London: Routledge 1994). I have considered Derrida's notions of the messiah and the "monstrous" in my *Kabbalah and Postmodernism: A Dialog* (New York: Peter Lang, 2009), pp. 96-7.

[20] Martin Buber, "Religion and Modern Thinking," in his *Eclipse of God: Studies in the Relation Between Religion and Philosophy* (Amherst, New York: Humanity Books, 1988), p. 81.

Notes to Chapter 8

[1] Jay Sherry, "A Pictorial Guide to *The Red Book.*" (Downloaded from: http://aras.org/docs/00033sherry.pdf).

[2] Lévi-Strauss held that since all cultures organize thought and knowledge into binary oppositions, they end up producing contradictions that can only be reconciled through myth and symbols. For Lévi-Strauss, myth "provides a logical model capable of overcoming contradictions." Claude Lévi-Strauss, "The Structure of Myth," in *Structural Anthropology,* trans. Claire Jacobson and Brooke Grundfest (New York: Allen Lane, 1963. Originally published in the *Journal of American Folklore* LXVII, 1955, pp. 428-44).

[3] Jean-Paul Sartre, *The Psychology of the Imagination,* trans. Bernard Frechtman (New York: Washington Square Press, 1966).

[4] *Ibid.,* p. 124.

[5] *Ibid.,* p. 10.

[6] C.G. Jung, *Letters,* Volumes I and II, eds., Gerhard Adler, Aniela Jaffe, and R.F.C. Hull (Princeton, NJ: Princeton University Press, 1973), Vol. I, p. 33.

[7] Joseph H. Peterson, ed., *The Sixth and Seventh Books of Moses: Or Moses' Magical Spirit-Art Known as the Wonderful Arts of the Old Wise Hebrews, Taken from the Mosaic Books of the Kabbalah and the Talmud, for the Good of Mankind* (Lake Worth, FL: Ibis, 2008).

[8] What "eludes comprehension" might range from the depths of the unconscious psyche to the origins of the world.

[9] Daniel Matt, "Ayin: The Concept of Nothingness in Jewish Mysticism," in *Essential Papers on Kabbalah,* ed. Lawrence Fine (New York: New York University Press, 1995), p. 81.

[10] Murray Stein, "Carl Jung's Red Book," videotaped lecture, Asheville Jung Center (Asheville, NC), Jan. 22, 2010.

[11] C.G. Jung, *Letters,* Vol. I, p. 31; cf. C.G. Jung's *The Red Book, Liber Novus,* ed. Sonu Shamdasani, trans. Mark Kyburz, John Peck, and Sonu Shamdasani (New York: W.W. Norton & Company, 2009), p. 337, n. 24.

[12] Ludwig Wittgenstein, *Notebooks, 1914-16,* ed. and trans. George H. von Wright and G. Elizabeth M. Anscombe (New York: Harper & Row, 1961), p. 80e.

[13] Ludwig Wittgenstein, *The Tractatus Logico Philosophicus,* trans. David. F. Pears & Brian F. McGuinness (London: Routledge & Kegan Paul Ltd., 1961), proposition 6.52.

[14] *Ibid.,* proposition 6.522.

[15] *Ibid.,* Proposition 7.

[16] Azriel of Gerona, *Perush Eser* Sefirot, quoted in Isaiah Tishby & Fischel Lachower, *The Wisdom of the Zohar: An Anthology of Texts, I, II, & III,* arranged and rendered into Hebrew, English trans. David Goldstein (Oxford: Oxford University Press, 1989), Vol. I, p. 234.

[17] While these "accidental" properties are not rationally derivable in the manner of mathematical truths, it is unclear that they are "irrational", even in Jung's limited sense of this term, as each might be rationally explicable on the basis of one or more scientific axioms or theorems. One would need to turn to propositions of much wider scope, such as the fact "there exists anything at all", for a better example of something not grounded in reason.

[18] Murray Stein, "Carl Jung's Red Book," videotaped lecture, Asheville Jung Center (Asheville, NC), Jan. 22, 2010.

¹⁹ Gershom Scholem, *Origins of the Kabbalah*, trans. R.J. Zwi Werblowski (Princeton: Princeton University Press, 1987), pp. 441-2.

²⁰ *Hegel's Logic*, trans. William Wallace (Oxford: Clarendon Press, 1975), par. 48, Zusatz 1, p. 78.

²¹ James Kirsch, "Carl Gustav Jung and the Jews: The Real Story," reprinted in *Lingering Shadows: Jungians, Freudians, and Anti-Semitism,* ed. Aryeh Maidenbaum and Stephen A. Martin (Boston: Shambhala, 1982), p. 64.

²² C.G. Jung, "Diagnosing the Dictators," in *C.G. Jung Speaking,* ed. William McGuire and R.F.C. Hull (Princeton, NJ: Princeton University Press, 1977), p. 119.

²³ In H.L. Philip, *Jung and the Problem of Evil* (London: Rockliff, 1958, reprinted as "Jung and Religious Belief" in CW 18, pp. 702-744).

²⁴ Murray Stein, "Carl Jung's Red Book," videotaped lecture, Asheville Jung Center (Asheville, NC), Jan. 22, 2010.

NOTES TO CHAPTER 9

¹ Jung refers to "the extraneous world of the Kellipot" in a letter to James Kirsch, November 18, 1952, *The Jung-Kirsch Letters: The Correspondence of C.G. Jung and James Kirsch,* ed. Ann C. Lammers (London: Routledge, 2011), p. 144. See my "Jung, Kirsch, and Judaism: Mystical and Paradoxical Transformations," *Jung Journal: Culture & Psyche* 6/1 (Winter 2012): 35-55. On the Kellipot, see S. Drob, *Symbols of the Kabbalah*, Ch. 8.

² See Francis X. Charet, *Spiritualism and the Foundations of C.G. Jung's Psychology* (Albany, NY: State University of New York Press, 1993).

³ Marilyn Nagy, *Philosophical Issues in the Psychology of C.G. Jung* (Albany, NY: State University of New York Press, 1991), p. 134.

⁴ Yet in *Transformations and Symbols of the Libido* Jung had spoken of "typical myths" (CW B, §§ 56, 358, 549). Jung first made a clear distinction between the personal unconscious and the impersonal unconscious, or what he termed the "collective psyche," in his 1916 paper "The Structure of the Unconscious." CW 7, pp. 269-304, note especially § 456, which I have quoted above.

⁵ Wolfgang Giegerich, "*Liber Novus*, That is, The New Bible: A First Analysis of C.G. Jung's *Red Book*," *Spring: A Journal of Archetype and Culture* 83 (Spring 2010): 361-411, p. 373.

[6] This does not mean that Jung's material is not *archetypal*, only that if it is, it is so in the same manner as other works of philosophy, literature, and "documents of the soul." At any rate, it is too much to expect archetypal themes to emerge into Jung's (or anyone's) awareness in a manner that is independent of learning and cultural forms. Indeed, while I certainly believe that we are witness to archetypal or universal material in *Liber Novus*, it is probably an illusion to think that one can find evidence of the *innate* nature of an image, idea, or archetype by considering the fantasy productions of any single individual.

[7] Giegerich, "*Liber Novus*, That is, the New Bible: A First Analysis of Jung's *Red Book*," *Spring: A Journal of Archetype and Culture* 83 (Spring 2010): 361-411, p. 390.

[8] Early in his career Jung took an interest in forensic psychiatry (CW 1, pp. 157-205).

[9] Jung to Frau N., C.G. Jung, *Letters*, eds., Gerhard Adler, Aniela Jaffe, and R.F.C. Hull (Princeton, NJ: Princeton University Press, 1973), Vol. II, p. 343.

[10] I am indebted to Stanton Marlan for his clarification of this important issue.

[11] Giegerich, "*Liber Novus*, That is, the New Bible: A First Analysis of Jung's *Red Book*," *Spring: A Journal of Archetype and Culture* 83 (Spring 2010): 361-411, p. 392.

[12] As Stein points out, in the course of this episode Jung moves from his quest for independence and manhood to being a feminine womb, which is, of course, a receptacle for an other (Murray Stein, "Carl Jung's Red Book," videotaped lecture, Asheville Jung Center (Asheville, NC, January 22, 2010). However, this feminine, maternal state does not seem to last long as Jung soon again finds himself advocating solitude.

[13] Jay Sherry, "A Pictorial Guide to *The Red Book*." (Downloaded from: http://aras.org/docs/00033sherry.pdf, p. 20).

NOTES TO CHAPTER 10

[1] Ludwig Wittgenstein, *Notebooks, 1914-16*, ed. and trans. George H. von Wright and G. Elizabeth M. Anscombe (New York: Harper & Row, 1961), p. 80e.

[2] Sonu Shamdasani and John Beebe, "Jung Becomes Jung: A Dialogue on *Liber Novus* (*The Red Book*)," *Psychological Perspectives* 53, 2010, p. 420.

[3] *Ibid.*

[4] Sanford L. Drob, *Kabbalistic Visions: C.G. Jung and Jewish Mysticism* (New Orleans, LA: Spring Journal Books, 2010), pp. 198-200.

[5] This characterization came in a brief essay, "Religion and Psychology: A Reply to Martin Buber," in which Jung responded to Martin Buber's accusation that he was a disguised gnostic (CW 18, pp. 663-70).

[6] Thomas J.J. Altizer, *The Gospel of Christian Atheism* (Philadelphia: Westminster Press, 1966).

[7] Martin Buber, "Religion and Modern Thinking," in his *Eclipse of God: Studies in the Relation Between Religion and Philosophy* (Amherst, New York: Humanity Books, 1988), pp. 63-92.

[8] Richard Noll, *The Aryan Christ: The Secret Life of Carl Jung* (New York: Random House, 1997).

[9] Murray Stein, "*The Red Book*, Part II: Further Exploring Jung's Visionary Masterpiece," videotaped lecture, Asheville Jung Center (Asheville, NC), May 14, 2010.

[10] In the "Seven Sermons," Jung speaks of Abraxas as a transcendent deity separate from man, but identifies him with the inscrutable disorder and "cruelty" of nature (RB, p. 350b).

[11] *Jung's Seminar on Nietzsche's Zarathustra*, abridged edition, ed. James L. Jarrett (Princeton University Press, 1998), pp. 239-40.

[12] *Ibid.*, p. 240.

[13] Kurt Rudolph, *Gnosis: The Nature and History of Gnosticism*, trans. R.M. Wilson (San Francisco, CA: Harper, 1987), p. 93.

[14] *Zohar* V, 113a, *The Zohar*, trans. Harry Sperling and Maurice Simon (London: Soncino Press, 1931-4), Vol. 5, p. 153.

[15] C.G. Jung, "An Eightieth Birthday Interview," in *C.G. Jung Speaking*, ed. William McGuire & R.F.C. Hull (Princeton, NJ: Princeton University Press, 1977), pp. 271-2.

[16] R. Schatz Uffenheimer, *Hasidism as Mysticism: Quietistic Elements in Eighteenth Century Hasidic Thought* (Jerusalem: Hebrew University, 1993), p. 207; cf. Sanford L. Drob, "Jung, Kirsch, and Judaism: Mystical and Paradoxical Transformations," *Jung Journal: Culture & Psyche* 6/1 (Winter 2012): 35-55.

[17] Jung wrote, "I can hardly draw a veil over the fact that we psychotherapists ought really to be philosophers or philosophic doctors or rather that we already are so, though we are unwilling to admit it because of the glaring contrast between our work and what passes for philosophy in the universities. We could also call it religion *in statu nascendi,* for in the vast confusion that reigns at the roots of life there is no line of division between philosophy and religion" (CW 16, § 181).

[18] See Sonu Shamdasani, *Cult Fictions* (New York: Routledge, 1998), and Lionel Corbett, "Jung's *The Red Book* Dialogues with the Soul: Herald of a New Religion," *Jung Journal: Culture & Psyche* 5/3 (Summer 2011): 63-77.

[19] In his discussion of this passage in *The Red Book,* Stein points out that contemporary Western society is the first in history where the living pay little or no attention to their ancestors, and this has resulted in a certain impoverishment of our psyches. Stein, *"The Red Book,* Part II."

NOTES TO CHAPTER 11

[1] See, for example, Robert A. Segal, *The Gnostic Jung* (Princeton: Princeton University Press, 1992), and Stephen A. Hoeller, *The Gnostic Jung and the Seven Sermons to the Dead* (Wheaton, Illinois: Theosophical Publishing, 1982). On Gnosticism in general, see Giovanni Filoramo, *A History of Gnosticism,* trans. Anthony Alcock (Cambridge: Basil Blackwell, 1990); Kurt Rudolph, *Gnosis: The Nature and History of Gnosticism,* trans. R.M. Wilson (San Francisco: Harper, 1987); *The Nag Hammadi Library,* ed. James Robinson, 3rd ed. (San Francisco: Harper & Row, 1988). The latter volume contains English translations of the Gnostic texts that had recently been discovered in Egypt.

[2] Jung to Alphonse Maeder, January 19, 1917, C.G. Jung, *Letters, Volumes I and II,* eds., Gerhard Adler, Aniela Jaffe, and R.F.C. Hull (Princeton, NJ: Princeton University Press, 1973), Vol. I, pp. 33-4.

[3] Georg Wilhelm Friedrich Hegel, *Science of Logic,* trans. A.V. Miller (Amherst, NY: Prometheus Books, 1998), par. 132.

[4] The question was originally posed by Leibniz in his 1697 essay, "On the Ultimate Origin of Things." It was later asked by Schelling, Heidegger, and many others.

⁵ In *Black Book* 5, Jung writes that through the process of individuation, the Pleroma becomes concentrated and small: "The more concentrated the Pleroma becomes, the stronger the star of the individual becomes." C.G. Jung, *The Red Book, Liber Novus*, ed. Sonu Shamdasani, trans. Mark Kyburz, John Peck, and Sonu Shamdasani (New York: W.W. Norton & Company, 2009), Appendix C, p. 370b.

⁶ Jung writes, "the concept of an all-encompassing God must necessarily include his opposite. The *coincidentia,* of course, must not be too radical or too extreme, otherwise God would cancel himself out. The principle of the coincidence of opposites must therefore be completed by that of absolute opposition in order to attain full paradoxicality and hence psychological validity." C.G. Jung's *The Red Book, Liber Novus*, ed. Sonu Shamdasani, trans. Mark Kyburz, John Peck, and Sonu Shamdasani (New York: W.W. Norton & Company, 2009), p. 350, n. 101, referencing "The spirit of Mercurius", CW 13, § 256).

⁷ A better, if perhaps less transparent analogy, would be to the "morning" and "evening" stars, which the ancients thought to be distinct, but which we now know to be different appearances of the planet Venus.

⁸ Jacques Derrida, "Différance", in his *Margins of Philosophy*, trans. Alan Bass (Chicago: Chicago University Press, 1982, pp. 1-28. Original French edition, 1967).

⁹ Interestingly, while Derrida eschews all philosophical and mystical efforts to think or experience unity, he too allows for the possibility of transcending difference. He writes: "The efficacy of the thematic of *différance* may very well, indeed must, one day be superseded, lending itself if not to its own replacement, at least to enmeshing itself in a chain that in truth it never will have governed" (Derrida, *"Différance"*, p. 7).

¹⁰ For Hillman, the psyche's multiplicity is reflected in the many Gods, which in turn are conditioned by multiple sources of meaning, direction, and value. Thomas Moore summarizes Hillman's views when he writes:

> The psyche is not only multiple, it is a communion of many persons, each with specific needs, fears, longings, style and language. The many persons echo the many gods who define

the worlds that underlie what appear to be a unified human being. T. Moore, "Prologue, Introductions", in *A Blue Fire: Selected Writings by James Hillman*, introduced and edited by Thomas Moore. (New York: Harper Perennial, 1991)

Hillman holds that the so-called "individual" lives simultaneously within a variety of genres and narratives:

> For even while one part of me knows the soul goes to death in tragedy, another is living a picaresque fantasy, and a third is engaged in the heroic fantasy of improvement. James Hillman, *Healing Fiction* (Barrytown, N.Y.: Station Hill Press, 1983), p. 19; cf. *A Blue Fire*, p. 81.

[11] Murray Stein, "*The Red Book*, Part II: Further Exploring Jung's Visionary Masterpiece," videotaped lecture, The Asheville Jung Center, May 14, 2010.

[12] Stanton Marlan, personal communication.

[13] Renos Papadopoulos, "Jung's epistemology and methodology," in *The Handbook of Jungian Psychology: Theory, Practice and Applications*, ed. Renos Papadopoulos (New York: Routledge, 2006), pp. 7-53.

[14] An example is Jung's 1934 "The State of Psychotherapy Today" where he makes general statements about the ethnic psychologies of Germans and Jews (CW 10, pp. 157-173).

[15] Papadopoulos, "Jung's epistemology and methodology."

[16] Part of the difficulty here arises from the ambiguity of such concepts of "knowledge," "real," and "objective," as these might be applied to Jung's "objective psyche." An "experience" (e.g. one rooted in an archetype of the collective unconscious) may be "objective" and "real" in one sense, without having an "objective" and "real" referent beyond the psyche.

[17] Shamdasani cites Jung's *Vision Seminars*, June 7, 1933, Vol. 2, pp. 1041-2.

[18] On Derrida's use of "monstrous" and its relationship to the future, see Derrida, "Deconstruction and the Other," in *Dialogues with Contemporary Continental Thinkers*, ed. Richard Kearney (Manchester: Manchester University Press, 1984), p. 123; see also Jacques Derrida, *Points...Interviews, 1974-94*, ed. Elizabeth Weber, trans. Peggy Kamuf, et. al. (Stanford: Stanford University Press, 1995), p. 386-7. Derrida writes that the "future is necessarily monstrous: the figure of the future,

that is, that which can only be surprising, that for which we are not prepared, you see, is heralded by species of monsters. A future that would not be monstrous would not be a future." (pp. 386-7).

[19] In *Black Book* 5 Jung writes that Abraxas is the "creative drive," "matter and force," "light and dark," "creative and created," and "the life of the universe." (*The Red Book*, Appendix C, p. 370b). Christ himself "had to subjugate himself to the power of Abraxas and Abraxas killed him in a gruesome manner" (RB, p. 371a).

[20] *Jung's Seminar on Nietzsche's Zarathustra*, abridged edition, ed. James. L. Jarrett (Princeton University Press, 1998), pp. 199-200.

[21] Stanton Marlan, "The Philosopher's Stone as Chaosmos: The Self and the Dilemma of Diversity," in *Facing Multiplicity: Psyche, Nature, Culture: Proceedings of the Eighteenth International Congress for Analytical Psychology*, ed. P. Bennett (Einsiedeln: Daimon Verlag, 2010).

[22] In *The Red Book* draft Jung writes: "only one law exists, and that is your law. Only one truth exists, and that is your truth." C.G. Jung, *The Red Book, Liber Novus*, ed. Sonu Shamdasani, trans. Mark Kyburz, John Peck, and Sonu Shamdasani (New York: W.W. Norton & Company, 2009), p. 231, n. 27.

[23] Jung himself experienced a Kabbalistic *coniunctio* vision after his heart attack in 1944 (MDR, p. 294). I discuss this vision in relation to Kabbalistic erotic and wedding symbolism in Sanford L. Drob, *Kabbalistic Visions: C.G. Jung and Jewish Mysticism* (New Orleans, LA: Spring Journal Books, 2010), Ch. 3.

[24] "Adaptation, individuation and collectivity," CW 18, pp. 449-454; "The Structure of the Unconscious," CW 7, pp. 269-304.

[25] Jung later wrote of the Gnostic and Kabbalistic divine inner "spark" (CW 12, p. 301, n. 26) that must be liberated in order for the adept to achieve salvation. Jung further pointed out that the alchemist Gerhard Dorn held that there was an "invisible sun" in each man (CW 14, § 49). In his later writings Jung equated the sparks or scintillae with the luminosity of the collective unconscious (CW 14, p. 55, n. 116; cf. CW 8, § 388, where Jung says, "One such spark is the human mind"). In *Mysterium Coniunctionis* Jung wrote, "In the unconscious are hidden those 'sparks of light' (*scintillae*), the archetypes, from which a higher meaning can be 'extracted'" (CW 14, § 700).

²⁶ James W. Heisig, *Imago Dei: Jung's Psychology of Religion* (Lewisburg, PA: Bucknell University Press, 1979).

Notes to Chapter 12

¹ C.G. Jung, "Is Analytic Psychology a Religion?" in *C.G. Jung Speaking,* ed. William McGuire & R.F.C. Hull (Princeton, NJ: Princeton University Press, 1977), p. 98.

² Friedrich Nietzsche, *Thus Spake Zarathustra,* Part II, in *The Portable Nietzsche,* ed. Walter Kaufmann (New York: Viking Press, 1968), p. 197-8.

³ Nietzsche, *Zarathustra,* Part I, *Portable Nietzsche,* ed. Kaufmann, p. 124.

⁴ Nietzsche's comments on the demise of the one God may have influenced Jung's thinking in this section of *Scrutinies.* Nietzsche writes:

> For the old gods, after all, things came to an end long ago; and verily, they had a good gay godlike end. They did not end in a 'twilight,' though this lie is told. Instead: one day they *laughed* themselves to death. That happened when the most godless word issued from one of the gods themselves—the word: 'There is one god, Thou shalt have no other gods before me!' An old grimbeard of a god, a jealous one, thus forgot himself. And then all the gods laughed and rocked on their chairs and cried, 'Is not just this godlike, that there are gods but no God?' Nietzsche, *Zarathustra,* Part III, *Portable Nietzsche,* ed. Kaufmann, p. 294

⁵ According to James Hillman, "psychological polytheism provides archetypal containers for differentiating our fragmentation." James Hillman, *Revisioning Psychology* (New York: Harper & Row, 1975), p. 26.

⁶ Note the contradiction with Philemon's earlier pronouncement that the universe is not lawful and "God" names the reality of chance and "irregularity." C.G. Jung, *The Red Book, Liber Novus,* ed. Sonu Shamdasani, trans. Mark Kyburz, John Peck, and Sonu Shamdasani (New York: W.W. Norton & Company, 2009), p. 350b.

⁷ Nietzsche, *The Gay Science* 343, *Portable Nietzsche,* ed. Kaufmann, p. 448.

[8] Jung, *Seminar on Nietzsche's Zarathustra*, p. 172-3.

[9] Murray Stein, "*The Red Book*, Part II: Further Exploring Jung's Visionary Masterpiece," videotaped lecture, The Asheville Jung Center, (Asheville: NC), May 14, 2010.

[10] Sanford L. Drob, *Kabbalistic Visions: C.G. Jung and Jewish Mysticism* (New Orleans, LA: Spring Journal Books, 2010), Ch. 7.

[11] C.G. Jung, *Letters*, Volumes I and II, eds., Gerhard Adler, Aniela Jaffe, and R.F.C. Hull (Princeton, NJ: Princeton University Press, 1973), Vol. II, p. 157.

[12] In a commentary to Chapter IX of *Liber Primus*, printed as "Appendix B" in the English language volume, Jung writes that Elijah and Salome could just as easily have been called Simon Magus and Helena, the important thing being that they are "biblical figures." C.G. Jung, *The Red Book, Liber Novus*, ed. Sonu Shamdasani, trans. Mark Kyburz, John Peck, and Sonu Shamdasani (New York: W.W. Norton & Company, 2009), p. 368a.

NOTES TO CHAPTER 13

[1] Robert S. Henderson, "The Search for the Lost Soul: An "Enterview" with Murray Stein about C.G. Jung's *The Red Book*," *Jung Journal: Culture & Psyche* 4/4 (Fall 2010): 92-101, p. 94.

[2] For a critique of the view that dreams should be understood as compensations, see James Hillman, *The Dream and the Underworld* (New York: Harper Perennial, 1979), pp. 74-85.

[3] Wolfgang Giegerich, "The End of Meaning and the Birth of Man: An Essay about the State Reached in the History of Consciousness and an Analysis of C.G. Jung's Psychology Project," *Journal of Jungian Theory and Practice*, 6/1 (2004): 1-65. Available at: http://www.junginstitute.org/pdf_files/JungV6N1p1-66.pdf.

[4] In his exploration of the theological significance of *The Red Book*, John Hill writes: "ask yourself if you have dared probe the depth and intensity of your own God image. Have you simply taken over the traditional imagery of the fathers? Or have you rebelled against tradition, plunged into the emptiness of your own hinterlands?" John Hill, "Exile, Hell and the Becoming of God," *Jung Journal: Culture & Psyche*, 5/3 (Summer 2011): 38-53, p. 43. One might

say that each generation, and each person must indeed produce new images of the divine as well as resignify the images and conceptions of one's own tradition. Indeed, the very notion of *transcendence* suggests that one must break through the clearing of common discourse and enter the unknown and untamed forest of what has yet to be imagined. The shocking and uncanny nature of *The Red Book* may thus be one of its greatest gifts.

[5] See Sanford L. Drob, "Fragmentation in Psychology: A Dialectical Solution," *Journal of Humanistic Psychology* 43:4 (2003):102-123. Available at http://www.newkabbalah.com/frag.pdf.

Index

CPSIA information can be obtained
at www.ICGtesting.com
Printed in the USA
LVHW01s1813090817
544406LV00019B/609/P